HOSPITALITY
MARKETING MANAGEMENT

6e

David C. Bojanic
University of Texas at San Antonio

Robert D. Reid
AACSB International

ISBN 9781118988954 (pbk) | ISBN 9781119223122 (eval)

Library of Congress Cataloging-in-Publication Data:
Names: Reid, Robert D., author. | Bojanic, David C., author.
Title: Hospitality marketing management / David C. Bojanic, University of
    Texas at San Antonio, Robert D. Reid, AACSB International.
Description: Sixth edition. | Hoboken, New Jersey : John Wiley & Sons, Inc.,
    [2017] | Previous edition: Hospitality marketing management / Robert D.
    Reid, David C. Bojanic. | Includes bibliographical references and index.
Identifiers: LCCN 2016027511 (print) | LCCN 2016029926 (ebook) | ISBN
    9781118988954 | ISBN 9781119195153 (pdf) | ISBN 9781119195122 (epub)
Subjects: LCSH: Hospitality industry—Marketing. | Food service—Marketing. |
    Restaurants—Marketing.
Classification: LCC TX911.3.M3 R443 2017 (print) | LCC TX911.3.M3 (ebook) |
    DDC 657/.8370688—dc23 | LC record available at lccn.loc.gov/2016027511

The inside back cover will contain printing identification and country of origin if omitted from this page. In addition, if the ISBN on the back cover differs from the ISBN on this page, the one on the back cover is correct.

Printed in the United States of America

SKY10076567_060424

Dedication

I would like to dedicate this book to the memory of my mother, Betty Bojanic, who made life better for everyone around her.

David Bojanic

This book is dedicated with my sincere appreciation and admiration to my friends, family and the many professionals with whom I have had the privilege to work. Each has contributed in ways known and unknown to my own development. Thank you!

Robert Reid

Contents

8 Developing New Products and Services 164

9 Managing Products and Services 183

10 Distribution and Supply Chain Management 210

Preface

Today's hospitality marketing student needs to keep up with the constant changes in the hospitality and tourism industry, including consumer trends, revised industry standards, and environmental concerns. The *Sixth Edition* of *Hospitality Marketing Management* presents many new ideas along with established marketing principles, exploring not only the foundations of marketing in the hospitality world but also new trends in the industry. *Hospitality Marketing Management* explores marketing themes unique to hospitality and tourism. **Chapters 1 through 4** provide an introduction to marketing, including the importance of the marketing environment to hospitality and tourism operations. In addition, it provides insight into consumer behavior and how firms can segment markets and target customers. **Chapters 5 through 7** weave application with theory in the discussion of the marketing planning process and gathering information for marketing decisions, including pricing strategy. **Chapters 8 through 11** focus on developing and managing products and services, and the distribution of the products and services, including the world of e-commerce. **Chapters 12 through 15** explore strategies for promoting products and services, including advertising in different forms of media, personal selling, sales promotions, and public relations.

NEW TO THE SIXTH EDITION

The changes to this *Sixth Edition* were made with the goal of improving the text and keeping it up to date. They include:

- **New Chapter 2, "The Marketing Environment and Sustainability."** In keeping with current industry trends, a new chapter has been written to combine the components of the external marketing environment and sustainability practices in hospitality and tourism.

- **More coverage of the Internet and technology.** In this edition, the added coverage of the Internet and technology was continued, including a section on social media under advertising and promotion.

- **Streamlined content throughout the book.** One of the main goals of this edition was to reorganize the chapters and try to streamline the content to be user-friendly for students. There is one less chapter and the content was arranged within each chapter to be more cohesive. Additional topics were added based on reviewer's comments, and some less important topics were removed.

- **More coverage of the tourism industry within each chapter.** It was decided that it would be better for students if the content from the "destination marketing" chapter was integrated in the appropriate context throughout the book, rather than placed together in one chapter at the end of the book. The book now covers destination marketing in Chapter 1, "Introduction to Hospitality Marketing"; Chapter 6, "Information for Marketing Decisions"; Chapter 8, "Developing New Products and Services"; Chapter 9, "Managing Products and Services"; and Chapter 14, "Sales Promotions and Public Relations." In addition, there are new cases related to tourism.

- **More coverage of international marketing.** The importance of a global economy directly affects the hospitality and tourism industry. As in past editions, an effort was made to provide more international examples and references throughout the book to illustrate this trend.

- **New case studies.** Fourteen new case studies were added to this edition, and each chapter now contains two case studies.

PEDAGOGICAL FEATURES

- Each chapter begins with a list of chapter objectives to focus the reader and provide an overview of the chapter content, and then culminates with a more detailed summary of chapter objectives to bring the discussion full circle and reiterate key points.

- Each chapter also contains a list of key terms and concepts at the end. The terms and concepts appear in **bold** throughout the chapter, and definitions for each appear in a glossary as well as in the text margins at the point they are introduced.

11

Electronic Commerce

Courtesy of Mila Supinskaya/Shutterstock

Chapter Objectives

After studying this chapter, you should be able to:

1. Describe the impact of the Internet on the hospitality and tourism industry.
2. Discuss the attributes and scope of electronic commerce, including traits of a networked economy and security issues.
3. Explain the various strategies and business models used in electronic commerce.
4. Describe Internet marketing strategies for websites and e-mail campaigns.

228

---

184 CHAPTER 9 Managing Products and Services

Product levels
The varying levels of goods and services that combine to form the final product.

Product life cycle
A theory that describes how a product progresses from its infancy to its eventual decline.

Resource allocation models
Models used by firms to determine the most effective use of company resources within their product portfolio.

Core product
The most basic form of the product represented by the main benefit sought by consumers to fulfill their needs.

Peripheral services
Additional goods and services that expand the core offering and can be used to obtain a competitive advantage.

Facilitating products
Services that enable the customer to consume the core product by making it available where and when the customer wants it.

Supporting products
Additional goods and services that can be bundled with the core service in an attempt to increase the overall utility or value for consumers.

9.1 INTRODUCTION

Developing a sound marketing strategy is a cornerstone of successful marketing. When a company is successful and its marketing programs are the benchmarks among its competitors, it is often the result of a sound and well-developed marketing strategy. This chapter examines the key aspects of managing the product–service mix. The first area concerns the **product levels** and their importance in differentiating the product. The second area is the **product life cycle**. This advances the concept that all products and services progress through a life cycle, much as people do. The concept of the product life cycle is that different marketing strategies are best used at different stages in the life cycle. The third area involves the **resource allocation models** used by firms to determine the most effective use of company resources within their product portfolios. Most firms have a limited amount of resources, and it is necessary to prioritize their expenditures based on potential returns and company goals.

Finally, this chapter examines the various issues surrounding managing services. The characteristics that distinguish services from goods create different challenges for managers. It is important to manage supply and demand in service industries because of the inability to maintain inventories for intangible products. Basically, there are four product levels: the core product, the facilitating products, the supporting products, and the augmented product. The **core product** is the basic form of the product. In other words, it is the main benefit sought by customers in an attempt to satisfy their needs as recognized by the gap between the ideal state and actual state. For example, for a restaurant, the core product is the food that will resolve the consumer's state of hunger.

As our case see, there are many ways that this need can be satisfied. Similarly, consumers in the lodging industry are looking for guest rooms with a shower. Two of the other product levels can be referred to as **peripheral services**. These services expand the core offering and can be used to obtain a competitive advantage. Peripheral services must meet or exceed customer expectations if customers are to be satisfied. The **facilitating products** are services that enable the customer to consume the core product. They must be present to make the product available where and when the customer wants it. Hotels have front desks and reservations departments, and restaurants have hosts or hostesses and wait staff. **Supporting products** are additional goods and services that can be bundled with the core service in an attempt to increase the overall utility or value for consumers. Examples of supporting products within the hotel industry include concierge service, multilingual staff, 24-hour room service, and complimentary newspapers for business travelers.

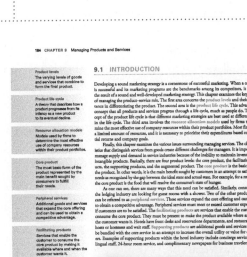

Supporting services such as a hotel gym add value for guests.

Courtesy of Wavebreak Media/Shutterstock

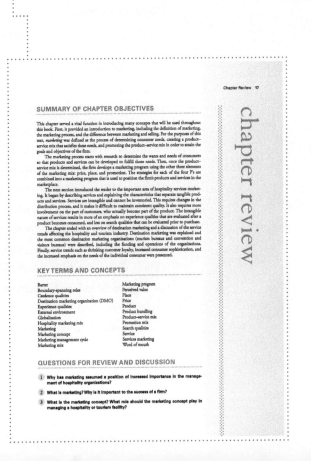

Chapter Review 17

chapter review

SUMMARY OF CHAPTER OBJECTIVES

This chapter served a vital function in introducing many concepts that will be used throughout this book. First, it provided an introduction to marketing, including the definition of marketing, the marketing process, and the difference between marketing and selling. For the purposes of this text, *marketing* was defined as the process of determining consumer needs, creating a product–service mix that satisfies these needs, and promoting the product–service mix in order to attain the goals and objectives of the firm.

The marketing process starts with research to determine the wants and needs of consumers so that products and services can be developed to fulfill those needs. Then, once the product–service mix is determined, the firm develops a marketing program using the other three elements of the marketing mix: price, place, and promotion. The strategies for each of the four P's are combined into a marketing program that is used to position the firm's products and services in the marketplace.

The next section introduced the reader to the important area of hospitality services marketing. It began by describing services and explaining the characteristics that separate tangible products and services. Services are intangible and cannot be inventoried. This requires changes in the distribution process, and it makes it difficult to maintain consistent quality. It also requires more involvement on the part of customers, who actually become part of the product. The intangible nature of services results in more of an emphasis on experience qualities that are evaluated after a product becomes consumed, and less on search qualities that can be evaluated prior to purchase.

The chapter ended with an overview of destination marketing and a discussion of the service trends affecting the hospitality and tourism industry. Destination marketing was explained and the most common destination marketing organizations (tourism bureaus and convention and visitors bureaus) were described, including the funding and operations of the organizations. Finally, service trends such as shrinking customer loyalty, increased consumer sophistication, and the increased emphasis on the needs of the individual consumer were presented.

KEY TERMS AND CONCEPTS

Barter	Marketing program
Boundary-spanning roles	Perceived value
Credence qualities	Place
Destination marketing organization (DMO)	Price
Experience qualities	Product
External environment	Product bundling
Globalization	Product–service mix
Hospitality marketing mix	Promotion mix
Marketing	Search qualities
Marketing concept	Service
Marketing management cycle	Services marketing
Marketing mix	Word of mouth

QUESTIONS FOR REVIEW AND DISCUSSION

1. Why has marketing assumed a position of increased importance in the management of hospitality organizations?

2. What is marketing? Why is it important to the success of a firm?

3. What is the marketing concept? What role should the marketing concept play in managing a hospitality or tourism facility?

Finally, there are questions and case studies provided at the end of each chapter to give students a chance to test their knowledge of the material. Instructors can use the questions to initiate class discussions, or to review for exams. In addition, each chapter contains case studies that connect theory and practice, and can be used as group projects or for individual class assignments and discussions. The cases are based on real-world situations, whether they reference an actual company or disguise the name for proprietary reasons. The *Instructor's Manual* contains answers for the questions and the case studies for easy reference.

SUPPLEMENTARY MATERIALS

The *Instructor's Manual* has been updated, and is available to qualified instructors on the companion website at www.wiley.com/college/bojanic. In addition, **PowerPoint slides,** a downloadable **Test Bank,** and additional **Case Studies** can be accessed from the same website.

We hope you find these improvements and changes to the *Sixth Edition* of *Hospitality Marketing Management* useful in your quest to learn about the exciting world of marketing in the hospitality and tourism industry.

ACKNOWLEDGMENTS

We are grateful for the assistance of these talented educators who have contributed, to this edition as well as previous ones, through their constructive criticism:

Robert Ambrose, Burlington County College

Jeffrey A. Beck, Michigan State University

Kimberly A. Boyle, University of Alabama

Steve Fixman, J. Sargeant Reynolds Community College

Valerian A. Ginter, Fiorello H. LaGuardia Community College of the City University of New York

Zaher A. A. Hallab, California State University, East Bay

Amy Hart, Columbus State Community College

Jungsun Kim, Texas Tech University

Kyungmi Kim, Southern Illinois University

Stuart Levy, Florida International University

Lauren Maguire, Bunker Hill Community College

Ian McVitty, Algonquin College

Juline Mills, Purdue University

Shaun M. Murie, Florida Gulf Coast University

Emily Grace Newkirk, Sandhills Community College

Kathryn Pounders, University of Nevada, Las Vegas

Scott Richardson, Valencia College

Susan Stafford, State University of New York

Introduction to Hospitality Marketing

Courtesy of San Antonio Convention and Visitors Bureau.

Chapter Objectives

After studying this chapter, you should be able to:

1. Explain the importance of marketing to the success of a hospitality operation, including the definition of the term *marketing* and the marketing process.

2. Understand the hospitality marketing mix and the differences between the traditional marketing mix and the hospitality marketing mix.

3. Explain how marketing intangible services is different from marketing tangible goods.

4. Identify the role of a destination marketing organization.

5. Explain the service trends that are affecting the hospitality and tourism industry.

1.1 INTRODUCTION

In recent years, most of the growth in the hospitality industry has occurred in chain operations or in the industry's corporate segment. The hospitality industry leaders, such as Marriott International, Hyatt, Hilton, McDonald's, Subway, Choice International, and Starwood Lodging, continue to increase their share of the market at the expense of smaller chains and independent operators. While independent operators have continued to prosper, especially in the food service sector, the marketplace is much more competitive. An increased level of competition has meant greater emphasis on marketing. No longer is it possible for an individual to open and operate a food service facility successfully on good food alone. To ensure a steady flow of customers, a hospitality manager must possess a thorough understanding of marketing. Without the marketing management skills the hospitality industry demands, a hospitality manager is less likely to achieve success today. With this continual change and increased competition, what are the marketing functions that a successful hospitality manager must fulfill? This chapter introduces basic marketing definitions and concepts, including the marketing mix, the marketing environment, the marketing management cycle, and the role of marketing within the operation of a hospitality and tourism organization.

1.1.1 Marketing Defined

Marketing
The process of creating, pricing, promoting, and distributing products and services to consumers in a mutual exchange of value.

Product
A good, idea, information, or service created to satisfy a consumer's want or need.

Product–service mix
The strategic blend of a firm's tangible and intangible attributes.

Service
An intangible product that is sold or purchased in the marketplace.

The term **marketing** encompasses many different activities, so it is necessary to discuss some of the terms used in the definition of *marketing,* and throughout the text. First, the term **product** refers to all the goods and services that are bundled together and offered to consumers. For example, computers and automobiles are sold as tangible goods, but they include warranties and service contracts as part of the overall product. Therefore, the term *product* refers to both goods and services, but it is often thought of as a good or commodity. Nearly every product sold includes both tangible and intangible elements. Another term that is used to refer to the product as a bundle of goods and services, and eliminate the confusion, is the **product–service mix**.

A **service** is defined as an intangible product that is sold or purchased in the marketplace. A meal purchased at a fast-food restaurant or an occupied room in a hotel is considered a part of the service segment. Why? Simply stated, after the meal is consumed and paid for or after the individual checks out of the hotel, the individual leaves the facility and does not have a tangible product in exchange for the money spent. This individual has consumed a service that is a part of the hospitality and travel industry, one of the largest service industries.

Each year, millions of individuals spend billions of dollars vacationing and traveling for business and pleasure; when the trip is over, nothing tangible remains. To more clearly reflect the role of service industries, such as the hospitality and tourism industry, the definition of *marketing* can be expanded to include references to services. This will eliminate the confusion caused by the semantic differences between products, goods, and services, discussed earlier. According to the American Marketing Association, "Marketing is the activity, set of institutions, and processes for creating, communicating, delivering, and exchanging offerings that have value to customers, clients, partners, and society at large."[1]

The vast majority of hospitality establishments, however, are operated to generate a satisfactory return on investment in the form of profits or excess revenue. These profits are used to pay dividends to stockholders and are reinvested by the organization to promote expansion and further development. Even nonprofit hospitality operations, such as selected hospitals, nursing homes, college or university hospitality operations, and government-run hospitality operations, must be concerned with marketing. Managers of nonprofit operations must still understand the wants and needs of their consumers and provide goods and services at a satisfactory level to as many individuals as possible. A universal concern of all hospitality managers is the financial condition of the organization. Whether a manager is trying to achieve a 20 percent annual return on investment (ROI) or is instead aiming to break even on a very limited budget, the overriding concern is still financial.

Another factor that any definition of *marketing* must include is a focus on the exchange that takes place between a producer and a consumer. In order for an exchange to take place, both parties must receive something they are satisfied with. In most cases, consumers give producers money in exchange for products and services that meet the consumers' wants and needs. However, the exchange can include anything of value to the parties. Before there was a monetary system, people would barter, or exchange goods and services rather than money. There are still companies that engage in bartering today. For example, PepsiCo chose to exchange its soft-drink product with a company in Mexico for wine and other products to avoid incurring the foreign exchange risk associated with the peso, which was devalued at the time.

1.1.2 The Marketing Process

The process of marketing can be best understood by examining the diagram presented in Figure 1.1. As you can see, the target market, or those groups of consumers that the firm chooses to target with its marketing efforts, is at the center of the process. The marketing concept is based on the premise that firms determine customer wants and needs and then design products and services that meet those wants and needs while at the same time meeting the goals of the firm. This concept is an extension of earlier concepts that focused on the production process as a means to design products and services, or the selling of already produced products and services. Today, most firms realize the value of customer input in the new product design process. The issues unique to marketing services are discussed later in this chapter, Chapter 3 focuses on the behavior of hospitality consumers, and Chapter 4 discusses the process of market segmentation and positioning products in the market.

In Figure 1.1, the first layer around the target market, or consumers, is referred to as the marketing mix. The marketing mix has four components: price, product, place, and promotion. These are often referred to as the four P's of marketing, and they are the variables that managers can control. Firms will manipulate the marketing mix variables to formulate strategies that are combined in a marketing program for a product or service. This program is the basis on which the firm's products and services compete with the offerings of other firms in the competitive environment. The marketing mix will be discussed in more detail later in this chapter. The product component is covered in Chapters 7 and 8, the price component is discussed in Chapter 9, the place (distribution and delivery) component is presented in Chapters 10 and 11, and the promotion component is addressed in Chapters 12 through 15.

Barter
A process of exchanging goods and services rather than money.

Marketing concept
The marketing concept is based on the premise that firms determine customer wants and needs, and then design products and services that meet those wants and needs, while also meeting the goals of the firm.

Marketing mix
The four components (price, product, place, and promotion) that are controlled by organizations and used to influence consumers to purchase goods and services.

Marketing program
The set of strategies based on the manipulation of the marketing mix to meet target market preferences.

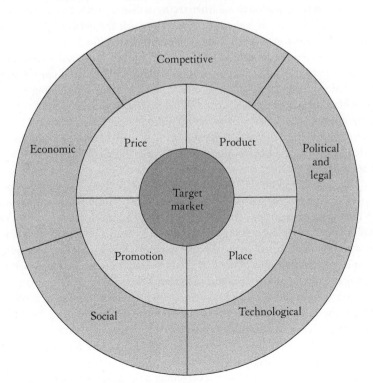

FIGURE 1.1 • The marketing mix and external environment.

External environment
The outside influences on the marketing process that are not under the control of the organization.

Marketing management cycle
The dynamic process involving marketing planning, execution, and evaluation.

The outside layer of the diagram of Figure 1.1 represents the external environment that influences the marketing process. The state of the economy, trends in society, competitive pressures, political and legal developments, and advances in technology all affect the performance of a product or service. Firms cannot control these environments, but they must monitor the changes and trends in the respective environments and look for opportunities and threats. The components of the external environment and some of the current trends that affect hospitality and travel firms will be examined in more detail in Chapter 2.

Firms must continually monitor environments and make changes in their marketing programs. The marketing management cycle involves marketing planning, marketing execution, and marketing evaluation. This cycle is discussed briefly in this chapter, and Chapter 5 covers the marketing planning process in depth. To be successful in marketing planning, firms need to conduct research and collect information that can be used to evaluate their programs. Chapter 6 discusses the marketing research process used to gather information to be stored in marketing information systems and used to make marketing decisions.

1.1.3 The Emergence of the Marketing Concept

If a hospitality organization is to market its product–service mix successfully, it is essential that the marketing concept be thoroughly understood and fully implemented. Understanding the marketing concept is not difficult, but implementing it may prove to be very challenging for management. Simply stated, the marketing concept is a consumer-oriented philosophy that focuses all available resources on satisfying the needs and wants of the consumer, thereby resulting in profits. As an old rhyme states, "To sell Jane Smith what Jane Smith buys, you've got to see things through Jane Smith's eyes." Clearly, it is difficult to sell something to someone who has no need for it. If the firm adopts a consumer-oriented marketing philosophy, however, the product–service mix will be designed in direct response to unsatisfied consumer needs. As a result, very limited actual selling will be necessary. In such instances, supply and demand are in balance, and both the consumer and the hospitality providers are satisfied.

Table 1.1 illustrates the two different philosophies of the marketing concept that are often practiced in the hospitality and tourism industry. One demonstrates the actions of a manager who applies the marketing concept; the other demonstrates actions that are not consistent with the marketing concept. The key question to ask when trying to distinguish between the two approaches is: Are consumers given priority or is the operation run to suit the needs of the employees, management, or owners? A manager of a hospitality operation has a difficult series of daily challenges. First, a manager is expected to successfully satisfy the needs of the hospitality consumers. Second, the owners expect a manager to maintain the level of expenses within certain predetermined limits that are usually defined in actual dollars or as a percentage of sales. Third, a manager is expected to generate a satisfactory return on investment (ROI) for the owners.

This return might be the break-even point in a nonprofit operation or a 10, 15, or 20 percent rate of return in a commercial operation. Whatever the expected return, a manager is faced with a series of difficult objectives to achieve, and these objectives often conflict with one another. Even in the most successful companies, there are limited resources that must be used to accomplish seemingly unlimited goals and objectives. Regardless of how well the company has performed in the past, owners and senior management will always expect a little more in the future. Guests develop ever-increasing expectations for all aspects of the product–service mix. Owners want increased profits, and the employees want a little more each year. The manager's task is to balance the three objectives mentioned in the preceding paragraph. Managers often view profitability as the single-most important objective of the firm. Yet, for the long-term financial well-being of the firm, profits may not be the most important objective. It is quite possible, as many shortsighted owners and managers have demonstrated, to achieve high levels of short-term profitability at the expense of long-term consumer satisfaction and long-term profits. After a period of time, however, consumers will perceive that they are not receiving a high level of value for their money, and the operation will develop a reputation for being overpriced and/or offering poor service. As a result, the number of patrons is likely to decline, and so will profitability.

By contrast, if management establishes a consumer orientation and places customer satisfaction as the number-one priority, the firm's products and services are more likely to meet customers'

DECISIONS	WHEN THE MARKETING CONCEPT IS APPLIED	WHEN THE MARKETING CONCEPT IS NOT APPLIED
Menu design	"Let's conduct focus group interviews using our current and target market customers to determine which potential new menu items we should add to our menu."	"Let's add two steaks to the menu; that's what I like to eat."
Pricing	"How do you think our guests will perceive the price value of our new weekend package if we increase the price by 5 percent?"	"Let's increase the price by 5 percent; that's what we did last year."
Guest service	"I'm very sorry that you had to wait 20 minutes for your breakfast this morning. May I offer you a complimentary breakfast today, or would you like the credit applied toward your breakfast tomorrow?"	"I'm sorry you had to wait, but we were short-handed today. One of the servers called in sick."
Guest requests	"We don't have any rooms with a king bed available at this time, but I can have one ready for you in 30 minutes. Can I have the bell staff check your bags until then?"	"We don't have any rooms with a king bed left. You'll have to take a room with two double beds."
Reactions to negative guest comments	"That is a very good idea. I'll talk about it at our staff meeting tomorrow and see if we can use your suggestion to improve service. Thanks for suggesting that."	"Your idea isn't feasible, and besides, it's against our policy."

TABLE 1.1 • **Marketing Concept Philosophies**

expectations. As a result, they will return more frequently to the hospitality operation, and this will have a positive influence on long-term sales and profits. In addition, by telling their friends and acquaintances about their positive experiences, satisfied consumers are likely to influence others to patronize the establishment. This **word of mouth** passed on by satisfied customers can become a very important part of a firm's promotional efforts. It doesn't cost anything, yet it can be a very powerful influence on sales, and as sales increase, so does profitability. Experience shows

Word of mouth
A spoken communication between consumers that involves their perceptions about a product or service.

Courtesy of The Melting Pot.

To remain competitive, hospitality organizations must keep up with the ever-changing market.

that when the marketing concept is understood and applied by all of a firm's employees, substantial changes have often been made in the establishment's manner of operation, and the financial results have often been improved significantly.

1.2 THE MARKETING MIX

Marketing managers have used the term *marketing mix* for a long time. The concept of the marketing mix has gained universal acceptance. It is important for hospitality marketing students to understand this concept, both conceptually and strategically. This section outlines the major components of the traditional marketing mix, and the next section covers the hospitality marketing mix that was offered as an alternative for the industry. We will explain the similarities and differences between the two approaches. A successful hospitality organization is one that focuses on the needs and wants of the consumers and markets the product–service mix of the operation. Management of this type of operation involves integrating the components of the marketing mix into a marketing program that will appeal to potential consumers and meet the goals and objectives of the firm. The following sections will introduce the components of the marketing mix, which will be discussed in more detail in Chapters 7 through 15.

1.2.1 The Traditional Marketing Mix

The marketing mix, many believe, consists of four elements, often called the four P's of marketing: price, product, place, and promotion.

Price
Price refers to the value placed by a firm on its products and services.

1.2.1.1 PRICE. The price component refers to the value placed by a firm on its products and services. Some of the decisions involve pricing the product line, discounting strategies, and positioning against competitors.

1.2.1.2 PRODUCT. This component refers to the unique combination of goods and services offered by a firm to consumers. The product includes both the tangible and intangible elements of the service offering. Product decisions involve product attributes such as quality, the breadth and mix of the product line (i.e., the number and type of products and services offered by a firm), and services such as warranties and guarantees.

Place
This component, sometimes called *distribution,* refers to the manner in which the products and services are being delivered to consumers. It involves decisions related to the location of facilities and the use of intermediaries.

1.2.1.3 PLACE. The place component of marketing refers to the manner in which the products and services are being delivered to consumers. This component is sometimes referred to as distribution, and it involves decisions related to the location of facilities and the use of intermediaries. In addition, the marketing of services includes the decision regarding customer involvement in the production process.

Promotion mix
The basic elements (advertising, public relations, sales promotions, and personal selling) used by organizations to communicate with consumers.

1.2.1.4 PROMOTION. This component refers to the methods used to communicate with consumer markets. The promotion mix includes advertising, personal selling, sales promotions (e.g., coupons, rebates, and contests), and publicity. These are the vehicles that can be used to communicate the firm's intended messages to consumers. The decisions for promotion involve the amount to be spent on each component of the promotion mix, the strategies for each of the components, and the overall message to be sent.

To achieve success in marketing a hospitality operation, a manager must closely examine and understand all the components of the marketing mix. To be successful, these components must be combined into well-conceived marketing programs and managed properly. There is no magical formula that will guarantee success. If there were, no hospitality operation would ever fail or go out of business. Yet each year, many hospitality operations fail because managers are unable to combine the elements of the marketing mix into effective marketing programs, or the marketing mix is not implemented properly.

Courtesy of Red Lobster Restaurants, Orlando, Florida.

Hospitality firms use the elements of the marketing mix to establish a competitive position in the market.

1.2.2 The Hospitality Marketing Mix

Just as researchers have demonstrated distinct differences between goods and services, some researchers believe that the traditional four P's approach to the marketing mix does not apply to the hospitality industry. Rather, a modified marketing mix is more appropriate. This **hospitality marketing mix** consists of five components:[2]

1. Product–service mix

2. Presentation mix

3. Communication mix

4. Pricing mix

5. Distribution mix

Hospitality marketing mix
Hospitality marketing mix consists of five components: product–service mix, presentation mix, communication mix, pricing mix, and distribution mix.

1.2.2.1 PRODUCT–SERVICE MIX.   The product–service mix is a combination of all the products and services offered by the hospitality operation, including both tangible and intangible elements. For example, it includes such things as the type of guest room, the amenities offered, and the broad array of elements offered to the consumer. Section 1.3 addresses further the unique nature of services. Keep in mind that once a hospitality consumer leaves the hotel or restaurant, there is nothing tangible to show. Because the consumer has purchased and consumed the service, the largest part of the hospitality industry product–service mix is indeed the intangible elements of service.

1.2.2.2 PRESENTATION MIX.   The presentation mix includes those elements that the marketing manager uses to increase the tangibility of the product–service mix as perceived by the consumer. This mix includes physical location, atmosphere (lighting, sound, and color), and personnel.

1.2.2.3 COMMUNICATION MIX.   The communication mix involves all communication that takes place between the hospitality operation and the consumer. It includes advertising, marketing research, and feedback about consumer perceptions. The communication mix should be viewed as a two-way communication link, rather than as a simple one-way link with the hospitality operation communicating to the consumer. This two-way link allows for the traditional advertising and promotion that flow from the seller to the buyer, but it also allows for marketing research and other data collection vehicles. In these cases, the seller is seeking information and data from the consumer, thereby establishing open communication with the various market segments.

There are some similarities and differences between the traditional marketing mix and the hospitality marketing mix. In the hospitality version, the product component is expanded to include some aspects of distribution. People are part of the production process in services, and distribution occurs in the presence of the consumer. The communication mix is almost identical with the promotion component in the traditional marketing mix, although it does include some additional communications such as marketing research. Finally, the presentation mix represents the largest departure from the traditional marketing mix. It includes price and some of the aspects of the place component such as location, and it adds elements such as atmosphere and the personal contact between customers and employees.

1.2.2.4 PRICING MIX. In addition to the actual price a firm charges, the pricing mix encompasses the consumer's perception of value. The pricing mix includes such variables as volume discounts and bundling multiple products together for an overall discounted price. This bundling approach is used extensively by fast-food chains as a method to increase spending per customer.

1.2.2.5 DISTRIBUTION MIX. The distribution mix includes all distribution channels available between the firm and the target market. Historically, distribution occurred at the point of production, such as the restaurant where the food was produced. This has changed as a result of newer distribution channels, such as the Internet and e-commerce; the importance of the distribution mix has increased.

The marketing mix, whether designed in the traditional or modified hospitality services format, is an important concept for managers of marketing functions. Initially, the marketing mix is used to formulate a marketing strategy and plan (see Chapter 5), but it pervades all aspects of marketing management. Several external factors can reduce the effectiveness of the manager's efforts to successfully implement all the components of the hospitality marketing mix. These factors, which may have either direct or indirect influence, are consumer perceptions, attitudes, and behavior; industry practices and trends; local competition; broad national and international trends; and government policy and legislation.

1.3 SERVICES MARKETING

The growth in the service sector of the worldwide economy has been phenomenal in the last several decades. In the United States, services currently account for more than 75 percent of the gross domestic product (GDP), which is a popular measure of an economy's productivity. Similarly, on an international scale, services continue to account for an ever-increasing percentage of economic activity. Most new jobs are created in the service sector, and the growth in the hospitality and tourism industry is a major contributor.

From the 1940s until the mid-1980s, the emphasis within the marketing community was on products. Today, services have surpassed products and have taken on a more important role in marketing. Services, such as those offered by providers in the hospitality and tourism industry, have developed marketing strategies and practices that are unique. It has been established that the strategies, tactics, and practices that have been used successfully for product marketers do not always work successfully for those who market services. With the distinct differences between products and services in mind, the field of services marketing has evolved.

Services marketing
The use of marketing principles to create and deliver intangible items to consumers.

1.3.1 Services Defined

Unlike products, which are tangible, services are intangible. A service is not a physical good; rather, it is the performance of an act or a deed and does not result in the physical ownership of anything. This performance often requires consumers to be present during the production or delivery of the service. Service industries, including hospitality and tourism, are actually selling consumers an experience. Services vary based on numerous criteria: the degree of tangibility, the degree of customization, the skills of the service provider, the amount of customer contact, and whether they are services for people (e.g., restaurants and health care) or services performed for goods (e.g., dry cleaning and equipment repairs).

Service employees such as front-desk agents, housekeepers, hostesses, wait staff, car rental agents, flight attendants, and travel agents are responsible for creating positive experiences for customers. These frontline employees are critical to the success of service firms and play **boundary-spanning roles** because of their direct contact with customers. These roles are important because customers' perceptions of service firms are formed as a result of their dealings with these employees who represent the company and its intangible product.

Several reasons underlie the remarkable growth in services. Two leading services marketing experts, Christopher Lovelock and Lauren Wright, cite numerous reasons for this growth. The following is a list of reasons that pertain to hospitality and tourism:[3]

- **Changing patterns of government regulation.**   The reduction in government regulation has paved the way for the growth of services. The trend is for government to take a less active role in the regulation of business activities, such as removing barriers to entry and relaxing (or removing) regulations governing marketing elements such as price. For example travel firms such as airlines and hotels have been able to implement models that adjust price continuously in an attempt to sell excess capacity that cannot be inventoried. This is basically a legal form of price discrimination that cannot be used for tangible goods.

- **Privatization of some public and nonprofit services.**   Privatization is a process whereby the government allows an industry or business to change from governmental or public ownership or control to a private enterprise. This transformation is necessary in a market-driven economy where meeting consumer needs is a main priority and cost containment is necessary. For example, many countries have released the control of airlines and other travel-related agencies to private firms to improve service quality and make the operations more efficient.

- **Technological innovation.**   Technology continues to alter the way firms do business and interact with consumers. In all types of businesses, consumers take a more active role in the service delivery process. For example, in an effort to reduce labor costs and increase speed of service to customers, airlines have aggressively promoted self–check-in, both at ticket counter kiosks and through their websites prior to arrival at the airport. Customers may print boarding passes, receipts, and other documents without intervention by an airline employee.

Boundary-spanning roles
Roles that frontline employees (e.g., front-desk clerks, waiters, flight attendants, travel agents) perform.

Racorn/Shutterstock

The front-desk agent often sets the tone for guest service.

Perceived value
The worth or utility of a product or service held in the minds of consumers.

Express checkout for hotel guests has been in place for many years, but hotel chains continue to experiment with ways to enhance the service, thereby reducing labor costs and/or increasing the customers' perceived value. In other settings, touch-screen computers collect feedback from guests, in much the same manner that comment cards have been used previously. The ease with which a company can maintain and access a database has permitted the development of proficient reservation systems and has led to more enhanced frequent traveler programs. The use of more sophisticated reservations and property management systems has allowed hospitality and tourism firms to improve the level of service provided to guests. Guest history data serve as another example of how a hospitality organization can use technology to gain a competitive advantage. If a hotel guest requests a specific type of pillow, for example, staff can record this preference within the individual's guest history file. When this guest checks into another hotel operated by the chain, the items that were previously requested can be waiting, without the guest even having to request them.

- **Growth in service chains and franchise networks.** Much of the growth in service firms, including the hospitality industry, has been the direct result of franchising efforts by some of the major companies. Notable lodging organizations such as Choice Hotels International and Marriott International, as well as food service firms such as McDonald's, Burger King, Subway, Taco Bell, and Wendy's, have all used franchising as a major vehicle for growth. The continued growth of the hospitality industry by means of franchising has put additional stress on independent owners and operators. In fact, each year the percentage of hospitality and tourism operations that are independently operated decreases.

Globalization
Firms expand outside of their traditional domestic markets (i.e., expanding worldwide).

- **Internationalization and globalization.** Increasing shareholder value often remains directly associated with increasing company sales and profits, and globalization is one means of achieving this. As more and more of the prime locations are developed domestically, companies look internationally for expansion opportunities. This has been particularly true for fast-food franchisors; a significant proportion of their expansion during the last few years has occurred outside of their traditional domestic markets.

- **Pressures to improve productivity.** There is stiff competition in many of the service industries, including hospitality, and the pressure from investors for higher returns on capital has led to an increased emphasis on improving productivity and reducing costs. In many cases, managers seek to reduce labor costs by running leaner operations or using technology to replace humans for some tasks. An example of this is how airlines encourage passengers to check in via the Internet, thereby reducing the number of passengers who need to check in at the airport. Although increasing productivity and profits remains a highly desirable goal, it must not be done at the expense of long-term customer satisfaction. Without long-term satisfaction, future profitability is at risk.

- **The service quality movement.** With the advent of consumerism, the public's perception is that service quality has declined. In response, successful firms are using the customers' perceptions of quality to set performance standards, rather than relying solely on operationally defined standards for service quality. Companies often conduct extensive research to determine the key elements that impact the customers' perceptions of service quality. When Ritz-Carlton won the Malcolm Baldrige National Quality Award, this was tangible evidence that paying careful attention to customers' service expectations can have a dramatic effect on the firm.

- **Expansion of leasing and rental businesses.** The expansion of businesses that lease equipment and personnel to firms has been a contributing factor in the growth of the service sector. More and more firms are looking to outsource elements of their operation, and they often start with elements that are not part of the firm's core product or business. For example, most hotels that host meetings and conventions have outsourced the servicing of the audiovisual needs of groups to a company that specializes in that type of business. The company, in turn, leases the audiovisual equipment to groups that are holding meetings in the hotel. The company is able to provide more up-to-date and specialized equipment to groups than the hotel might if it provided the service itself. The hotel does not have to maintain an inventory of equipment, and therefore capital costs are reduced.

- **Hiring and promotion of innovative managers.**   In the past, managers in the service industries often spent their entire careers within a single industry segment, or perhaps even with the same firm. This situation has changed, especially at the corporate level of management. Firms often hire individuals from other industries to provide a fresh perspective and new ideas. Many of the large lodging chains hire key executives from other industries that can provide valuable insight in areas like human resources, sales, marketing, and finance.

1.3.2 The Nature of Services: Differences between Goods and Services

Along with the growth in services, an appreciation for the ways in which services are different from products has developed. The traditional ways of marketing tangible products are not equally effective in services marketing. In many industries, marketing involves tangible manufactured products, such as automobiles, washing machines, and clothing, whereas service industries focus on intangible products such as travel and food service. However, before exploring how services get successfully marketed, we need to examine the ways services differ from products. Lovelock and Wright have identified nine key differences:[4]

1. **No ownership by customers.**   A customer does not take ownership when purchasing a service. There is no transfer of assets.

2. **Service products as intangible performers.**   The value of purchasing services lies in the nature of the performance. For example, if you decide to celebrate a birthday or anniversary by dining at an expensive restaurant, the value lies in the way in which the service actors (i.e., waiters and waitresses) perform. When servers come to the table and present all the entrees simultaneously, the choreographed presentation appears in the same manner as a choreographed play or performance.

3. **Greater involvement of customers in the production process.**   Because consumers tend to be present when receiving service within a hospitality operation, they remain involved in the service production. In many instances, they are directly involved through the element of self-service. Examples of this can be seen in fast-food restaurants when customers poor their own drinks, or in airports when customers check-in at kiosks. In any case, a customer's level of satisfaction depends on the nature of the interaction with the service provider, the nature of the physical facilities in which the service gets provided, and the nature of the interaction with other guests present in the facility at the time the service is provided.

4. **People as part of the product.**   People or firms that purchase services come in contact with other consumers as well as the service employees. For example, a hotel guest waits in line at the front desk or the concierge desk with other guests. In addition, the guests share facilities such as the pool, the restaurant, and the fitness center. Therefore, service firms must also manage consumer interactions to the best of their abilities to ensure customer satisfaction. For instance, a hotel's sales office would not want to book a nondrinking religious group at the same time as a high school senior trip. The two groups are significantly different in behavior, and the expectation is that they would not mix well within the facilities at the same time.

5. **Greater variability in operational inputs and outputs.**   In a manufacturing setting, the operational production can be controlled very carefully. For example, staff accurately manage inventory and precisely calculate production times. Services, however, are delivered in real time, with many variables not being fully under the control of managers. For example, if a guest has been promised an early check-in but all of the guests from the preceding night are late in checking out, it becomes more difficult for the hotel to honor the arriving guest's request. In other words, it is more difficult to control quality and offer a consistent service experience than manufacturing a product. Service firms try to minimize the amount of variability between service encounters, but much of the final product stays situational. There are many uncontrollable aspects of the delivery process such as weather, the number of consumers present, the attitudes of the consumers, and the attitudes of the employees.

6. **Harder for consumers to evaluate.** Consumers can receive considerable information regarding the purchase of products; however, they often do not obtain it for services. Prior to buying a product, a consumer can research the product attributes and performance and use this information when making a purchase decision, especially an important one. In contrast, it is difficult to evaluate a service until after it is consumed. For example, travelers normally book hotel rooms and cruise vacations months in advance and have to wait until after the trip to evaluate the experience.

7. **No inventories for services.** Due to the intangible nature of services, they cannot be inventoried for future use. Therefore, a lost sale can never be recaptured. When a seat remains empty on a flight, a hotel room stays vacant, or a table stays unoccupied in a restaurant, the potential revenue for these services at that point in time becomes lost forever. In other words, services are perishable, much like produce in a supermarket or items in a bakery. It remains critical for hospitality and tourism firms to manage supply and demand in an attempt to minimize unused capacity. For example, restaurants offer early-bird specials and hotels offer discounted room rates in an attempt to shift demand from peak periods to nonpeak periods, thereby increasing revenue and profits.

8. **Importance of time.** Hospitality services are generally produced and consumed simultaneously, unlike tangible products, which are manufactured, inventoried, and then sold at a later date. Customers must be present to receive the service. There are definite limits to the amount of time that customers are willing to wait to receive, or consume, a service. Service firms study the phenomenon of service queues, or the maximum amount of time a customer will wait for a service before it has a significant (negative) impact on his or her perception of service quality. This is a common issue at tourist attractions. For example, amusement parks offer priority passes as either a restricted component of the basic ticket purchase, or at an additional price, that allows visitors to go through shorter ride lines.

9. **Different distribution channels.** The distribution channel for services is usually more direct than the traditional channel (i.e., manufacturer-wholesaler-retailer-consumer) used by many product firms. The simultaneous production and consumption normally associated with service delivery limits the use of intermediaries. The service firm usually comprises the roles of both the manufacturer and the retailer, with no need for a wholesaler to inventory its products. Consumers are present to consume the meals prepared in a restaurant, to take advantage of the amenities in a hotel, and to travel between cities by plane.

Intangible products, such as a cruise vacation, are the basis of services marketing.

Courtesy of Carnival Cruise Lines.

1.3.3   Search, Experience, and Credence Qualities

Consumer behavior is covered in greater depth in Chapter 3, but a brief introduction to the subject as it relates to services becomes useful at this point. When consumers make purchase decisions, they move through a series of steps that explain the thought process leading up to and following the purchase of a product or service. Prior to making a purchase decision, consumers look for information about the product or service. Search qualities are attributes that the consumer can investigate prior to making a purchase. When purchasing hospitality and tourism services, consumers rely heavily on word of mouth and on promotional elements such as advertising and publicity. Because services are intangible, search qualities can be difficult to evaluate. However, advances in technology and the increase in consumer advocacy groups have resulted in more information being available to consumers prior to purchase.

The second set of qualities consumers use to evaluate services are experience qualities. These refer to the attributes that can be evaluated only after the purchase and consumption of a service. The intangible nature of services forces consumers to rely heavily on experience qualities in the final evaluation of services. Therefore, a high risk remains associated with the purchase of services. For example, consumers who want to purchase an automobile will test-drive the car and review and consult the consumer performance data that are available on that model. Conversely, consumers who rent cars cannot evaluate their purchases until after they have committed their payment. Few consumers will take the time or make the effort to test-drive potential rental cars prior to making a decision at the time of rental. Similarly, consumers are taking a risk when they choose a restaurant because they cannot sample meals before they are purchased.

Finally, credence qualities are those attributes that are difficult to evaluate even after the service is consumed. Even though you arrive safely at your destination after a flight, you cannot evaluate the pilot's work in any real depth. In many cases, you know a service was not performed correctly only when an obvious mistake exists. For example, bacteria often appear on food served in restaurants, but the public becomes aware of it only when major ramifications such as food poisoning or deaths get publicized.

Purchase decisions related to services are more difficult to make because of the lack of search qualities and the difficulty in evaluating credence qualities. Consumers tend to rely on their own past experiences and those of others when making purchase decisions. Therefore, service firms must obtain as much feedback from consumers as possible. If consumers do not return, the firm may not know why, and the consumers will probably tell others about their experience. Service firms should know if consumers are not satisfied so that appropriate actions can be taken to improve the quality of service and increase repeat business.

1.4   DESTINATION MARKETING

A tourism destination offers both tangible and intangible products. The tangible products include the tourist attractions and facilities for lodging, dining, shopping, and parking. The intangible product is the image of the destination. The complexity of destination marketing is that tourists usually select among destinations based on the total set of destination attributes, not an individual firm's marketing effort. Therefore, in the increasingly competitive marketplace, marketing alliances between the private and the public sectors can create economies of scale for the destination. In the United States, tourism marketing alliances are often formed by a combination of agencies such as the convention and visitor bureaus, Chambers of Commerce, local governments, and tourism operators.

According to the Destination Marketing Association International (DMAI), destination marketing organizations (DMOs) are primarily concerned with promoting the long-term development and marketing of a destination, focusing on convention sales, tourism marketing, and service.[5] The two most common forms of DMOs are convention and visitors bureaus (CVBs) and tourism bureaus. In fact, DMAI changed its name from the International Association of Convention and Visitors Bureaus (IACVB) to better represent the function (i.e., destination marketing), rather than just one of the organizations involved in marketing destinations. Destination

Search qualities
Attributes that the consumer can investigate prior to making a purchase.

Experience qualities
Attributes that can be evaluated only after the purchase and consumption of a service.

Credence qualities
Attributes that are difficult to evaluate even after the service is consumed.

Destination Marketing Organization (DMO)
Government or nonprofit organization responsible for developing and promoting tourism and visitation to a destination.

marketing organizations market their destinations to business travelers, tour operators, meeting and event planners, and individual tourists.

Tourism bureaus are mainly government organizations that are funded through the government's revenue sources such as state and federal taxes. (This could be referred to as provinces and national, respectively, in other countries.) These organizations are part of the government system that includes other divisions such as education, transportation, and defense. In the United States, convention and visitors bureaus are typically not-for-profit organizations that are funded through a combination of hotel taxes and membership dues. A small percentage (15 to 20 percent) of CVBs are either a government agency or a division of the Chamber of Commerce. Other funding sources include government grants, revenues from advertising and visitor center services, and donated services. However, convention and visitors bureaus do not normally charge customers for their services. Finally, the major expense for CVBs is advertising and promotion (including personal selling).

The membership of a CVB consists of organizations from the various stakeholders. The stakeholders for CVBs are those businesses who sell products or services that are attractive to associations and corporations that hold meetings and events, as well as the individual travelers. For example, obvious stakeholders would be hotels and other lodging facilities, convention centers, restaurants, and tourist attractions. Other, less obvious, stakeholders would be event organizers, shopping facilities, and convention services suppliers such as decorators, entertainment companies, destination management companies (DMCs), and local transportation companies. Convention and visitors bureaus are governed by a board of directors that follows a published list of bylaws. The major goals of CVBs are the following:[6]

- To encourage associations and corporations to hold meetings, conventions, and trade shows in the area.
- To assist associations and corporations coordinating their conventions, seminars, and trade shows in the area.
- To provide services to tour planners, both domestic and international.
- To provide leadership for the visitor industry, build the image of the area, and encourage marketing activities.
- To provide additional support to travel writers to help sell the area.

1.5   SERVICE TRENDS AFFECTING THE HOSPITALITY AND TOURISM INDUSTRY

Identifying trends within any business is one of the keys to success. Being in a position to identify what is occurring and what is likely to occur in the future remains very important. When studying trends in a broad sense, one should examine five major areas: the competitive environment, the economic environment, the political and legal environment, the social environment, and the technological environment. This is referred to as the external environment and is covered in detail in Chapter 2.

Several issues and trends are critical to understanding hospitality and tourism marketing. They help put into proper perspective what occurs within the competitive marketplace. Three trends that are having an impact on the hospitality industry and will continue to do so are shrinking customer loyalty, increasing customer sophistication, and increasing emphasis on the needs of individual customers.

1.5.1   Shrinking Customer Loyalty

Advertising and promotion for the hospitality and tourism industry's product–service mix have traditionally focused on the product, the services provided, and the physical plant or atmosphere in which the customer enjoys the product–service mix. Today, many hospitality and tourism firms focus their promotions on price; that is, heavy price competition exists along with a good deal of discounting. Unfortunately, price discounting exists as a short-term strategy that seldom builds brand loyalty. Consumers often shop around for the best deal and are loyal only to organizations that give them a consistently superior one. Recognizing this, companies have sought ways to increase brand loyalty, especially among heavy users of the product–service mix. The best examples of this approach are the frequent-flyer programs promoted by the airlines and the frequent-traveler programs promoted by the lodging companies. These loyalty programs are commonplace in the lodging industry; all of the major chains use loyalty programs to encourage and reward frequent guests. The strategy behind loyalty programs is to hook the customer with points that can be redeemed for products or services. The more frequently the customer stays at a hotel operated by the company, the more points are earned. The basic concepts common to all of these programs are as follows:

- Identify individuals who frequently purchase your product–service mix.
- Recognize the contribution those individuals make to the success of your company.
- Reward those individuals with awards and incentives that will increase their loyalty to your company and its brands.

Tie-ins with other companies providing travel-related services are also frequently used. For example, airlines, hotels, and car rental companies frequently offer bonus points within their programs if the traveler uses the services offered by one of the companies participating in the tie-in. Both the airlines and the hotel companies are constantly making minor alterations to their programs.

1.5.2   Increasing Consumer Sophistication

The budget segment of the lodging industry has undergone significant growth in the last several years. This growth has been fueled by the consumer demand for affordable accommodations that provide good value. In fact, consumers focus more on value and less on quality or price alone. Consumers have become more sophisticated and understand the concept of value at any price level. Companies have responded with brands that offer good quality at an affordable price (e.g., Hampton Inn, Comfort Inn, Holiday Inn Express, and Fairfield Inn). Each of these brands features nicely appointed guest rooms, limited or no public meeting space, limited or no food service provided on the hotel site, and a complimentary continental breakfast for guests. These limited-service brands incur lower development and operating expenses and thereby can provide guests with a lower price and good value, something that all consumers are seeking.

Hotels in the upscale segment are also trying to increase the consumer's perception of value. They continually provide a broad assortment of amenities, such as health clubs on the property, business centers, rooms that provide more work space for business travelers, and personalized concierge service. These properties are striving to become "one-stop" destinations, providing a complete product–service mix that includes many food and beverage outlets, in-house office services, a wide variety of meeting room configurations, and other services, such as recreation, that will appeal to potential guests. Within the fast-food service segment, companies often "bundle" their products in an attempt to increase sales and provide a better value for their customers. For example, they combine a sandwich, a large order of french fries, and a large soft drink at a price lower than what the items would cost if purchased separately. Similarly, tour operators and travel agents attempt to provide customers with more value by "bundling" the various components of travel (e.g., airline ticket, hotel room, car rental, and tickets for tourist attractions) at a price lower than the sum of the individual components. This approach is known as **product bundling**.

Product bundling
An approach where goods and services are combined into one offering, typically at a lower price than if the individual goods and services were purchased separately.

1.5.3   Increased Emphasis on the Needs of Individual Customers

The markets within both hospitality and tourism segments have been segmented for a long time. In the past 20 years, this trend has become even more pronounced. Mass marketing has become a thing of the past as more firms extend their product lines to meet the specific needs of smaller segments of travelers and diners. This phenomenon has become most apparent in the lodging industry.

Hotels provide amenities, such as health clubs, to increase the consumer's perception of value.

During the last decade, most of the major lodging chains developed several new brands or types of lodging properties to appeal to market segments that they were not currently serving. In addition, many hotel chains have merged with, or acquired, other hotel chains that focus on different market segments. For example, Marriott purchased the Ritz-Carlton chain in the 1990s to have better access to the luxury hotel market.

Improvements in technology have given firms the ability to maintain large databases that detail consumer purchasing behavior and preferences. This information can be used to direct marketing efforts toward individual customers or market segments. Instead of relying on the mass media for promotions, a marketer can target past customers through direct mail and e-mail with special promotions and incentives that have a higher probability of being successful. There is more customization of products and promotions and less wasted coverage with media campaigns.

chapter review

SUMMARY OF CHAPTER OBJECTIVES

This chapter served a vital function in introducing many concepts that will be used throughout this book. First, it provided an introduction to marketing, including the definition of marketing, the marketing process, and the difference between marketing and selling. For the purposes of this text, *marketing* was defined as the process of determining consumer needs, creating a product–service mix that satisfies these needs, and promoting the product–service mix in order to attain the goals and objectives of the firm.

The marketing process starts with research to determine the wants and needs of consumers so that products and services can be developed to fulfill those needs. Then, once the product–service mix is determined, the firm develops a marketing program using the other three elements of the marketing mix: price, place, and promotion. The strategies for each of the four P's are combined into a marketing program that is used to position the firm's products and services in the marketplace.

The next section introduced the reader to the important area of hospitality services marketing. It began by describing services and explaining the characteristics that separate tangible products and services. Services are intangible and cannot be inventoried. This requires changes in the distribution process, and it makes it difficult to maintain consistent quality. It also requires more involvement on the part of customers, who actually become part of the product. The intangible nature of services results in more of an emphasis on experience qualities that are evaluated after a product becomes consumed, and less on search qualities that can be evaluated prior to purchase.

The chapter ended with an overview of destination marketing and a discussion of the service trends affecting the hospitality and tourism industry. Destination marketing was explained and the most common destination marketing organizations (tourism bureaus and convention and visitors bureaus) were described, including the funding and operations of the organizations. Finally, service trends such as shrinking customer loyalty, increased consumer sophistication, and the increased emphasis on the needs of the individual consumer were presented.

KEY TERMS AND CONCEPTS

Barter
Boundary-spanning roles
Credence qualities
Destination marketing organization (DMO)
Experience qualities
External environment
Globalization
Hospitality marketing mix
Marketing
Marketing concept
Marketing management cycle
Marketing mix

Marketing program
Perceived value
Place
Price
Product
Product bundling
Product–service mix
Promotion mix
Search qualities
Service
Services marketing
Word of mouth

QUESTIONS FOR REVIEW AND DISCUSSION

1 Why has marketing assumed a position of increased importance in the management of hospitality organizations?

2 What is marketing? Why is it important to the success of a firm?

3 What is the marketing concept? What role should the marketing concept play in managing a hospitality or tourism facility?

chapter review

4   What is the marketing process? Briefly explain the process and its elements.

5   Discuss the components of the traditional and hospitality marketing mixes. What role does the hospitality manager play in managing the marketing mix? How is the marketing mix used?

6   What factors can affect the marketing mix? How might these factors affect the marketing mix? How might a manager anticipate the impact that these factors might have?

7   What are services? Do you believe that services marketing should be studied separately from product marketing? Why or why not?

8   List and discuss several of the reasons behind the growth in services. Which of these do you consider to be the most important? Why?

9   How do services differ from tangible goods?

10   What are destination marketing organizations? What is their major function?

11   What are the two most common types of destination marketing organizations? How are they funded?

12   Describe the service trends that are affecting the hospitality and tourism industry.

NOTES

[1] American Marketing Association Dictionary website, www.ama.org/AboutAMA/Pages/Definition-of-Marketing.aspx.

[2] Leo Renaghan, "A New Marketing Mix for the Hospitality Industry," *The Cornell Hotel and Restaurant Administration Quarterly* (April 1981), pp. 31, 35; Robert C. Lewis, Richard E. Chambers, and Harsha E. Chacko, *Marketing Leadership in Hospitality: Foundations and Practices*, 2nd ed. (New York: Wiley and Sons, 1994), pp. 394–395.

[3] Christopher H. Lovelock and Lauren Wright, *Principles of Service Marketing and Management*, 1st ed. (Englewood Cliffs, NJ: Prentice-Hall, 1999), pp. 7–14.

[4] Ibid., pp. 14–17.

[5] Destination Marketing Association International, www.destinationmarketing.org/page.asp?pid=21.

[6] Richard. B. Gartrell, *Destination Marketing for Convention and Visitor Bureaus*, 2nd ed. (Dubuque, IA: Kendall/Hunt, 1994).

CASE STUDY

Campus Center Hotel

A large state university in a college town in the Northeast owns and operates a 120-room hotel on its campus. There is a hotel manager who reports to the Campus Center building manager. The Campus Center building also has a bookstore, retail food operations, a post office, a barbershop, and several other small retail stores geared toward students. In addition, there is meeting space operated by Conference Services that is independent of the hotel, but the two enterprises work closely to attract groups for conferences and seminars. There isn't a dedicated parking area for the hotel, but there is a parking garage within walking distance that is connected through an underground tunnel. However, it takes about 10 to 15 minutes to get to the garage from the hotel, and there is an $8.00 daily fee for parking. All the off-campus competitors have free parking in lots adjacent to the hotels.

In terms of competition, there are several limited service hotels (e.g., Econo Lodge, Holiday Inn Express, and Hampton Inn) and a Marriott Courtyard within 2 to 5 miles of the campus. However, none of those hotels has as much meeting space as the Campus Center Hotel, nor do they have the level of catering services that the campus can offer. Unfortunately, the Campus Center Hotel does not have a full-service sit-down restaurant like those in close proximity to some of the competitors' hotels. Guests have to leave the campus to find anything more than quick service–style food. Most of the restaurants in the area are quick service or casual dining, although there are a few restaurants that would be considered fine casual or fine dining. Some are within walking distance of the campus (about 1 mile to the small downtown area), but that isn't a good option from November through February when the weather is cold.

Recently, the hotel manager was asked to assess the hotel's current operation and determine what could be done to better compete with the other hotels for the transient and corporate markets, as well as some of the sports teams and smaller groups that frequent the area. Luckily, the hotel manager had a degree in hospitality management and studied hotel marketing. He knew that the Campus Center Hotel had a relatively lower average room rate than the other hotels because of the group business and the discounts given to the university's students and departments. He also knew that the other hotels were newer and had relatively nicer accommodations for guests. Finally, the manager knew that the other hotels also had larger advertising budgets because they were affiliated with known brands through a franchise agreement. The Campus Center Hotel relied on word-of-mouth through students and alumni, Conference Services salespeople, and the university's website.

Case Study Questions and Issues

1. How can the marketing mix be applied to this situation? Discuss each of the four traditional components (i.e., 4P's) and how they can be used to increase occupancy and revenues for the Campus Center Hotel.

2. What other information would be useful for this task and how can it be obtained?

3. How would this type of marketing mix analysis be different if it was for a tangible good such as a computer instead of a hotel (service)?

case study

CASE STUDY

Location, Location, Location?

Bruce Adams stood in the parking lot facing an empty restaurant building. The restaurant had closed 60 days earlier, after being in business for about 8 months. As he visually surveyed the area, he noticed several things of interest. The building itself was fairly new, having been built 10 years ago by a franchisee of a national budget steakhouse chain. In the current configuration, the building had three separate dining areas, with seating for 40, 50, and 30 in the respective areas. In addition, there was a lounge that had 12 seats at the bar and space for an additional 16 seats. The quality of the building was very good, and the equipment, although not new, was certainly better than what he'd seen in other locations.

Bruce, who owned three other restaurants in another city within the state, believed that the local area offered potential. A successful 130-room, four-story Days Inn was located next to the restaurant, and it was positioned at an interchange of an interstate highway. A small residential community north of the restaurant consisted of approximately 100 single-family homes priced slightly above the average for the city. To the east and south of the restaurant were over 1,500 apartments, occupied predominantly by students attending a local university. The city in which the building was located had a rapidly growing population of 50,000, and the effective trading area population for businesses in the city was over 200,000. Several universities and a community college were within a 10-mile radius of the restaurant.

The local industrial base consisted of a number of small manufacturing operations. The largest employers manufactured parts for the automotive industry, published books for national and international distribution, manufactured equipment for the agricultural industry, produced beer for one of the nation's largest brewers, and provided trucking and transportation services. In addition, there was a growing service economy, and the city was home to a regional medical center and a strong professional community. At the present time, overall economic conditions in the area were good. Unemployment was very low, less than 2 percent, well below both the state and national levels.

As he stood in the parking lot, Bruce discussed the restaurant site with a business associate and a commercial real estate agent. He asked what he felt was an obvious question: "With what appear to be so many positive attributes for this location, why hasn't anyone been successful here?" In the 10 years since the building was constructed, there had been five different restaurant concepts, none of them successful. The failed concepts included a budget steakhouse, a southern barbecue restaurant, two different midpriced casual dining concepts, and most recently a somewhat upscale fine-dining concept. All had proven to be unsuccessful. Most closed their doors within 9 to 12 months. The longest-running restaurant remained open for 22 months. The only individuals making any money from this location were the commercial real estate agents. As the discussion continued, Bruce wondered aloud, "What type of product–service mix might be successful here? What type of concept might attract and retain customers? How might we approach the development of a successful restaurant?"

Case Study Questions and Issues

1. How can the marketing concept be applied to this situation?

2. Should Bruce be considering the potential product–service mix for a restaurant at this location at this time? Or should he be focused on other issues? If so, what might they be?

3. What information does Bruce need in order to make a decision about the possible purchase or lease of this site?

case study

The External Environment and Sustainability

Courtesy of LEGOLAND® California. LEGO, LEGOLAND, the LEGO and LEGOLAND logos and the brick configuration are trademarks of the LEGO Group and are used here with special permission. © 2004 The LEGO Group.

Chapter Objectives

After studying this chapter, you should be able to:

1. Discuss the external environments that influence the hospitality marketing process.

2. Describe the concept of sustainable development.

3. Describe how to manage for sustainable development and communicate initiatives.

2.1　INTRODUCTION

During the past decade, many changes have had an impact on the hospitality industry in the United States. The industry has confronted and adapted to such diverse situations as economic recession, overbuilding, increased competition, increased emphasis on technology, increased emphasis on the environment, newer forms of distribution and sales using technology, increased foreign ownership of previously American brands, changes in dining habits, changes in food consumption patterns, the ever-increasing globalization of the hospitality and tourism industry, and the impact of international terrorism. Each of these external forces has brought with it changes that hospitality firms have had to make to survive and remain competitive in a global marketplace. This relates to the concept of sustainability that refers to the ability of an organization to function efficiently and effectively and remain competitive over the long term.

Initially, the business community focused on economic sustainability, but now the world has embraced an approach that seeks to ensure environmental and social sustainability as well. In other words, there is an emphasis on people and the planet, as well as profits. The hospitality and tourism industry is heavily affected by this initiative because it relies, to a large extent, on travel between destinations. Although visitors are a good positive source of economic impact on a destination, there are also negative impacts on the environment and the local community. Therefore, it is necessary for destinations to manage the positive and negative impacts related to their economies, environments, and society. This chapter will start with a discussion of the external environment that affects hospitality and tourism firms, and then address the issue of sustainability.

Sustainability
The ability of individuals or organizations to endure and function over the long term.

2.2　THE EXTERNAL ENVIRONMENT

When marketing managers consider changes in marketing strategy or tactics, they often examine the changes in five major components of the external environment: economic, social, competitive, political and legal, and technological. Firms cannot directly influence their external environment, but they can monitor changes and be somewhat proactive. It is critical for firms to engage in some level of environmental scanning, so they can take advantage of marketing opportunities while anticipating any threats to their business. Environmental scanning can be a formal mechanism within a firm, or merely the result of salespeople and managers consciously monitoring changes in the environment. The larger the firm, the more likely it will have a structured approach to scanning the environment and documenting trends. The following section contains brief descriptions of each of the external environments.

Environmental scanning
Environmental scanning can be a formal mechanism within a firm, or merely the result of salespeople and managers consciously monitoring changes in the environment.

2.2.1　The Economic Environment

The goal of all marketing activity is to create and satisfy customers. Consumers' purchasing power, or ability to purchase products and services, is directly related to the economic health of the city, state, and country. As marketers study the economic environment, they are concerned about such things as inflation, recession, unemployment, resource availability, interest-rate trends, personal income growth, business growth and performance, and consumers' confidence in the economy. There are other key economic terms that relate to marketing and will be used throughout the text. The consumer price index (CPI) is a measure of the relative level of prices for consumer goods in the economy. As this measure rises, there are more concerns about inflation and a poor economy. The term disposable income refers to the portion of an individual's income that is left for spending after required deductions such as taxes. Discretionary income is probably a more important measure for most marketers because it refers to the income that is available for spending after deducting taxes and necessary expenditures on housing, food, and basic clothing.

Purchasing power
The extent to which consumers have the ability to purchase products and services.

Consumer price index (CPI)
A measure of the relative level of prices for consumer goods in the economy.

Disposable income
An individual's income that remains for spending after required deductions such as taxes.

Discretionary income
An individual's income that is available for spending after deducting taxes and necessary expenditures on housing, food, and basic clothing.

Courtesy of Wyndham Worldwide.

Hotels such as the Wingate Tulfarris Hotel and Golf Resort in County Wicklow, Ireland, offer a range of room rates and amenities for guests with differing levels of purchasing power.

Here are some examples of issues and trends related to the economic environment that affect the hospitality and travel industry:

- The percentage of independently owned hospitality operations has declined, resulting in a concentration of power among large hospitality chains. In turn, these chains have become large, multinational firms based in the United States or abroad.

- An increase in the amount of discretionary income has resulted in an increase in the percentage of the household food budget spent outside the home. Food away from home as a share of household food expenditures has risen steadily since 1970, reaching 43.1 percent in 2012.[1]

- After a period of excess supply due to overbuilding in the 1980s, hotel occupancy percentages fell to the low 60s. This trend later reversed itself because of the strong economy and business growth. Following a recession in the early 1990s, occupancy and profitability reached all-time highs for many lodging companies. Then, in the 2000s, the events of September 11 and the global recession caused hotel occupancies to decrease and many properties suffered operating losses. The hospitality industry, like most other industries, experiences these business cycles resulting in periods of expansion and recession.

- Variations in consumer purchasing power have led the hospitality and travel industry to offer products and services at different price levels. For example, most of the major lodging chains now have established multiple brands, ranging from economy to luxury, based on prices and amenities. Each brand targets a specific market segment.

Some of the issues in the economic environment are closely related to the trends in the social environment, which will be discussed next.

2.2.2 The Social Environment

There are constant changes in the social environment as consumers evolve. The social environment is affected by all the other environments. Changes in the economy, advances in technology, competitive actions, and government regulations all shape the way consumers view the world. These changes may be sudden, or they may take place over a number of years or even decades.

Demographics
Characteristics that describe the population such as age, income, education, occupation, family size, marital status, and gender.

First, there have been changes in demographics, or characteristics that describe the population, such as age, income, education, occupation, family size, marital status, and gender. Second, there have been changes in consumers' attitudes, interests, and opinions that determine their lifestyles.

Some issues related to the social environment affect the hospitality and travel industry:

- The increased discretionary income and time pressures experienced by two-income families have an impact on their lodging, dining, and travel behaviors. These families take more but shorter vacations to fit their busy lifestyles. Also, they are quality-conscious and focus on brand names.

- The proportion of older Americans and their purchasing power are continually increasing. Senior citizens are becoming a very important market segment because people are living longer. Furthermore, there is an improved quality of life among seniors, and their disposable income continues to increase. This segment has specific needs, and the American Association of Retired Persons (AARP) is one of the strongest political lobbying organizations in the nation.

- The dietary habits of the American people have also changed, and in some ways are bipolar: the percentage of individuals characterized as overweight or obese is at an all-time high, yet many individuals are showing an increased concern for their health. The trend has been toward healthier, more natural foods. In support of this, the United States Department of Agriculture publishes *Dietary Guidelines for Americans,* which outlines the dietary goals for the nation. The American Heart Association provides menu review and recipes that meet their dietary guidelines for good health. Many food service operations now feature menu items that have been approved by this organization. The National Restaurant Association has also been active in this area, especially in educating its members.

Fast-food restaurants, extended-stay hotels, and the growth in the cruise industry are all the result of changes in the social environment. These changes can offer opportunities for new products and services, while posing a threat to existing companies. For example, the increasing emphasis on brand names has resulted in tremendous growth in restaurant chains such as Outback Steakhouse, Starbucks, Panera Bread, Subway, Chili's, and Applebee's. This growth of regional and national brands has come at the expense of many independent restaurants.

Competitive structure
A combination of buyers and sellers in a market.

Monopoly
A competitive structure in an industry with one seller and many buyers.

Perfect competition
A competitive structure in an industry with many buyers and sellers of homogeneous products that are almost exactly the same.

Oligopoly
A competitive structure in an industry with a few sellers and many buyers.

Monopolistic competition
A common, competitive structure where there are many buyers and sellers with differentiated products.

Price elasticity of demand
A measure of the percentage change in demand for a product resulting from a percentage change in price.

2.2.3 The Competitive Environment

Within all markets, a variety of competitors seek to win the favor of the consumer. Each offers what it believes will be the best combination of products and services designed to result in maximum consumer satisfaction. The competitive structure in an industry can range from a monopoly, with one seller and many buyers, to perfect competition, with many buyers and sellers of homogeneous products that are almost exactly the same. In between, there is the oligopoly, with a few sellers and many buyers, and the most common form of competitive structure, monopolistic competition, where there are many buyers and sellers with differentiated products. The price elasticity of demand is a measure of the percentage change in demand for a product resulting from a percentage change in price. The price elasticity of demand normally increases as the competitive structure changes from monopoly to oligopoly to monopolistic competition and ends with perfect competition. The hospitality and tourism industry is highly competitive, with new companies entering the industry every day. In the business world, four levels of competition must be considered in order for firms to be able to protect their positions in the market:[2]

- **Product form competition exists among companies that provide similar products and services to the same customers at a similar price level.** For example, McDonald's competes with Burger King and Wendy's; Delta Airlines competes with United Airlines and US Airways; Hertz competes with Avis and National; and Four Seasons Hotels competes with Ritz-Carlton and other luxury hotels.

- **Product category competition exists among companies that make the same class of products.** In this case, McDonald's competes with other fast-food restaurants such as Pizza Hut, Taco Bell, and KFC; Delta Airlines competes with charter airlines and commuter airlines; Hertz competes with all the local rental car companies; and Four Seasons Hotels competes with nonluxury hotel chains such as Marriott and Sheraton.

- **General competition exists among companies that offer the same basic service that fulfills the same basic consumer needs.**   For example, McDonald's competes with all restaurants as well as with convenience stores and supermarkets; Delta Airlines and Hertz compete with all forms of transportation, such as bus and rail; and Four Seasons Hotels competes with all forms of lodging, such as bed-and-breakfasts and boutique hotels.

- **Budget competition exists among all companies that compete for consumers' disposable incomes.**   Most consumers have limited budgets that can be used for purchasing products and services, and all companies compete for these consumer dollars, especially discretionary income. The hospitality and travel firms discussed earlier would compete with department stores, movie theaters, health clubs, and financial institutions for consumers' limited resources.

As companies examine the competitive environment, three important questions need to be addressed. The questions may seem straightforward, but the answers are often difficult to determine, and many firms do not make the correct decision:

1. Should we compete?

2. If we compete, in what markets should we compete?

3. What should our competitive strategy be?

The response to the first question should be based on such things as the firm's resources and objectives. The company must examine the level of potential sales, potential profitability, and the overall feasibility of competing. A firm may decide that it should not compete if the risks outweigh the potential returns or if the projected returns are not as high as it would like to see.

The second question relates to the markets in which a firm wishes to compete. Most firms elect not to compete in all potential markets. For example, although many firms, such as Marriott International, have developed brands that compete in all price segments of the lodging industry (economy through luxury), others, such as Hyatt Hotels and Resorts, initially did not choose to compete in all price segments. Owners believed that the single-brand strategy would serve the firm's best long-term interests. More recently, Hyatt has adopted the multi-brand strategy.

The following information was posted at www.hyatt.com:

Hyatt Brands and Affiliates in Addition to Hyatt Hotels

Andaz: Boutique-style hotels

Hyatt Place: Upscale select-service hotels

Hyatt House: Upscale all-suite hotels with full kitchens for extended stay guests

Hyatt Residence Club: Collection of generously appointed luxury residences in exclusive destinations

Hyatt Zilara and Hyatt Ziva: All-inclusive resorts

The third question relates to marketing strategy. How should the firm attempt to gain a competitive advantage? These decisions, which will be explored in much greater depth throughout the text, are related to issues such as products and services, pricing, distribution, and promotion.

2.2.4 The Political and Legal Environment

Understanding the political and legal environment means understanding the rules and regulations by which the competitive game is played. At all levels of government—local, state, national, and international—there are laws and regulations that businesses must follow. To compete successfully, a firm must understand not only the current laws and regulations but also any new ones that might come into play in the future. Most professional hospitality and tourism managers belong to one or more professional associations. One of the goals of these associations is to help members

Affordable price and familiar brands are important in a global market.

not only understand developing laws and regulations but also to have influence in how they are written through lobbying efforts with politicians and government officials. Two examples of hospitality industry associations are the National Restaurant Association (NRA) and the American Hotel & Lodging Association (AH&LA). Here are some examples of issues related to the political and legal environment that affect the hospitality and tourism industry:

- **Changes in the federal tax codes have made hotel development less desirable than under previous tax codes.**   So-called passive investments, in which the investor is not an active participant in the daily management of the facility, are not treated as favorably under the new federal tax codes as they were in the past. As a result, future hotel development decisions are based more on operational feasibility and less on the real estate investment aspects of the project.

- **As a means to reduce the federal budget deficit, costs are being shifted to state and local governments.**   To raise tax revenues at the local level without incurring the disapproval of local voters, many localities have implemented or increased taxes on lodging and restaurant meals. These user taxes serve to increase consumer perceptions of the prices for hospitality and travel products and can have a major negative impact on operations.

- **Changes in nutrition labeling and food handling requirements affect the food service industry.**   The Food and Drug Administration and other federal, state, and local agencies enact rules that requires food service providers to display nutritional information on their menus, and use safe food handling procedures to protect consumers.

- **National, state, and local governments also pass laws that can affect firms' operations without using taxes.**   For example, the federal government in the United States has chosen to stay on the sidelines, local and state governments are taking on the issue of smoking in public places such as restaurants. This directly affects the competitive structure of the industry when regulations do not affect all firms equally.

The idea of a level playing field is critical when governments evaluate new taxes and regulations. It is often difficult for firms to address social issues as a priority over profits, especially small firms with very limited resources. However, governments can make sure that their laws and regulations do not distort the balance of competition.

Smoking bans have affected hospitality firms and consumers. This is a smoking zone in the Munich Airport.

2.2.5 The Technological Environment

We live in an increasingly technological and interconnected society. With the evolution of the personal computer from an expensive desktop machine to other devices such as laptops, smartphones, and tablets and the pervasive access to the Internet via cellular data plans and wifi connections, our lives have changed in ways we perhaps could not have even dreamed about before. The power of computers doubles roughly every 18 to 24 months, with prices constantly dropping. Computers are being used for more and more applications every day. Although the hospitality and tourism industry remains a highly labor-intensive and personal-contact–oriented industry, computers and technology have had and will continue to have an impact. The area in which technology will have the greatest impact in the next 10 years is in **digital marketing** where a product–service provider can reach individual customers on the Internet through corporate websites and social media. This allows marketers to monitor guests' purchasing behavior and then tailor service offerings to meet their needs.

Digital marketing
The marketing of products and services using the Internet and other forms of electronic media.

The following are some examples of issues related to the technological environment that affect the hospitality and travel industry:

- **New technologies have helped to combat labor shortages and the high cost of labor by enabling hospitality and travel firms to shift some of these duties to consumers through self-service operations.**   Examples include automated check-in and check-out. This is occurring within all segments of the industry, from fast-food restaurants to luxury hotels and resorts. The very competitive environment in which commercial airlines operate has made them leaders in cost-saving applications of technology.

- **The increasing sophistication and decrease in price of computer technology have had a significant impact.**   Most of the larger firms maintain relational databases and use resource management systems that can provide managers with the potential to better serve customers. This technology is becoming more accessible to smaller firms through service contractors and consultants.

- **The development and growth of the Internet has changed the competitive structure in the hospitality and travel industry.**   Even small firms can now market on a national or international basis. Selling on the Internet also reduces the costs associated with service delivery, thereby increasing the profit potential for service firms. The trend toward consumers' evaluating service alternatives and making online purchases has been significant.

The hospitality industry has experienced growth due to these changes. Most of the leading hospitality experts project continued industry growth, albeit a somewhat slower rate. Certainly, a few large obstacles loom on the horizon. Existing economic cycles will cause some upward and downward shifts in the hospitality industry, and further changes in the tax codes may have some negative impact on business travel and entertaining.

2.3 SUSTAINABLE DEVELOPMENT

Sustainable development
Development that meets the needs of the present without compromising the ability of future generations to meet their own needs.

In general, the focus of **sustainable development** is on operating companies and tourism destinations in a way that ensures future generations will benefit economically, will have a clean environment, and will preserve society, including the well-being of individuals and the community. The most commonly cited definition is the from the Brundtland Report:

Sustainable development is development that meets the needs of the present without compromising the ability of future generations to meet their own needs. It contains within it two key concepts:

- the concept of *needs,* in particular the essential needs of the world's poor, to which overriding priority should be given; and

- the idea of *limitations* imposed by the state of technology and social organization on the environment's ability to meet present and future needs.[3]

Figure 2.1 illustrates the relationship between the three components of sustainable development: environment, economic, and social. Sustainable development occurs where among all three components overlap, as shown in the diagram. This demonstrates a balance among people, planet, and profit. The overlap between the environment and the economic components suggests that hospitality organizations are able to achieve adequate profits while still preserving nature and the environment. The overlap between the environment and social components suggests that society benefits from having a better quality of life. However, that doesn't ensure that society benefits as a whole economically. For example, when tourism destinations promote sustainability, one of the goals is to reduce poverty and have people with lower incomes benefit from increased tourism. Unfortunately, this normally does not occur; wealthier people and organizations usually reap the benefits and sometimes remove the money from the local economy. Finally, the overlap between the economic and social components suggests that business practices result in economic prosperity for society as a whole, including the poor and other disadvantage.

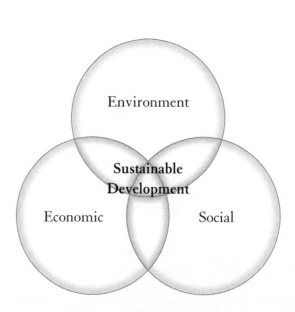

FIGURE 2.1 • Sustainable development.

2.3.1 Environmental Sustainability

The area that gets the most attention in discussions about sustainability is the environment. Environmental sustainability is the ability to maintain reasonable levels of renewable and nonrenewable energy, waste, water, and pollution indefinitely. In particular, people and government agencies are concerned about the greenhouse emissions that affect climate change. Carbon footprint is a term used to refer to the total amount of greenhouse gas emissions caused by people, organizations, products, and events through everyday activities. This basically includes all carbon dioxide (CO_2) and methane (CH_4) emissions, as well as nitrous oxide (N_2O) and fluorinated gases.

Numerous sources may be used to measure the carbon footprint for an individual or organization (e.g., U.S. Environmental Protection Agency website and EarthLab.com). After an individual or organization determines its carbon footprint, action can be taken to offset the impact. Carbon offsets are measured in metric tons and can be as simple as planting trees or donating to a nonprofit organization that focuses on activities to reduce greenhouse emissions. Hospitality firms, especially large hotels and resorts, are heavy users of water and energy in the creation and delivery of their services. In addition, hospitality firms create a lot of waste. Typically, companies that engage in "green" practices try to save energy, minimize waste, conserve water, and reduce pollution.

Environmental sustainability
The ability to maintain reasonable levels of renewable and nonrenewable energy, waste, water, and pollution indefinitely.

Carbon footprint
The total amount of greenhouse gas emissions caused by people, organizations, products, and events through everyday activities.

2.3.1.1 ENERGY MANAGEMENT. Some of the practices used by hotels to save energy are the installation of energy-efficient appliances, the use of energy-efficient lightbulbs, central controls for heating and air conditioning, and encouraging guests to turn off lights and reuse linens. Another recommendation is to power down unused equipment and turn off lights in unoccupied rooms (e.g., install occupancy sensors). Similarly, restaurant companies and owners could install energy-efficient appliances and lightbulbs, and power down equipment at night. Also, restaurants and hotel firms can purchase organic foods that are produced using renewable resources. In fact, hospitality firms can save energy by using more renewable energy sources such as solar, wind, geothermal, biomass, and water to create electricity and provide power for their own operations. In addition to the energy from the sun (solar) and wind, the flow of water can create energy, as can the heat from Earth (geothermal) and burning organic or living matter (biomass). Traditionally, companies relied on nonrenewable energy sources such as oil, coal, nuclear, and natural gas.

A *nonrenewable resource* is a natural resource that cannot be remade or regrown at a scale comparable to its consumption. For example, nuclear fission uses uranium to create energy, but once the uranium is used, it is gone forever. Fossil fuels such as oil, coal, and natural gas are considered nonrenewable because it takes a long time to replenish them after they are used. Conversely, renewable resources—solar, wind, and water, for example—can be replenished in a short period of time. Unfortunately, the decision often comes down to money. The use of renewable energy sources can require an initial capital investment in new equipment that can be cost prohibitive for some companies, especially those that don't understand the long-term cost savings from using alternative energy sources.

Regarding restaurants and hotels, gas stoves are the most efficient regarding carbon emissions and are more consistent in distributing heat to food. Propane is even more efficient, but the downside is that propane is significantly more expensive to use than natural gas. The other option is to use a renewable energy source such as solar or wind to efficiently provide energy for an electric stove. Newer refrigerators and coolers can be costly, but the improvements in efficiency will not only help the environment but it will also reduce operating costs.

2.3.1.2 WASTE MANAGEMENT. Hospitality firms can also help the environment through waste management programs. This is accomplished by creating programs to reduce waste by reusing products and recycling. The best way to manage waste is to purchase supplies that are biodegradable, and recycle any nonbiodegradable materials. It is also important to properly dispose of hazardous substances. Hospitality firms can purchase products (e.g., soap and shampoo) for guest consumption that are in biodegradable packaging. In addition, guests can be encouraged to reuse soap and shampoo instead of opening new containers each day and discarding the unused portions. Another area where hotels and restaurants can reduce waste is by composting leftover food items. It is estimated that 50 percent of restaurant waste is food, and 65 to 75 percent of all waste in landfills consists of organics that could be composted or recycled. Finally, firms can recycle paper, glass, and plastic to reduce waste in landfills and avoid incineration. It should be noted that the U.S. Food and Drug Administration does not allow food-grade plastic to be made from recycled material. Also, chemicals and energy are used to recycle plastics, and most of the plastics are recycled in China and could involve transportation—all having negative effects on the environment.

2.3.1.3 WATER CONSERVATION.

Once again, hotels and other lodging facilities are heavy users of water. There can be hundreds or thousands of guests staying at a large hotel and all of them are taking showers and using the toilet. Therefore, there is a great deal of water usage per square foot of space relative to one's home or apartment. In fact, it isn't uncommon for hotel guests to consume more water when traveling than when at home. They assume the room price includes unlimited usage and they tend to take more showers after swimming, working out, going to the beach, and/or sightseeing. Hotel swimming pools are another major source of water usage. Every effort should be made to reduce water waste. For instance, low-flow showerheads and low-flow toilets can be installed in hotels in an effort to reduce water usage. Also, pool temperatures could be set cooler and pool covers might be used to reduce evaporation. Using recycled water from lakes and ponds to water the fairways and the greens of golf courses at resorts would also conserve water. Finally, guests can be encouraged to reuse linens and towels to reduce the amount of laundry, and hotels can purchase laundry equipment that minimizes the use of water (e.g., ozone laundry system).

Restaurant dishwashers should be filled before use, and the staff can scrape off leftover food and presoak pots and pans before putting them in the dishwasher. Use of low-flow toilets and installation of water-efficient aerators on sinks will conserve water. All hospitality employees should check for leaks and make sure water isn't continually running from faucets or toilets. Another practice that can be useful is to fill guests' water glasses only when requested. However, there can be a trade-off between being environmentally friendly and keeping customers satisfied. Finally, for watering outdoor plants and grass, restaurants and hotels can reuse "gray water" that comes from showers and sinks, as well as rainwater collected from roofs and paved surfaces.

2.3.1.4 MANAGING POLLUTION.

The Environmental Protection Agency (EPA) in the United States is concerned about the quality of air, as well as other effects on the environment from business operations, including the hospitality industry. Most developed countries, and many developing countries, have similar organizations to monitor the country's environmental health. Both lodging and food service operations contribute to the pollution problem by using cleaning supplies, synthetic materials, and paints that release toxic air pollutants and volatile organic compounds (VOC) that eventually work their way into the outdoor environment. In addition, hospitality firms release ozone-depleting substances such as chlorofluorocarbons (CFCs) through improperly maintained heating, ventilation, and air conditioning (HVAC) equipment and refrigeration units.

The EPA has suggested several practices that could be employed by hospitality firms to reduce air pollution:[4]

1. **Change cleaners.**   Use nontoxic products whenever possible, purchase cleaners with low toxic air pollutant and VOC content, and choose pump-style sprays.

2. **Maintain buildings.**   Use water-based or other less toxic paints and coatings, only refinish those portions of floors where the most wear occurs, and use indoor furniture made of wood instead of pressed wood products

3. **Control ozone-depleting substance emissions.**   Check for leaks in HVAC units and refrigeration systems regularly, recover and reuse ozone-depleting substances, replace old equipment with more efficient equipment, and inspect fire extinguishers frequently for leads (especially if they contain halon).

2.3.2   Economic Sustainability

Economic sustainability
The ability to support a given level of economic production indefinitely.

Economic sustainability can be defined as the ability to support a given level of economic production indefinitely. The basic premise of economic sustainability it to utilize an organization's existing resources efficiently and responsibly in an attempt to continue operating profitably over the long run. In the restaurant industry, one could argue that another goal could be survival, given the failure rates. However, economic sustainability is normally associated with monetary goals such as maintaining adequate profit margins, providing an acceptable return on investment for

Olivier Le Moal/Shutterstock

Hotels have found that sustainability efforts can increase profits by reducing costs.

owners and shareholders, and being able to service debt requirements. One of the main criticisms of corporations is that they sacrifice long-term environmental sustainability for short-term profits.

From a more global perspective, countries and regions are usually compared based on gross domestic product (GDP) per capita, gross national income (GNI) per capita, or some other measure of income that can be used as an indicator of the standard of living. This type of assessment is more relevant when looking at tourism destinations and countries as a whole. Sustainable development in the tourism industry is particularly important because destinations use government funding to generate revenue that gets channeled back to the government through taxes and used to support social programs. It is also a way to help those in society that are less fortunate (e.g., community-based tourism).

2.3.3   Social Sustainability

Social sustainability can be defined as the ability of a country or a society to maintain an adequate standard of living indefinitely. This concept, which is often referred to as *human development,* is monitored on a global level by keeping statistics on things such as the percentage of the population at the poverty level, access to quality water, access to medical facilities and disease control, life expectancy, and literacy. Two of the underlying themes in social sustainability are equity and diversity. The notion of *equity* focuses on the ability and willingness of a community to provide opportunities and resources to all its members, regardless of race, religion, gender, income level, and so on. In other words, all members of the community should have access to the same level of education and health care, and there should be affordable housing and employment opportunities. The related notion of *diversity* focuses on the extent to which society welcomes members from all walks of life. It not only refers to one's race and income but also to one's political and religious views.

Hospitality firms can help accomplish society's goals by providing good-paying jobs and careers for local residents rather than bringing in all of their own managers and staff from outside the community. In addition, they can offer training programs and skills development for lower-income and at-risk members of the community. Hotel and restaurant businesses have many jobs available to those without higher education. Hotel taxes and sales taxes generated by visitors and local residents provide revenues for the local community to use for social programs. The tourism industry is also good for bringing outside money into the community and providing a positive economic impact in the way of jobs and tax revenues. However, one of the complaints with the tourism industry is that there are "leakages" from the community because travel-related companies are headquartered in other areas and don't always reinvest the profits in the community. Other criticisms are that tourists can have a negative impact on the local culture by changing social norms and exposing residents to outside influences, and that tourists have access to resources (e.g., clean water and energy) that the residents don't have (i.e., in developing countries).

Social sustainability
The ability of a country or a society to maintain an adequate standard of living indefinitely.

2.3.3.1 CORPORATE SOCIAL RESPONSIBILITY. *Corporate social responsibility* can be defined as the continuing voluntary commitment by corporations to behave ethically and to contribute to the economic development, social equity, and environmental protection of society as a whole. Some of the key aspects of the definition are:

1. It is a continuing commitment, or a long-term initiative.

2. It is voluntary, suggesting that organizations need to self-regulate and encourage participation among both internal and external stakeholders.

3. It focuses on the triple bottom line—economic, social, and environmental impacts.

The goal is to create shared value between the organization and society. In other words, organizations should be able to achieve their economic goals while, at the same time, protect the environment and contribute to the social welfare of the community. However, it is not uncommon for organizations to find that they must comply with social and/or environmental standards that the government, or industry regulatory body, imposes on them.

2.4 MANAGING FOR SUSTAINABILITY

It is important to train employees to adhere to the sustainability initiatives created by hospitality firms and tourism organizations. In addition, management has to have a monitoring process in place that includes some way to evaluate performance in terms of sustainability. If an organization is going to deliver economic prosperity, environmental quality, and societal well-being, it is necessary to integrate the three components into the strategic planning process of the organization. Also, the organization needs to be transparent regarding its operations and activities. Finally, there has to be some level of measurement and reporting of the organization's performance in terms of sustainability. The **triple bottom line** is an accounting and recording system used by firms to monitor sustainability performance on all three components—people, planet, and profits. Table 2.1 contains a summary of the three components and some examples of measures that can be used to monitor performance for the hospitality and tourism industries.

Triple bottom line
An accounting and recording system used by firms to monitor sustainability performance on all three components—people, planet, and profits.

COMPONENT	HOSPITALITY MEASURES	TOURISM MEASURES
Environmental (Planet)	• Greenhouse emissions • Energy consumption • Water consumption • Solid and toxic waste	• Air and water quality • Energy consumption • Water consumption • Natural resources • Solid and toxic waste
Economic (Profits)	• Revenues and profits • Operating costs • Employee compensation • Job creation • Community investments	• Personal income and level of poverty • Unemployment rate • GDP per capita • Job growth
Social (People)	• Workforce diversity • Employee turnover • Health-care coverage • Incidents of discrimination • Employee training and education • Workplace injuries	• Life expectancy • Violent crimes per capita • Incidence of diseases • Medical facilities and doctors • Education of population

TABLE 2.1 • Sustainability Indicators

2.4.1 Communicating Sustainability Initiatives

It is important for organizations to make sure employees are aware of their sustainability goals in order to achieve those goals. In addition, the sustainability initiatives of the firm should be communicated to external stakeholders such as customers, suppliers/vendors, stockholders/investors, the government, and the community. The human resources department in larger companies is responsible for internal communications regarding the sustainability initiatives, as well as training and socialization of employees to the sustainability culture. Stakeholder engagement is also important in determining the organization's sustainability initiatives.

In addition to words, statistics, and data measurements, it is important to create more visual and compelling elements to convey an organization's commitment to sustainability. The following five suggestions were provided in an article published on the *GreenBiz.com* website:[5]

1. Communications that you can see, touch, or even listen to provide a tangible measure of sustainability success. It is recommended that firms provide this tangible evidence in newsletters, annual reports, and other supplemental materials available online and distributed in hard copy.

2. Develop a brand/identity to represent and highlight your efforts in sustainability. It should be consistent with the overall brand, but have its own unique characteristic(s) to create interest among target markets. This will help with employee recruitment and retention, employee engagement, and customer loyalty.

3. Create a memorable theme and title that ties closely with an organization's core competencies. It should be creative and be related to the corporate name and/or corporate culture.

4. Many sustainable measures can be taken with a printed piece. For example, if an organization carries out its sustainability initiatives, it might be possible to add a certification logo to its collateral materials.

5. Take advantage of the technology that exists today. This can be done through the use of social media, QR codes, and online polls and surveys. Firms can promote their sustainability efforts through these vehicles.

Global sustainability requires organizations, governments, and individuals to change the way they think and act in regard to the environment and society. It is the responsibility of firms to educate consumers and encourage them to purchase environmental-friendly products and services. Additionally, it is necessary for organizations to communicate their efforts as a means of obtaining a competitive advantage with customers who value firms with "green practices." The United Nations Environment Programme (UNEP) developed a report to help organizations produce effective campaigns for communicating sustainability.[6] The UNEP provides an eight stage sustainability communications planning process (see Figure 2.2).

The first stage involves doing research to get a better understanding of the situation so that you can increase your chances of success. One means of obtaining pertinent information is to scan the external environments (competitive, economic, political and legal, social, and technological) to determine if there are any issues that might affect your campaign. This will put your situation in the proper context. Also, look at other sustainable development campaigns in your market. The second stage involves doing additional research on your target audience. Segment your market and prioritize the segments. Then, determine what motivates your target audience and how best to reach them with print and broadcast media. Finally, identify potential opinion leaders and influencers who can help distribute your message.

After you have completed your research, the third stage involves setting objectives for your campaign. This should be completed before you launch your communications campaign. The objectives should be clear, concise, and measurable. They should be specific, including what is to be accomplished and the timeframe in which to achieve the results (e.g., reduce water consumption by 10 percent within the next year). The fourth stage is to decide on a strategic approach to achieve your objectives. This involves developing a list of possible alternatives and then evaluating the alternatives to determine which would have the best potential for success in meeting your objectives. It is important to establish a budget and do a cost/benefit analysis to make sure that the alternative provides positive benefits (both tangible and intangible) that exceed the costs

FIGURE 2.2 • **Sustainable communications planning process.**

(both monetary and nonmonetary) of pursuing the alternative. It is also helpful to include stakeholders in this process so that they "buy into" your campaign.

The fifth stage involves developing the message(s) that will appeal to your target audience(s) and create a basic theme for your campaign. You can develop a unique brand for this purpose and use a specific logo and branded statements in all your communications. The message(s) can be adjusted, or tailored, to appeal to various segments. The sixth stage involves choosing the proper channels, or media vehicles, to use in distributing the message(s) to the target audience(s). You can use the research from the second stage to help in this regard.

The seventh stage is one of the most important stages. It involves determining who is responsible for managing the campaign and establishing a final budget and time line for the campaign. You need to develop a list of required resources (e.g., people, materials, and money) and create a project schedule that can be used to allocate resources and monitor the project stages. Additionally, you should develop a crisis management plan that can be implemented in the event something unexpected occurs. The eighth and final stage involves the measurement and evaluation of the campaign. Every effort should be taken to obtain measurable results that can be used to assess the success, or failure, of the various components of the campaign. Measurement can address the process of delivering the message(s), the outcome(s) of the campaign related to changes in awareness, attitudes, or behaviors, and the impact of the campaign on sustainable development initiatives.

2.4.2 Sustainability Programs and Certifications

One other issue for management to consider is whether or not to obtain some type of sustainability or "green" certification to recognize the organization's efforts in this area. The benefit of having a certification is that it lends credibility to the firm because it has met the standards and criteria of an objective organization. Most of the certification groups provide a logo or "seal of approval" that firms can display on their websites and facilities that can add value to marketing campaigns. Also, it encourages firms to track their performance, and it can help motivate staff and employees to support the firm's sustainability initiatives. However, there is usually a review process that requires the firm to keep records and document its performance. This additional effort and the cost of the certification might outweigh the benefits for some hospitality and travel organizations.

Currently, there are three main organizations that provide certification for the restaurant industry. The Green Restaurant Association is a nonprofit organization located in Boston, Massachusetts. The cost of the certification starts at $300 per year based on the term of the contract, the restaurant size, and the number of locations involved. The organization performs an environmental assessment to create a baseline and then works with the restaurants to improve their standards to meet the criteria for the Green Restaurant 4.0 certification. The Sustainable Restaurant Association is based in London and has recently started to provide certifications in the United States. The certification involves restaurants addressing 14 focus areas across three sustainability categories: sourcing, environment, and society. The process is handled mainly online and costs $295. The U.S. Healthful Food Council is a nonprofit organization located in Washington, DC. This certification is based on the U.S. Green Building Council LEED certification program and the cost starts at $400. The REAL (Responsible Epicurean and Agricultural Leadership) certification includes a nutrition component, unlike the other certifications.

According to Green Lodging News[7], 27 states, Puerto Rico, five cities, and two regions currently have some form of green-lodging program. Certification programs are offered through U.S. organizations such as TripAdvisor from Newton, Massachusetts; the U.S. Environmental Protection Agency (EPA); Green Seal from Washington, DC; and Audubon International in New York. In addition, there are global organizations such as Sustainable Travel International. Some of the certifications are tourism based and include lodging facilities—for example, the Certification for Sustainable Tourism in Costa Rica, Green Globe in California, and EarthCheck in Australia. Agenda 21, a nonbinding sustainable development action plan started by the United Nations in 1992, created a platform for nations, states, cities, and regions to use in developing sustainable tourism programs.

2.5   SUMMARY OF CHAPTER OBJECTIVES

This chapter covered the external environment that is part of the marketing process introduced in Chapter 1. The external environment consists of the areas that affect the marketing process, but are not under the direct control of marketing managers. The five major marketing environments are economic, social, competitive, political and legal, and technological. Firms use environmental scanning to keep abreast of changes in the external environment that could result in opportunities or threats to the organization. Some of the external environments can be indirectly controlled through obtaining patents, creating barriers to entry, and/or lobbying for favorable government regulation.

The second part of this chapter focused on sustainability. The three major components of sustainability in hospitality and tourism operations are social, environmental, and economic. These are often referred to as people, planet, and profits, respectively. The goal of today's organizations should be on managing this triple bottom line to ensure that, while making adequate profits, businesses leave the planet and society in the same, or better, condition. This has led to a field of inquiry that addresses corporate social responsibility. All organizations should strive to be good community citizens by establishing sustainability initiatives, measuring them with sustainability indicators, and communicating their results to their various stakeholders (e.g., employees, investors, suppliers, customers, and the local community).

KEY TERMS AND CONCEPTS

Carbon footprint
Competitive structure
Consumer price index (CPI)
Demographics
Digital marketing
Discretionary income
Disposable income
Economic sustainability
Environmental scanning
Environmental sustainability

Monopolistic competition
Monopoly
Oligopoly
Perfect competition
Price elasticity of demand
Purchasing power
Social sustainability
Sustainability
Sustainable development
Triple bottom line

QUESTIONS FOR REVIEW AND DISCUSSION

1   What are the key variables in the marketing environment? In your opinion, which is the most important? Why?

2   Of the variables in the marketing environment, is there one or two that you believe a marketing manager can influence or predict more easily than the others? If so, which one(s), and why?

3   What changes in technology will impact the hospitality and tourism industry in the next 5 years? What specific positive and negative impacts from technology do you foresee?

4   Define sustainable development. What are the three major components of sustainable development?

5   Which component of sustainable development receives the most attention from hospitality and tourism organizations? Explain your answer.

chapter review

6 What is environmental sustainability? Discuss the various areas where hospitality and travel firms can address environmental sustainability.

7 What is a carbon footprint? What can organizations do to mitigate their impact on the environment in this regard?

8 What is corporate social responsibility? Do you think hospitality firms do a good job in this area? What more could they do?

9 What are some of the more common sustainability indicators used by hospitality and tourism organizations to monitor sustainability performance?

10 How can hospitality firms communicate their sustainability initiatives to stakeholders?

NOTES

[1] Economic Research Service, U.S. Department of Agriculture (USDA), Food Expenditures, www.ers.usda.gov/data-products/food-expenditures.aspx.

[2] Donald R. Lehman and Russell S. Winer, *Analysis for Marketing Planning*, 2nd ed. (Homewood, IL: Richard D. Irwin, 1991).

[3] World Commission on Environment and Development (WCED), *Our Common Future* (Oxford: Oxford University Press, 1987), p. 43.

[4] "Reducing Air Pollution from the Hospitality Industry (Lodging Sector)," *EPA Community Information Sheet*, September 12, 2005.

[5] Melissa Wicinski and Jennifer Griffith, "5 Ways to Communicate Sustainability beyond Words," *GreenBiz.com*, May 1, 2013. www.greenbiz.com/blog/2013/05/01/5-ways-communicate-sustainability-beyond-words.

[6] "Communicating Sustainability: How to Produce Effective Public Campaigns," prepared by Futerra Sustainability Communications for the United Nations Environment Programme (UNEP), 2005.

[7] Hasek, Glenn. 2014. "Number of State Level Certification, Recognition Programs Stands at 27." *Green Lodging News,* February 12. Available at www.greenlodgingnews.com/number-of-state-level-certification-recognition-programs.

chapter review

CASE STUDY

Arizona Hotel Resort and Spa

You have recently been hired as the general manager for a luxury resort hotel in Scottsdale, Arizona, that boasts one of the nicest spas in the country. However, the hotel has done very little planning in the past and has relied mainly on its reputation. As the new general manager, you decide to engage in an environmental scanning task to determine the impact of the external environment on your hotel's operation.

Case Study Questions and Issues

1. Discuss the potential impact of each of the external environments on your hotel and spa.

2. What, if anything, can be done to address these potential impacts?

CASE STUDY

Bushwood Country Club

Ty Webb was recently hired as the general manager at the Bushwood Country Club. One of his main initiatives as the new GM is to improve the club's sustainability efforts and find ways to become a more environmentally friendly country club. The country club has a fine dining restaurant and a clubhouse grill to service its members. In addition, there is an 18-hole professional golf course. The area where the country club is located often has droughts and water shortages throughout the summer months and the local residents and businesses face certain water restrictions. Therefore, it would greatly benefit the course to reduce its water usage. Carl Spackler is the golf superintendent responsible for the maintenance of the course. He has been attending conferences on golf course sustainability and is excited about the opportunity to implement some of the practices presented at the conferences.

The restaurants haven't implemented any "green practices" to date, and there is definitely room for improvement. Danny Noonan is the clubhouse manager in charge of the restaurant and bar business. He doesn't share Mr. Spackler's enthusiasm and feels that it is a waste of time and money to incorporate the necessary changes to become a "green" facility. Also, Ty Webb has to sell the members on having a special assessment to raise the money necessary to implement the new programs. This isn't easy, seeing as the annual dues are already on the high side and members won't be willing to pay additional fees unless they see a direct benefit. There is a Board of Directors elected by the members that will make the final decision about a special assessment based on their discussions with the members.

Case Study Questions and Issues

1. What is the first thing Ty Webb should do before meeting with the Board of Directors?

2. What are some of the recommendations that can be made for the golf course?

3. What are some of the recommendations that can be made for the restaurants?

4. Who is the target audience(s) for communicating the sustainability initiatives?

5. Develop an outline of a communications plan that Ty Webb could use, including specific objectives, messages, channels, and so on.

Understanding the Behavior of Hospitality Consumers

Courtesy of Carnival Cruise Lines.

Chapter Objectives

After studying this chapter, you should be able to:

1. Define consumer behavior and explain why it is important to study.

2. List and discuss the external and internal factors that influence consumer behavior.

3. Describe the consumer decision-making model.

4. Explain the problem-solving process strategies employed by consumers.

5. Outline the three levels of consumer problem solving.

6. List characteristics unique to organizational buying.

3.1 INTRODUCTION

Successful marketing managers focus on understanding their consumers' wants and needs as clearly as possible. Thorough marketing research has allowed marketing managers of tangible products, such as automobiles, toothpaste, laundry detergent, and most other products, to understand their customers. More recently, marketers have begun to better understand the subject of consumer behavior as it relates to the consumption of services. This knowledge enables marketing managers to develop sophisticated marketing programs aimed at very specific target market segments.

One of the most perplexing problems confronting hospitality managers is to understand why hospitality consumers behave as they do. This chapter explores several important aspects of consumer behavior, including the internal and external factors that influence consumer behavior, the way in which consumers make purchase decisions, the satisfaction of hospitality consumers, and how continuous quality improvement can be used as a marketing tool. In general, *consumer behavior* can be defined as the study of how an individual's thoughts, feelings, attitudes, opinions, and patterns of behavior affect what he buys, when he buys, why he buys, and how he uses the product or service he purchases. The study of consumer behavior focuses on understanding consumers as they purchase products or services. This behavior takes place within the larger context of the environment in which each person operates. Therefore, consumer behavior examines the roles and influences that others have on the behavior of individual consumers.

Understanding the behavior of hospitality and tourism consumers is among the most important challenges facing management. It is critical that managers remain in constant communication with those who consume the products and services. Equally critical is the importance of managers to pay close attention to consumer needs so that they will be ready to change elements of the marketing mix when consumer preferences, wants, or needs change. For example, in recent years many consumers have demonstrated an increasing emphasis on healthier diets. This concern has led them to request—even, in some cases, demand—menu choices that are healthier. Restaurants have responded by providing menu choices that are lower in fat and salt and adding more fresh fruits, vegetables, and grains. The products and services made available to consumers must respond to the changing needs of the target market segments.

The study of consumer behavior is based on two fundamental ideas: (1) consumer behavior is rational and predictable and (2) marketers can influence this behavior. Contrary to what some may think, the behavior of consumers is not irrational or random. Consumer behavior that appears to be irrational to the outside observer is very rational to the individual making the purchase decisions. As we've noted, restaurants are increasing the number of healthier menu choices because restaurant guests were demanding them. Yet, at the same time, the sale of desserts and other sweets has also increased. Is this rational? Does it make sense from a consumer's point of view? How can consumers appear to exhibit this conflicting, and perhaps irrational, behavior?

Consider it from the restaurant guest's point of view and it is very rational. Suppose that a particular customer has made healthy menu choices all during the week. However, when dining out on Friday evening, she indulges in a high-calorie, high-fat dessert, saying to her friends, "It's been a long, hard week, and I'm going to treat myself to the mocha swirl cheesecake." This is not irrational behavior in the mind of the consumer. She believes that she has cut back on calorie and fat consumption all week and in fact deserves a special treat at dinner on Friday. The challenge for restaurant marketers is to recognize the trends in consumer behavior and provide the products and services that consumers demand.

3.1.1 Describing Consumer Behavior

Consumer behavior can be described, and to some extent it can be predicted, based on theory. James McNeal, in his classic book *Consumer Behavior,* advances the idea that human behavior is influenced by several factors: social setting, social forces, roles, and attitudes relative to roles.[1]

3.1.1.1 SOCIAL SETTING. All consumers make decisions and take actions within the larger social setting and, in doing so, are influenced by their peers. In addition, the same consumers will, in turn, influence the actions of other consumers. Social settings will vary greatly. For example,

Corepics VOF/Shutterstock

Trekking in a large city is influenced by different social forces than hiking in the mountains.

the social setting of a consumer living in New York City is very different from that of someone living in Ames, Iowa; Paris, France; or an Eastern European country.

3.1.1.2 SOCIAL FORCES.

Forces within the society set the standards of acceptable behavior. These rules are both written and unwritten, and they are established by those within the society with the most influence. For example, the behavior that a college student exhibits at a party on campus is likely to be quite different than the behavior exhibited while at home during break. Different social forces are at work in these two situations.

3.1.1.3 ROLES. A *role* is a pattern of behavior associated with a specific position within a social setting. All individuals assume a variety of roles, some professional, others personal. Each role brings with it a set of expectations for behavior. For example, when a person is in a position of authority, such as the manager of a hotel, employees look to the manager to provide direction, make decisions, and help the operation run smoothly. However, when this manager leaves work and goes home, he or she may assume a less active decision-making role when interacting with his or her children. For example, at home, the manager may defer to the children the decision about what type of activity they will engage in during a day that they spend together.

3.1.1.4 ATTITUDES RELATIVE TO ROLES. Within each of the roles that we play are attitudes and knowledge that we gain about the setting. Attitudes are defined as consistently favorable or unfavorable evaluations of objects or situations. *Knowledge* is defined as facts that we gain about objects or situations. Attitudes are directly tied to a consumer's needs. These needs, which are the cause for all consumer behavior, are linked to an individual's attitudes and knowledge.

Attitudes
Learned predispositions to act in a consistently favorable or unfavorable manner.

3.1.2 Reasons to Study Consumer Behavior

Why should you study consumer behavior? First, knowledge of consumer behavior is important because managers in the hospitality industry come into direct contact with many consumers on a daily basis. One of the primary goals for each of these managers is to create and maintain satisfied consumers. Without a working knowledge of their wants and needs, it will be much more difficult to satisfy them. Keep in mind that the fundamental reason for being in business is to create and satisfy consumers.

Second, if a company is to grow and prosper, management must anticipate the wants and needs of consumers. For example, if a hospitality company is considering whether to build a new hotel, appropriate personnel must anticipate a particular location's demand for hotel rooms, meeting space, and food and beverage services. In doing so, they are likely to project demand for several years into the future. One of the ways to help make a better decision in this case is to understand more thoroughly the current and future behavior of consumers.

3.2 FACTORS THAT INFLUENCE CONSUMER BEHAVIOR

Consumers do not make purchase decisions in a vacuum. Rather, they are subject to both external and internal factors that influence them.

External influences
External influences include culture, socioeconomic status, reference groups, and household.

3.2.1 External Influences on Consumer Behavior

External influences include culture, socioeconomic level, reference groups, and household.

3.2.1.1 CULTURE. Culture is defined as the patterns of behavior and social relations that characterize a society and separate it from others. It conveys values, ideals, and attitudes that help individuals communicate with each other and evaluate situations. It is important in viewing culture to draw legitimate generalizations about a given culture or subculture without resorting to stereotyping. An individual's culture provides a frame of reference concerning acceptable behaviors, and as such, culture is a learned set of arbitrary values. The dominant culture in the United States today stresses equality, use of resources, materialism, individualism, and youth.

Culture
Patterns of behavior and social relations that characterize a society and separate it from others.

Differences in cultures are most apparent when a hospitality and tourism firm attempts to expand into international markets. There are significant differences between, for example, the way that Europeans make purchase decisions and exhibit travel behavior and the way that Americans do so. In much of Europe, for instance, it is very common for a family to take an extended vacation that might last for 2, 3, or more weeks. In France, it is very common for businesses to shut down for much of August while the entire country is on vacation. In the United States, the opposite trend is prevalent. Families are less likely to take a vacation of more than 1 week and are more likely to take a series of mini-vacations that extend over 3-day weekends. In fact, in the early 1990s, the phrase "break-ation" was introduced to describe the mini- or getaway-vacations that have become common in the United States.

In addition to the general culture of the United States, marketers must also be concerned with subcultures. Subcultures include groups of people within the larger culture who share common beliefs or interests that differ from the majority based on common life experiences. Subcultures in marketing are often based on race, ethnicity, religion, or nationality. However, they can also be based on geographic location, age, and sexual orientation. Two markets that have received a good deal of attention in the travel industry are the lesbian, gay, bisexual, and transgender (LGBT) population and millenials (those born between 1980 and 2000) because of their distinct differences relative to the overall society. For example, millenials constitute a large percentage of the labor force for hospitality organizations, but owners and managers have a difficult time relating to these individuals because of their different value systems. In general, millenials are more open to change and more creative than previous generations, but they are also more narcissistic and individualistic. Millenials often want flexible hours and job enrichment, and they change jobs frequently because there is no sense of loyalty. This lack of loyalty is also present in millenials as consumers. In addition, they rely more heavily on word of mouth and objective product reviews than on traditional advertising.

3.2.1.2 SOCIOECONOMIC LEVEL.

Socioeconomic level has a large influence in consumer decision making. Marketing managers have long attempted to correlate socioeconomic level with dining-out habits and travel patterns. Hospitality managers must identify the relative socioeconomic levels to which the operation appeals and target those groups directly with a customized marketing mix. For example, an upscale and expensive four- or five-star resort property will target its promotional efforts to those in upper-income groups. These resorts are likely to advertise in publications read by professionals and those who are in the top 25 percent of annual household income—in other words, the resorts' target market.

The Internet is a successful tool for firms to reach various socioeconomic groups. For example, online travel agents are able to reach price-sensitive consumers who tend to have relatively lower incomes than most frequent travelers. These consumers use websites such as Expedia.com and Travelocity.com to find good deals and bargain prices for flights, hotels, rental cars, and tourist attractions. Hotels also have their own websites that are used to reach frequent travelers who accumulate points and redeem them for free hotel rooms and vacation packages.

3.2.1.3 REFERENCE GROUPS.

A reference group is a group with whom an individual identifies to the point where the group dictates a standard of behavior. Reference groups exert tremendous influence on consumers' hospitality and tourism purchase decisions. Every individual is influenced directly and indirectly. Marketing research has identified three types of reference groups: comparative, status, and normative. The two most common types of reference groups are comparative and normative.

> **Reference group**
> A group with whom an individual identifies to the point where the group dictates a standard of behavior.

Celebrities such as sports figures and popular entertainers serve as comparative referents by providing standards and influencing consumers' behaviors. One example of this is the popularity of certain restaurants in major cities such as New York City and Los Angeles. The media report the dining behaviors of the celebrities, and other consumers who aspire to be like those celebrities dine at the same "trendy" restaurants frequented by the celebrities. There is also a status component to reference groups. Restaurant critics provide their reviews of restaurants and many consumers want to "be seen" at the highest-rated restaurants. It is important to note that comparative referents are merely observed and there is no direct interaction between the referent and the individual being influenced.

Acquaintances such as parents, teachers, and peers serve as normative referents by providing individuals with norms, values, and attitudes through personal interactions. For example, children might continue to vacation at the same destinations that were popular among their parents and other relatives throughout their childhoods. Another example would be "Spring Break" destinations. College students often choose destinations that are popular among the other students at their colleges or universities (e.g., fraternity brothers or club members).

Opinion leaders
People whose opinions impact the lifestyle choices and purchasing behaviors of others.

A hospitality manager can also influence consumer behavior through the use of opinion leaders. Opinion leaders include formal and/or informal leaders of reference groups, and their opinions normally influence opinion formation in others. Common opinion leaders are leaders within the community, such as doctors, lawyers, and politicians, and those who are viewed as subject matter experts. For example, a travel agent is clearly an opinion leader for travel-related products. Potential travelers often seek advice from a travel agent because they believe that the agent has knowledge far superior to their own. Another example is the food critic who writes for a local newspaper, or the writer for a travel magazine or television show. The opinions that the critic expresses in a newspaper column have direct and immediate influence on readers. The survival of restaurants in competitive markets (e.g., New York City, Las Vegas, Los Angeles) is greatly influenced by critics, and a favorable review is a necessity. Similarly, travel writers can have a significant impact on the number of visitors to a tourism destination.

Hospitality managers often strive to create their own reference groups and opinion leaders. Frequent guests can be rewarded with complimentary samples of new menu items or perhaps a complimentary flavored coffee or bottle of champagne. The champagne creates excitement and is very likely to increase sales, as individuals sitting at other tables want to become part of the excitement and often order a bottle for their own table. The desired result is of course a snowball effect among many tables, which results in increased sales. Frequent guests can also be used for feedback about potential new menu items or new services. If they are favorably impressed with the new products or services, they will tell their friends and colleagues, and increased business can result.

3.2.1.4 HOUSEHOLD. A *household* is defined as those individuals who occupy a single living unit. There are more than 115 million households in the United States, and within every household certain characteristics, leadership, and norms exist. Leadership is normally rotated among members of the household. For example, the children may decide which breakfast cereal to eat or which fast-food restaurant to patronize, while an adult selects the type of living accommodations. Hospitality marketing research points out that leadership is often shared. For example, the parents normally decide when the household will go out to eat, but it is the children who decide which restaurant will be patronized.

All external influences discussed can affect the decision-making process of a consumer whenever a decision about hospitality and tourism products and services is made. The culture, socioeconomic level, reference groups, and household members influence directly and indirectly, consciously and unconsciously, the dining habits of all consumers.

3.2.2 Internal Influences on Consumer Behavior

Internal influences
Personal characteristics, beliefs, and experiences that guide a consumer's decision-making.

In addition to external influences, internal influences affect consumers' choices as well—personal needs and motives, experience, personality and self-image, and perceptions and attitudes. The exact influence of internal factors is less well known than the external factors, as internal factors are not as observable and therefore are not as well documented and understood.

Need
A lack of something or the difference between someone's desired and actual states.

3.2.2.1 PERSONAL NEEDS AND MOTIVES. A need is defined as a lack of something or the difference between someone's desired and actual states. Motive is defined as a person's inner state that directs the individual toward satisfying a felt need. For example, consumers may be hungry and tired (their actual state), yet they desire to be well fed and rested (desired state). This felt need would therefore cause them to have the motivation to seek out a restaurant where this need could be satisfied.

Motive
A person's inner state that directs the individual toward satisfying a perceived need.

Despite years of consumer behavior research, it is very difficult, if not impossible, to fully explain all of the needs consumers feel. Figure 3.1 illustrates the role of needs in consumer

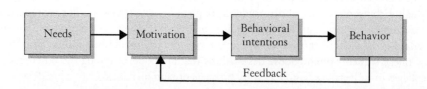

FIGURE 3.1 • Needs related to consumer behavior.

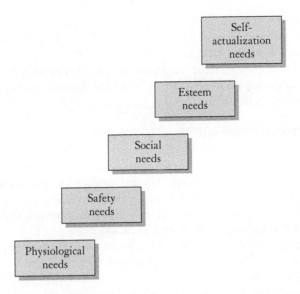

FIGURE 3.2 • **Maslow's hierarchy of needs.**

behavior. Simply stated, needs lead to motivation, which leads to behavioral intentions, which ultimately lead to observable behavior. Following behavior, feedback affects and may change a consumer's motivation. To continue our earlier example, once the consumer had been to a particular restaurant, if the meal was satisfying and met prior expectations, then the feedback would be favorable and the consumer would likely plan to return to this particular restaurant. If, however, the meal was not satisfying or did not meet prior expectations, then the individual's negative feelings would likely result in not returning to this particular restaurant. It is important to remember that successful marketing is about identifying and then meeting or exceeding the expectations of consumers.

In the mid-1900s, Abraham Maslow, an American psychologist, developed a model identifying five classes of needs; today, the model remains one of the influential cornerstones of consumer behavior. As shown in Figure 3.2, Maslow's hierarchy of needs is arranged in the following order, from the lowest to highest level: physiological needs, safety needs, social and belonging needs, esteem needs, and self-actualization needs.[2] Individuals are believed to satisfy the lower-level needs before they move to the higher-level needs.

Maslow's hierarchy of needs
Five motivational needs that individuals seek to fulfill, progressing in order from basic to complex.

3.2.2.2 PHYSIOLOGICAL NEEDS. Physiological needs are primary needs for food, shelter, and clothing, which one must have before thinking about higher-order needs. Nearly all products and services offered to consumers by hospitality and tourism firms address these needs.

3.2.2.3 SAFETY NEEDS. These second-level needs include personal security and protection from physical harm. The movement toward greater security and safety within the hotel industry has addressed these needs. Electronic door locks, increased lighting, outside entrances that are locked after dark, and more sophisticated fire detection devices all are designed to meet safety needs.

3.2.2.4 SOCIAL AND BELONGING NEEDS. After needs at the lower two levels are satisfied, consumers look toward achieving social acceptance by others. From the hospitality and tourism perspective, we cater to consumers who want to join private clubs that offer a variety of social and recreational activities. We also make consumers feel like they belong by making special products and services available for frequent guests. Hotels that target longer-term guests, such as Marriott's Residence Inns, will often schedule social events for their guests in order to satisfy the social needs of those who are away from family and friends for an extended period of time.

3.2.2.5 ESTEEM NEEDS. When consumers feel accepted, they seek to enhance their self-esteem. Hospitality and tourism companies cater to these individuals by providing a higher level of personal service. For example, airlines provide first-class and business class, in addition to coach. Airlines also provide special lounges and waiting areas for frequent travelers and for individuals who purchase memberships in their "airline clubs." Another example is expensive restaurants that offer only the finest food, beverages, and service. They provide a level of products and services that cater to the esteem needs of guests, and they expend a good deal of effort to make guests feel very special and important.

3.2.2.6 SELF-ACTUALIZATION NEEDS.

The highest-level needs within Maslow's hierarchy focus on an individual's need to reach his or her full potential. For the most part, these needs are often beyond the scope of what hospitality and tourism marketers can expect to fulfill. However, there are examples from within the hospitality and tourism industry regarding a consumer's attempt to satisfy self-actualization needs. For example, when guests are attracted to sports programs at five-star resorts focusing on how to play the best golf or tennis possible, they are seeking to reach a state of self-actualization with regard to the sport.

An alternative approach combines the work of Maslow with the work on personality development by Erik Erikson.[3] In this model, adults pass through three life stages, and each stage will help determine the kinds of experiences will seek as consumers (see Figure 3.3). Consumers purchase products either because they need them, because they desire them, or both. Consumer satisfaction is achieved mainly through desire-driven, or discretionary purchases.

In the first stage, young adults (age 40 or younger) are seeking satisfaction through purchasing *possession experiences* in their early career-development and family-building years. Examples of products purchased during this stage are cars and houses. Then, as they grow older (age 40 to 60), consumers focus more on purchasing *catered experiences* such as travel, restaurants, education, and sports. Finally, the third stage (age over 60) finds consumers shifting their focus toward *being experiences* associated with interpersonal relationships and simple pleasures. In this context, hospitality services would be purchased more in the second stage, although they would be purchased merely for survival throughout a consumer's life span. Some resorts, spas, and travel destinations target the third stage as well. For example, some destinations market themselves to older travelers who are seeking a more spiritual experience.

Psychologist David McClelland identified three social motives: achievement, affiliation, and power.[4] Achievement causes an individual to work harder to reach a goal. Affiliation causes individuals to belong to groups or to seek the approval of others. Each person has the need to belong and to be accepted. Finally, McClelland identified individuals' need for power. Individuals want to feel that they have some control over their immediate environment.

3.2.2.7 EXPERIENCE.

Experience is also a major internal influence on consumer behavior. As individuals encounter new situations, such as dining in a particular restaurant for the first time, they integrate their perceptions into an experience framework that influences future decisions. The adage, "First impressions are important," applies directly to the hospitality and tourism industry. If consumers are turned off the first time they walk up to the front desk in a hotel or are greeted by a host in a restaurant, they are unlikely to return. One of the factors that have led to the success of Walt Disney World is that the staff, called "cast members," focus on the guests'

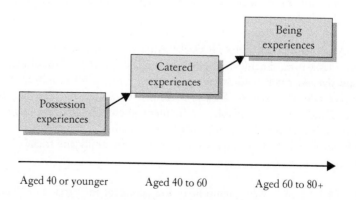

FIGURE 3.3 • Consumer discretionary purchasing over a life span.

needs from the moment they arrive on site until they depart. In the morning, when carloads of excited families arrive, they are greeted by smiling parking-lot cast members who help get everyone's day at Disney off to a memorable start. These initial impressions are the start of a great day for the guests and leave an impression.

Hospitality managers must remember that people (consumers) are products of their environments. Each new experience is integrated into a frame of reference against which new situations are evaluated. This frame of reference includes each individual's beliefs, values, norms, and assumptions. Consider the following example. A guest who travels more than 100 days each year checks into a hotel at which she has not previously stayed. As the guest checks in, she is evaluating the quality of the service received against prior check-in experiences. Based on her prior experience, she may believe that the check-in process should not take more than 60 seconds to complete. Any amount of time in excess of 60 seconds will likely result in dissatisfaction with the hotel. In this example, the guest has a belief that check-in should be accomplished quickly and easily. This is the norm against which she will judge all check-ins.

3.2.2.8 PERSONALITY AND SELF-IMAGE.

Each individual consumer develops a unique personality and self-image over a period of time. For marketing purposes, individual personality types can be grouped into various classifications such as swingers, conservatives, leaders, and followers. The important thing for hospitality managers to remember is that no hospitality operation can be all things to all people. Firms must select one or more target markets that are subsets or segments of the total market and then appeal directly to these consumers. Many hospitality organizations experience difficulty when attempting to appeal to too wide a segment of the total market. The result is quite predictable: failure to satisfy any of the target markets, which leads to poor financial performance and often failure.

> **Personality**
> An individual's distinctive psychological characteristics that lead to relatively consistent responses to his or her environment.

One example of this type of thinking involved a restaurant that featured a beef and seafood menu, with moderate to high prices and a semiformal atmosphere. This restaurant had been successful, but the owners and managers felt that more profits could and should be generated. In an attempt to broaden the target market, the atmosphere was made more informal, and the menu was changed to include hamburgers, snacks, sandwiches, and pizza, as well as steaks and seafood. In only 30 days after the change was made, sales volume had increased by 15 percent. Within 3 months, however, volume had fallen by 38 percent, and what had once been a profitable operation was now running a deficit. Following careful examination of the performance of several hospitality organizations, one finds that it is normally those with well-defined target markets that are the most successful. Those attempting to be all things to all people often fail.

3.2.2.9 PERCEPTION AND ATTITUDE.

Each day, consumers are exposed to thousands of stimuli. Some of these stimuli are consciously received, resulting in a thought process, whereas others are simply ignored. Perception is the process by which stimuli are recognized, received, and interpreted. Each individual consumer perceives the world differently. Perceptions are manifested in attitudes. As stated earlier in the chapter, attitudes are learned predispositions to act in a consistently favorable or unfavorable manner. For example, some individuals' attitudes are that fast-food meals are very good because they are of high quality and low cost and come with fast and courteous service. Other individuals' attitudes are that fast-food meals are of low nutritional value and poor culinary quality and that they are not visually attractive. Both types of individuals hold attitudes based on their perceptions. Their perceptions may or may not be valid, but it is important for the marketing manager to remember that perceptions are the way an individual sees the world. In the mind of the individual consumer, the perceptions and resulting attitudes are correct and valid. It is very difficult to change the perceptions and resulting attitudes that individuals have developed over time.

> **Perception**
> The process by which stimuli are recognized, received, and interpreted.

3.2.3   Consumer Adoption Process

Hospitality consumers today are demanding more sophisticated dining and lodging experiences. Consumers are better educated, earn more money, and are more confident when they travel and dine outside the home. Today's hospitality consumers are seeking products and services tailored to meet their specific needs. They are more concerned about nutrition and safety, and they know more about value. Some of the following trends in individual behavior are affecting consumerism:

- Receiving instant gratification rather than the concept of self-denial
- Feeling terrific rather than feeling responsible
- Improvising rather than planning
- Choosing simplicity over complexity
- Showing concern for status rather than egalitarianism

These trends shape the way firms develop and market their products and services. There are consumer models that aid marketers in understanding consumers and determining strategies.

Individuals have been classified according to willingness to change. Some are not upset by change, whereas others resist change in any form. Figure 3.4 illustrates the diffusion of consumers over a typical product life cycle. Consumers will adopt new products at different rates depending on their level of aversion to risk and change. When a new hospitality operation opens, it is very important that individuals representing the innovators and early adopters are reached by marketing efforts. These individuals offer excellent potential as early customers, for if they are satisfied, they will tell friends and associates, and these people, in turn, may become customers. People falling into the early and late majority categories will not usually try a new hospitality operation until they have heard positive comments from others.

This process of influencing the innovators and early adopters is called *diffusion and adoption*. The key is to get the consumers who are most likely to try new products and services to make a trial purchase—that is, to dine at the restaurant, stay in the hotel, rent a car, or purchase a flight. If they are satisfied with the products and services received, they will then help spread the positive word to others, and the number of customers will increase over time. How quickly consumers adopt a new product depends on the actual need for the product and the risk associated with the product's purchase.

First, products that are necessary will be adopted more readily than products that are not essential. For example, a fine-dining restaurant may take longer to build a clientele than a fast-food restaurant in a growing suburb. Second, the more risk involved with a product's purchase, the slower the adoption process. Several types of risk are associated with the purchase of a product or service:

- **Financial risk.** The monetary loss that would result from a wrong decision

- **Performance risk.** The chance that the product or service will not meet a consumer's expectations

- **Physical risk.** Any mental or physical harm that could occur

- **Social risk.** The possibility that the product will not meet the approval of one's peers

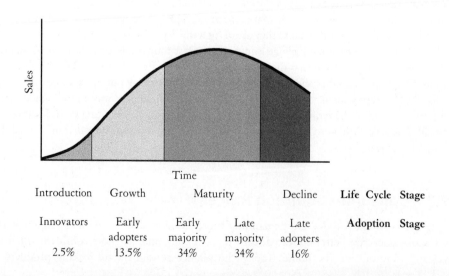

FIGURE 3.4 • Diffusion and adoption across the product life cycle.

For example, a cruise can be expensive, it carries a certain prestige, and consumers have high expectations. Also, there have been instances in which passengers have been harmed or even killed, as the result of fires, taking on water, and terrorists.

3.3   CONSUMER DECISION-MAKING MODEL

When consumers make decisions concerning the purchase of goods and services, a very complex decision-making process takes place. Numerous variables influence this decision-making process, as the many models of consumer behavior demonstrate. Figure 3.5 draws together several theories into a model that shows both the external and internal influences we have just discussed, as well as the process by which consumers make purchase decisions.

This model illustrates the major steps in the decision-making process, as well as the role external and internal influences play as the individual makes purchase decisions. Because both external and internal variables influence consumers' decision-making processes, hospitality managers need to develop awareness of the specific influences that are most important to their particular target market segments. Figure 3.5 shows five key elements in the decision-making model: problem recognition, information search, evaluation of alternatives, purchase decision, and postpurchase evaluation. Each element is affected by external and internal influences.

3.3.1   Problem Recognition

The decision-making process begins with problem recognition, which occurs when a consumer realizes a difference between her actual state and her desired state. Thousands of different stimuli can trigger the awareness of a need or a problem. For example, if one feels hungry when driving down an interstate highway, this may trigger a need to search for a restaurant to satisfy the hunger need. In another situation, the need to feel important and be treated with the utmost respect may lead a potential guest to search for an upscale hotel with a concierge floor when making a reservation. The need may not begin within a single individual. For example, if a couple comes home after both have worked all day, and one says to the other, "Let's go out tonight; I'm too tired to cook," this manifests a joint need that only one of the individuals may have felt. Hospitality marketing managers should recognize the wide variety of needs that consumers are attempting to satisfy when they dine out.

3.3.2   Information Search

After the need is raised to a conscious level, the model holds that consumers seek to retrieve information. This search can involve a variety of information sources, including reference groups and members of the immediate household, as well as the mass media in the form of advertising. Table 3.1 provides a comparison of information sources based on the effort required and the credibility of the source.

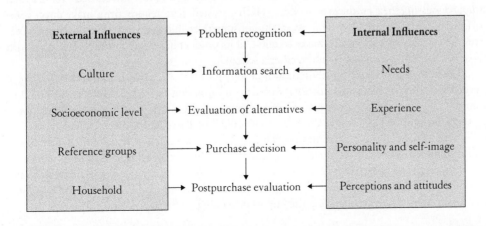

FIGURE 3.5 • A consumer decision-making model.

INFORMATION SOURCE	EFFORT REQUIRED	CREDIBILITY
Internal (past experience)	Low	High
External		
Personal (friends and family)	Low	High
Marketing (advertising, promotions, salespeople)	High	Low
Public (consumer information, Internet)	High	High

TABLE 3.1 • Comparison of Information Sources.

If the felt need is as basic as the need to eat because of hunger, the information retrieval process is likely to be brief. That is, the restaurant facility selected in this case is likely to be chosen primarily because of convenience, and the number of sources of information consulted is likely to be quite small. In other situations, the number of sources consulted could be much larger. Consider the meeting planner who is coordinating the annual meeting for a professional association. This individual is likely to consult several sources of information before selecting an appropriate hotel for this important event. The important thing for the hospitality marketing manager to remember is that consumers rely to a certain extent on the mass media for information.

The amount of information to research and the length of the consumer decision-making process will increase with the consumer's level of involvement. Consumers tend to be more involved when there is a greater perceived risk of making a wrong choice, which is normally associated with products or services with higher prices, more visibility, or greater complexity. Consumers tend to compare the benefits of search (e.g., value, enjoyment, self-confidence) with the costs (e.g., money, time, convenience) to determine the perceived risk. There are also many other situational factors that will affect the amount of information search, such as product knowledge, demographics (e.g., income and education), and the market environment.

3.3.3 Evaluation of Alternatives

After the consumer has gathered a sufficient amount of information, the third element in the decision-making process is to evaluate alternatives. Consumers who ask, "At which one of several possible restaurants should I dine tonight?" go through a cognitive process in answering this question, whereby they weigh the positive and negative aspects of each alternative. They also examine the attributes of the product–service mix of each restaurant. Consumers consider the relative importance of each attribute of the product–service mix by making trade-offs between the various attributes and their levels. The final result is an **evoked set**, or a group of brands that will be considered in the final purchase decision.

Marketing managers in other industries have long recognized this cognitive process and have used it to their advantage in advertising and promoting their products and services. Rather than simply discussing their products or services as if they existed in a vacuum, firms make direct comparisons with the competition. This assists the consumer's cognitive process of evaluating alternatives. Of course, every advertiser makes certain that its product or service compares favorably with those of the competition based on the criteria selected.

The following example illustrates how a hospitality firm can gain a better understanding of the consumer decision-making process. Assume the information in Table 3.2a represents one consumer's evaluation of the importance of hotel attributes and the ratings of three competing hotels on those attributes. (This is the kind of data that could be collected using a comment card or some other type of survey.) The first column under each hotel represents the actual rating and the second column represents the weighted rating based on the importance assigned to the attribute by the consumer. The consumer was instructed to divide 100 points between the three attributes based on their relative importance. The figures were converted to decimals and the weighted rating was computed by multiplying the importance rating by the actual rating. The final average

Evoked set
The qualified set of brands that will be considered in the final purchase decision.

ATTRIBUTE	IMPORTANCE	HOLIDAY INN		MARRIOTT		FOUR SEASONS	
		ACTUAL	*WEIGHTED*	*ACTUAL*	*WEIGHTED*	*ACTUAL*	*WEIGHTED*
Price	0.5	4.0	2.0	3.0	1.5	2.0	1.0
Location	0.3	3.0	0.9	3.0	0.9	4.0	1.2
Service Quality	0.2	2.0	0.4	3.0	0.6	4.0	0.8
Average		3.00	3.30	3.00	3.00	3.33	3.00

TABLE 3.2a • **Evaluation of Alternative Hotels.**

for the weighted rating is simply the sum of the scores for each attribute. The ratings were based on a four-point scale: 1 = poor, 2 = fair, 3 = good, 4 = excellent.

The hospitality manager can see from the information in Table 3.2a that this consumer feels that price is the most important factor in choosing a hotel, followed by location, and then service quality. The manager can also tell how each hotel is perceived on the same list of attributes. In this example, the consumer prefers the Holiday Inn based on his or her perceptions of the hotel and his or her relative importance rating for each of the attributes. The Holiday Inn received the highest weighted average total across the three attributes (price, location, and service quality). This same process can be used for a market segment by combining the scores of a sample of consumers and using the aggregate figures. However, the section on consumer problem-solving strategies explains how consumers employ different heuristics for making purchase decisions.

3.3.4 Purchase Decision

The fourth stage in the consumer decision-making model is the purchase decision. It is at this point that the individual actually makes the decision. All external and internal variables come together to produce a decision. This decision is made based on the perceived risk associated with each alternative and the willingness of the individual to take risks. This risk factor offers a tremendous competitive advantage for hospitality chains. When consumers step through the front door of a McDonald's, Burger King, Red Lobster, or any other nationally recognized chain, they are taking a much smaller risk than if they entered an independent restaurant about which they knew very little. There is less risk with the chain operation because the product–service mix is well known to customers. Independent hospitality operations must work very hard to establish themselves and thereby reduce some of the risk that consumers associate with patronizing a restaurant where the product–service mix is not well known.

There are other factors, in addition to perceived risk and risk aversion, that affect the consumer's purchase decision. The actual purchase is based on the consumer problem-solving strategy used by each individual. Some consumers base the decision on their evaluation of all the product or service attributes simultaneously, whereas others evaluate the attributes one at a time. Also, it depends on the consumer's involvement with the product or service category and the resultant problem-solving technique. Both of these topics are discussed in the next section, following the final stage in the consumer decision-making process—postpurchase evaluation.

3.3.5 Postpurchase Evaluation

Following the product–service mix consumption, the final stage is postpurchase evaluation. How did the actual experience compare with the expectations prior to purchase? Was the product–service mix better than or not quite up to the standards anticipated? Postconsumption feelings are based on two factors: the consumer's expectations and the actual performance by the hospitality operation. For this reason, it is very important for any hospitality operation to deliver the product–service mix promised in advertising promotion or personal selling. Failure to perform at or above the level anticipated by the consumer is likely to lead to negative postconsumption feelings.

These negative feelings produce dissatisfaction and reduce the level of repeat patronage. From a management perspective, it is important to promise less and deliver more—underpromise and overdeliver. This is a key concept in producing satisfied customers.[5] Finally, there is a period of time between the purchase of hospitality or tourism services and when they are consumed. During this period, consumers may have second thoughts or negative feelings about the purchase; this hesitancy is referred to as cognitive dissonance. That is why it is important for hospitality firms to run advertisements that depict satisfied customers.

Consumer decision-making is extremely complex. Marketing managers constantly strive to learn more about the way consumers reach decisions. As with other forms of human behavior, consumer behavior may never be totally understood.

Cognitive dissonance
Stress or discomfort experienced by a consumer because of conflicting beliefs or second thoughts after they have purchased a product or service.

3.4 CONSUMER PROBLEM-SOLVING PROCESSES

Consumers, either consciously or subconsciously, employ certain processes to integrate the information that they have obtained over time to evaluate and choose among the various alternatives. These formal integration strategies can be termed compensatory, noncompensatory, or a combination of the two.

3.4.1 Compensatory Strategies

When consumers use compensatory strategies, they use a product's strength(s) in one or more areas to compensate for deficiencies in other areas. In other words, consumers view products and services as bundles of attributes. The set of alternatives that a consumer is considering for purchase will contain products or services that have various combinations of these attributes and their levels. This multiattribute approach assumes that consumers are capable of evaluating each of a product's attributes and then arriving at an overall assessment, or score, for the product that can be compared to alternative products. It is believed that consumers make these complicated comparisons and trade-offs and then choose the product that achieves the highest rating.

Compensatory strategies
Consumers use a product's strength(s) in one or more areas to compensate for deficiencies in other areas.

For example, the consumer information in Table 3.2b can be used to illustrate the differences between the various consumer problem-solving processes. According to the information in the table, if all of the attributes were equally weighted, the consumer would choose the Four Seasons because it received the highest average score (3.33) based on the actual ratings. Even though the hotel received a lower rating for price, its higher ratings on location and service quality compensated for the deficiency. However, if the weighted averages are used, the Holiday Inn received the highest average score because this consumer (or market segment) is relatively price sensitive and Holiday Inn's higher rating on price offset the lower ratings on location and service quality.

ATTRIBUTE	IMPORTANCE	HOLIDAY INN		MARRIOTT		FOUR SEASONS	
		ACTUAL	*WEIGHTED*	*ACTUAL*	*WEIGHTED*	*ACTUAL*	*WEIGHTED*
Price	0.5	4.0	2.0	3.0	1.5	2.0	1.0
Location	0.3	2.0	0.6	3.0	0.9	4.0	1.2
Service Quality	0.2	2.0	0.4	3.0	0.6	4.0	0.8
Average		2.66	3.00	3.00	3.00	3.33	3.00

Compensatory Strategy: highest average score
Conjunctive Strategy: all scores above minimum threshold of 3.0 for all attributes
Disjunctive Strategy: highest score on most important attribute (price)
Lexicographic Strategy: highest score starting with most important attribute (price)

TABLE 3.2b • Evaluation of Alternative Hotels.

3.4.2 Noncompensatory Strategies

When using **noncompensatory strategies**, consumers do not allow product strengths in one area to compensate for deficiencies or weaknesses in another area. Instead, consumers place more emphasis on individual attributes and in some cases develop minimum thresholds to use in evaluating products and services. There are three main noncompensatory strategies that are used by consumers: conjunctive, disjunctive, and lexicographic.

3.4.2.1 CONJUNCTIVE.

A conjunctive approach involves setting minimum thresholds for each attribute and eliminating brands that do not surpass this threshold on any one salient attribute. The consumer determines which attributes will be important in choosing between brands. For example, a certain individual might consider location, food quality, food variety, and price to be the salient attributes in choosing a restaurant while on vacation. By examining the menus that are posted in the windows of restaurants in a busy tourist area, the individual can quickly eliminate restaurants that are deficient on menu variety or have prices that are too high. In addition, restaurants with good reputations for food quality and menu variety that are within the acceptable price range will be eliminated if they are not within walking distance.

Referring to the example in Table 3.2b, assume that the consumer has a minimum threshold of 3.0 (good) for all the attributes. Even though the Four Seasons received the highest scores for location and service quality, it did not meet the threshold for price. Therefore, the consumer would choose the Marriott if he or she was using a conjunctive strategy. It is the only hotel that received a minimum of 3.0 on all the attributes.

3.4.2.2 DISJUNCTIVE.

Some consumers do not get as involved in the purchase process and may prefer to take a less complicated approach to making purchase decisions. With the disjunctive approach, consumers still establish minimum thresholds for their salient attributes. However, a brand will be acceptable if it exceeds the minimum standard on at least one attribute. Consumers applying this approach tend to have only one or two salient attributes, the products or services tend to be very similar, and they are not as highly involved in the decision-making process. For example, a truck driver might consider price, location, and basic quality in choosing a hotel or motel to stop for the night. However, it is not unusual for truck drivers to choose the closest hotel or motel when they are starting to get tired. Similarly, an international tourist might choose the first hotel that looks clean or fits her or his price range.

Once again, the information in Table 3.2b can be used to illustrate the thought process behind a disjunctive strategy. Assume that the consumer was concerned about only one attribute. In this case, it would probably be price, because it received the highest importance rating. The consumer would choose the hotel that received the highest rating for price, which would be the Holiday Inn. This strategy would assume that location and service quality weren't as important, given that the Holiday Inn received the lowest ratings on both.

3.4.2.3 LEXICOGRAPHIC.

The lexicographic approach falls somewhere between conjunctive and disjunctive choice processes in terms of complexity. Just as in the other two approaches, the consumer determines a set of salient attributes, or choice criteria. Next, he or she places these choice criteria in rank order from most important to least important. Then the consumer evaluates the alternative brands, starting with the most important attribute. The brand that rates the highest on the most important attribute will be selected. If two or more brands tie or are closely rated, then those brands are evaluated by using the second-most important attribute. This continues until one brand remains or the list of attributes is exhausted—forcing a choice between the remaining brands. It is important to note that all brands are not evaluated on all criteria. For example, a business traveler might rank the most important attributes in airline travel to be convenience, comfort, food quality, and price, in that order. Depending on the airport where the flight originates, the traveler might be able to narrow the choices down to two airlines that offer direct flights at the preferred time. The final choice might then be made based on the fact that one of the airlines is perceived by the traveler to provide better service or comfort.

Finally, the information in Table 3.2b can be used to demonstrate this last noncompensatory strategy. This strategy would make use of the actual ratings based on the importance, or priority, assigned to each of the attributes. The consumer puts the attributes in order of price, location, and service quality based on importance (highest to lowest). Therefore, the first step is for the consumer to evaluate all three hotels on price. Because the Holiday Inn received the highest rating for price, the consumer would choose that hotel. However, if one of the other hotels also received a 4.0 rating for price, the consumer would have eliminated the one that didn't and move to the next attribute. This process would be repeated until there was one alternative left.

3.4.3   Combination Strategies

One of the main questions regarding problem-solving strategies is the ability of consumers to obtain, integrate, and evaluate the information available on the myriad brands in most product categories. The compensatory approach is particularly cumbersome in this respect, as can be non-compensatory approaches such as conjunctive or lexicographic strategies. And in many cases, the disjunctive approach would seem overly simplistic. Therefore, it could be argued that consumers actually use a combination of approaches in an attempt to adapt to the purchase situation and simplify the decision process. For example, using a conjunctive strategy, a family might eliminate all restaurants that don't have children's menus. Then the remaining restaurants could be evaluated using a more complicated compensatory strategy or a more simple disjunctive strategy.

3.5   CONSUMER PROBLEM-SOLVING TECHNIQUES

The consumer decision-making process differs in the length of time and effort expended on each stage based on the consumer's level of involvement and experience with a product category. Also, the level of involvement may change depending on the purchase situation. For instance, a young man's choice process for a restaurant could differ greatly when it is for a date versus a dinner with his buddies. Table 3.3 provides a comparison of the three levels of problem solving: routine response behavior, limited problem solving, and extended problem solving.

3.5.1   Routine Response Behavior

For some products, consumers exert very little effort in the decision-making process. Some marketing professionals believe that consumers actually skip stages of the process, whereas others feel that consumers merely move through all of the stages very quickly. This routine, or habitual,

CHARACTERISTICS	ROUTINE RESPONSE BEHAVIOR	LIMITED PROBLEM SOLVING	EXTENDED PROBLEM SOLVING
Amount of search	Minimal	Moderate	Substantial
Number of brands considered	One	Few	Many
Number of attributes evaluated	One or two	Few	Many
Cognitive processing	Minimal	Moderate	Substantial
Number of external information sources used	None	Few	Many
Level of involvement	Low	Medium	High
Total amount of effort	Low	Medium	High

TABLE 3.3 • Problem-Solving Techniques.

response involves very little information search or cognitive processing because the decision is almost automatic. Routine response behavior is typical for low-priced, frequently purchased products where consumer involvement is low. The amount of effort that consumers exert in the problem-solving process tends to decrease over time as they learn more about a product category and gain experience through consumption. An example of this behavior would be workers choosing the employee cafeteria for lunch.

3.5.2   Limited Problem Solving

Many consumers' purchase decisions involve limited problem solving because of some product differentiation and alternative brands. There is some information search, including external sources, unlike in routine response behavior. Consumers have a low to moderate level of involvement, and they consider a moderate number of attributes in making the purchase decision. At this point, the consumer usually has some knowledge and experience with regard to the product category. Consumers are willing to exert some time and effort to ensure a good choice. For example, choosing a restaurant for everyday dining is a limited problem-solving task for most consumers. Similarly, the choice of airline or rental car agency usually involves a few salient attributes, and the choice of alternatives is easily reduced to two or three brands.

3.5.3   Extended Problem Solving

Extended problem solving is most often associated with high-priced products that are purchased infrequently. Consumers need to engage in an extensive search process to identify salient attributes and alternative brands. Consumers are highly involved and exert a good deal of time and effort because of the price and risk of making a bad choice. The cognitive process is substantial because consumers need to evaluate the alternative brands using many attributes. For example, a couple planning a cruise will talk to friends, as well as a travel agent, and take their time to evaluate the various cruise lines based on price, accommodations, destinations, cabin availability, service, and quality.

3.6   ORGANIZATIONAL BUYER BEHAVIOR

Purchase decisions differ between organizations and individual buyers, but both types of buyers are trying to satisfy their particular needs. The buying process for organizations is much more structured and formal in comparison to the individual buying process. The most common organizational markets in hospitality and tourism are the meetings market for hotels and the tour market for travel. In addition, food service companies will offer catering services to groups such as corporations and institutions, wedding parties, and tour buses. Finally, hospitality firms purchase supplies needed for their operations from various vendors. For example, restaurants and hotels purchase uniforms, computer hardware and software, paper, and large food quantities. This section highlights some of the main characteristics of organizational buying.

3.6.1   Characteristics of Organizational Buying

The **organizational buying** process includes the stages used by organizations to determine needs (problem recognition), search for information, evaluate alternatives, make a purchase, and evaluate the purchase (postconsumption evaluation). In general, organizations go through the same decision-making process as individual consumers. However, there are some major differences between the activities within the stages:

Organizational buying
The process organizations follow to acquire the goods and services they use to produce and deliver their own products and services.

- **Larger-volume purchases.** Organizational buyers usually purchase in large volumes. Meeting planners, for example, book anywhere from 10 to 1,000 or more rooms, and tour operators package trips for groups of 10 or more.

- **Derived demand.**   The demand for organization products is derived from the demand for consumer products. For example, when the demand for insurance increases, insurance companies have more sales meetings and sponsor more incentive trips. Corporations and associations tend to have larger travel budgets when their industries are doing well.

- **More emphasis on specifications and service.**   The products in organization markets tend to be more technical in nature, and buyers are more concerned about specifications and service after the sale. For example, meeting planners are concerned about meeting room dimensions, audiovisual equipment, room temperature control, and conference service. Rarely do transient customers go into detail about the room dimensions and other specifications.

- **Professional buyers and more negotiation.**   Organization buyers tend to be professionals with an extensive knowledge of the product. Therefore, the purchase process tends to be longer and more involved for organizations than for regular consumers. Also, when buying large volumes, organization buyers have more power and can negotiate. Hotels and tour operators, for example, are willing to make more concessions in the price and product–service mix to sell higher volume to one buyer.

- **Repeat business.**   One of the benefits of selling to organizations is that they tend to become repeat purchasers. For example, corporations will use the same hotel throughout the year to amass higher volume and receive more concessions. Then, if the corporation is pleased with the service, it will use the hotel for meetings in subsequent years.

- **Multiple buyers.**   Often, more than one individual is involved in the buying process and making the ultimate purchase decision for organizations. A **buying center** or **buying unit** is a group of people that influences buying decisions for organizations. For example, many associations have site selection committees that choose destinations and hotels for future meetings.

Buying center or buying unit
Groups of people that influence buying decisions for organizations.

Table 3.4 provides a comparison of the stages in the buying process between consumers and organizations. The example involves the purchase of hotel services and provides a step-by-step summary of the possible activities at each stage.

3.6.2   Members of the Buying Unit

As mentioned earlier, organizations will normally have buying centers or buying units that influence their purchase decisions. Five specific roles have been identified for individuals constituting a buying unit: user, influencer, buyer, decider, and gatekeeper. In some instances, there is more than one person in each role, or the same person occupies more than one role.

- **Users.**   These are the people in the firm who actually use the product. For example, front-desk personnel will use a reservation system, waiters will use a point-of-sale system, and meeting attendees will use hotel facilities.

- **Influencers.**   These are the people who have some expertise in the product area and help define the necessary specifications. For example, computer systems personnel would help choose a reservation system or a point-of-sale system, and human resources personnel often influence site selection for meetings.

- **Buyers.**   These individuals have the formal authority and responsibility for making the purchase decision. For example, an employee at the corporate office for a hotel or restaurant chain will purchase reservation systems or point-of-sale systems, and a meeting planner will sign a contract for hotel facilities.

- **Deciders.**   These people have the authority to select or approve a supplier. They are often top executives within the organization who have the formal power to make decisions, but they are normally involved only with high-dollar purchases. For example, general managers, CEOs, directors, and presidents usually have this type of authority.

STAGE IN THE BUYING PROCESS	CONSUMER PURCHASE OF A WEEKEND HOTEL ROOM	ORGANIZATIONAL PURCHASE OF HOTEL FACILITIES FOR AN ASSOCIATION MEETING
Problem Recognition	A couple feels like getting away for a weekend.	An association has to hold its annual meeting for members to elect officers.
Information Search	Based on past experience, they may contact a travel agent or rely on word of mouth and other forms of promotion.	The planner looks through information on file, contacts the local conventions and visitors bureaus and hotel salespeople, considers past experience, looks at websites, or looks at meeting magazines or other advertising materials.
Evaluation of Alternatives	They use routine or limited problem solving based on a few salient attributes.	The planner reviews hotel specifications, makes site visits, and talks to salespeople. Many attributes are important.
Purchase Decisions	A specific hotel is chosen and the room is charged to a credit card.	The meeting planner negotiates with a salesperson, the terms are determined, and a contract is signed.
Postpurchase Evaluation	There is some time before the actual visit for cognitive dissonance, but it is difficult to evaluate the service before it is consumed.	Association meetings are planned 3 to 5 years in advance, leaving time for cognitive dissonance. The hotel or the city could undergo some major changes within that period.

TABLE 3.4 • A Comparison of Consumer and Organizational Buying.

- **Gatekeepers.** These individuals control the flow of information that is relevant to a purchase decision. For example, administrative assistants or receptionists have the ability to restrict the flow of information to buyers and other members of the buying unit. Hotel salespeople must often rely on administrative assistants to get information to meeting planners.

3.6.3 Factors That Influence Organizational Buying

Most of the factors that affect consumers' buying behavior are also relevant to organizational buying behavior. This includes external influences such as environmental factors (i.e., political/ legal, technological, economic, and competitive), reference groups (e.g., trade associations and certification boards), and cultural differences. Cultural differences can be external, such as "individualism versus collectivism," social gender roles, "long-term versus short-term orientation," and the society's level of risk aversion. For example, Asian countries such as Japan and South Korea tend to have more of a long-term business focus than the United States, and many developed countries are individualist societies, whereas developing countries tend to be more collectivist.

In addition, cultural differences can be internal influences, such as the characteristics of the organization (e.g., size, level of technology, and the internal reward system), the characteristics of the individuals in the buying unit (e.g., personality, motivation, and education), and the characteristics of the buying unit as a whole (e.g., size, authority, leadership, and structure). The Ritz-Carlton hotel chain, for example, focuses on quality, and it stresses quality in its training and reward structure. Buying decisions are based on the willingness of suppliers to adhere to this same concept and support the chain's quality goals.

SUMMARY OF CHAPTER OBJECTIVES

This chapter provided a broad overview of the complex subject of consumer behavior. Management must constantly strive to learn more about consumer behavior, for this will allow managers to better serve the needs of customers. In this way, sales and profits can be increased and a competitive advantage can be gained.

A variety of factors influence consumers' purchase decisions. External influences include culture, socioeconomic status, reference groups, and household. All of these entities affect the way a consumer progresses through the five stages of the decision-making process: problem recognition, information search, evaluation of alternatives, purchase decision, and postpurchase evaluation. In addition, internal influences such as needs, experiences, personality, perceptions, and attitudes affect the decision-making process.

In theory, consumers are believed to apply certain processes, or strategies, when they evaluate alternatives. Compensatory strategies allow product strengths to compensate for weaknesses, whereas noncompensatory strategies reduce the number of salient attributes to streamline the process. However, it is possible that consumers use a combination of more than one approach or strategy. There are various problem-solving techniques that consider the consumers' level of involvement and explain how the decision-making process may differ across product categories. The level of problem solving ranges from routine response behavior to limited problem solving to extended problem solving, depending on the situation.

KEY TERMS AND CONCEPTS

Attitudes
Buying center
Buying unit
Cognitive dissonance
Compensatory strategies
Culture
Evoked set
External influences
Internal influences

Maslow's hierarchy of needs
Motive
Need
Noncompensatory strategies
Opinion leaders
Organizational buying
Perception
Personality
Reference group

QUESTIONS FOR REVIEW AND DISCUSSION

1 **What are some of the internal and external influences on consumer purchases?**

2 **List and discuss the five stages in the consumer decision-making process.**

3 **What are the differences between compensatory strategies and noncompensatory strategies for problem solving?**

4 **Give an example of how a consumer would use a combination of problem-solving processes.**

5 **What are the three problem-solving techniques used by consumers? Explain how they differ, using the stages of the consumer decision-making process.**

chapter review

6 How would a hospitality marketer use the consumer adoption process in planning a promotional strategy?

7 How does the decision-making process differ between consumers and organizations?

8 What are the five components of the buying unit? Give an example of a buying unit in hospitality or tourism.

NOTES

[1] James U. McNeal, *Consumer Behavior* (Boston: Little, Brown, 1982), pp. 5–15.

[2] Abraham H. Maslow, *Motivation and Personality*, 2nd ed. (New York: Harper and Row, 1970).

[3] David B. Wolfe, "The Ageless Market: The Key to the Older Market Is to Forget Age and Focus on Consumer Wants and Needs," *American Demographics* 9, 7 (July 1987): 26(6).

[4] David C. McClelland, "Toward a Theory of Motive Acquisition," *American Psychologist* 20 (1965): 321–333.

[5] Kenneth Blanchard and Sheldon M. Bowles, *Raving Fans: A Revolutionary Approach to Customer Service* (New York: William Morrow, 1993), p. 101.

chapter review

CASE STUDY

Spring Break Vacation

Every year, students flock to popular "Spring Break" locations in southern United States to enjoy surf, sun, and sand vacations. This is particularly true of students who attend colleges in the northern part of the United States where the weather is still cold in late February and March. Some of the more popular destinations are Cancun (Mexico), Panama Beach (Florida), and South Padre (Texas). In addition to these popular destinations, students are also visiting less traditional locations such as ski resorts, casinos, and cities on other continents (e.g., Europe and South America).

The other option is for students to participate in an alternative "Spring Break" program. These programs are for students who want to volunteer to help less-developed countries focus on social issues such as poverty, education reform, and the environment. The programs are typically run by nonprofit organizations and are "alcohol-free." The goal is for the students to help communities in need and, in the process, the students receive a positive experience with a feeling of accomplishment. Also, some of these programs focus on destinations within the United States, such as working on rebuilding New Orleans after Hurricane Katrina, or working with Habitat for Humanity to build homes for low-income families.

The number of available options has changed drastically over the years. For example, in the late 1970s and early 1980s, most students went to Fort Lauderdale or Daytona Beach in Florida. Very few even considered leaving the country, doing volunteer work, or visiting a destination with a cold climate. Also, most of the students drove to Florida instead of flying, and they stayed in economy or average-priced hotels, often having 5 to 8 people in a room. The majority of the students' time was spent laying on the beach or by the pool, drinking in bars, and sleeping late in the mornings. Today, students visit popular attractions, eat at nice restaurants, and engage in other outdoor activities for an additional fee.

Case Study Questions and Issues

1. Briefly describe how a typical student would go through the consumer decision-making process. What would she or he do at each stage?

2. What external influences would likely affect the process?

3. What internal influences would likely affect the process?

4. What caused the changes that occurred since the early 1980s?

case study

CASE STUDY

Tempura Garden

Tempura Garden restaurant offers Asian cuisine consisting of Japanese and some Korean dishes. The meals are competitively priced ($7 to $10 for lunch and $8 to $16 for dinner) compared with other full-service restaurants in the area, but the location and parking are a problem. The restaurant is located away from the main traffic area, and there is limited parking available. Fortunately, the restaurant is doing fairly well because it is one of the few places in town that offers sushi and other Japanese and Korean dishes. However, the downturn in the economy has affected the full-service restaurant market, and the owner is concerned about competing in the new environment.

The restaurant has a group of loyal customers who live nearby, as well as some of the local Asian population. The owner is concerned about keeping these customers satisfied, but he must also find a way to attract new customers to continue to be profitable. Therefore, he decides that the first step would be to survey his current customers to determine how they had first heard about Tempura Garden and what is important to them when choosing a restaurant. The following are the results to the first question.

HOW DID YOU FIRST BECOME AWARE OF TEMPURA GARDEN?	
Newspaper advertisement	10%
Radio advertisement	5%
Word of mouth	55%
Val-Pak	10%
Drove by	20%

This provided some useful insight into how people became aware of the restaurant. Apparently, word of mouth was the main vehicle, which is consistent with other studies reported in trade publications. The owner didn't do much radio advertising, but he did place ads in the newspaper and Val-Pak (various retail coupons combined and delivered through direct mail) on a regular basis.

The other area of concern is the importance of various attributes or characteristics in choosing a restaurant. In particular, the owner wanted to know if his location was a major weakness relative to other full-service restaurants in the area. In addition, he could determine what characteristics were most important to customers when choosing a restaurant. The survey contained a section for respondents to rate the importance of a list of characteristics on a seven-point scale ranging from 1 = not important at all to 7 = very important. The following contains the mean importance ratings.

CHARACTERISTIC	IMPORTANCE RATING	PERFORMANCE RATING
Timeliness of service	5.64	4.17
Quality of service	6.21	4.36
Cleanliness	6.43	4.37
Quality of food	6.63	4.50
Menu variety	5.29	4.32
Employee friendliness	5.91	4.46
Atmosphere	5.44	4.11
Convenience of location	5.08	4.23
Value for the price paid	6.01	4.18

In addition to the importance ratings, respondents were also asked to rate Tempura Garden's performance on a five-point scale ranging from 1 = poor to 5 = excellent. The mean performance ratings appear in the third column in the preceding list. The owner must now examine the results and make some decisions based on his analysis.

Case Study Questions and Issues

1. How did people first become aware of the restaurant? How does this affect the owner's approach to creating awareness and getting people to try the restaurant? What strategies would you recommend?

2. What are the most important factors in choosing a restaurant? How does Tempura Garden rate on these factors?

3. Discuss the owner's potential responses to the ratings for each of the consumer problem-solving processes.

4. What additional information would be useful?

case study

4

Market Segmentation and Positioning

Courtesy of Julius Kielaitis/Shutterstock.

Chapter Objectives

After studying this chapter, you should be able to:

1. Define and explain the term *market segmentation*.

2. List variables that are commonly used to segment markets.

3. Outline the four-step process used to segment potential markets.

4. Explain the relationship between market segmentation and the development of marketing strategies.

5. Define *positioning* and describe its role in gaining a competitive advantage.

4.1 INTRODUCTION

Competitive advantage
An advantage over competitors gained by offering greater relative value based on lower prices and/or higher quality.

Market segmentation
Pursuing a marketing strategy where the total potential market is divided into homogeneous subsets of customers, each of which responds differently to the marketing mix.

Gaining and maintaining a competitive advantage in the broad consumer market for hospitality and travel products is a very difficult task. It is much easier to be successful if a firm tries to carve out a smaller niche or segment of the market, in which the firm can establish a competitive uniqueness; hence, the development of market segmentation. Marketing managers have long used market segmentation to separate the market into smaller, relatively homogeneous groups. Therefore, a simple definition for market segmentation is pursuing a marketing strategy where the total potential market is divided into homogeneous subsets of customers, each of which responds differently to the marketing mix of the organization.

For many years, most hospitality and tourism organizations attempted to serve the needs of a fairly wide variety of markets. These groups included broad segments that cut across much of the spectrum of age, gender, income, geography, ethnicity, and education. Today, many hospitality chains serve the needs of markets in all 50 states and several foreign countries. Therefore, it is imperative that they use some type of segmentation strategy. These firms must keep in mind the differences between various consumer groups that represent their target markets. For example, a national fast-food chain should take into consideration the differences among individuals living in different regions of the United States. In addition to geographic location, firms must also consider differences in lifestyle and consumer behavior, all of which add special challenges to the marketing of the product–service mix for hospitality and tourism organizations.

Segmentation can be used effectively in all facets of the hospitality and tourism industry, even in areas that may appear to be less suitable for segmentation. For example, airline travel may not appear to be well suited to segmentation. Each year, millions of travelers will board aircraft that will take them to their destination. At first glance, one might assume that airline travel is a fairly homogeneous product serving the same basic need for most travelers. However, airlines have been successful at segmenting based on price sensitivity and frequency of use. Within many aircraft today, you will find three levels of service: first class, business class, and coach. Each level offers differences in seat size and comfort, the level of amenities, and the ratio of flight attendants to passengers. The individual consumer is able to select the level of service desired and is charged a different price for each. Airlines also segment the market based on frequency of travel.

4.1.1 The Nature of Market Segmentation

Why is it desirable to segment markets? Many owners and managers of hospitality organizations ask this question. Often, they believe that they need to appeal to *all* potential customers, and that by segmenting the market they will weaken their competitive position and profits. They believe that if they segment the market and target their marketing and promotional efforts to just a few selected segments, their sales volume will fall. This approach is shortsighted and fails to consider the reasons underlying a market segmentation approach. The basic premise of segmentation is to allocate limited resources so that return on investment can be maximized.

Market segmentation, when done properly, can improve sales and profits because it allows the organization to target specific market segments that are much more likely to patronize the organization's facilities. This approach permits the company to more effectively allocate scarce marketing resources aimed at those market segments with the highest probability of purchasing the organization's products and services. Using market segmentation, companies can identify those market segments that are heavy users of their products and services. At the same time, segments that hold little potential for using a company's products receive little or no attention, so the marketing resources that are available are not wasted on chasing after market segments with little sales potential.

When the market is segmented, different product–service mixes can be promoted to meet the needs of the different segments. For example, a hotel's bar and restaurant can be used to attract a variety of market segments by varying the type of entertainment offered. Management could try to increase sales volume by establishing specific nights of the week, such as "jazz night," "oldies night," "country night," and so on. Each of these events offers a specific type of entertainment that appeals to a specific clientele. Within the lodging segment of the industry, hotels that cater to the business traveler are usually busy on Monday through Thursday nights and are often quite slow on the weekends. Therefore, one of the marketing communications and promotional goals is to target those market segments with the most potential for boosting weekend occupancy. Each hotel chain attempts to present the total package of amenities, room, and food and beverage in an appealing manner. By attempting to appeal to those target segments seeking a getaway weekend or a mini-vacation at a good price, the hotel is able to boost occupancy and total revenue during a time when the hotel would normally not be operating at full capacity (i.e., 100 percent occupancy).

4.1.2   Criteria for Effective Segmentation

As firms attempt to segment markets, they have many methods from which to choose. However, it is important to know when to segment and how far the segmentation efforts should go in targeting specific markets. There is a point where a market can be segmented too much, with the resulting subset being too small to be profitable. Or it may not be efficient to develop several different marketing programs for the various market segments when one or two could be used for the entire market. When any segmentation efforts are undertaken, four criteria should be used to evaluate the effectiveness of the market segmentation strategy:

1. Substantiality

2. Measurability

3. Accessibility

4. Actionability

First, consider substantiality—in other words, determine whether the market segment is large enough. As the market is segmented, a hospitality manager manipulates the elements of the marketing mix to meet the needs of the individual segments and to achieve the marketing objectives of the firm. The size of each of these segments must be large enough to warrant this special attention. For example, two decades ago, very few restaurants had sections of their menus dedicated to healthier foods because there weren't enough customers to justify it. Since then, even fast-food restaurants have added healthy menu items, and today, many restaurants have items targeting a specific diet segment—such as the Atkins diet. This demonstrates the importance of having a large enough population to warrant targeting a specific market segment.

Substantiality
The size of the segment must be large enough to warrant special attention to meet the needs of the segment and to achieve the marketing objectives of the firm.

Second, each of the segments must pass the measurability test. Measurability should be assessed from two perspectives: the overall size of the target market segment and the projected total demand or purchasing power of the target market. Minimum cutoff points should be established relative to the size and projected demand of any target market segments. If the number of consumers or projected total demand within a given segment falls below these cutoff points, target market segments can simply be combined.

Measurability
The overall size of the target market segment and the projected total demand or purchasing power of the target market.

Third, look at accessibility. It must be possible to reach the large target market segments through a variety of marketing communications efforts. Marketing communication can involve a wide variety of approaches, including but not limited to advertising, promotion, direct marketing, telemarketing, and personal selling. Without accessibility, there is very little reason for segmenting the target market. A major purpose for segmenting the market is to isolate viable segments of potential business and to direct marketing communication efforts related to specific aspects of the product–service mix toward these segments. Without accessibility, this is not possible, and segmenting the target market is of little value.

Accessibility
The target markets must be reachable, or accessible, through a variety of marketing communication efforts.

Fourth, firms must be able to create marketing programs that are effective in attracting buyers from the market segment (i.e., getting them to act). In other words, actionability refers to the notion that customers within a particular market segment should share similar characteristics, and react in a similar faction to a particular marketing program tactic or strategy. For example, if a restaurant offers an early-bird special, it should appeal to certain target segments and not others. Families and senior citizens might be willing to eat earlier to save money and avoid crowds, whereas consumers in other segments aren't as price-sensitive and aren't willing to compromise on convenience for a discount. If all consumers reacted the same to a firm's marketing program, then there wouldn't be any need to segment the market.

Actionability
Consumers in the same market segment should react similarly to the marketing program used to target them.

4.2   SEGMENTATION VARIABLES

Marketing managers can use five basic types of variables when segmenting consumer markets: geographic, demographic, psychographic, behavioral, and benefits. These segmentation variables can be used alone or in combination with one another, depending on the level of segmentation that is desired. Figures 4.1a to 4.1d illustrate the basic concept of market segmentation. Figure 4.1a shows a market that has not been segmented. In other words, no attempt has been made to divide the large, heterogeneous market into smaller, homogeneous subsets. Figures 4.1b and 4.1c illustrate markets that have been segmented using one variable, and Figure 4.1d shows a market that has been segmented using two variables. In practice, it is normally best to use at least two or more of the following types of variables to segment markets.

4.2.1   Geographic Variables

Geographic segmentation
Segmentation technique that focuses on the consumer's geographic area of residence.

A **geographic segmentation**, as the name implies, relates to the consumer's geographic area of residence. Markets are often segmented by dividing the country into regions such as Northeast, Mid-Atlantic, North-Central, Southwest, and Northwest. Segmentation is also accomplished by examining the population of a given area. According to the United States Census Bureau, the total U.S. population was 316.1 million in 2013, and it is projected to surpass 400 million by 2040. However, this population is not evenly distributed; it is concentrated in major metropolitan areas. According to the World Bank, the percentage of the U.S. population living in metropolitan areas remained at 81 percent from 2010 through 2014.[1]

In addition to population density, there are differing patterns of population migration. For example, the metro areas with the largest annual population growth in the United States from 2000 through 2013 were all in, or around, the Sunbelt (e.g., Florida, Texas, Arizona, Nevada, California, and the Carolinas). Interestingly, 7 of the top 10 metro areas were on the list from 1980 through 2000 as well. The other current trend is that people are moving more toward middle-density areas (e.g., suburbs) rather than large cities and rural areas. This is different from the trend in the 1950s, when people from the south moved north to find jobs, and the trend in the 1970s, when people moved back to rural areas.

Metropolitan statistical area (MSA)
A self-contained urban area with a population of at least 50,000 that is surrounded by rural areas.

Several different terms are used to describe cities and metropolitan areas, but in marketing, the most popular term is **metropolitan statistical area (MSA)**. This refers to the smallest urban

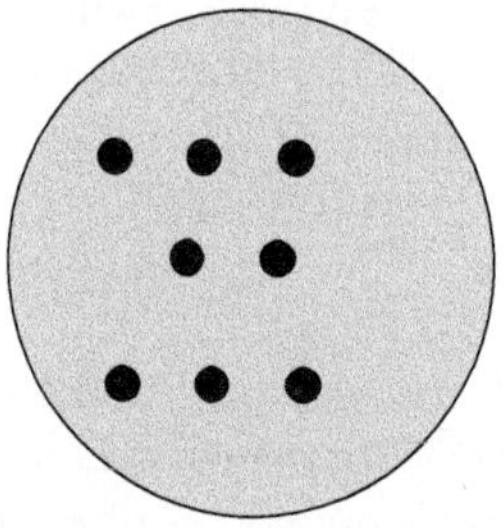

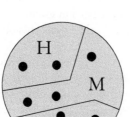

FIGURE 4.1a • **A nonsegmented market.**

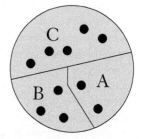

FIGURE 4.1b • **A market segmented by age (A = 18 – 34, B = 35 – 49, C = above 49).**

FIGURE 4.1c • **A market segmented by income (H = high, M = moderate, L = low).**

FIGURE 4.1d • **A market segmented by age and income.**

Courtesy of Mobile Bay CVB.

Residents of and visitors to Mobile, Alabama, can enjoy a scenic trip along the Mobile River in a stern-wheeler. Mobile is an example of a metropolitan statistical area (MSA).

area with an urban center population of 50,000 and a total metropolitan population of more than 100,000. Metropolitan statistical areas are normally urban areas that are self-contained and surrounded by rural areas. Examples of MSAs include Roanoke, Virginia, and Peoria, Illinois. The next category of urban area is **primary metropolitan statistical area (PMSA)**. A PMSA is an urbanized county or multicounty area with a population of more than 1 million individuals. Examples of PMSAs include Cook County in Illinois and Nassau County in New York. Finally, the very largest cities such as New York, Chicago, and Los Angeles are known as **consolidated metropolitan statistical areas (CMSAs)**. A CMSA must include at least two PMSAs.

Geographic variables are used extensively by the print and broadcast media to define and describe their readers and audience. It is also vital to know the geographic areas your business is in. For example, nearly 50 percent of all room nights in the hotel industry are generated by the top 25 CMSAs, PSMAs, and MSAs. Segmenting a hotel's market based on the origin of the guests by using their zip codes is an effective way to identify those areas that merit the heaviest concentration of advertising and promotion.

Primary metropolitan statistical area (PMSA)
An urbanized county or multicounty area with a population of more than one million individuals.

Consolidated metropolitan statistical area (CMSAs)
The largest type of metropolitan statistical area, consisting of at least two PMSAs.

4.2.2 Demographic Variables

Markets are often varied based on **demographic segmentation** such as age, gender, income and expenditure patterns, family size, stage in the family life cycle, educational level achieved, and occupation. When these variables are used in defining consumers within the hospitality and tourism industry, certain trends emerge. For instance, as family size increases, the number of times per week that a family dines outside the home tends to decrease. Also, when families do dine out, their choice of restaurant changes as the family composition changes. This is important because the size of the average family in the United States has decreased over the years. In 2012, the average family size was 2.55 persons, down from 2.63 in 1990 and 2.59 in 2000.[2] Disposable income per capita increased from \$18,435.80 in 1992 to \$53,869.60 in 2012.[3]

The **family life cycle** provides a good example of how variables can be combined to create categories that can be used for segmentation. The family life cycle uses age, marital status, and the number of children to create categories sharing common discretionary income levels and purchasing behaviors. The traditional family life cycle proposes that as individuals become adults and enter the workforce, they tend to be single and have lower incomes, resulting in lower levels of discretionary income—income available after covering current expenses for necessity items such as food and

Demographic segmentation
Segmentation technique that focuses on consumer demographics such as age, income, gender, and ethnicity.

Family life cycle
A concept that attempts to describe how purchasing behaviors change as consumers pass through various life stages.

housing (see Figure 4.2a). However, these young singles do not have many obligations or responsibilities and so are able to spend money on items that are not necessities. Individuals begin to increase their incomes as they age, and young married couples without children will have increasing amounts of discretionary income. However, after married couples have children, their discretionary incomes begin to decrease, until the children are older and move out. At this point, the couples are said to have an "empty nest," and discretionary income begins to increase again. Finally, as individuals reach their so-called golden years, they retire and see their incomes start to decrease.

This traditional family life cycle has changed over time and now includes several extensions. First, many people are waiting longer to get married, thus extending the single stage. In addition, more people are choosing not to marry, and some single adults adopt children. Second, the increase in the divorce rate has resulted in more single parents and second marriages that involve older parents with younger children. Third, there are more same-sex couples, and organizations are beginning to recognize this partnership for benefits and adoptions. Finally, people are living longer, resulting in a higher percentage of solitary survivors, many of whom form relationships later in life. Figure 4.2b provides an example of a modernized family life cycle.

Segmentation using demographic variables is very common. In fact, firms should always collect demographic information on their customers so that they can construct a basic profile of heavy users. Demographic information is easy to collect and understand. Also, aggregate data collected by the government at all levels can be used for comparisons in surveys and targeting potential markets. Finally, demographic classifications are widely used by various media to describe viewers, listeners, and readers. This allows firms to select media vehicles that will reach individuals fitting the profile of a typical customer.

The senior market, often referred to as the "gray market," is growing faster than any other market in America. By the year 2050, it is expected that one in three Americans will be age 55 or older. The senior market has been expanding and is becoming more attractive because older Americans have a good deal of free time, they are healthier and live longer, and they have more discretionary income than ever before. These trends make the senior market particularly attractive to firms in the hospitality and tourism industry. However, although the age of 55 is a common cutoff used for describing this market, the American Association for Retired Persons (AARP) accepts members starting at 50 years of age, and many firms use a figure in the range of 60 to 65 when offering discounts to the senior market. Regardless, this market is growing in size as well as clout when it comes to influencing the government and marketers. It is quite possible that AARP is the most influential association in Washington, DC, and most hospitality and tourism firms offer some type of discount to senior citizens.

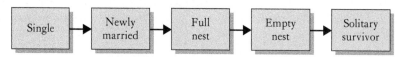

FIGURE 4.2a • **Traditional family life cycle.**

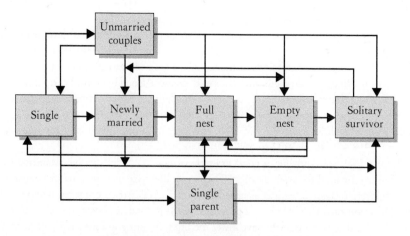

FIGURE 4.2b • **Modernized family life cycle.**

If a firm chooses to target the senior market, it should determine the attributes that are important to this market segment in purchasing its types of products and services. Products and services could then be designed and marketed specifically to seniors. For example, hotels should provide luggage carts or bell service so seniors can get help with heavy luggage. In addition, rooms should have wide aisles, telephones, and remote controls with larger numbers, simple alarm clocks with large numbers, and easy-to-use facilities in the bathroom, including bars near the toilet and in the bathtub that can be used for getting up and down. Similarly, restaurants should provide menus with large print, meals that are healthy and have smaller portions, and adequate lighting so that seniors can read the menus. Finally, hospitality and tourism firms should realize that seniors like to travel in tour groups for the companionship and security, they are very value-conscious, and they require frequent stops for resting, eating, and using restroom facilities.

4.2.3 Psychographic Variables

Psychographic segmentation is another commonly used method to segment markets. *Psychographics* refers to segmentation based on lifestyle, attitudes, and personality. The development of psychographic segmentation is based on lifestyle profiles normally derived from survey responses to AIO (attitudes, interests, and opinions) statements. Psychographics has the following characteristics:

Psychographic segmentation Segmentation technique that focuses on consumers' lifestyles, attitudes, and personalities.

- Generally, psychographics may be viewed as the practical application of the behavioral and social sciences to marketing research.
- More specifically, psychographics makes use of research procedures that are indicated when demographic, socioeconomic, and user–nonuser analyses are not sufficient to explain and predict consumer behavior.
- Most specifically, psychographics seeks to describe the human characteristics of consumers that may have bearing on their response to products, packaging, advertising, promotion, and public relations efforts. Such variables may range from self-concept and lifestyle to attitudes, interests, and opinions, as well as perceptions of product attributes.

Psychographics is used primarily to segment markets, but it can be used for other purposes as well. For example, it is useful when selecting the most effective advertising vehicles, in that the vehicle(s) selected can be matched with the interests, attitudes, opinions, and personalities of the target market segment. Psychographics is also helpful when designing advertising and promotion messages. Illustrations, pictures, and the actual copy can be designed with the needs of a specific market segment in mind. By pinpointing the target market in this manner, the advertising and promotional messages and images are likely to be more effective, resulting in increased sales and profits.

A good example of psychographic segmentation is the VALS™ framework, a marketing tool developed by Strategic Business Insights to segment the consumer marketplace based on personality traits that drive consumer behavior. The framework contains eight VALS segments based on a consumers' primary motivations and resources: innovators, thinkers, achievers, experiencers, believers, strivers, makers, and survivors. The basic tenet of VALS is that consumers' purchasing behaviors are expressions of their personalities. The VALS framework allows marketers to identify meaningful market segments based on consumers' personality traits and provides a means to predict purchasing behaviors. Innovators and achievers, for instance, would be target market segments for upscale hotels and restaurants, whereas thinkers, believers, and makers would be target market segments for popular midscale chain hotels and casual dining restaurants. Additionally, innovators and experiencers would be the segments most likely to try new hotel and restaurant concepts, and makers would be the segment most likely to be loyal to independent operators. There is an Internet exercise at the end of this chapter that will provide students with a detailed understanding of the VALS segmentation framework.

It should be evident at this point that the division of the market into segments should not be based solely on easily quantified demographic variables such as age, sex, or income.

Rather, the division should be based on less easily defined psychographic factors, such as lifestyle, attitudes, opinions, and personality. Individual firms can define their target markets and address the needs of those markets with products and promotional campaigns. For instance, tour operators could design various overseas tour packages that would appeal to different social value groups.

4.2.4 Behavioral Variables

Behavioral segmentation
Segmentation technique that focuses on the purchasing behaviors exhibited by consumers in the marketplace.

Another type of variable that can be used to define markets is behavioral segmentation, which focuses on the behaviors that consumers exhibit in the marketplace. For example, are consumers loyal or are they easily persuaded by competitors' marketing communications and promotional efforts? How frequently do consumers dine out? Would they be considered light, medium, or heavy users of various types of hospitality products? When they travel on business, at what types of lodging facilities do they stay? When they travel for pleasure, do they stay at the same types of lodging facilities as when they travel on business?

One of the best uses of the behavioral variables is to identify those individuals who are heavy users, meaning that they dine out frequently, stay in hotels many more nights per year than the average person, or account for a large percentage of air travel. If these individuals can be identified, then a marketing plan can be formulated to increase loyalty and frequency of use even further. For example, most airlines offer a frequent traveler program to encourage brand loyalty. Within each program are varying levels of membership. Anyone can join, but the rewards are commensurate with the level of use. Airline miles can be redeemed for free flights or a variety of other travel services. Many hotels and restaurants offer similar programs, and often, hotels and airlines develop strategic alliances and combine their programs.

Frequent traveler programs
Loyalty programs that reward customers commensurate with their level of purchase and use.

Each year, more and more research is undertaken to help companies more fully understand consumer behavior. Behavioral variables represent an excellent segmentation tool, for as data are collected concerning the manner in which consumers actually behave in the marketplace, the information will allow hospitality managers to gain a better understanding of consumer behavior. As marketing managers increase their understanding of what motivates consumers to buy, it will facilitate the development of product–service mixes that will better satisfy the needs of consumers.

4.2.5 Benefits Sought

Finally, market segmentation can be based on the benefits that consumers are seeking when they purchase a product. Once a firm has determined the benefits sought by consumers, it can use this information to design products and services and to create promotional materials that focus on these benefits. Market research can be used to identify the benefits that are important to various types of consumers. This marketing information allows management to employ benefit segmentation, which is based on benefits sought, as well as demographic, psychographic, or behavioral variables.

Benefit segmentation
Segmentation technique that focuses on benefits sought by consumers when purchasing a product.

For example, airlines segment consumers based on the benefits those consumers seek. Business travelers are most concerned about convenience when choosing flights. They will make reservations at the last minute and want to travel at a convenient time with short routes. Conversely, leisure travelers will book further ahead and sacrifice some convenience to get a better price because it is the most important benefit. Similarly, airlines offer first-class and business-class seats with additional amenities for a higher price, and hotels offer a concierge or business-level room for consumers who want additional amenities at a higher price.

Another example involves the rental car industry. Rental car companies carry several models of cars and trucks in order to accommodate the needs of all types of travelers. Families are looking for larger cars or vans that are economical, business travelers prefer larger cars with more options, and younger travelers might prefer convertibles or sportier cars. Rental car companies have a vehicle for any customer, no matter what benefit(s) the customer is seeking.

Courtesy of The Breakers, Palm Beach, Florida.

Consumers can be seeking different benefits from the same resort or hotel.

4.3 MARKET SEGMENTATION DECISIONS

When faced with market segmentation decisions, a hospitality and tourism marketing manager should use a systematic approach that employs critical thinking and careful analysis. Figure 4.3 presents a four-step process that can be used by marketing managers in segmenting potential markets: (1) identify segmentation bases, (2) develop profiles for each segment, (3) forecast performance for each market segment, and (4) select the best market segments.

4.3.1 Identify Segmentation Bases

The first thing a marketing manager must do is to identify one or more characteristics that can describe the target market segment. Any of the previously discussed segmentation criteria can be used to accomplish this. In almost all cases, several characteristics will be used. For example, a new

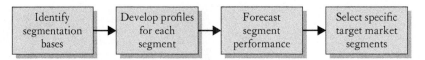

FIGURE 4.3 • **Market segmentation decision process.**

restaurant might elect to target a consumer market consisting of the following individuals: 25 to 40 years of age, living in cities with a population greater than 500,000, who have annual incomes greater than $35,000.

The objective of identifying the segmentation bases is to develop a relatively homogenous market segment made up of individual consumers who will respond in a similar manner to the marketing strategies and marketing communications efforts of the firm. It is also important that the members of the selected target markets place a high value on the combination of attributes that the firm has used in the product–service mix. For example, the economy segment of the lodging industry has experienced exceptional growth in recent years by offering basic amenities at a relatively low price, resulting in a high level of perceived value to consumers. However, it would not make sense for this type of lodging chain to target the midlevel and senior executives of Fortune 500 companies. These individuals, for both business and personal reasons, normally elect to use full-service hotels for their lodging and meeting needs.

4.3.2 Develop Profiles for Each Market Segment

After the target market has been identified, it is very important to compile as much information about the target market consumers as possible. The overall goal is to match the stated wants and needs of the targeted segment with the product–service mix offerings and marketing communications that the firm uses. The importance of matching consumers' wants and needs with the marketing offerings and communication efforts of the firm cannot be overemphasized. It is also important to identify the similarities and differences among and between various target markets. People within the same market segment should share similar characteristics and react in a similar fashion to changes in marketing programs. When developing a profile of the target markets, it is necessary to use the various segmentation variables described earlier in this chapter.

This can be illustrated using the popular early-bird concept from the restaurant industry. The idea of offering early-bird specials is to shift demand from peak periods when the restaurant operates at full capacity to the earlier time period (e.g., 4:00 to 6:00 P.M.) when there is less demand. This allows the restaurant to avoid turning customers away during the peak time period and develop another market for the people who are willing to dine at the less-demanded earlier time period. The new market consists of various market segments, including senior citizens, families with young children, and other people who are price-sensitive. A lower price is the main benefit sought by all of these segments, but restaurants offer smaller, healthier portions for seniors, kids' meals for families, and package deals including appetizers and/or desserts for other price-sensitive consumers.

4.3.3 Forecast Performance for Each Market Segment

Margin of error
The difference between forecasted value and actual value.

Market demand
The total volume that would be bought by a clearly specified customer group in a defined geographic area in a defined period.

To forecast the sales potential of a given market segment or an entire market for any given product–service mix is an extremely difficult task. Computer models and statistical approaches have facilitated the process somewhat, but it is still very difficult to account for all of the variables that can influence consumer demand. Even the best forecasts may be subject to a margin of error of several percentage points in either direction. However, marketing managers must have some knowledge of the level of market demand in order to plan for short- and long-term contingencies as well as day-to-day operations. Without reasonably accurate forecasts, managers must operate by the seat of their pants. The demands of the competitive situation in the hospitality and tourism industry today will not permit this casual approach.

Market demand can be defined as potential consumers having both purchasing power and motivation. Many variables can affect the demand within any given segment. Variables such as consumer motivation are often difficult to quantify. Market demand for a product or service is the total volume that would be bought by a clearly specified customer group in a defined geographic area in a defined period. Only when clear definitions are available for each of these variables can market demand be precisely calculated. Determining total market demand is an important marketing function because so many other assumptions are based on its forecast. Hospitality managers should be able to examine forecasts for market demand and understand their uses and limitations. *Primary demand* is the demand for the entire product class; *secondary demand* is the demand for a particular brand. For example, hotels in the same area are normally members of the convention and visitors bureaus and work together to bring tourists and meetings to the local area. This will benefit all the hotels, which can then compete for the various market segments based on their particular needs.

Projected demand for the product–service mix is calculated based on the total market demand multiplied by the market share, or the percentage of the market that the firm's product–service mix will capture. Market share is calculated by dividing the firm's sales by the total industry sales. Determining the projected market share is an imprecise science. It should be based on a thorough and objective assessment of the firm's capabilities, the relative competitiveness of those also targeting the same consumers, and marketing strategies used by all firms. When decisions have been made about the specific marketing strategies and tactics that will be used, then resource needs can be determined to market the product–service mix to specific target market segments. There is a more detailed discussion of sales forecasting in Chapter Five.

Projected demand
The total market demand multiplied by the firm's market share for a particular product-service mix.

Market share
The percentage of the market that the firm's product–service mix will capture.

4.3.4 Select the Best Market Segments

Based on the steps previously discussed, those responsible for developing and implementing the marketing plan must decide on the specific target market segments that are selected. Although the use of data and factual information is very important, the judgment, insight, and experience that a seasoned marketing manager brings to the decision are also valuable. The overall goal is to limit the uncertainty surrounding market segmentation decisions. Decisions should be based on a careful analysis of the data and how the forecasts of projected demand and market share were determined. It is imperative that the marketing manager examine the projected return on investment (ROI) that the target market will provide. One may calculate the ROI by dividing return, or net profit, by the amount of the investment. Firms will normally have target ROIs for their investments, but the higher the ROI, the better the investment.

Return on investment (ROI)
Data calculated by dividing return, or net profit, by the amount of the investment.

4.4 MARKET SEGMENTATION STRATEGIES

After specific target markets have been identified, the marketing managers must begin to develop broad marketing strategies. In general, there are three segmentation strategies that can be applied: a *mass-market strategy,* a *differentiated strategy,* and a *concentrated strategy.*

4.4.1 Mass-Market Strategy

A mass-market strategy calls on a firm to develop one product–service mix that is marketed to all potential consumers in the target markets. This approach considers the market to be one homogeneous market segment with similar wants and needs. There is no reason to develop more than one marketing program, because consumers are alike and react in a similar fashion to the components of the marketing program. For example, when McDonald's first opened, the firm offered a very limited menu that was consistent across the entire organization. It featured only a couple of hamburger choices, milkshakes, soft drinks, and french fries. No other choices were available, and all stores offered the identical menu. This strategy was also used by hotel chains (e.g., Holiday Inns), airlines (e.g., United Airlines), and tourism destinations (e.g., cities and countries) in the early stages of their life cycles.

McDonald's uses a mass-market strategy to compete in different countries throughout the world.

However, in reality, few products or services appeal to all segments of the market. Since its inception, McDonald's has changed this strategy in response to trends in the demographic and social environments. The fast-food restaurant now offers chicken sandwiches, salads, and other menu items that appeal to a more health-conscious market segment. Hotels, airlines, and other hospitality and travel firms have moved away from mass marketing as well. The largest threat when using this strategy is that competitors will tailor their product–service mix and take away market share because they are better able to meet the needs of smaller target market segments of consumers.

4.4.2 Differentiated Strategy

When a firm elects to follow a differentiated strategy, it is following a strategy that calls for the firm to appeal to more than one market segment with a separate marketing program for each segment. The overall objective of this approach is to increase sales and market share by capturing sales from several smaller market segments. Each of the marketing programs, including the product–service mix, is tailored to the specific needs of a market segment.

Perhaps the best example of this approach within the hospitality and tourism industry is the strategy followed by Choice Hotels International. The hotel chain has developed numerous product–service mixes or brands, each targeting a different market. Among the brands offered by Choice Hotels are Clarion Hotels and Suites, Quality Inns and Suites, Comfort Inns and Suites, Sleep Inns, Econo Lodge, and Travelodge. Each of the brands offers a different array of amenities at various price levels in an attempt to have at least one brand that will appeal to any consumer in the economy or mid-priced market segments.

A differentiated strategy can also be used at the unit or property level. Consider a hotel that is targeting the following markets:

- Individual travelers, including those traveling for both pleasure and business during the week.
- Group meetings, representing corporations, associations, social, and other smaller segments.
- Tour and travel groups, including those traveling by motor coach.

Each of these target markets has needs and wants that differ from the other markets. Those responsible for the marketing efforts of the hotels will, using a differentiated strategy, develop a product–service mix that meets the needs of the individual market segments. Most successful firms use some type of a differentiated marketing strategy. Although the marketing costs associated with a differentiated strategy are higher in most cases, the return on investment is also higher. Targeting the needs and wants of specific target markets and communicating directly to these target markets with separate marketing programs mean that overall sales usually increase.

4.4.3 Concentrated Strategy

A concentrated, or focused, strategy calls on firms to develop modifications of one or more product–service mixes that are marketed to one or relatively few market segments with limited changes in the marketing program. This strategy can be used successfully by smaller firms that don't have the resources to compete in a broader market. Consider that many firms in the lodging industry have developed multiple product–service mixes and brands targeting many markets, but companies such as Hyatt Hotels and Resorts and Renaissance Hotels have not taken this approach. Instead, these two hotel chains concentrate marketing efforts on business travelers and those who need full-service lodging. It is not a question of which company is correct. Rather, it is a question of which strategy is the most appropriate in light of the firm's mission and long-term goals.

4.5 POSITIONING THE PRODUCT–SERVICE MIX

When the market segments have been selected, management must develop a positioning strategy for its products and services in each target market. Put simply, **positioning** is the process of determining how to differentiate a firm's product offerings from those of its competitors in the minds of consumers. This requires the firm to know how important certain attributes are to consumers in purchasing the firm's product, and the consumers' perceptions of how well the firm and its competitors are doing with respect to these attributes.[4] Marketers want to position their products so consumers purchase them instead of competing products.

Positioning
The process of determining how to differentiate a firm's product offerings from those of its competitors in the minds of consumers.

Generally, firms have choices on the positioning of their products, and it is important to consider the alternatives. For example, there was a famous advertising campaign war between two car rental companies based on market position that started in the 1960s. Hertz stressed the benefits of using the number-one rental car company to satisfy consumer needs, and Avis positioned itself against Hertz using the "We try harder" slogan because they were number two in the industry. Meanwhile, Enterprise stressed pick-up service, and Budget stressed a specific product feature (i.e., price). Interestingly, Enterprise recently passed both Hertz and Avis (who merged with Budget) because of their emphasis on service and choice of markets (e.g., downtown locations and insurance companies). Other bases for positioning could be specific usage occasions or user category. For instance, Marriott positions its Residence Inns for extended stays and its Courtyard Hotels for business travelers. Also, firms could base their positioning on intangibles such as the food or ambience. Applebee's has used the slogans "Eating good in the neighborhood," "There's no place like the neighborhood," and "See you tomorrow" to create a personal atmosphere, and Subway uses the slogan "Eat fresh" to focus on food quality. Finally, it is also possible to use more than one basis for positioning when targeting a specific market.

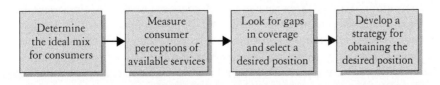

FIGURE 4.4 • The positioning process.

TABLE 4.1 • Important Attributes for Hospitality and Travel Firms

TYPE OF FIRM	LIST OF ATTRIBUTES
Restaurant	Price, value, quality of food, type of food, service quality, menu variety, employee friendliness, location, atmosphere, speed of service, cleanliness, parking
Hotel	Price, value, room quality, restaurant quality, location, number and types of restaurants, other facilities (e.g., pool and fitness center), cleanliness, atmosphere, employee friendliness, speed of check-in and check-out, amenities (e.g., valet parking and room service), service quality
Airline	Price, value, service quality, employee friendliness, on-time performance, baggage handling, direct routes, cities served, scheduled flights, frequent flyer programs
Rental Car	Price, value, service quality, convenience, location, types of cars, condition of cars, speed of service, pickup and drop-off policies

Several factors will affect a firm's decision regarding which positioning bases it should use. First, a firm's current market position and the positions of its competitors are important. Second, a firm should consider the compatibility of a desired position with the needs of consumers and the goals of the firm. Third, a firm must have the resources necessary to communicate and maintain the desired position. Figure 4.4 provides a four-step process that considers these factors and can be used in positioning a firm's products.

4.5.1   Determine the Ideal Mix for Consumers

The first step in the process is to determine what consumers are looking for when they purchase a specific product or service. After a firm establishes this *ideal mix* of attributes, it can begin to examine the ability of its product–service mix to meet the needs of consumers. Normally, there are a few **salient attributes** that are important to consumers in evaluating the alternative products or service offerings. These attributes will differ by product or service, but Table 4.1 provides some of the more important attributes for hospitality and tourism products.

Salient attributes
Attributes that are the most important to consumers in evaluating the alternative products or service offerings.

As you can see, many of the attributes are important for all products and services. Price is not always the most important attribute, but is almost always one of the top three. Service quality is another attribute that is important to consumers in choosing service providers, and it is commonly used to differentiate between brands. Other attributes are more specific to a particular type of firm. For example, food quality is very important to consumers in choosing a restaurant, and room quality is important in choosing a hotel.

It is necessary for firms to obtain importance ratings from consumers using some type of research method. These methods will be discussed in more detail in Chapter 6, but the most common method is to conduct some type of survey. Normally, individuals are asked to rate a list of attributes using an importance scale. For example, a restaurant's comment card may ask a customer to rate the quality of food on a scale of 1 to 5, with 1 being "not important at all" and 5 being "very important." The answers to these ratings are combined to provide an average rating for each desired target market. The averages for all of the attributes can then be examined and used to construct an ideal mix for the product. In other words, what are consumers looking for?

4.5.2   Measure Consumer Perceptions of Available Services

After the ideal mix is determined, the next step is to examine the current offerings of your firm and its competitors to evaluate their abilities to meet consumer needs. More important, it is necessary to obtain consumer perceptions of your service and your competitors' services. Even if a firm believes its product–service mix offers good value to consumers, it is only true if consumers believe it to be true. In marketing, *perceptions are everything*. It would be a critical mistake for a firm to assume that it knows what consumers want and that its products are meeting consumers' wants

TABLE 4.2 • **Competitive Benefit Matrix**

POTENTIAL BENEFITS	OUR OPERATION	COMPETITOR A	COMPETITOR B
Value for price			
Quality of food			
Quality of service			
Atmosphere			
Location			
Menu variety			

and needs. Once again, it is essential for firms to evaluate consumer perceptions through the use of consumer surveys and other research methods. Table 4.2 provides an example of a competitive benefit matrix that can be used by restaurants to compile consumer perceptions for the firm and its closest competitors.

At this point, it may be helpful for a firm to be able to visualize the information in the competitive benefit matrix by using a **perceptual map**. Perceptual mapping is a technique used to construct a graphic representation of how consumers in a market perceive a competing set of products relative to each other. Because of the difficulties associated with graphing and understanding multidimensional presentations, in evaluating competing products managers must determine which two or three dimensions consumers consider most important, and use these dimensions to construct the perceptual map. For example, Figure 4.5 provides a hypothetical perceptual map for hotel chains.

The perceptual map was constructed using perceived price and perceived quality as the two dimensions. Assuming the ratings for the hotel chains on these dimensions were collected using consumer research, the placement of the firms in the perceptual space depicts their relative positions in the market. The results of perceptual mapping can be used for the following purposes:

- To learn how consumers perceive the strengths, weaknesses, and similarities of the alternative product–service mixes being offered.

- To learn about consumers' desires and how these are satisfied or not satisfied by the current products and services in the market.

Perceptual map
A technique used to construct a graphic representation of how consumers in a market perceive a competing set of products relative to each other.

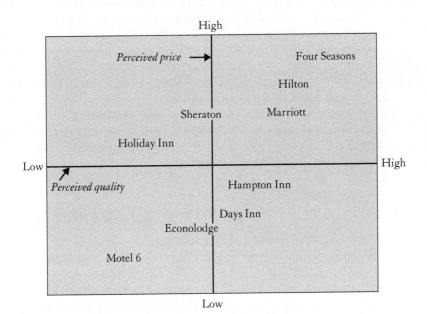

FIGURE 4.5 • **Perceptual map for hotel service.**

• To integrate these findings strategically to determine the greatest opportunities for new product–service mixes and how a product or service's image should be modified to produce the greatest sales gain.

Several methods can be used to construct a perceptual map. Similarity-dissimilarity data involve asking consumers to make direct comparisons between alternative brands. For example, consumers might be given the names of restaurants and asked to select the ones that are most similar or the ones that are least similar. Preference data involve asking consumers to indicate their preferences for a list of alternative brands. For example, consumers might be asked to rank-order a short list of restaurants or rate a specific restaurant on a 1 to 5 scale, with 1 being "least preferred" and 5 being "most preferred." Attribute data involve asking consumers to rate the alternative brands on a predetermined list of attributes. For example, consumers might be asked to rate a given restaurant based on a series of attributes.

After the data are collected, sophisticated statistical techniques are used to reduce the list of attributes into two or three dimensions for easier presentation and interpretation. Management can then use these perceptual maps to fine-tune current product–service mixes and uncover gaps in market coverage between the ideal mix and the alternative offerings.

4.5.3 Look for Gaps in Coverage and Select a Desired Position

After the consumers' perceptions are obtained, measured, and plotted on a perceptual map, the third step in the process is to examine the map for gaps in coverage. In other words, are there any areas on the map depicting ideal mixes that are not being adequately served by the brands in the market? Or is there a difference between the position sought by management and the position perceived by consumers? For example, Subway entered the market in response to a lack of variety (including healthier options) in foods being offered by fast-food restaurants such as McDonald's and Burger King. Similarly, extended-stay hotels were created in response to consumers who had to travel for extended periods and did not like staying in typical hotels. They wanted the ability to cook, do laundry, avoid crowded lobbies, and stay in a more residential setting.

The results of the consumer research and perceptual mapping enable firms to develop a positioning statement. The positioning statement should differentiate the organization's product–service mix from that of the competition. For many years, hotels and restaurants have advertised and promoted "fine food," "prompt, courteous service," "elegant atmosphere," "first-class accommodations," and "top-flight entertainment." As might be expected, these promotional approaches are not as effective as they could be. Consumers usually do not believe these statements because they have heard them many times before and have often been disappointed when they patronized the properties that had made these promotional claims. Also, these statements do little to separate the organization's product–service mix from that of the competition. If other hospitality organizations are promoting "fine food" or similar benefits, then all the promotion and advertising is basically the same.

The key to success in positioning is to establish some unique element of the product–service mix and promote it. This allows management to differentiate the product–service mix from that of the competition and thereby gain a competitive advantage. This approach is known as establishing a unique selling proposition (USP). With a USP, every effort should be made to link the benefits with tangible aspects of the product–service mix. In this way, consumers have something tangible with which to associate the hospitality operation.

4.5.4 Develop a Strategy for Obtaining the Desired Position

The final step in the positioning process is to develop strategies for obtaining the desired position that results from the analyses performed in the first three steps. As with any other discussions of strategy in this text, marketing managers must use the components of the marketing mix to develop marketing programs that can be used to achieve the firm's objectives. In this case, decisions regarding price, product–service mix, promotion, and distribution must be made to help the

---

Similarity-dissimilarity data
Data that involve asking consumers to make direct comparisons between alternative brands based on the degree of similarity.

Preference data
Data obtained by asking consumers to indicate their preferences for a list of alternative brands.

Attribute data
Data that involve asking consumers to rate alternative brands on a predetermined list of attributes.

Positioning statement
The positioning statement is used to differentiate the organization's product–service mix from that of the competition.

Unique selling proposition (USP)
Promoting a unique element of the product–service mix.

firm achieve its desired position. It should be noted that the easiest changes in the marketing mix involve price and promotion. Changes to the product–service mix and distribution are more complicated and often involve expensive changes in tangible elements.

One of the most effective ways to change consumer perceptions of the product–service mix is through promotion and advertising. There are many examples of how products have been positioned or repositioned using advertising and promotional campaigns. For instance, Burger King attempted to differentiate its product–service mix as superior to those of other hamburger restaurants in the fast-food industry. The focus of Burger King's advertising is on charbroiling, its method of cooking hamburgers. The objective of the advertising campaign is to promote the unique process as providing a better-tasting burger of higher quality than that of its competitors.

A second example of using product–service mix positioning is the manner in which Taco Bell used price and packaging to gain a competitive advantage. At a time when the typical meal at a fast-food restaurant cost between $3.50 and $4.00, Taco Bell took a very different positioning strategy. It introduced a line of value-priced products and meals at price points between 59 and 99 cents. The focus of all promotions and point-of-purchase displays was on low price and value. As a result of these promotions, Taco Bell was able to increase its market share, largely at the expense of other fast-food restaurants.

Finally, Enterprise Rent-A-Car trailed market leaders Hertz and Avis and needed to develop its own unique position in order to gain market share. Enterprise analyzed the market and realized there was a gap for lower-priced rental cars in larger cities and surrounding communities at locations other than airports. In response, the company decided to expand in more suburban and rural areas and has since grown to be the largest car rental agency in North America. In addition, the company was the first to offer customers a free pick-up service as a facilitating service in the marketing exchange.

Al Ries and Jack Trout provide a useful set of guidelines to use in developing positioning strategies in their text titled *Positioning: The Battle for Your Mind*.[5] The authors formulated six questions that should be used to guide your thinking:

1. *What position do you own?* The first step is to determine how your product is viewed in the minds of consumers, relative to your competitors based on salient attributes.

2. *What position do you want?* Once you have determined your perceived position in the marketplace, you can decide if it is consistent with position you would like to have based on your firm's capabilities. This could be the market leader, or you could carve out a niche that is easier to "own" and defend.

3. *Whom must you outgun?* It is necessary to take your competitors into account when you are developing your strategies. As previously mentioned, it is how your product is perceived relative to the competition. Make sure you have the skills and competencies to compete directly with close competitors. If you don't have an advantage, then try to avoid direct competition.

4. *Do you have enough money?* Market leaders enjoy the benefit of spending less money to defend market share than challengers need to spend to take it away. Therefore, you need to make sure you have adequate resources for launching your attack, or defending your position.

5. *Can you stick it out?* Once again, it is necessary to have the funds to protect your position. In addition, it is necessary to have some type of competitive advantage or uniqueness that is defendable. If others can refute your claims or easily imitate your products and services, then you won't be able to sustain your position over the long term.

6. *Do you match your position?* It is critical that the position you choose is consistent with the mission and vision of the firm, and the products and services that the firm produces and delivers. Otherwise, consumers will be confused and your marketing campaigns will be ineffective.

chapter review

SUMMARY OF CHAPTER OBJECTIVES

Market segmentation is defined as pursuing a marketing strategy whereby the total potential market is divided into homogeneous subsets of customers, each of which responds differently to the marketing mix of the organization. Market segmentation involves considering several segmentation variables as well as segmentation criteria. Criteria for effective segmentation are substantiality, measurability, and accessibility to the selected target markets. Variables that can be used to segment markets include geographic, demographic, psychographic, behavioral, and benefits sought.

After potential target markets have been identified, decisions must be made concerning which market segments offer the best opportunity to succeed; once determined, these should be pursued. A four-step process was introduced to accomplish this. Firms need to identify segmentation bases, develop profiles for each segment, forecast potential demand, and select specific target market segments.

The important link between target market segmentation and marketing strategy was also introduced. The vast majority of firms follow one of three broad strategies: a mass-market strategy, a differentiated strategy, or a concentrated strategy. The market segmentation strategies differ in the number and type of marketing programs and target markets.

Positioning is a very important aspect of the marketing efforts of any hospitality organization. The positioning statement, and thus the promotional messages, should clearly reflect image, benefit package and support, and differentiation of the product–service mix. Only when all three of these elements are reflected in the hospitality organization's advertising and promotion does the organization realize its full potential. The positioning statement should be supported with tangible clues, rather than the intangible and ineffective "fine food" or "excellent service" slogans used by many firms.

Hospitality and tourism firms should go through the positioning process by (1) determining the ideal mix for consumers, (2) measuring consumer perceptions of available services, (3) looking for gaps in coverage and selecting a desired position, and (4) developing a strategy for obtaining the desired position. Consumer research is vital in this process of collecting information on consumer perceptions regarding the brands in the market. Perceptual maps can be constructed that provide a graphical representation of the consumer preferences and resulting brand positions. Then firms can select their desired positions and devise strategies for obtaining those positions.

KEY TERMS AND CONCEPTS

Accessibility

Actionability

Attribute data

Behavioral segmentation

Benefit segmentation

Competitive advantage

Consolidated metropolitan statistical areas (CMSAs)

Demographic segmentation

Family life cycle

Frequent traveler program

Geographic segmentation

Margin of error

Market demand

Market segmentation

Market share

Measurability

Metropolitan statistical area (MSA)

Perceptual map

Positioning

Positioning statement

Preference data

Primary metropolitan statistical area (PMSA)

Projected demand

Psychographic segmentation

Return on investment (ROI)

Salient attributes

Similarity-dissimilarity data

Substantiality

Unique selling proposition (USP)

chapter review

QUESTIONS FOR REVIEW AND DISCUSSION

1 What is market segmentation?

2 Of what value is market segmentation to marketing managers?

3 What variables are used to segment target markets?

4 Which of the variables from question 3 do you see as most and least useful to a manager working in the hospitality and tourism industry?

5 Cite and discuss the criteria for effective segmentation.

6 Is it possible to oversegment a market? If so, provide an example.

7 What are the four steps in the market segmentation decision process?

8 Explain and give examples of each of the three market segmentation strategies.

9 What is positioning? Why is it important?

10 Describe the four steps in the positioning process.

11 What is perceptual mapping?

12 Internet Exercise: The VALS™ Survey is the instrument used to gather the data necessary to identify the various market segments used in the VALS framework. Use the following link to access the Strategic Business Insights website where you can take the VALS survey and determine your VALS segment or type:

www.strategicbusinessinsights.com/vals/presurvey.shtml

Then, you can use the following link to get a thorough description of each VALS type:

www.strategicbusinessinsights.com/vals/ustypes.shtml

- Do you think the VALS type determined by the survey is consistent with the way you perceive yourself?

- Talk to your friends and relatives and see if they have a different perception of you regarding your personality traits and purchasing behavior.

NOTES

[1] The World Bank, data.worldbank.org/indicator/sp.urb.totl.in.zs.

[2] United States Census Bureau, www.census.gov/hhes/families/data/cps2012avg.html.

[3] Bureau of Labor Statistics, United States Department of Labor, www.bls.gov/emp/ep_table_410.htm.

[4] James H. Martin and James M. Daley, "How to Develop a Customer-Driven Positioning Strategy," *Business* 39 (October–December 1989), p. 11.

[5] Al Ries and Jack Trout, *Positioning: The Battle for Your Mind* (New York: McGraw-Hill, 1981).

chapter review

CASE STUDY

Destination Market Segments

The four primary market segments for conventions and visitors bureaus (CVBs) are associations, corporations, tour operators, and individual travelers. Associations consist of social, military, education, religious, and fraternal (SMERF) groups, as well as industry trade groups. These groups can be local, regional, or national, and they all have meetings and events throughout the year. *Associations* hold conferences, which are smaller meetings normally focused on education and training, and *conventions,* which are large annual meetings for the national membership. *Trade shows* are conventions that include exhibitors that sell products to the association's members and their organizations. Many of these conventions are large enough to "sell out" a city and use most of the hotel rooms that are available. The most popular destinations for the largest conventions are Las Vegas, Chicago, Orlando, and Los Angeles because they have the necessary square footage for exhibitors and enough hotel rooms to accommodate all the attendees.

Corporations also hold meetings and events throughout the year for sales training, advertising campaigns and product launches, board of directors, shareholders, and so on. Most of these meetings have less than 100 attendees, but there are a large number of these meetings relative to association meetings and conventions. Corporations are less price-sensitive than the other meeting groups and individual travelers. In addition, there is a better opportunity for more frequent repeat visitation. These characteristics all add up to make the corporate market a lucrative market for destinations that can acquire their business and loyalty. Corporations also hold picnics and holiday parties for their employees that are valuable pieces of business for members or local partners of the destination marketing organizations (DMOs).

Tour operators develop travel packages that they sell to individual travelers. These packages typically include airfare, lodging, and tickets to local attractions. Travel agents are also part of this market segment because they function as intermediaries between the tour operators and the final consumer when the tour operator doesn't sell directly to the consumer via mail, telephone, or the Internet. *Conventions and visitors bureaus* are responsible for organizing familiarization (Fam) tours for the tour operators and travel agents. The CVB approaches its local members (e.g., hotels and restaurants) to obtain donations in order to host the intermediaries free of charge. The goal is to "familiarize" the tour operators and travel agents with the destination so that they will promote the area to their clients and potential customers.

In addition, *destination marketing organizations* are concerned with providing information and promotional materials focused on the individual leisure traveler. Generally, DMOs promote events such as festivals and sporting events, cultural and heritage sites such parks and museums, and recreational activities such as amusement parks, shopping facilities, and golf facilities. This is accomplished through mass communications rather than using the DMOs sales force. Placements in magazines and articles by travel writers are popular forms of marketing communications directed at this target segment.

Case Study Questions and Issues

1. What segmentation variables are used to create the destination market segments that are described in this case study?

2. What types of hotels would cater to each of these market segments? What variables would be used to segment the hotels?

3. What cities would appeal to each of the segments? Explain your answer.

CASE STUDY

Segmenting and Positioning in the Cruise Industry

The cruise industry has increased in popularity over the past two decades. This has led to higher volume, including more market segments than just affluent travelers. However, the cruise lines have to be careful that they don't try to mix too many different groups of customers on the same ship. In response, the cruise lines have added more ships and designed them to appeal to the varied customer segments. Also, there are many outlets for purchasing cruise travel, including traditional travel agents, online travel agents, airline agents and websites, and the cruise line agents and websites.

The purpose of this exercise is to research the various distribution outlets and determine the makeup of the cruise line industry. That is, identify the popular cruise lines in the United States, how they are positioned, and what market segments they serve. The following is a description of how you can find this information through two of the more popular online travel agents, but you can use other sources as well. You should limit your search to Bahamas cruises of 3 to 6 nights/days. It doesn't matter what month you use, so long as it is a popular cruising month for the Florida ports (i.e., Fort Lauderdale, Miami, and Tampa).

First, you can go to www.expedia.com and click on "Cruises." Put in the criteria listed in the previous paragraph (i.e., Bahamas, 3 to 5 nights, all lines) and choose a month. Next, click on "Choose and Continue" for the various selections and scroll down to "About the Ship."

Next, you can go to www.travelocity.com and click on "Cruises." Put in the same criteria (except it is 3 to 6 nights) and choose the same month. Then, click on "More Info" for each of the selections, followed by "Reviews."

Case Study Questions and Issues

1. What cruise lines are available, and how are they positioned in the market? Explain your answer based on actual evidence and construct a simple perceptual map based on price and quality.

2. What are the primary market segments for cruise lines based on your review of the websites? What ships are available within the Carnival Cruise Line, and how are they targeted to each of these segments?

3. What other websites are available for obtaining useful information for how the cruise lines, and their ships, are segmented?

case study

Developing a Marketing Plan

Courtesy of Frank Gaertner/Shutterstock.

Chapter Objectives

After studying this chapter, you should be able to:

1. Describe the typical marketing management cycle.

2. Differentiate between strategic and tactical marketing plans, and describe the advantages and disadvantages of planning.

3. Describe the four steps of the marketing planning process.

4. Explain the qualitative and quantitative techniques for developing sales forecasts, and the criteria used to select the appropriate sales forecasting techniques.

5.1 INTRODUCTION

Marketing is an ongoing process. It needs constant attention to be successful. Management must regularly obtain feedback and use it to revise strategic plans. Management's role in the marketing effort is critical, for without diligent effort, the results will be less than satisfactory. Large hospitality and tourism organizations normally have a director of marketing who is responsible for the management of all marketing activities. However, in most hospitality and tourism units, and especially in independent firms, the marketing function is the responsibility of an operations manager who must be concerned with other functions as well. This, together with the lack of a sizable budget, results in a low priority for marketing in these situations. The successful marketing of a hospitality operation is not something that can be accomplished overnight or with only a few hours of attention each week. Establishing and maintaining a successful marketing program requires significant management time and effort. The management activities in marketing a hospitality operation can be divided into three major areas that form a **marketing management cycle**: marketing planning, marketing execution, and marketing evaluation (see Figure 5.1). Marketing planning is the focus of this chapter; the topics related to marketing execution and marketing evaluation are discussed in subsequent chapters.

Marketing management cycle
The dynamic process involving marketing planning, execution, and evaluation.

5.1.1 Marketing Planning

There are three basic questions that should be addressed during **marketing planning**. The first question is, "Where are we now?" A situation analysis should be performed to determine the company's strengths and weaknesses. This information is based on past trends and historical performance, and it should include an analysis of the market and the competition. In addition, it is necessary to scan the environment for opportunities and threats. Once the company has a good grasp of the situation, it is time to move on to the next question.

Marketing planning
The process of analyzing potential markets and developing marketing programs using marketing mix strategies to compete in chosen markets.

The second question is, "Where do we want to go?" It is at this point that a company must set its goals and objectives for operating in the future. These goals and objectives should be clear, concise, and measurable over a specific time frame. All employees and stakeholders should be made aware of the strategic direction of the firm. Also, these goals and objectives become targets for evaluating the performance of the company's employees. Finally, the goals and objectives should be consistent with the company's mission statement.

The third question is, "How are we going to get there?" After the company determines its direction for the future, it is necessary to devise strategies and action plans that can serve as a road map. Basically, marketing managers develop marketing programs that are consistent with the goals of the firm. The components of the marketing mix are under the direct control of managers, and they can be used to form strategies that will help the company reach its goals. The actions taken with price, the product–service mix, promotion, and distribution should be integrated and lead to a common end.

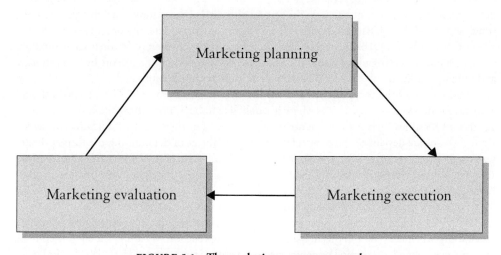

FIGURE 5.1 • The marketing management cycle.

5.1.2 Marketing Execution

After the objectives and strategies are determined, the next step is to implement the action plans developed during the planning process, using the specific timetable that was part of the marketing plan. This is accomplished using the promotional, advertising, personal selling, and direct marketing materials and methods that were devised in the planning stage. Employees should be informed about the company's plans for its service offerings and receive additional training if necessary. Unit managers and franchisees should be made aware of the changes in the marketing plan so that they can implement them in their respective units.

5.1.3 Marketing Evaluation

The final step in the marketing management cycle is to monitor and control the elements of the marketing plan. Data are collected and evaluated using a variety of marketing research methods and stored in forms that allow for easy retrieval. Organizational performance needs to be analyzed in comparison with goals and objectives, looking for the underlying reasons for the difference between stated performance goals and actual performance. Specifically, the company should analyze the effectiveness of its marketing programs, including its strategies for pricing, promoting, and distributing its products and services. The firm's performance can be evaluated relative to its competitors, using measures such as sales, market share, and customer satisfaction. Finally, at this point, firms can return to the planning stage of the marketing management cycle and make any desired changes in their objectives or their strategies.

5.2 MARKETING PLANS

Planning focuses on the future. It involves assessing current environmental trends and determining what is most likely to occur in the future. People who are responsible for developing marketing plans chart a course of action that they believe will allow the firm to achieve its stated objectives. Planners can never be 100 percent certain that they will achieve their stated objectives, but well-developed plans have a much higher probability of accomplishing the desired results.

In general, a marketing plan is a written document that contains the outline for a business unit's marketing programs and resource allocations over a specific planning period. Marketing plans are written documents, requiring managers to analyze the company, its products and services, and the environment so that they can prepare well-organized documents to guide their companies. Second, marketing plans are written for the appropriate business center as defined by the organization. A **strategic business unit (SBU)** consists of products that share common characteristics and have the same competitors. For example, within a large multibrand lodging company such as Marriott International, an SBU might be classified as one of the brands, such as Fairfield Inns or Courtyard. Finally, marketing plans are developed for a specific time period that varies from product to product or unit to unit based on the scope or breadth of the planning activity. For example, strategic plans are broad, have far-reaching implications, and often extend 3 or more years into the future. Conversely, tactical plans are more short-term in focus, with an emphasis on implementation.

Strategic marketing plans result from a careful examination of a firm's core business strategy and primary marketing objectives. When involved in this type of planning, firms should focus on key areas, starting with the type of business the firm is in or wishes to be in. Next, the firm should ask where it is now and whether it is where it would like to be. If not, what should the firm do to get there? Questions such as these are not easy to answer, but they are the foundation on which strategic plans are developed. Strategic planning is the process of determining the firm's primary goals and objectives and initiating actions that will allow it to achieve those goals and objectives. All types of hospitality and tourism firms conduct strategic marketing planning, but it is an absolute necessity for multiunit firms or chains.

Tactical marketing plans focus on implementing the broad strategies established in the strategic plan. For example, if a hotel's strategy is to increase occupancy by 2 percent by focusing on a specific target market, how will this market segment be approached? What specific steps need to be taken to achieve the stated goal? The actual methods used are part of the tactical plan. Tactical plans

---

Strategic business unit (SBU)
Business centers consisting of products that share common characteristics and have the same competitors.

Strategic marketing plans
These plans result from a careful examination of a firm's core business and primary marketing objectives.

Tactical marketing plans
These plans focus on implementing the broad strategies that are established in the strategic marketing plan.

typically cover a period of one year and primarily focus on specific activities that must be implemented if the firm is to achieve the goals and objectives stated in the longer-range strategic plan. One of the focal points for tactical plans is the allocation of resources to achieve the stated objectives. Tactical plans may get modified, based on the actions of the primary competitors and the availability of resources, but strategic plans are normally not modified without considerable reflection.

Within small chains and independent operations, the unit management is often granted great autonomy. Within larger chain organizations, most aspects of the marketing function are tightly controlled, and the manager of an individual unit is more involved in implementing rather than planning. Planning is conducted at a higher level within the organization to ensure coordination of marketing efforts and consistency throughout the chain. Corporate-level marketing managers normally work with managers of the individual units to help them formulate and implement tactical plans that allow the unit to remain successful, while supporting the overall corporate marketing strategic plan.

Tactical plans prepared for a one-year time horizon are based on the answers to questions similar to those listed here:

- What is our market share? Is it increasing or decreasing?
- How have the strengths and weaknesses of our firm changed in the last year?
- How has our mix of guests changed in the last year?
- What advertising and promotions were the most and least successful during the last year?
- What types of promotions and sales efforts should we use to build business during our slow periods?
- What specific promotion and advertising schedules will lead to success?
- What in-house promotions should we schedule?

5.2.1 Advantages and Disadvantages of Marketing Plans

Formulating an organized and well-conceived marketing plan can have a tremendously positive impact on a hospitality firm. There are five main advantages of marketing planning:

1. **It helps the firm cope with change more effectively.** If the competitive environment changes rapidly, a firm that has developed strategic plans with several contingency options is in a better position to effectively deal with the change.

2. **Developing marketing plans ensure that the firm's objectives are achieved.** The plans serve as guides to help the firm achieve the objectives. If, in some unforeseen circumstances, the objectives are not attainable, objectives and plans can be modified. This is done after a very careful analysis of the situation, investigating why the original objectives could not be achieved.

3. **Establishing a marketing plan aids management in making important decisions.** The established plans can easily serve as a point of reference for management to consult when confronted with a difficult decision. Given the alternatives, managers can decide which ones will contribute the most to the achievement of their objectives.

4. **Planning forces managers to examine the firm's operations.** Marketing plans make it necessary for managers to relate employee tasks and resource allocation to the firm's objectives. There must be a clear delineation of how the use of resources and employee time will help the firm achieve its objectives.

5. **Developing both strategic and tactical marketing plans helps management when evaluating the marketing efforts.** Results of marketing efforts are compared with projected results, giving management a control process for the marketing function.

Although establishing a marketing plan has many advantages, there are also some disadvantages associated with marketing planning. Five main disadvantages of marketing planning follow:

1. **Establishing objectives and formulating a marketing plan are very time consuming.** The time that management invests in planning can be expensive, and the results of planning

must be cost-effective. The overall benefits of these efforts, however, normally far exceed the cost to the firm.

2. **If planning is to be successful and have the desired impact on an organization, it must have the support and commitment of the top management.** If those involved in the planning process perceive that they are merely going through the motions and that their activities will not have any impact, they will have a negative opinion about planning. Under these circumstances, managers perceive the planning process as an extra duty. Therefore, they give it a low priority, resulting in an inferior plan.

3. **If managers develop poorly conceived plans or plans based on false assumptions, the plans may be inaccurate or ineffective.** For this reason, some managers feel that planning is of little value. Additionally, unplanned scenarios can develop rapidly, rendering marketing plans much less effective.

4. **Because plans often need to be prepared within a short period, it may not be possible to conduct as much background work as necessary for a high-quality plan.** In addition, the planning task is often assigned to a manager who has other duties and responsibilities, limiting the amount of time the manager has for planning. Managers must view the development of a plan as a means to an end, such as increased sales and profits, not as an end unto itself.

5. **Many firms do not have the personnel with the required knowledge and expertise in planning.** Many aspects are involved in marketing planning (discussed later in this chapter); hence, the employee responsible for planning should have some level of formal training. Often, managers are focused on day-to-day operations and do not have the time or ability to step back and view the business from a strategic perspective. If plans are to be successful, it is important to adopt a longer-term, strategic perspective.

5.2.2 Why Marketing Plans Fail

Despite the best efforts of marketing planners and all those involved in the planning process, some plans fail to fully achieve the desired results because of tactical shortcomings. The following are the most common reasons that some plans fail, based on the findings of several research studies:

- **Managers do not integrate strategic planning into the day-to-day activities of the firm.** In these cases, managers view the plan as an end in itself, rather than a means to achieve a desired result. Often, plans are carefully prepared, but they are not implemented because employees are either unable or unwilling to implement them. The planning process functions as a dynamic, ongoing process. Plans should be implemented, evaluated, revised, and implemented again. Only when this cycle is continual can planning truly succeed.

- **Those responsible for planning do not understand the planning process.** When managers develop a marketing plan, they must take time to work through all steps of the planning process. Sometimes managers want to jump ahead and draw conclusions before all environmental variables are considered and before a clear consensus is determined. Managers must avoid this tendency, for the results are usually unreliable. Every member of the planning team must fully understand the steps involved in the planning process and should actively contribute during each step.

- **There is a lack of input from line managers.** For a marketing plan to succeed, managers who have major responsibilities in areas other than marketing must implement the plan. In some cases, professional marketing managers assume responsibility for developing marketing plans, while implementation is left to line managers who are concerned mainly with day-to-day operations. These managers did not participate in the planning process and do not see the advantages or importance of planning. In addition, the planners did not benefit from the operational knowledge possessed by the line managers.

- **Financial projections are not marketing plans.** Some hospitality and tourism firms make revenue projections or sales forecasts and call this activity *marketing planning*.

Projections by themselves are not plans. Only when plans contain clearly defined tactics or action plans for achieving the desired objectives does planning take place.

- **Input is inadequate and there is insufficient consideration of all environmental variables.**   Although it remains impossible to consider every single variable, the real danger is basing decisions and plans on an insufficient amount of information. Managers often want to rush to a conclusion rather than gather information and make informed decisions. This type of information is available through environmental scanning and the use of the firm's marketing information systems.

- **The managers' planning focuses too heavily on short-term results.**   Managers must emphasize formulating plans that will allow the firm to move toward the achievement of long-term goals. Too frequently, the managers emphasize short-term profits at the expense of long-term objectives and profits.

- **No procedures are established to monitor and control the planning process.**   It is important to establish procedures to monitor the planning process from beginning to end. This will allow the firm to make necessary changes based on new information or problems that may arise. There are many other reasons why plans fail to achieve the desired results. However, if the members of the planning team clearly focus their attention on the initial stages of the planning process, the later stages will become much easier to complete, and the probability of success will increase. It is important to avoid the temptation to rush through the initial steps in order to produce quick results.

An old saying that still holds true notes that there are three types of companies:

1. Companies that make things happen.
2. Companies that watch things happen.
3. Companies that wonder what happened.

Companies that make things happen are generally engaged in planning. They have established a mission statement as well as goals that lead to the formation of overall strategies that result in success. Becoming overly concerned with day-to-day operations causes the downfall of many hospitality organizations. The result is that managers become so engrossed in meeting the daily demands of their positions that they fail to see the big picture—they cannot see the forest for the trees.

Because of this myopic perspective, managers are not aware of trends, and when the competitive environment does change, they are not prepared for it. Successful planning is a key element in the financial success of all firms. Hospitality and tourism firms that allocate human and monetary resources for planning are much more likely to reach their financial goals than firms that do not engage in planning.

5.3   THE MARKETING PLANNING PROCESS

Successful marketing begins with careful assessment of the competitive environment, followed by the development of a marketing plan. The sections that follow provide a framework for this process.

5.3.1   Framework for Marketing Plans

Marketing plans are normally developed for both short-term and long-term time frames. Short-term plans are normally for a period of up to 1 year, whereas long-term plans for a period of greater than 1 year, often for 2 or more years.

One-year plans are fairly tactical in nature. The plans are specific in terms of the action plans and the activities that will be undertaken to achieve the stated objectives. Budgets are included, and the allocations of resources to each action plan is usually stated. Performance metrics will be used to gauge the success attained for each objective. These performance metrics are normally monitored monthly, or at least quarterly. If the performance targets are not being achieved, changes in the action plans and tactics will be necessary to increase the likelihood of achieving the stated objectives.

Long-term plans, normally for a period of longer than 1 year, are developed with a more strategic focus. These plans generally follow a framework similar to the following:

I. Executive Summary. This is a summary that provides an overview of the entire plan.

II. Situation Analysis

   A. Market Summary

   1. Target markets. What specific markets are targeted? Why are these specific segments the best targets? How have the target markets changed over time?

   2. Market analysis. Where does current business come from? How has this changed in the past 1 to 2 years?

   3. Market demographics. Describe the customers demographically. Where do they come from geographically? What travel or consumption behavior do they exhibit?

   4. Market needs. What needs are customers trying to satisfy? How have these needs changed in the past 1 to 2 years? When customers are asked why they buy from your organization, what would they say?

   5. Market trends. How has the market or competitive behavior changed? Have there been changes in either supply or demand?

   6. Market growth. What has been the annual growth in the market in the past 1 to 2 years? How does this growth compare to other similar situations?

   B. SWOT (Strengths, weaknesses, opportunities, or threats) Analysis

   1. Strengths. What are the internal strengths of the operation? What does the organization do well? In what ways is the organization stronger than its competitors?

   2. Weaknesses. What are the internal weaknesses of the operation? What does the organization need to improve? In what ways is the organization weaker than, or at a competitive disadvantage to, competitors?

   3. Opportunities. In what ways is the organization positioned to gain a competitive advantage?

   4. Threats. In what ways is the organization at a competitive disadvantage when external factors are examined?

   C. Competition. Who are the major competitors? How has this competitive set changed in the past 1 to 2 years? Have competitors taken actions that create challenges or opportunities?

   D. Service Offerings. What is the primary product–service mix of the organization? Has this changed in the past 1 to 2 years?

III. Marketing Strategy

   A. Mission. What is the mission statement of the organization? Does the mission statement need to be reviewed or modified?

   B. Objectives. What is the overall strategy of the organization? How is this strategy operationalized? What specific objectives will execute the strategy? How will performance against the objectives be measured? Are the objectives reasonable? Are time parameters to accomplish the objectives stated? What resources will be required to achieve the objectives?

   1. Marketing. What are the specific objectives related to the marketing strategy?

   2. Financial. What are the specific financial performance objectives? These are normally associated with each of the marketing objectives. What level of performance is desired?

   C. Target Marketing. What strategies and tactics are associated with each targeted market segment?

D. Positioning. How is the organization positioned? How will this positioning strategy be implemented?

E. Marketing Mix. How will each of the marketing mix elements be implemented?

F. Marketing Research. Is any research necessary to execute future marketing plans?

IV. Financials, Budgets, and Forecasts

A. Sales Forecast. What is the monthly sales forecast for each target market?

B. Expense Forecast. What is the monthly budget for each item in the marketing budget?

V. Controls

A. Implementation Milestones and Metrics. What are the monthly milestones? How will these be monitored? What action(s) will be taken if performance falls below the milestones?

B. Contingency Planning. What action(s) will be taken if performance falls below the milestones? How will decisions regarding changes in the marketing plan be made? Who will be involved in this review and analysis?

No magic formula will guarantee success for a firm in the hospitality and tourism industry. Even well managed firms can fail to achieve the desired level of success. However, managers can take steps that will increase the probability of success. Figure 5.2 illustrates the basic steps in the marketing planning process. If managers focus on these elements, they are more likely to lead the firm in a direction that will accomplish its goals.

Before actually beginning the marketing planning process, each firm should establish a **mission statement**. A firm's mission statement defines its purpose and how to differentiate it from its competitors. It should provide managers with the general guidelines for decision making. First, mission statements typically are brief, often only a sentence or two and always less than two paragraphs; they define the scope of business for the corporation, and they answer the question, "What business are we in?" For example, if a corporation defined its mission as providing outstanding hospitality services in the budget-priced segment of the market, this would be its primary focus. This is the message that is conveyed to the firm's internal stakeholders: owners/investors, managers, and employees. Second, those involved in the planning process often create a series of value statements, which describe what the firm believes in and how it will attempt to execute the mission statement. Finally, managers create a **position statement**, which describes this mission to the firm's external stakeholders (customers, suppliers, and the general community) in terms of the public's perceptions of the benefits offered.

Mission statement
Expresses the firm's purpose and the qualities that differentiate the firm from its competitors.

Position statement
Describes the firm's mission to its external stakeholders in terms of the benefits of the firm's offerings.

FIGURE 5.2 • The marketing planning process.

This idea of focus, or purpose, is important when proceeding with the marketing planning process. A firm's mission is a function of its available resources and capabilities. It is difficult to operate outside these parameters and still remain successful. For example, the budget hotel mentioned earlier would not be able to compete for customers with full-service hotels that offer a wide array of amenities and services that are not available at budget properties. Budget hotels know that they appeal to price-sensitive customers who want a nice room that is clean and safe. If the hotel adheres to its mission, there will be no confusion among the stakeholders, and there is a better chance for success. Once the mission statement is established, the firm can begin the planning process. Samples and information on creating mission statements can be found at http://www.missionstatements.com/and http://onstrategyhq.com/resources/topic/mission-statement/.

5.3.2 Conducting a Situation Analysis

The first step in the marketing planning process requires a firm to perform a situation analysis. The firm must first look at its history, and then objectively assess its strengths and weaknesses relative to competitors. The planning process should include an analysis of the potential opportunities and threats posed by the changes in the firm's external environment. The situation analysis provides the background information necessary to make decisions regarding the future direction of the firm. It answers the questions, "Where are we now?" and "How did we get here?" Managers engaged in planning can gain a better understanding by studying the history of an organization.

Historical appraisal
An examination of the current trends in the market's size and scope, and the market shares of competitors.

5.3.2.1 HISTORICAL APPRAISAL. The **historical appraisal** starts by examining the market, looking at its size, its scope, and competitors' market shares. It is important to look at the trends in the market to understand how the firm arrived at its present position. The firm should examine internal data regarding its sales history, including costs and profits. It is helpful to see the trends in sales, costs, and profit margins that resulted from changes in marketing programs and the environment. This provides insight into possible future directions based on the current position of products in the market. Many trends can be attributed to changes in the external environment. For example, changes in technology and government regulation have forced firms to rethink their strategies and react appropriately. Traditional travel agents once dominated the travel planning market, but now they compete with online travel agents such as Expedia.com, Priceline.com, and Hotels.com, as well as online reservations directly through the service provider (e.g., United.com, Marriott.com, and Hertz.com).

Firms must also examine sales histories for changes in consumer purchasing patterns. Consumers usually change their buying procedures and practices over time. For instance, there may be changes in frequency, quantity, or timing of their purchases. Understanding these changes remains crucial for firms that want to be competitive at getting products to consumers how and when they want them. Firms will undoubtedly use this information to gain competitive advantages through pricing and product design. Firms should communicate these advantages to consumers through advertising and promotions. For example, restaurant managers may notice that a larger percentage of customers are dining earlier as a result of the aging population and the increase in families with small children. Similarly, resort managers may find that consumers are taking more vacations of shorter duration. All types of hospitality and tourism firms will benefit from conducting a formal situation analysis, beginning with a historical appraisal.

Management should conduct a consumer analysis to identify the buyers and users of the product and to assure they are the same. In some cases, the person who purchases the product is not the user (e.g., meeting planners, tour operators). In addition, it is important to identify the individuals who may influence a purchase (e.g., family members, buying centers). Next, firms must identify other factors that could influence the purchase (e.g., demographics, socioeconomic status, lifestyle) and any variations in purchase behavior (e.g., seasonal or cyclical variations). Related areas include determining what motivates consumers to purchase this type of product, deciding how the markets can be segmented, and identifying the most frequent purchasers. After management identifies the salient attributes and the end benefits that consumers are seeking, they can determine if any unmet needs can be targeted.

Next, management should conduct an industry analysis to determine actual and potential industry size, historical growth rate and future predictions, industry structure (including costs and distribution), industry trends, and key success factors. It may be useful to rank competitors by market share and identify both direct and indirect competition. For example, restaurants face competition from supermarkets, convenience stores, and delivery services. The next section will elaborate on the process of assessing the internal strengths and weaknesses of firms, relative to the competition, and the opportunities and threats posed by the environment.

5.3.2.2 SWOT ANALYSIS.   The next part of the situation analysis involves a detailed examination of the firm's internal strengths and weaknesses, and the external opportunities and threats. This analysis is often referred to as a SWOT analysis. Figure 5.3 illustrates the various components of a SWOT analysis and their relationships with one another.

The strengths and weaknesses components of a marketing plan reflect an evaluation of the firm's internal situation. What are the things that the firm does well, and where are they below standard? The opportunities and threats reflect an assessment of the external environment that the firm faces. Strengths and opportunities represent positive attributes that the firm can use to gain a competitive advantage. If items that appear as strengths and opportunities for the firm are similar to weaknesses and threats for the competitors, then the firm has a distinct competitive advantage to leverage for gains in sales and market share. Similarly, weaknesses and threats are viewed as problem areas. Firms need to compensate for weaknesses until they can eliminate them, and if possible, threats need to be anticipated so strategies can be developed to minimize their impact.

As shown in Figure 5.3, strengths and opportunities are items that can be leveraged to gain a competitive advantage. For example, if a food service operation found that there would be minimal competition for an off-premise catering business in addition to its existing restaurant operation, this would represent an opportunity—an area for potential growth. Using the same example, a food service operation might find that if it decided to enter the off-premise catering business, competition might follow. This potential competition represents an external threat.

Inherent in this analysis is the need for managers to examine what the business does well and what could be improved. At the same time, a critical assessment of the market is needed to determine, as specifically as possible, the threats and potential opportunities that exist outside the firm. Management must ask, "What do we have or offer that is different, unique, or superior to what the competition offers consumers?" Management must also examine the organization's shortcomings by asking, "What do we provide that is below average?"

The process of identifying internal strengths and weaknesses or external threats and opportunities is similar to examining a balance sheet with assets and liabilities. The strengths and opportunities are used to promote the business and to make decisions about new directions that should be taken. Conversely, managers must make every effort to correct or neutralize the weaknesses and threats. Many managers find it difficult to identify an organization's weaknesses or threats clearly, tending to overlook or downplay negative factors. Successful managers can usually predict the future and adapt to meet the changes that are occurring in the marketplace. Although this may not be entirely true, those who are successful seem to know what will occur in the marketplace before it actually happens. Is it luck or successful planning? One definition of *luck* is "preparation meeting opportunity." Successful managers are students of trends. They carefully watch the broad marketing environment discussed in Chapter 2, looking for subtle changes in the economic, political and legal, social, and technological environments that may potentially influence their businesses.

SWOT analysis
The analysis of a firm's strengths and weaknesses relative to competitors, and the potential threats and opportunities posed by the external environment.

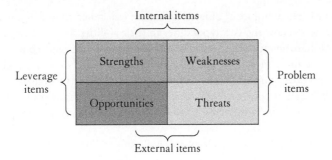

FIGURE 5.3 • SWOT analysis.

They carefully study the moves made by their competitors and do everything they can to stay close to their customers. In doing so, they attempt to match their product–service mix to the constantly changing needs and wants of their customers and potential customers.

5.3.3 Defining the Firm's Goals and Objectives

A firm's goals and objectives should evolve from the mission statement. Goals are broad statements of what the firm seeks to accomplish. For example, a firm may develop a goal that states, "We are seeking to achieve the number-one market share in the mid-Atlantic region." The goal does not tell how the results are to be achieved; rather, it states, in broad terms, the desired result. Objectives are more detailed statements, or refinements, of what the firm intends to accomplish. A good objective includes (1) what will be accomplished in measurable terms, (2) within what specific time frame it will be accomplished, (3) which individual or group will be responsible for achieving the objective, and (4) how the results will be evaluated.

5.3.3.1 PURPOSE OF OBJECTIVES.

The objectives serve several functions. For one thing, they enable management to arrive at a consensus concerning the primary activities of the organization. In addition, responsibility for specific objectives gets assigned to specific managers, thereby establishing accountability. If a well-defined objective is assigned to a specific manager, that individual assumes responsibility for following through and seeing that the objective is completed. Therefore, the results are likely to be more positive than if no one individual is assigned responsibility.

For objectives to achieve their greatest purpose, they must be established with the input of many individual managers. The process of defining objectives can serve as a brainstorming and motivational tool. When individuals have input into formulating the organizational marketing objectives, they develop a sense of ownership and allegiance toward the objectives. As a result, employees are likely to work more diligently to achieve stated objectives. Formulating well-written and measurable objectives takes time, and care should be taken to ensure that the objectives remain feasible. Several characteristics of good objectives follow:

- **Objectives should be specific and easy to understand.** They should not be too broad and difficult to define. Everyone involved in formulating the objectives should clearly understand the precise objectives toward which the organization seeks to move.

- **Objectives should identify expected results.** They should be quantitative so that no gray area will exist for purposes of evaluation. When managers state an objective in quantitative terms, the expected results are more readily understood.

- **Objectives must be within the power of the organization to achieve.** When establishing objectives, management must keep in mind the relative abilities of the organization.

- **Objectives must be acceptable to the individuals within the organization.** Management must come to a consensus concerning the objectives. It is extremely difficult for a firm to achieve the stated objectives if the managers, who have input into the formation of the objectives, do not agree.

Table 5.1 provides examples of objectives that are well stated as well as some that are poorly stated. It is easy to see how the two types differ in their abilities to steer firms and allow for the measurement of performance. The well-stated objectives are clear and concise. They provide a specific time frame for completion, and they contain quantified targets. In addition to stating objectives, it is necessary for firms to explain how the results will be evaluated and who has the actual responsibility for attaining the objective. Finally, adequate resources must be committed to achieving each objective, including personnel, facilities, and financial resources.

5.3.3.2 TYPES OF OBJECTIVES.

Objectives are grouped into four main categories: financial, sales, competitive, and customer. Table 5.2 contains a list of specific objectives that can be used under each of the four categories. *Financial objectives* focus on the firm's ability to generate enough

Goals

Goals are broad statements of what the firm seeks to accomplish.

Objectives

Objectives are more detailed statements of what the firm intends to achieve.

WELL-STATED OBJECTIVES	POORLY STATED OBJECTIVES
Our objective is to increase occupancy rate from 70 percent to 75 percent within 1 year by decreasing group rates by 5 percent .	Our objective is to increase occupancy rate.
Our objective is to increase our awareness rating from 60 percent to 70 percent within one year by allocating $200,000 to advertising for an awareness campaign.	Our objective is to increase awareness over the next year.
Our objective is to increase the average check by 10 percent within 6 months by providing waiters with a 2-hour suggestive selling training program.	Our objective is to increase the average check by training waiters.

TABLE 5.1 · Examples of Objectives

money to pay its bills, offer investors an adequate return, and retain some of the earnings for investing in the firm. *Sales objectives* focus on the level of sales in units or dollars, and the firm's sales relative to its competitors (i.e., market share). *Competitive objectives* focus on the firm's ability to compete in the marketplace. The firm positions itself against the competition, determines the best strategies for survival, or tries to keep pace with the competition in terms of sales growth, market share, and/or marketing expenditures. Finally, *customer objectives* focus on the firm's ability to make consumers aware of its products, provide them with a product–service mix that meets their expectations, and create a level of goodwill among customers and other stakeholders.

Firms can use a combination of objectives, such as a desire to maximize profit and increase customer satisfaction. In most situations, objectives do not conflict, so the firm can work at attaining both. However, it is necessary to prioritize multiple objectives and allocate resources appropriately. One potential problem with multiple objectives is that there could be a conflict between them. For example, consider the case of a firm that wants to increase market share and maximize profit. In the short run, increases in market share are accomplished by lowering price and/or increasing marketing expenditures on changes in the product–service mix and promotion. Either decreasing price or increasing marketing expenditures will result in a decrease in short-term profits. The firm must rethink its objectives or make a distinction between short-term and long-term profits.

MAIN CATEGORY	SPECIFIC OBJECTIVES
Financial	Maximize profit
	Target rate of return
	Increase cash flow
Sales	Increase or maximize sales revenues
	Increase volume (number of units sold)
	Increase or maximize market share
Competitive	Position against competitors
	Long-term survival
	Maintain competitive parity (market share or marketing expenditures)
Customer	Increase market awareness
	Increase customer satisfaction
	Improve or change perceived image
	Create goodwill

TABLE 5.2 · Types of Objectives

Subway Restaurants offer special promotional prices as a market penetration strategy.

5.3.4 Formulating Marketing Strategies and Action Plans

A *strategy* is the manner by which an organization attempts to link with, respond to, integrate with, and exploit its environment. In other words, a firm's strategies integrate its mission, goals, objectives, and action plans. When well formulated, strategies help firms maximize the use of their resources. This, in turn, puts them in a viable position within the competitive environment. Timing is everything. Managers must always look for a strategic window, or a limited period when marketing opportunities present themselves and the firm is in a position to take advantage of those opportunities. For example, imagine that your firm had stockpiled a large supply of frozen beef tenderloins and your major competitor had not. Due to weather conditions in the major growing areas, a beef shortage occurred. Prices escalated rapidly and supplies of beef tenderloins were low. This occurrence would offer your firm a strategic window in which to gain a competitive advantage. You could undercut competitors' prices for the product and run a promotion that your competition would be unable to match.

When developing a marketing strategy, a manager first selects the markets the firm will target and then blends the elements of the marketing mix, which includes the product–service mix, price, promotion, and distribution. Strategic options for each of the marketing mix areas will be discussed in more detail in later chapters. However, various frameworks can be used by firms to aid in general strategy formulation. One of the more popular frameworks provides four basic strategies for achieving growth based on whether the products are new or currently exist and whether the markets are new or are currently being served. These growth strategies appear in Table 5.3.

A market penetration strategy focuses on selling the existing product–service mix to the existing target markets. Most firms will attempt to increase the quality and consistency of the product–service mix as a means of increasing customer satisfaction, promoting brand loyalty, and increasing sales and market share. For example, if a McDonald's franchisee continued to expand by opening stores in a rural part of the country, this could represent a market penetration strategy.

In an effort to increase sales, management attempts to increase the rate of repeat patronage, building on a solid client base. Another part of this strategy is to increase initial patronage among

Strategic window
Limited periods of time when marketing opportunities present themselves and the firm is in a position to take advantage of those opportunities.

Market penetration strategy
A market penetration strategy focuses on increasing the market share of existing products in current markets.

	EXISTING PRODUCT	NEW PRODUCT
Existing Market	Market Penetration	Product Development
New Market	Market Development	Product Diversification

TABLE 5.3 • Product Development Strategy Options

members of existing markets who have not previously patronized the hospitality operation. Management can accomplish this by attracting patrons from competing operations, thereby increasing the market share. The overall goal is twofold: to increase sales and to increase market share. Managers frequently select this strategy during periods of economic uncertainty, such as when the inflation rate is high. As it becomes more expensive to borrow capital for physical expansion, one of the best ways to grow is to increase sales within existing units. In this manner, a larger percentage of the increased sales will eventually become profits.

The basis of a **product development strategy** is the idea of developing new products for existing markets. As new elements of the product–service mix get introduced, management ensures the long-term financial viability of the firm by increasing sales. Examples of this strategy are common within the hospitality and tourism industry. For instance, noncommercial food service firms such as Aramark and Sodexo have long managed the food service operations for host firms, companies whose primary business is not providing a final food product (e.g., businesses, hospitals, colleges and universities, and other government and nonprofit organizations). Building on the successful relationship that has been established through running the food service aspects of the business, Aramark and Sodexo have expanded into facilities management (i.e., managing all aspects of stadiums and arenas for events). Another possible product development strategy for contract food service firms is to manage university housing and dining services.

> **Product development strategy**
> A strategy that focuses on achieving growth by developing new products for existing markets.

No hospitality or tourism firm can remain unchanged for too long and expect to prosper. Markets change, consumer needs and wants change, and so, too, must the product–service mix of any hospitality and tourism firm. For example, consider the product development of any of the fast-food chains. New menu items have been added continually over the years to increase unit sales and expand the total market. McDonald's was the first to put breakfast items on its menu, adding significantly to total sales of the individual units and the total corporation. Later, it added drive-through service. Then it added soft-serve ice cream and salads in order to expand the product–service mix and total sales. Although McDonald's is no longer as dominant as it once was in the fast-food market, the company has continually sought ways to expand its product–service mix and increase sales.

A **market development strategy** focuses on developing new markets for existing products and services. In the case of hotels and restaurants, this normally involves building new units and expanding into new markets. One of the most lucrative growth areas within the hospitality and tourism industry is outside the United States. As growth rates slow within the domestic market, large hospitality and tourism marketers look to grow internationally. Hyatt Hotels and Resorts has targeted many Asian countries for its expansion, while other hotel chains have focused on European countries. Foreign markets offer attractive growth prospects because many are virtually untapped. However, this potential for high return is counterbalanced by risks associated with the political and economic environments in foreign countries. Most local and regional hospitality firms still choose to add units in other regions within the United States before attempting overseas expansion. Or a hospitality firm may form a partnership or strategic alliance with another firm that has a stronger international presence. For example, when Marriott International acquired the Renaissance Hotels chain, it secured many international locations that enjoyed both a strong image and profitable hotels. In doing so, Marriott International did not have to establish a Marriott-branded hotel in these locations.

> **Market development strategy**
> A strategy that focuses on achieving growth by pursuing new markets for existing products and services.

A **diversification strategy** involves introducing new products and services into new markets. This strategy offers the most long-term potential, but it is also the strategy with the greatest degree of risk. The upside potential is important because any sales generated will be new sales. They will not take sales away from existing products and services. When existing customers buy new products and services rather than existing products and services, this is called *cannibalization*. When a firm introduces new products and services into new markets, there is no potential for cannibalization. However, the risk, and potential downside, is that actual sales will lag the company's forecasted sales and not meet profit projections. In this case, a diversification strategy would fail.

> **Diversification strategy**
> A strategy for growth that involves introducing new products and services into new markets.

Other popular frameworks offer baseline strategies based on the firm's competitive position, or business strengths, and the growth rate in the market, or industry attractiveness. In general, firms with weak competitive positions should look for ways to improve their status, either by concentrating on a single business or through mergers and acquisitions. Firms in markets with slow growth rates should look for new markets or form alliances with other firms to strengthen their positions. This allows them to survive and prosper, whereas other firms find it necessary to divest or liquidate.

Many hospitality and tourism firms, particularly small organizations, often do not devote the human and monetary resources necessary to develop adequate strategic marketing plans. Without such plans, the marketing strategy can easily become reactionary; the organization merely reacts to each new competitive force and lacks an overall sense of direction and purpose. Conversely, an organization that develops well-defined strategic marketing plans has laid the groundwork necessary for a proactive marketing effort that takes the initiative instead of allowing competitors to control the environment.

5.3.5 Implementing Action Plans and Evaluating Performance

Once management selects the best strategic alternatives, it must develop action plans and a timetable for implementation. Action plans are developed, indicating the specifics of what will happen, when it will be done, and how the marketing plan will be implemented. This does not mean that it is inflexible, but a clear implementation plan remains important. Action plans should contain the following information:

- Who will assume primary responsibility for each part of the action plan?
- How will these individuals (teams) proceed to implement the action plan?
- When should these individuals (teams) have the action plan completed?
- What resources will be necessary to fully implement the action plan?
- How will the results of the plan be evaluated?
- What specific metrics will be used to measure success?

Following the development of the action plans but before implementing them, managers must complete two activities. First, an *implementation schedule* must be developed. Because not all the action plans will be implemented at the same time, an orderly timetable or schedule will determine when the various actions should be carried out. Second, a set of *performance criteria* for evaluating the relative success of the action plans must be established. Performance criteria should be measurable. It is important to remember that marketing planning is a continuous process requiring monitoring and adapting based on actual performance. Four key control areas exist to evaluate performance: sales, costs, profits, and consumers. These control areas closely relate to the types of objectives discussed earlier in this section.

Sales control data should focus on the firm's sales by market segment, market share, and sales input. The quantified sales objectives should be broken down on a quarterly basis by *market segment* and used as a standard against which actual sales results can be compared. Managers should evaluate differences in terms of absolute dollar amount, as well as percentages that allow for easier comparisons. Firms should determine why there are variances between the targeted sales figures and the actual sales figures, even if the actual figures are better than expected. Then the elements of the marketing plan can be adjusted to reflect the changes that are deemed necessary.

Another measure of a firm's performance in terms of sales is *market share*. Market share data provide the firm with a comparison of its performance relative to its competitors. The formula to determine market share is the firm's sales divided by total industry sales. Market share is expressed as a percentage of sales in the total marketplace. The first step in performing market share analysis is to define the market. For example, a hotel chain could calculate its market share based on sales in the entire lodging industry or based on sales in its key segment(s), such as economy, luxury, extended stay, or all suites. The firm's sales figures would remain the same, but the denominator, which reflects the basis for comparison, would change. Therefore, the definition of the market is critical in the overall analysis.

The final type of sales control data involves the firm's *sales input*. In other words, what resources were used to obtain sales, and how efficiently is the firm using its resources? Mainly, sales input data deal with the various components of the promotion mix: advertising, personal selling, sales promotions, and publicity. First, firms need to examine the amount of time and money spent by its sales force. How much time is spent in selling and nonselling activities, how many calls are sales personnel making per day, what are their expenses, and what is their conversion rate with

Sales control data
Data focused on the firm's sales by market segment, market share, and sales inputs.

customers? For example, hotels can determine averages, or benchmarks, to evaluate the performance of their salespeople.

Salespeople are assigned quotas that can be evaluated on an annual, quarterly, or monthly basis to determine their progress. Second, the firm can look at the effectiveness of its advertising and sales promotions (publicity is difficult to assess because it is free and not easy to control). How many consumers in their target markets are reached, and with what frequency? What is the cost per thousand of reaching those consumers, and how many inquiries are received in response to the promotion? For example, a restaurant may put a discount coupon in the Val-Pak that local residents receive. It is important to keep track of the redemption rate to determine the net impact of the promotion. What did it cost to run the promotion? How much new business was generated? To what extent did discounted business cannibalize existing business?

Cost control data are another form of data used to evaluate performance. Firms should compare their forecasted budgets with actual budgets to determine where there are large deviations. Normally, sales forecasts are the basis for establishing budgets for various expense items and are usually expressed as a percentage of sales. This cost information is determined on an annual basis, but most often managers evaluate it either monthly or quarterly. Any large discrepancies are reviewed to determine the cause, and adjustments are made. Some of the more common expense ratios are profit margins, selling expense ratio, cost per sales call, and advertising expense ratio. In most cases, the various expense items are divided by total sales. However, as with sales control data, it is important to analyze the data by market segment. This will help the firm identify the profitability of its products and market segments. The standards for some of these cost items are based on the historical performance of firms within the industry. For example, a common rule of thumb in the restaurant industry is to keep food costs between 25 and 35 percent of the total costs of operation. When the actual percentage exceeds this range, it should alert the management of a potential problem.

Cost control data
Data focused on the firm's costs and expenses for each market segment.

Profit control data are a function of sales and costs and should be broken down by market segment as well. To perform this type of analysis, it is important to understand basic accounting and income statements. Here is a typical income statement:

Profit control data
This is a function of sales and costs and should be broken down by market segment.

Sales revenue	$1,100,000
– Cost of goods sold	560,000
= Gross profit	540,000
– Selling expenses	175,000
– Depreciation	100,000
– Administrative overhead	150,000
= Operating profit	115,000
– Interest expense	30,000
= Pretax profit	$85,000

It is crucial that firms examine the income statement to determine why net profit is negative or does not meet the target set in the marketing plan. Often, firms approach profitability from a cost perspective without having a good understanding of pricing strategy. Chapter 7 covers pricing in detail, but it is important to know how consumers' price sensitivity impacts a firm's products and services. There is no simple solution for obtaining desired profit levels. It is not easy to maximize sales revenue and minimize costs simultaneously. Decreases in costs can lead to lower quality and decreased sales and profits. In some cases, sales revenue can increase when the firm incurs additional costs to improve the product–service mix and raises prices. The income statement is a very useful tool for marketers. It should be studied carefully to determine the level of profitability, and if the desired results are not being achieved, the source of the problem can be determined by tracing it back through the sections of the income statement to determine the cause or causes. Once the cause is identified, a plan for corrective action can be developed.

Consumer feedback
Information received directly from consumers regarding their experiences with a product or service.

Consumer feedback is the final area of performance evaluation, and it is a key element in understanding the results of the financial analyses. Consumer feedback provides firms with information regarding awareness, knowledge, attitudes, purchasing behavior, and customer satisfaction.

Chapter 3 discussed consumer behavior, and Chapter 6 discusses the research methods used to obtain this information. In many cases, the financial data are merely a symptom of problems within the firm. It is often necessary to obtain consumer feedback to gain a true understanding of the problem.

It can be detrimental if managers focus too much on numbers and not enough on consumer needs. For example, a hotel in Boston was experiencing a decrease in occupancy rate in relation to other hotels in the area. Management tried to approach the issue by discounting prices, but it had very little effect. After speaking with customers, the hotel realized that business travelers found the rooms too small. Business travelers are not as price-sensitive as other travelers, but they are quality-conscious, which explained the ineffectiveness of the price discounting strategy. As a result, the hotel decided to focus on the government market because of the hotel's location.

The government market is price-sensitive (there is an allowable per diem) and not as quality-conscious, and the hotel could selectively discount to this large-volume market. Once again, it is important to point out that marketing planning is a continuous process. Marketing managers must evaluate the situation and adapt to changes that occur. Evaluating the success of the marketing plan is the moment of truth. Managers develop a plan to increase the probability of success, and once the plan is implemented, it is important for management to monitor the results. Any variance from the predicted results should be identified, evaluated, and corrected.

As the environment changes or the results vary, management may need to return to the appropriate step to reformulate marketing strategy or the action plans. The marketing planning process continues as a dynamic procedure, with sufficient flexibility allowing for changes in strategies, action plans, or implementation schedules.

5.4 SALES FORECASTING

Sales forecasting
The process for determining current sales and estimating future sales for a product or service.

One of the most critical components of a marketing plan is the forecast for sales. Sales forecasting is the process for determining current sales and estimating future sales for a product or service. The success of the firm often results from the accuracy of forecasts. The decisions about the elements of the marketing mix that are made during the situation analysis are based on sales forecasts.

5.4.1 Sales Forecasting Techniques

Causal analysis
Analysis techniques that look for cause and effect relationships between two or more variables.

Sales forecasting techniques are separated into two broad categories: quantitative techniques and qualitative techniques. *Quantitative* techniques use past data values and employ a set of rules to obtain estimates of future sales. *Qualitative* techniques rely on judgment or intuition and tend to be used when data are not readily available. Quantitative methods can be further classified as either causal or time series. Both types of quantitative methods use trends in historical data to predict future sales; however, causal analysis techniques establish a cause and effect relationship between variables and the results using historical data to establish the relationship between sales and other factors that are believed to influence sales. These techniques model the relationships between sales and other variables that can help predict changes in sales. Time series techniques extrapolate future sales estimates based on the trend in historical sales. In other words, past sales are used to predict future sales, assuming all other factors that affect sales will continue to have a similar effect in the future. The forecasting techniques described in this chapter are presented in a conceptual framework. Use of these techniques requires a sound statistical background. The techniques are presented so that marketing managers will have a better understanding of the range of techniques that are available.

5.4.1.1 QUALITATIVE FORECASTING TECHNIQUES. The goal of qualitative forecasting techniques is to forecast changes in the basic sales pattern as well as the pattern itself. Qualitative techniques are often difficult to apply, and they tend to be very time-consuming and costly. Therefore, these techniques are used mainly for long-term forecasts and in situations that are of major importance to the firm. It is important for firms to predict changes in sales patterns so they can take advantage of opportunities and minimize the impact of threats. To predict these changes, firms enlist the aid of experts, or individuals with an intimate knowledge of the product and its markets. The following basic approaches are classified as qualitative forecasting techniques:

- **Expert opinion.** Marketers look to a panel of experts with knowledge of the industry and the marketplace to provide a forecast. A variety of sources are consulted, and the results are combined to form a consensus forecast based on expert opinion. These experts can be from within the firm or from outside the firm. Often, secondary sources, such as forecasts published in major trade journals or business journals, are used. The resulting forecast can be obtained by simply averaging the individual forecasts, or a more complicated weighting system can be used based on the experience and knowledge of the panel members.

- **Delphi technique.** The Delphi technique involves several rounds of forecasting and review by a panel of experts. It can be very time-consuming, but it is often quite accurate. This technique involves collecting forecasts, developing composites, and sending the data to those participating several times until a consensus results. The Delphi technique is normally used when the decision is an important one and there are no time constraints. Panel members are able to adjust their forecasts after seeing the forecasts of others on the panel.

- **Sales force forecast.** The sales force forecast technique aggregates the sales forecast of each salesperson or unit, depending on the level of the forecast. For example, a hotel may have each of its salespeople provide a forecast for his or her territory and then combine the forecasts to obtain an overall estimate. Alternatively, a hotel or restaurant chain may have each unit provide a forecast and then combine the forecasts to obtain an overall estimate for the chain. The rationale for using this technique is that it may be more accurate to forecast the sales for each territory or unit rather than to obtain a higher-level forecast and break it down for operational purposes. Each salesperson, or unit manager, is in touch with the customers and changes in the environment.

- **Survey of buying intentions.** Firms can use marketing research to ask potential customers about their future purchase intentions and then estimate future sales. This type of forecast, or survey of buying intentions, is very subjective because there is no clear relationship between purchase intentions and actual purchase behavior. However, this kind of information is readily available from published sources such as *Sales & Marketing Management*.

The experts employed in these methods may base their judgment on prior experience, or they may use sophisticated quantitative techniques to model the effects of other factors that influence the level of sales. However, the ultimate outcome is to predict changes in sales patterns.

5.4.1.2 QUANTITATIVE FORECASTING TECHNIQUES. The common element in quantitative forecasting techniques is that they are based almost exclusively on historical data. These forecasting techniques tend to be quicker and less costly because the data are readily available through existing sources. Quantitative forecasting techniques are also gaining in popularity due to their level of proven accuracy and improvements in computer technology. Many spreadsheet software packages, such as Microsoft Excel, have statistical applications that can be used for quantitative forecasting, and other statistical programs and forecasting packages are available at a reasonable price. In addition, these programs are easy to use, and many are compatible with software for preparing reports and charts. The two basic quantitative forecasting techniques are time series analysis and causal methods.

5.4.1.3 TIME SERIES ANALYSIS. The time series analysis method uses statistical techniques to fit a trend line to the pattern of historical sales. The trend line is expressed in terms of a mathematical equation that can be used to project the trend forward into future periods and predict sales.

Expert opinion
Marketers look to a panel of experts with knowledge of the industry and the marketplace to provide a forecast.

Delphi technique
The Delphi technique involves collecting forecasts, developing composites, and sending the data to those participating several times until a consensus results.

Sales force forecast
This technique aggregates the sales forecast of each salesperson or unit.

Survey of buying intentions
Firms use marketing research to ask potential customers about their future purchase intentions and then estimate future sales.

Time series analysis
This method uses statistical techniques to fit a trend line to the pattern of historical sales.

The trend line can be linear (a straight line) or nonlinear (a curved line) depending on the pattern of the historical data. Four major components of a time series should be considered in choosing a technique: (1) trend, or the long-term pattern; (2) cycle, or medium-term changes due to business and economic changes; (3) seasonal, short-term movements based on buying patterns; and (4) residual, unpredictable influences or disturbances. Here are the most common methods of time series analysis:

Trend extrapolation
The simplest method for forecasting sales is the linear projection of past sales.

- **Trend extrapolation.** The simplest method for forecasting sales is the linear projection of past sales, or trend extrapolation. It assumes that the factors that influenced sales in the past will have the same effect on future sales, and all data points are weighted equally. This is somewhat naive, but firms' basic marketing programs and competitive situations normally do not change drastically from year to year. This method is very simple, the data requirements are minimal, and it can be very accurate for products in industries with low growth rates.

Moving average
This technique uses short-term forecasts (e.g., monthly) and takes the average of the most recent periods to predict future sales.

- **Moving average.** The moving average technique uses short-term forecasts (e.g., monthly) and takes the average of the most recent periods to predict future sales. For example, next month's sales are forecast using the average of the monthly sales for the last 3 or 4 months. This method is simple and can be used when sales are fairly stable throughout the year, with only small fluctuations.

Exponential smoothing
This technique uses the trend line to predict future sales; however, it places more weight on the most recent periods.

- **Exponential smoothing.** The technique of exponential smoothing uses the trend line to predict future sales; however, it places more weight on the most recent periods. This method is better at picking up trends than the previous time series methods, and there are more complex formulas that allow for cycles and seasonal effects.

There are more sophisticated time series techniques, but they are beyond the scope of this text. For example, there is a group of methods referred to as autoregressive moving averages (ARMA), which express forecasts as a linear combination of past actual values and/or past errors. These methods are becoming more widespread, but they require more than a rudimentary knowledge of forecasting.

5.4.1.4 CAUSAL METHODS. Causal methods are often referred to as explanatory methods because they use historical data to establish the relationship between sales and other factors that are believed to influence sales. The other factors, or causal factors, can differ based on the level of the forecast. The higher the level or the more macro-oriented the forecast, the more likely the variables are to be economic, such as disposable income, unemployment, and consumer prices. As the forecast becomes more specific, or micro-oriented, the causal factors become more specific, such as price, advertising expenditures, and competitors' prices and advertising.

However, to forecast sales based on these causal factors, one must forecast the causal variables as well. In addition, the data requirements for causal methods are more extensive than for qualitative or time series forecasting techniques. The two most common causal methods are as follows:

Regression analysis
This technique identifies the causal factors, or independent variables, that can be used to predict the level of sales, or the dependent variable.

1. **Regression analysis.** A regression analysis identifies the causal factors, or independent variables, that can be used to predict the level of sales, or the dependent variable. Single regression analysis uses one independent variable, and multiple regression analysis uses more than one independent variable. Trend extrapolation is actually a simplified form of regression analysis that uses time as the independent variable and sales as the dependent variable. For example, a manager might want to study the impact that the growth rate of the economy or intensity of competition has on annual sales.

Econometric models
This model uses statistical techniques to solve a simultaneous set of multiple regression equations.

2. **Econometric models.** In econometric models, statistical techniques are used to solve a simultaneous set of multiple regression equations. In this case, a causal factor may be predicted as a dependent variable from several other causal factors and then used as an independent variable in an equation to predict sales. This method is more complicated and requires some expertise in statistical modeling. In addition, this technique requires the largest amount of data because of the number of variables being used in the various equations. Econometric models are best used within a corporate or multiunit competitive situation and are not readily adaptable for use at the single-unit level.

5.4.2 Selecting a Forecasting Technique

All of the sales forecasting techniques discussed earlier have advantages and disadvantages based on the situation. Therefore, it is important to apply a set of selection criteria in choosing the appropriate technique. The following criteria can be used in forecasting to evaluate the situation and to select the technique that is best suited to the firm's needs:

- **The time horizon.** The period of time over which a decision will have an impact will clearly affect the selection of the most appropriate technique. Time series methods perform best for short-term (1 to 3 months) and medium-term (3 months to 2 years) forecasts, whereas qualitative techniques are best for long-term (more than 2 years) new product forecasts. Causal methods perform best in the short term, but they can also be used quite effectively for medium-term forecasts.

- **The availability of data.** The type and amount of data available can have a major effect on the choice of technique. If only historical sales data are available, then time series methods would be most appropriate. However, if very little data are available (e.g., for new products), then the qualitative techniques would be most appropriate. If data are available for a large range of variables, then causal methods can be employed, providing a good deal of information regarding relationships between variables.

- **The pattern of the data.** The majority of quantitative forecasting techniques assume a particular pattern in the data to be forecast. Time series methods work best when there are defined patterns (trends), including cycles and seasonal changes. However, causal methods and qualitative methods work best in high-growth markets and when there may be turning points in the pattern.

- **The desired level of accuracy.** The desired level of accuracy will vary based on the use of the forecast. Forecasts for control purposes tend to be short term and need to be more precise, whereas forecasts for planning tend to be longer term and can be less precise. Causal methods will normally be the most accurate in the short term under various conditions. However, time series methods can be very accurate when there is a strong trend in the data. Qualitative methods will tend to be most accurate for long-term forecasts because they use the combined forecasts of experts.

- **Cost.** It is necessary to trade off the benefits of the various methods based on the other criteria with the cost involved in using the technique. Cost will be a function of data collection, storage, and analysis. The time series methods require the least amount of data and expertise, resulting in the lowest cost. Causal methods can be costly because they require the most data and expertise, whereas qualitative methods incur a large expense for data collection.

- **Ease of application.** The ease with which the various forecasting techniques can be employed depends on factors such as the firm's computer capabilities, the expertise of its employees, and the availability of data. Time series methods are the easiest to employ, whereas causal methods and qualitative methods are somewhat more complicated.

When making decisions, managers must use all of these criteria in selecting the appropriate forecasting technique. Certain interrelationships among the criteria may help simplify the selection task. For example, when good historical data are available, time series methods provide accuracy for short-term forecasts. Choosing the best forecasting technique is important because many of the elements of the marketing plan are based on the sales forecasts.

5.5 SUMMARY OF CHAPTER OBJECTIVES

This chapter has discussed the role of marketing planning in the marketing management cycle and the essential process for formulating marketing plans. Strategic marketing planning (i.e., building on the firm's mission) focuses on goals and objectives to develop long-term plans. Conversely, tactical planning is more short term and implementation-oriented. Effective marketing planning includes both strategic and tactical components. Although there are numerous advantages and disadvantages to planning, several research studies have clearly demonstrated that firms that engage in marketing planning hold a decisive advantage over the competition and exhibit improved financial performance.

The marketing planning process includes four important stages: (1) conducting a situation analysis, (2) defining the firm's goals and objectives, (3) formulating marketing strategies and action plans, and (4) implementing action plans and evaluating performance. The situation analysis includes a historical appraisal and a SWOT analysis to determine where the firm is in terms of internal strengths and weaknesses, and external opportunities and threats. These SWOTs are the basis on which strategic marketing plans are developed.

Strengths and opportunities are leverage items on which firms develop competitive advantages. Conversely, weaknesses and threats are problem areas that must be minimized if the firm is to achieve maximum success. Goals are broad statements of what the firm seeks to accomplish. Objectives are more detailed statements of what the firm wants to achieve. Well-written objectives should state (1) what will be accomplished in measurable terms, (2) within what specific time frame it will be accomplished, (3) which individual or group will be responsible for achieving the objective, and (4) how the results will be evaluated. The firm's marketing strategies will guide the firm to achieve its objectives, and the entire process should be monitored and the performance evaluated so that necessary changes can be made.

The last section of the chapter reviewed sales forecasting, including both qualitative and quantitative techniques. Sales forecasts are crucial in establishing objectives and strategies and are used to set budgets for marketing planning. Firms must understand the advantages and disadvantages of the various forecasting techniques so they can select the appropriate technique for a given situation. The selection of a forecasting technique is based on the time horizon, availability of data, pattern of data, desired level of accuracy, cost, and ease of application.

KEY TERMS AND CONCEPTS

Causal analysis	Objectives
Consumer feedback	Position statement
Cost control data	Product development strategy
Delphi technique	Profit control data
Diversification strategy	Regression analysis
Econometric models	Sales control data
Expert opinion	Sales force forecast
Exponential smoothing	Sales forecasting
Goals	Strategic business unit (SBU)
Historical appraisal	Strategic marketing plans
Market development strategy	Strategic window
Marketing management cycle	Survey of buying intentions
Marketing planning	SWOT analysis
Market penetration strategy	Tactical marketing plans
Mission statement	Time series analysis
Moving average	Trend extrapolation

chapter review

QUESTIONS FOR REVIEW AND DISCUSSION

1. What is the marketing management cycle? Explain and discuss the major activities with which a manager must be concerned.

2. What is the difference between strategic and tactical marketing plans? Provide examples of the types of questions tactical marketing plans seek to answer.

3. What are the advantages and disadvantages associated with planning?

4. Why do marketing plans fail? What steps might a marketing manager take to increase the probability of success?

5. Illustrate and discuss the steps in the marketing planning process.

6. What is a SWOT analysis? How can SWOTs be leverage or problem items?

7. Conduct a SWOT analysis for a restaurant located in your area. How might this restaurant leverage elements of its SWOTs?

8. What are the criteria for well-written objectives?

9. What are the four product development strategy options? Provide examples and justification of hospitality and tourism firms that you believe use each of the four options.

10. What are the types of control data that are used to evaluate performance?

11. What is sales forecasting? Why is it important?

12. Explain the difference between qualitative and quantitative forecasting techniques.

chapter review

CASE STUDY

Kilts and Ale

Three investors started a new restaurant concept in Southern California. The restaurant is basically an American version of the pubs found in the United Kingdom. The waitresses wear kilts and the menu consists of popular pub fare such as bangers and mash, corned beef and cabbage, shepherd's pie, and fish and chips. In addition, the restaurant carries a wide assortment of beers from England, Ireland, Scotland, Germany, and Belgium. The atmosphere matches that of an Irish pub with darts and televisions carrying soccer games and rugby matches. The concept was popular at first and the owners opened up several restaurants. However, it seems the area has become saturated and the sales per store are starting to become stagnant. Therefore, the owners are looking for ways to increase sales for the organization.

One of the problems is that Kilts and Ale has several restaurants within a relatively small geographic area. The other issue is that a few competitors have entered the market with similar concepts. Most of the competitors are one-unit operations, so Kilts and Ale has been able to maintain a strong market share and a competitive advantage in terms of per unit costs based on volume and economies of scale. The restaurants main target markets are workers during lunch and younger couples or middle-aged couples without children during dinner and weekends. In addition, the chain has some restaurants near college campuses that are frequented mainly by students on nights and weekends. The restaurants also get good crowds of expatriates and students from the United Kingdom and Europe to watch notable soccer games and rugby matches.

The owners enjoyed strong growth and profits over the years and they are now concerned how to invest that money to maximize their return on investment. They realize that it is important to maintain some level of growth, both per store and for the chain as a whole. However, they aren't sure if it would be wise to invest more money into the same concept, or within the same geographic area.

Case Study Questions and Issues

1. How could the owners achieve growth using a market penetration strategy? Give some specific details on actions they could take.

2. How could the owners achieve growth using a market development strategy? How would they determine the new markets?

3. How could the owners achieve growth using a product development strategy?

4. How could the owners achieve growth using a diversification strategy?

5. Which of the four strategies would you recommend and why? How did you arrive at your opinion?

case study

CASE STUDY

Planning at the Westwind Resort

When Wendell Adams became the general manager at the Westwind Resort, he knew that it would be a challenge. His predecessor, Manfred Gunlock, was highly regarded and had been in the position for more than 20 years. During that time, the resort enjoyed success by building a new lodge, adding more than 1,000 time-share units, and adding more snow-making equipment that extended the ski season. During Mr. Gunlock's tenure, Westwind Resort became a four-season resort. The golf course was very good, with golfers playing more than 25,000 rounds annually. These rounds were divided evenly between resort guests and year-round permanent residents.

The resort catered to families, as it featured a modest pricing structure and a focus on providing maximum value for them. About 60 percent of the resort business came from families. Many of them had children between the ages of 5 and 17.

Wendell also knew that the resort faced challenges. Westwind Resort had begun to slip. Sales were down 4 percent, and the quality of the product–service mix was perceived to have declined slightly as well. While still profitable, the resort was not producing the level of cash flow that it had in previous years. When Wendell accepted the job, he worried that maybe Manfred Gunlock had retired because he saw trouble ahead for Westwind Resort. Wendell had taken some very positive first steps. He assembled the management team for a half-day off-site planning session. Westwind had been run in a very entrepreneurial fashion, with Mr. Gunlock making all the important decisions without much input from other managers or even the board of directors. Although this approach had been successful in the past, Wendell believed it was time to implement a more systematic approach. He wanted to develop a mission statement and a complete marketing plan for the resort.

"Without a road map, how will we know where we are going?" he told his staff during the planning meeting. Wendell had hoped to develop a mission statement during the planning meeting, but the members of his management team felt it would be better to complete an assessment of the resort's current position prior to developing a mission statement. They also believed that the mission statement should come from the board of directors, not from the managers. In the end, Wendell agreed with them, and they developed a SWOT analysis. The results of their work are shown here.

Summary of the Strengths, Weaknesses, Opportunities, and Threats (SWOTs) for Westwind Resort

Strengths

More than 1,500 year-round residents reside in private homes at the resort.

The resort has a good reputation for food and beverage service.

Westwind offers four-season sports, including skiing and golf.

The airport on the property is suitable for up to six-passenger turboprop aircraft.

There is low turnover among staff.

Westwind Resort is located approximately 90 minutes from a major metropolitan area.

The resort carries only a small amount of long-term debt. The mortgage on the lodge (built 15 years ago) is paid off.

Opportunities

Westwind has established a reputation as being a family-oriented resort.

No competing resort has an airport.

The four-season recreational offerings can be expanded.

Weaknesses

Lodge occupancy has declined slightly, to 65 percent year round. Peak weekends during the ski season are overbooked.

The average daily room rate for lodge guests has not kept pace with inflation for the past 3 years.

There has been some management turnover since the retirement of Manfred Gunlock.

Due to the location of the resort in the mid-Atlantic region, the ski season is limited to approximately 60 to 75 days.

The lodge, although only 15 years old, lacks a freshness in the decor. It appears to be older than 15 years.

Although cash flow is positive, it is lower than in past years, due to a decline in profits.

Threats

Two other four-season resorts are located within a 90-minute drive of Westwind. Both are newer and offer more amenities.

Sales of time-share units have slowed in recent years, as buyers have sought time-share units offered by major chains rather than independent resorts.

Of the three competing resorts within a three-hour driving radius, two are owned by major corporations with significant resources and borrowing capacity.

Having completed the SWOT analysis, the managers were feeling very good. This was the first time that many of them had ever been involved in such an activity. They enjoyed having the opportunity to talk about the future of the resort and how their individual contributions could positively impact the future.

Case Study Questions and Issues

1. What should the mission statement for Westwind Resort be?

2. How should the mission statement be developed? Who should review it and have input?

3. How could Wendell use the SWOTs that the management team had developed to form the basis for a marketing plan?

4. How should he lead the team in the development of a marketing plan? What should be the next steps?

5. What additional components of the marketing plan need to be developed? What additional data and input would be necessary to complete the plan?

case study

Information for
Marketing Decisions

Courtesy of mama_mia/Shutterstock.

Chapter Objectives

After studying this chapter, you should be able to:

1. List and explain the components of a marketing information system.

2. Identify primary and secondary data sources for gathering marketing information.

3. Describe the marketing research process in detail.

4. Identify ethical issues surrounding marketing research and information systems.

6.1 INTRODUCTION

Since the advent of personal computers, the world has experienced an information explosion, and all industries have made substantial advances in information collection, analysis, storage, and retrieval. The hospitality industry was very much a part of this trend. As the external environment becomes more intricate and more competitive, informational needs become more complex. Organizations that employ a systematic approach to collecting, analyzing, storing, retrieving, and using information effectively and efficiently are likely to be the most successful in the future. Without the proper types of information available on a timely basis, management is more likely to make decisions that will adversely affect the performance of the organization. The new versions of hotel reservation systems and restaurant point-of-sale systems are capable of obtaining more forms of data that can be used in making managerial decisions. Revenue-management and yield-management software are available to help organize data for pricing decisions, and statistical programs are available for analyzing data and making forecasts.

6.1.1 Marketing Information Systems

Marketing information systems (MIS)

The structure of people, equipment, and procedures used to gather, analyze, and distribute information used by an organization to make informed decisions.

A **marketing information system (MIS)** is the structure of people, equipment, and procedures used to gather, analyze, and distribute information needed by an organization. These are the data to be used as a basis for marketing decisions. *Marketing information system* is a broader and more encompassing term than *marketing research*, which is just one component of a *management information system.* Market research is focused on acquiring information for a specific research objective or project, representing a one-time use. For example, a potential restaurant owner may undertake a feasibility study and use market research to determine whether to build a new restaurant in a certain location based on the demographics of the area. Such an information-gathering study is designed to answer a very specific question: "Should we open this type of restaurant in this area?"

A marketing information system, by contrast, is part of an ongoing data-gathering process involving initial data collection as well as routine and systematic data collection procedures. For example, a hotel manager may choose to collect data by means of a zip code analysis of guest registration information to determine the geographic profile of the guests of a hotel. This systematic and routine information gathering is not intended to address one specific question but is instead part of an overall system designed to monitor the degree of marketing success that the operation is able to achieve.

A well-designed marketing information system satisfies four basic criteria:

- It must include a structured organization or established system of people and information-gathering procedures.
- The system should be designed to generate a continuous flow of information to provide accurate and current marketing information for management.
- Information should be gathered from inside and outside the organization. External information-gathering methods include consumer surveys, whereas internal information-gathering methods involve employee meetings, guest comment cards, analyzing point-of-sale data, all guest registration information, and in-house guest surveys.
- Information should be compiled so that management can use it as a basis for marketing decisions.

It would be extremely difficult for the management of a hospitality organization to make decisions without accurate and up-to-date marketing information. Professional management demands that decisions be based on sound information. Managers can reduce the uncertainty surrounding marketing decisions when valuable information is available.

A key component of an effective marketing information system is having accurate information about the environment. The foundation for this data collection is environmental scanning, which refers to a process whereby external factors that could affect an organization are continually evaluated. A conceptual model of the components of a marketing information system is shown in

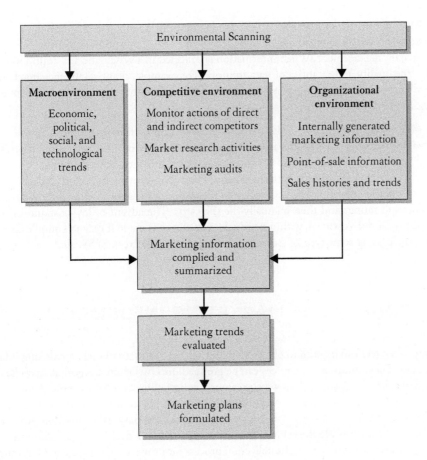

FIGURE 6.1 • **Components of a marketing information system.**

Figure 6.1. Data are generated for each of the three subenvironments (the macroenvironment, the competitive environment, and the organizational environment). The data are then compiled, summarized, and stored until needed by management. At the appropriate time, management can readily retrieve data summaries, evaluate marketing trends, and formulate marketing plans and strategies. There are three overriding objectives of a marketing information system:

1. To collect relevant data concerning each of these subenvironments.

2. To compile, summarize, and store the data.

3. To have data readily available for management on a timely basis.

6.1.2 Requirements for a Successful Marketing Information System

The basic task of gathering data is important to an organization, but an effective marketing information system is one that is able to organize this task and supply the firm with useful information. To generate data that are useful for managers and decision makers, a marketing information system should fulfill three requirements:

1. **A MIS should be objective.**   Management should be able to quantify and analyze the information gathered. Management needs as much purely objective data as possible to create metrics and make sound decisions. Too many hospitality managers rely heavily on subjective opinions for decision-making purposes, and their decisions are often incorrect. Decisions based on purely personal opinion are often less than successful when implemented. Decisions based on a combination of data and managerial insight and experience generally yield higher-quality decisions.

2. **A MIS should be systematic.**   The marketing information system is not an on–off process; it is a system that should be designed to provide a continuous stream of information source for management. When information is collected in a systematic and continuous manner, the quality and quantity of data improve. For example, many conference hotels receive feedback only from meeting planners on an ad hoc basis, rather than develop a system requiring feedback from each meeting.

3. **A MIS should be useful.**   Many studies produce information that is of little value. This is obviously not the purpose of a marketing information system. One rule of thumb to follow is this: collect, compile, and store information only if it is used actively; do not collect information and then file it away without using it. For example, many hotels still collect comment cards without inputting the results in the computer. Managers simply read over the comments and ratings and then manually file the cards. The advent of low-cost and increased-capacity hard disk storage within personal computers has made it easy to compile data to be examined using some type of analytical software (e.g., MS Excel, SPSS, etc.).

6.2 SOURCES OF MARKETING INFORMATION

A variety of sources can be used to obtain the information necessary to fuel a marketing information system. These information sources can be grouped into two main categories: secondary data and primary data. **Secondary data** were previously collected for another purpose. **Primary data** are generated for a specific purpose when the information is not available elsewhere. It is normally advisable to search for secondary data before engaging in a primary data collection process. The secondary data may provide the information necessary to make a decision, and even if they don't, they may be useful in developing the collection process for primary data. Figure 6.2 illustrates the possible sources of information for marketing decisions.

Secondary data

Data that have already been collected by another source and made available to interested parties either for free or at a reasonable cost.

Primary data

Data that are collected for a current study or project and tailored to meet the specific information needs for that study or project.

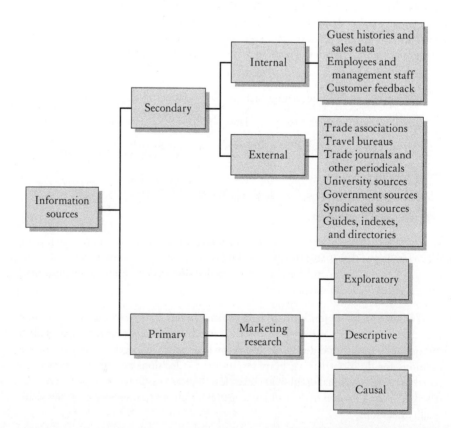

FIGURE 6.2 • Information sources.

6.2.1 Secondary Data

As already mentioned, secondary data are already available from other sources and summarize information about operations, marketing, human resource management, financial performance, and other topics of interest to management. A shrewd manager will make a thorough check of all available secondary data sources before undertaking primary data collection. The major advantages of using secondary data are:

- **Cost.** It is much less expensive to obtain information from existing sources than to develop entirely new data. These existing sources may require a nominal charge for the information, but it will be much less than the cost of undertaking primary data collection.

- **Timeliness.** Secondary data are available almost instantaneously. A manager can have access to data very quickly and does not have to wait weeks, or perhaps months, for primary data to be collected, analyzed, and summarized. By using secondary data whenever possible, a manager avoids the time and effort of developing the research design, designing the data collection instrument, and collecting the data. Instead, a manager can merely locate the appropriate source and access the information desired. This process can be completed in a few hours or days, whereas primary data collection can take weeks or months to complete.

However, secondary data collection does have the following disadvantages:

- **Limited applicability.** A manager has no assurance that information gathered by others will be applicable to a particular hospitality operation. For example, information obtained about consumer restaurant preferences in the United States might not be useful to a restaurant manager in New York City, given the unique nature of the market.

- **Information may be outdated.** Managers need current and accurate information on which to base decisions. All too often, secondary data are not as useful as they might be merely because they are not current. For example, the results of a consumer attitude survey conducted by a restaurant 4 years ago might be of limited value to a manager making plans today. This is a common problem with using U.S. Census data to get the demographics for geographic regions because the Census is only conducted every 10 years.

- **Reliability.** Whenever a hospitality operator uses secondary data as the basis for a decision, the manager runs the risk that the information may not be reliable and accurate. A manager would do well to determine who collected the data and what method of data collection was used. Information is only as good as the individuals who collect it and the methods they use. If a study is administered without following a sound scientific process, or there isn't any information given about the research process, the results and conclusions should be viewed with caution.

There are two main types of secondary data that can be used by managers within a firm (see Figure 6.2). *Internal data* exist within the firm and can be obtained with minimal time and effort. Advances in computer technology have made it easier to obtain this information and provide it to managers in a form that is useful. *External data* are not readily available within the firm. Managers must obtain these data by spending more time and/or money contacting outside sources. The Internet has made this a much easier task, but there is still a fair amount of effort involved. The various sources of internal and external data are discussed next.

6.2.1.1 INTERNAL DATA. The component of a marketing information system that is the simplest to design and implement is an internal system, or the component designed to collect data from within the organizational environment. When considering the organizational environment, management needs to be concerned only with information available from within the physical confines of the organization's units, whether they are hotels or restaurants. This component of a marketing information system requires less time and money than does the competitive environment or externally generated marketing information.

The internal component of a marketing information system is very valuable to management because it provides a wealth of information. Management has three main sources of internal marketing information: guest histories and sales data, employees and management staff, and customer feedback:

- **Guest histories and sales data.** Within a hotel operation, the minimum records that should be maintained are both individual and group guest histories. These will permit management to monitor changes in zip code origin of guests, length of stay, guest expenditure per day, and other pertinent data concerning guests. Within a restaurant operation, the records maintained should include customer counts for each meal period and sales for each menu item over a specified period of time. Many larger organizations have a sophisticated management information system in place. However, for the smaller organizations, the design of a management information system is much easier than it has been in the past. Many point-of-sale terminals interface with personal computers, making the transfer of data to off-the-shelf database management and accounting software like Microsoft Office relatively easy.

- **Employees and management staff.** All too often, hospitality management ignores the wealth of information that is informally gathered by line employees such as front desk personnel, housekeepers, telephone operators, restaurant service people, and hosts and hostesses. These individuals are in constant contact with guests, yet they are rarely asked to relay customer comments and reactions to managers. These employees represent an excellent source of information, although the information they provide may not be totally objective. It is a good idea for management to meet with employees on a regular basis to discuss problems and opportunities.

- **Customer feedback.** The focus of the marketing concept is the hospitality operation's clientele. All aspects of the entire operation should be aimed at satisfying these individuals. The purpose of using an internal marketing information system is to solicit opinions and comments from the current clientele. This can be done in a number of ways, such as having the manager talk with a few of the customers, offering a feedback system (e.g., online or toll-free number), surveying past guests/diners, or having service personnel ask the customers directly. For example, cards are placed in guest rooms or are provided to the guests upon check-out or when they have finished a meal in a restaurant. The purpose is to solicit their opinions and comments concerning the operation's quality.

All three internal sources of marketing information are very valuable. Together, they can provide a great deal of useful information with which to make decisions. Historically, hospitality managers have failed to use these sources to maximal advantage, but the current competitive situation in the hospitality industry dictates that all sources of information be used to gain a competitive advantage and to earn maximal financial rewards.

6.2.1.2 EXTERNAL DATA. Although externally generated marketing information is extremely valuable, it is normally not collected on a daily basis, as is the case with internally generated marketing information. This is due to a much larger investment of time, money, and other scarce resources required for externally generated information. Management should consider using a wide variety of sources of external marketing information. Literally thousands of sources are available, and these sources are limited only by management's own efforts to locate them. Several typical sources of external marketing information are:

- **Trade associations.** Many industries form trade groups that provide data for their members. These trade associations collect information from their members and then provide industry averages that can be used as benchmarks to measure a firm's relative performance. Some of the popular trade associations for the hospitality industry are the National Restaurant Association, the American Hotel & Lodging Association, and the Hospitality Sales and Marketing Association International. Data for the tourism industry are collected by the World Tourism Organization (WTO) and government travel bureaus.

- **Travel bureaus.** Cities, states, and countries usually form organizations that are responsible for promoting travel to the area, and often provide destination-specific research reports and statistics for members and/or the general public. Most cities have a chamber of commerce that is responsible for promoting business in the city and, in some cases, tourism as well. Larger cities and regions form convention and visitors bureaus (CVBs) for the sole purpose of promoting business and leisure travel to the region. Similarly, most states and countries have government travel and tourism bureaus that are responsible for promoting travel to that state or country.

- **Trade journals and periodicals.** Many industry, or trade, journals are available to firms. Trade associations often publish their own journals, but many other organizations publish periodicals covering certain industries. Some of the more popular hospitality publications are *Restaurants & Institutions, Restaurant Hospitality, Nation's Restaurant News, Restaurant Business, Lodging Hospitality, Lodging Magazine,* and *Hotel & Motel Management.* The articles in these publications provide information on new products and advertising campaigns, as well as current trends in the industry.

- **Other periodicals.** In addition to trade journals that specialize in a certain industry, other publications cover business in a variety of industries. Some of the more popular business publications that cover the hospitality and tourism industries are *BusinessWeek, Wall Street Journal, Fortune, Barron's,* and *Forbes.*

- **Internet.** The growth in both the quantity and quality of information available on the Internet is well documented. Using one or more of the available Internet search engines will uncover information, some of which will be highly valuable for managers. A key consideration for managers is being able to determine the accuracy and usefulness of information gathered from the Internet.

- **University sources.** Universities and colleges have well-stocked libraries that can be a valuable resource for firms in the area. These institutions often have access to many of the other sources of external data. In addition, universities and colleges form centers to research specific areas such as hospitality. This information is often free to the public or available for a reasonable fee.

- **Government sources.** Local, state, and federal governments maintain detailed data on all aspects of the economy; the data are free or available for a nominal fee. The U.S. Census gathers detailed information about the population and retail business, and the *Statistical Abstract of the United States* contains similar information in abbreviated form. Census and statistical documents are now available in electronic form, enabling quicker searches and data retrieval. The federal government also collects information about foreign countries and provides specialists to answer specific questions and address inquiries.

- **Syndicated services.** Firms such as Harris and Gallup polls, Target Group Index, Nielsen, and W. R. Simmons specialize in collecting and distributing marketing information for a fee. These syndicated services provide information about consumer profiles and shopping behaviors, consumer responses to sales promotions and advertising, and consumer attitudes and preferences. This information is useful in focusing on market segments using aggregate data. These services often advertise in trade publications and marketing periodicals.

- **Guides, indexes, and directories.** Other valuable sources of external information include guides, indexes, and directories that are available at most university libraries and larger public libraries. Guides such as the *Business Periodicals Index* provide references by subject matter for articles in major journals and trade publications. Also, most major publications such as the *Wall Street Journal* and the *New York Times* have indexes that provide references by subject matter for articles that appeared in those particular sources. Finally, Lexis-Nexis is an excellent online resource for data about the performance of publicly traded companies.

There is a good deal of external information available for hospitality and travel firms. Therefore, it is important to create a systematic process for gathering information. The following process should be used when collecting external information:

- **State the known facts.** Before undertaking an external study, make an inventory of all data currently available. Managers can then decide what additional information is needed, and how to collect it, based on a cost/benefit analysis.

- **List specific goals and objectives.** After a base of information has been established, a plan must be formulated. Goals and objectives are the basis for this plan and they guide the rest of the data gathering process.

- **Collect all relevant data.**   At this point the actual legwork must be done to ensure an adequate sample. The information must be gathered in a way that ensures it is both valid and reliable. *Validity* is the degree to which the data gathered measure what they are supposed to measure. *Reliability* is the degree with which data consistently measure whatever they are designed to measure.

- **Summarize the data and analyze the situation.**   No matter which data collection method is used, some type of summary and analysis must be done to reduce the data into a manageable package. Then management can access the organized information and use it for a wide variety of decisions.

6.2.2 Primary Data

Primary data consist of original research done to answer current questions regarding a specific operation. For example, a food service manager may attempt to determine consumer attitudes toward new menu offerings or to solicit consumer perceptions of increased menu prices or different portion sizes. This type of data is very pertinent to an individual operation but may not be applicable to other situations.

The advantages of using primary data include the following:

- **Specificity.**   These data are tailored to one operation and can provide excellent information for decision-making purposes.

- **Practicality.**   Primary data can provide solid real-life information and a practical foundation to be used in the decision-making process.

However, using primary data has the following disadvantages:

- **Cost.**   For an individual manager, gathering primary data is extremely expensive. To gather primary data even from a city of 100,000 people may prove to be a monumental task for an operator and may cost too much in time and money.

- **Time lag.**   Marketing decisions often must be made quickly, yet it requires a good deal of time to conduct a thorough information-gathering study. While a manager is collecting the data, the competition may be driving the hospitality or tourism operation into bankruptcy.

- **Duplication.**   Although primary data are geared toward a specific operation, other sources of existing data may closely duplicate the information collected and would therefore be appropriate for decision-making purposes. This duplication of effort is very expensive, and primary data collection should therefore be undertaken only after all secondary data sources have been exhausted.

In general, the advantages of using secondary data tend to be the disadvantages of using primary data, and vice versa. Table 6.1 provides a comparison of primary and secondary data collection methods. As mentioned earlier, before collecting primary data, it is advisable to perform a secondary-data search to determine the necessity and scope of a primary-data collection effort. The next section covers the marketing research process that is followed when collecting primary data.

CHARACTERISTIC	SECONDARY DATA	PRIMARY DATA
Cost to collect data	Low	High
Time frame to collect data	Short	Long
Specificity of data	Low	High
Reliability of data	Unknown	High
Timeliness of data	Can be outdated	Recent

TABLE 6.1 • Comparison of Primary and Secondary Data Collection Methods

6.3   THE MARKETING RESEARCH PROCESS

The **marketing research process** is undertaken to answer a wide variety of questions, which might include: "Where do our guests come from? How frequently do people dine out in this area? In what types of restaurants do they most frequently dine?" In addition, hospitality and tourism organizations might want to address more specific questions such as the menu items to be offered, the price to charge, and the proper mix of transient and group travelers. Either way, it is necessary to use a systematic process for conducting research.

Conducting marketing research is not an inexpensive proposition, and when research is undertaken, care must be taken to ensure that proper methods are used. This is true whether the hospitality organization conducts its own marketing research or relies on external consultants. Marketing research data are only as good as the methodology used. If a poor methodology is used, the results are not likely to describe the situation accurately, and marketing decisions based on this information are not likely to be very appropriate. Figure 6.3 contains the five steps involved in the marketing research process.

> **Marketing research process**
> A process used to collect data about marketing programs, external environments, and consumer markets in an attempt to improve the quality of marketing decisions.

6.3.1   Step 1: Define the Problem

Before conducting any marketing research, a firm must decide whether marketing research is necessary and, if so, what kind. In general, marketing research should be undertaken if it addresses a specific problem that could affect your business—if it helps in selecting between alternatives for achieving marketing objectives, if it assists in gaining a competitive advantage, or if it provides useful information on your markets.[1] Marketing research may not be needed if the information is already available, there is insufficient time for marketing research, resources are not available, or costs of conducting the research outweigh the potential benefits of having the information.

If the decision is made to proceed with the marketing research, the research problem should be clearly defined. First, it is necessary to view the problem from the marketing manager's perspective. Normally, a problem is brought to the attention of a manager when there is a decrease in a performance measure such as sales volume, profit, or market share. It is important not to mistake

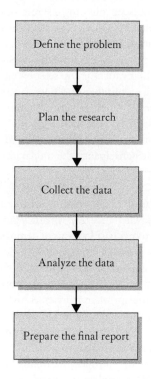

FIGURE 6.3 • **The marketing research process.**

this for the problem; instead, recognize it as a symptom of an underlying problem. For example, if a hotel's occupancy rate has suddenly fallen, there could be a number of causes. A new competitor may have opened, current competitors may be discounting prices or increasing advertising expenditures, consumers may be dissatisfied with the hotel, there might be construction in the immediate area, or there might be a downturn in the economy. Any one of these factors, or a combination of them, could be the cause of the decrease in performance.

6.3.2 Step 2: Plan the Research

Research design

A master plan specifying the methods and procedures for collecting and analyzing the needed information.

Exploratory research

Research used to determine the general nature of the problem.

Secondary data analysis

The process of reviewing existing information that is related to the research problem.

Focus group

A group of 8 to 12 people who represent the population being studied and are brought together in an informal setting to discuss the issues surrounding a research problem.

Descriptive research

Research that helps answer the questions who, what, where, when, why, and how.

Cross-sectional study

A study used to measure the population of interest at one point in time.

Longitudinal study

A study used to measure the same population over an extended period of time.

The second step in the marketing research process involves planning the research design for obtaining the desired information to address the research problem. The **research design** is basically a master plan specifying the methods and procedures for collecting and analyzing the needed information. There are three main categories of research designs from which to choose, based on the objectives of the research: exploratory research, descriptive research, and causal research.

6.3.2.1 EXPLORATORY RESEARCH. **Exploratory research** is used to gain background information when a firm doesn't have a good understanding of the nature of the problem. It can also be used to obtain additional information about a topic and to generate hypotheses that state the relationships between two or more variables. This research tends to be informal and unstructured, and it is mainly used to gain background information, define terms, and clarify problems. The hypotheses that are generated using exploratory research can be tested in future research efforts. Some of the more common methods for conducting exploratory research are secondary data analysis, experience surveys, case analysis, and focus groups. **Secondary data analysis** is the process of reviewing existing information that is related to the research problem.

Experience surveys are similar to the qualitative methods discussed in the sales forecasting section of Chapter 5. Basically, information is gathered from individuals who are believed to be knowledgeable about the research topic. *Case analysis* refers to the use of information about a situation that resembles the current situation surrounding the current research problem. Hospitality firms could benefit from the experiences of other firms in their industry, or of firms in other industries that faced similar circumstances.

One of the most common methods of exploratory research is the **focus group**. Focus groups consist of 8 to 12 people who represent the population being studied and are brought together in an informal setting to discuss the issues surrounding the research problem. The sessions generally last from 1 to 2 hours and are guided by a moderator who ensures that all the group's members give input and that all the pertinent topics are covered. Focus groups are valuable for testing new product designs and service concepts, testing advertising campaigns, and gaining insight into the market's basic needs and attitudes. Many focus group sessions are videotaped so they can be examined in more detail at a later date by a number of different people. The potential weaknesses of focus groups are that, given the small number of participants, the group may not completely represent the population of interest. Also, because the groups are unstructured, the information provided during the session is often very subjective and open to interpretation. Finally, it may be difficult and expensive to recruit the participants, the moderator, and a facility for a focus group.

6.3.2.2 DESCRIPTIVE RESEARCH. The second category of research design, **descriptive research**, is concerned with answering the basic questions of who buys the product, what customers do with the product, where they buy, when they buy, why they buy, and how they buy. Primarily, the researcher is trying to profile the customer base in terms of demographics, psychographics, attitudes, and purchasing behavior. There are basically two types of studies that can be used to collect this information: cross-sectional studies and longitudinal studies. A **cross-sectional study** measures the population at one point in time; it provides a snapshot of the population. This type of study is normally used to address a particular problem when it arises. A **longitudinal study** is used to measure the same population over an extended period of time. Generally, these studies use the same sample, referred to as a *panel,* and collect the same information over time (e.g., once a year). Longitudinal data are useful in determining trends and changes in consumer needs and attitudes. For example, many firms offering syndicated services will track the trends in an industry by constructing and maintaining a panel of consumers who complete an annual survey.

6.3.2.3 CAUSAL RESEARCH Causal research focuses on cause-and-effect relationships that are pertinent to a research problem. A series of if–then statements can be used to model certain elements of the hospitality service. For example, a hospitality firm may want to examine how a particular change in the marketing mix affects sales, market share, and/or customer satisfaction. The following relationships could be tested. If the quality of food is improved, customer satisfaction will increase. If on-time performance improves, market share will increase. If an additional salesperson is hired, occupancy rate will increase.

The potential benefits of understanding causal relationships are great. Firms could design better products, create effective advertising campaigns, and set prices that will maximize revenue. Unfortunately, many factors affect the consumer decision-making process, either alone or in combination, and it is almost impossible to understand them completely. In fact, many researchers argue that there is no such thing as true causality. Regardless, as managers' understanding of consumer behavior increases, the firm's performance will improve.

Causal research
Research used to define cause-and-effect relationships between variables.

6.3.3 Step 3: Collect the Data

Two major decisions must be made during this stage in the marketing research process. They involve choosing a data collection method and determining the sampling plan. Once a data collection method is chosen, the data collection instrument, or form (e.g., survey questionnaire or observation form) must be designed to fit that method and the research objectives. Designing data collection forms is discussed in more detail in the Appendix. Weaknesses in any of these areas can have a profound impact on the reliability and validity of the results. As previously noted, *reliability* refers to the consistency of responses to questions, and *validity* refers to the accuracy of the measure. It is possible to have reliability without validity, but for a measure to be valid, it must also be reliable. For example, a poorly written question can solicit consistent responses, but it may not be a valid measure of the construct that is being studied. Even with the best sample, a poorly designed collection form will result in inaccurate data. Similarly, a well-designed collection form is useless if the sample does not represent the population.

6.3.3.1 DATA COLLECTION METHODS. After the research design has been planned, it is necessary to determine the best method for collecting the data. The three possible methods for obtaining primary data are observation, surveys, and experiments. The appropriate method will depend on the research objectives and the research design. Exploratory research is most often accomplished using observation and surveys. Descriptive research uses all of the data collection methods, but it relies very heavily on information received from surveys. Finally, experiments are used almost exclusively for causal research. However, observation and surveys are also used to obtain information to study causal relationships.

Observation involves watching consumers and making organized notes to document or record the observed behavior. When doing this type of research, it is important that all individuals acting as observers record their observations in the same manner. *Direct observation* refers to the process of observing behavior as it actually occurs, by either a person or a mechanical device. For example, hotels and restaurants use "mystery shoppers" to experience the service firsthand and record their observations. Similarly, some amusement park chains have cameras and employees that are used to observe the behavior of the employees to make sure they are paying attention and adhering to safety procedures. *Indirect observation* refers to the process of observing behavior after the fact. For example, restaurants can examine the uneaten portion of meals to determine the eating behaviors of their guests. This *physical trace evidence* is useful in deciding which meal items to include and which ones to eliminate, or reduce the portion size. In most cases, the observation is disguised so as not to affect the consumer's behavior (e.g., observing visitors in line at an amusement park); however, there are instances, such as food testing, when subjects know they are being observed. One of the disadvantages of observation is that subjects' behavior can be difficult to interpret, especially the attitudes and motivation behind it.

Observation
A process involving watching consumers and documenting their behavior.

Surveys involve asking consumers to provide information regarding the issues surrounding the research problem on a questionnaire or comment card. The survey can be filled in by the researcher, completed with the aid of a computer, or completed by the respondent (self-administered). When used properly, the survey method can gather a great deal of useful information.

Surveys
Data collection instruments designed to gather specific information for a particular research problem through a series of questions and statements.

CHARACTERISTIC	DIRECT MAIL SURVEYS	TELEPHONE SURVEYS	PERSONAL INTERVIEWS	ELECTRONIC SURVEYS
Cost per respondent	Low	Medium	High	Low
Speed of response	Low	High	Medium	High
Response rate	Low	Medium	High	Low
Interviewer bias	Low	Medium	High	Low
Allows feedback	Low	Medium	High	Medium
Ability to handle sensitive topics	High	Medium	Low	Medium
Ability to handle complex questions	Medium	Low	High	Medium

TABLE 6.2 • Comparison of Survey Data Collection Methods

The survey method is adaptable to a variety of situations and is relatively inexpensive. Surveys may be accomplished using a number of different methods, including telephone surveys, direct mail surveys, personal interviews, or electronic surveys. A summary of the advantages and disadvantages of these methods is provided in Table 6.2.

Telephone surveys are the most common method of survey data collection because they are the easiest to implement and produce very quick results. Another major advantage of this type of survey is the cost. No travel is involved, and a single individual may contact and solicit answers from a large number of people in a fairly short period of time. However, there is no face-to-face contact, and people are often not inclined to answer questions over the phone, especially if they are complicated. Therefore, the reliability of the answers received over the telephone can be an issue. Another example is the national "do not call" list that prohibits telemarketers from contacting individuals who chose to be on the list, which can lead to a biased sample. However, political polls and noncommercial surveys are not included in the prohibition.

Direct mail surveys offer ease of completion, respondent anonymity, and a low cost per response. However, there are a few major drawbacks. First, the response rate is normally quite low, and the collection process is slow. Often, less than 25 percent of the surveys are properly completed and returned, and it may take up to 3 months, and 2 or 3 mailings, to obtain an adequate sample. With such a low response rate, there is a risk that the individuals who returned the surveys do not represent the population, and so any decisions based on the results could be biased. Second, direct mail surveys do not allow any in-depth questioning, and they do not allow for follow-up questions. The respondent merely sees the written questions and has no opportunity for clarification. This may make it more difficult to generate answers that reflect the complexity of opinion within the targeted market segments.

Personal interviews allow more in-depth questioning. An interviewer normally uses a guide sheet to direct the interview and may adjust the questioning to focus on a point of special interest or to follow up an answer given by the respondent. There are two drawbacks to personal interviews as a surveying technique. First, the major drawback is cost per interview. It is extremely expensive to have an interviewer spend a long period of time with each individual in order to gather information. An in-depth interview can last as long as an hour; hence, the number of individuals who can be interviewed is limited, and the cost per interview is quite high. The cost of travel also makes this type of survey expensive. Second, a good deal of training must be done for interviewers to be effective. In addition, supervision is required in order to have control over the interviewers. *Intercept interviews* are a form of personal interview conducted in major traffic areas such as shopping malls, in an attempt to eliminate some of the drawbacks associated with cost and speed of response.

Electronic surveys are increasing in popularity because of the availability of e-mail address lists and advances in technology. There are two basic types of electronic surveys: web-based surveys and e-mail surveys. Web-based surveys typically provide immediate feedback for the researcher, as well as simplify the data coding and editing process. E-mail surveys are either embedded within the e-mail message or attached to a message. They must be completed and returned to the researcher, and require data input and editing. Also, links to web-based surveys can be contained within an e-mail message. The major advantages of electronic surveys are the low cost per respondent to collect data (less than direct mail), the speed of response (most responses are collect within 2 weeks), and the ease of data input (if web-based). The major drawbacks of this approach are that e-mail addresses can be outdated and often filter incoming mail, and the response rate is low because of all the clutter and spam mail. However, this method combines the advantages of direct mail and telephone surveys. Popular web-based survey programs such as SurveyMonkey and Qualtrics are readily available to any size organization or individual, and the programs are easy to use.

Comment cards are a particular form of survey that is frequently used in the hospitality and tourism industry. They resemble a combination of an intercept based on the location and the direct mail survey based on its self-administered nature. The main objective of comment cards is to gather information from customers about their lodging or dining experience to determine if they are satisfied with the service. The card is normally placed in the guest's room in a hotel or on the table in a restaurant. This allows the customer to provide immediate feedback regarding the service and its delivery. In addition to immediate feedback, comment cards also have other benefits: (1) they are less expensive than other survey methods, (2) they can be tailored to the needs of the organization, (3) they can be standardized for easy analysis and comparisons, and (4) customer needs can be tracked over time. Figures 6.4a and 6.4b are examples of typical restaurant and hotel comment cards.

There are also some disadvantages associated with comment cards: (1) there is often a low response rate and the sample may not be representative of the population, (2) they can deal with only a limited number of issues because of their short length, and (3) there can be problems with reliability and validity. However, it is possible to improve the response rate by handing them out personally (e.g., wait staff or front-desk staff), keeping them simple (e.g., using closed-ended questions), leaving a space for comments, offering an incentive, and/or promising confidentiality (e.g., use a collection box or postage-paid return).

When conducting experiments, a researcher divides the sample of people into groups and exposes each group to a different treatment while trying to control for other extraneous factors that may affect the outcome. The treatment variable is referred to as the *independent variable,* and the outcome of the treatment is measured using a *dependent variable* because changes in the

Experiments

A data collection process used to compare a control group with one or more treatment groups to determine if there are any differences attributed to the variable(s) being tested.

Thank you for sharing your thoughts with us. Please return this card and place it in the comment box located at the entrance. We look forward to serving you again!

	Excellent	Good	Fair	Poor
Seating	☐	☐	☐	☐
Employee friendliness	☐	☐	☐	☐
Promptness of service	☐	☐	☐	☐
Menu variety	☐	☐	☐	☐
Food quality	☐	☐	☐	☐
Atmosphere	☐	☐	☐	☐
Value for price paid	☐	☐	☐	☐

What time of day did you visit the restaurant?_____

What day of the week did you visit the restaurant?_____

What meal did you order?_____

How could we make your experience more enjoyable?_____

FIGURE 6.4a • Restaurant comment card.

Please help us improve our service . . .

	Excellent	Good	Fair	Poor
How would you rate our hotel overall?	☐	☐	☐	☐

How would you rate the following?

Room reservation as requested	☐	☐	☐	☐
Check-in speed and efficiency	☐	☐	☐	☐
Cleanliness of room	☐	☐	☐	☐
Décor of your room	☐	☐	☐	☐
Check-out speed and efficiency	☐	☐	☐	☐
Value of room for price paid	☐	☐	☐	☐
Parking	☐	☐	☐	☐

How would you rate our hotel team in terms of friendly and efficient service?

Reservation staff	☐	☐	☐	☐
Front-desk clerk	☐	☐	☐	☐
Housekeeping staff	☐	☐	☐	☐
Telephone operators	☐	☐	☐	☐
Bellman	☐	☐	☐	☐
Management staff	☐	☐	☐	☐

Additional comments: _____
_____
_____

If a member of our staff was particularly helpful, please let us know so we can show that person our appreciation: _____

What did he/she do? _____
_____

What was your room number? _____

Optional:

Name: _____

Address: _____
_____

Please leave this card in your room or place it in the comment box in the lobby. Thank you for your time.

FIGURE 6.4b • Hotel comment card.

variable are dependent on changes in the treatment. In other words, there is a cause-and-effect relationship in which the independent variable is the cause and the dependent variable is the effect. Experiments can be conducted in the *field* under normal conditions or in a *laboratory* setting, where extraneous factors can be more easily controlled. For example, Marriott International experimented with its sales force to find the best approach. The hotel chain allowed some salespeople to work from home and sell multiple properties rather than sell one property from an office in the hotel. The performance of these two groups in terms of volume and revenues was then compared to determine the best approach based on the geographic area.

Test marketing is a common form of field experiment consisting of manipulations in the marketing mix at certain locations that represent the competitive environment and consumer profile of the overall population. For example, all of the national quick service restaurant chains use cities across the country as test market centers. In each city, the companies will introduce or "test-market" new products or marketing mix changes to obtain customer reactions and to project future sales. Sales may then be compared with those at other test-market centers to determine the popularity of new and old items and to decide which products will be introduced systemwide. Test markets are common for new restaurant concepts as well. Darden Restaurants' launched Seasons 52 in 2003. The marketing mix and menu were first tested near corporate headquarters in Orlando, Florida, and then expanded to other areas in Florida and Atlanta, Georgia, once the company was comfortable with the business model. After more than a decade, the concept is now located in several other states such as California, Massachusetts, New York, New Jersey, Texas, Alabama, Illinois, and Indiana.

6.3.3.2 DETERMINING THE SAMPLING PLAN.   *Sampling* is the process of using a small subset of the population to obtain information that can be used to make inferences about the total population. A population is the entire group, or target market, that is being studied for the purpose of answering the research questions. A sample is the subset of the population that is drawn in such a way so as to represent the overall population. Normally, the cost of a census, or the investigation of the entire population, is prohibitive, and the survey would take too much time to complete. Therefore, a sample is used in hopes that the results can be applied to the overall population. Whenever a sample is used instead of a census, there are some differences between the sample results and actual population measures. This difference is referred to as sampling error. The Appendix at the end of this chapter covers the sampling process in detail and explains how to determine the appropriate sample size. A sampling unit is the basic level of investigation. The sample unit could be an individual, a household, or an organization. For example, studies in the hospitality industry could look at a hotel's guest, a specific hotel property, or a hotel chain.

6.3.4   Step 4: Analyze the Data

Two basic forms of statistical analysis are used in marketing research: descriptive analysis and inferential analysis. Descriptive analysis uses aggregate data to describe the "average" or "typical" respondent, and to what degree respondents vary from this profile. The measures used for central tendency are the mode, median, and mean. *Mode* refers to the value that occurs most often. *Median* refers to the value that represents the middle of an ordered set of responses. In other words, the responses are ordered from high to low, or low to high, and then the middle value is determined. *Mean* refers to the arithmetic average, or the sum of all responses divided by the number of responses. The measures of variability are the frequency distribution, range, and standard deviation. The *frequency distribution* provides the counts for each value in the set of responses. The *range* is calculated by taking the difference between the highest value and the lowest value of the ordered set of responses. The *standard deviation* is a measure of variance between the observed values and the mean for the set of responses.

The second form of statistical analysis is inferential analysis, which is used to test hypotheses and estimate population parameters using sample statistics. Statistics such as the *t-statistic* and the *z-statistic* are used to test for differences between the sample mean and a hypothesized mean. These test statistics can also be used to test for differences between two groups, and *analysis of variance (ANOVA)* is used to test for differences between more than two groups based on their respective means and variances. *Correlations* and *cross-tabulations* are used to determine if an association exists between two variables. If so, the two variables will vary together either directly or inversely. Finally, *multivariate statistics* can be used to test for relationships between more than two variables. These forms of statistical analysis are beyond the scope of this text, and interested readers should refer to a marketing research text for more details.[2]

Test marketing
A common form of field experiment consisting of manipulations in the marketing mix at certain locations that represent the competitive environment and consumer profile of the overall target population.

Population
The entire group, or target market, that is being studied for the purpose of answering the research questions.

Sample
The subset of the population that is drawn in such a way so as to represent the overall population.

Census
A sample consisting of the entire population.

Sampling error
The difference between the sample results and actual population measures.

Sampling unit
The basic level of investigation in a research study.

Descriptive analysis
An analysis using aggregate data to describe the "average" or "typical" respondent, and to what degree respondents vary from this profile.

Inferential analysis
An analysis of cause-and-effect relationships used to test hypotheses.

6.3.5 Step 5: Prepare the Final Report

After the research is completed and the data are analyzed, it is necessary to prepare a final report that provides a detailed outline of the research design, summarizes the results, and provides some conclusions or recommendations. The researcher should consider the audience for the presentation when preparing the final report. Both written and oral reports have been criticized for things such as excessive length, impractical recommendations, and the use of complex terms. These mistakes can be avoided if the researcher determines the personality and requirements of the audience and takes them into consideration when preparing the report. For example, many clients prefer to be shown the results summarized in tables and charts rather than to read detailed discussions including statistics.

There are some guidelines that can be followed when preparing the final report that will improve the probability of client satisfaction, as well as success. First, the research team should plan to devote an adequate amount of time to preparing the report. In fact, the time for report preparation should be included in the time frame outlined in the proposal. Second, the original proposal should be examined and the research objectives should be addressed in the final report. Third, the research team must understand the needs of the audience and determine the content and length that are appropriate for the report. Fourth, it is important to anticipate possible objections or concerns and to address them in the report or presentation.

Most written reports follow a standard outline. The report normally begins with an executive or management summary that clearly and concisely states the project's objectives, methods, conclusions, and recommendations. Next, the actual body of the report begins with a detailed discussion of the research objectives, followed by an explanation of the research methodology, including its advantages and limitations. The research methodology section contains the elements of the research plan, including questionnaire design, sampling, data collection, and type of analysis. The next section contains a detailed description of the results, with references to charts, figures, and tables that summarize the results. Finally, the report ends with the conclusions, implications, and recommendations of the research team. Any tables, charts, figures, or other supplemental materials will appear in an appendix at the end of the report. Examples of supplemental materials would be an *annotated questionnaire* containing the results for each question, or a list of responses to open-ended questions.

6.4 DESTINATION RESEARCH

The goal of research is to reduce the uncertainty surrounding managerial decisions. These decisions are made on a regular basis and included in the organization's marketing plan. There are four main objectives of research regarding tourism destinations:

1. What is the profile of the visitors, or potential visitors, that compose the target market(s) for the destination?

2. What is the overall value, or economic impact, provided by the target market(s)?

3. What are the attributes or characteristics associated with the destination that attract visitors, and how does the destination compare with other destinations on those attributes?

4. How should the marketing mix be composed for each target market? For example, what types of marketing communications should be used to reach the target markets, and what should the message be?

Various research designs and methodologies may be used to obtain the necessary information to answer these questions. However, it is important for the destination marketing organization to weigh the benefits of collecting additional information against the costs of collecting it, in order to choose the appropriate cutoff point in order to make a decision.

Some of the information is needed on a continual basis (e.g., monthly visitor arrivals, occupancy rates, and average daily rates), whereas other studies are needed only on a periodic basis (e.g., economic impact and forecasting, destination image, and inquiry conversion). Most of the information that is required on a continual basis is obtained through basic tracking and reporting methods. The more complicated studies that are conducted periodically are discussed in the following sections.

6.4.1 Economic Impact Studies

Tourism in many countries or regions is an industry that brings significant economic effects to the local economy. Tourism not only contributes to the local economy monetarily by increasing foreign exchange and the purchase of goods and services but it also creates many job opportunities. In addition, tourism generates indirect effects to other industries that supply and support various tourism activities. There are several ways to estimate the economic impacts of tourism. An input–output model that multiplies total tourist expenditures by regional multipliers is the most commonly used method. The primary source of economic impact from tourism is derived from tourists' expenditures during their trips. The major categories of tourist expenditures are transportation, accommodations, meals, shopping, and tourist attractions. Changes in tourist expenditures can bring three types of effects to a local economy:

1. **Direct effect:** This refers to the effect brought to establishments and employees where tourists spend their money.

2. **Indirect effect:** This results from the need of tourism sectors to purchase from other industries in order to produce its output. Continuous interactions among sectors will be generated by these purchases until the money respent becomes negligible.

3. **Induced effect:** This is the income level increase as a result of tourism. A portion of the increased income will be respent on the final goods and services within the local economy.

Economic impacts of tourism come from the spending of tourists within the local area, change in regional incomes and changes in employment. To assess economic impacts, the local region is generally defined as all counties within a given radius of the destination, usually 30 to 60 miles. Satellite accounts and visitor survey input–output models are the two principal methods used for estimating the economic impacts generated from tourism.

The **satellite account method** identifies an overall estimate of tourism contribution to state and national economies by utilizing data from a country's System of National Accounts. Using existing economic data for the components of tourism in an accepted system of accounts is the advantage of the satellite accounting approach. However, the disadvantage is that it is relatively more difficult to gather complete information necessary to extract tourism activity from national economic accounts. Furthermore, it is more difficult to apply this method at the national level or for subcategories of tourism activities.

The **input–output model** is a more common approach for estimating the economic impacts of tourism by directly surveying tourists to obtain data on their spending habits. The direct survey method is more applicable in estimating the impacts of a particular action on the local economy. By adapting appropriate economic ratios and multipliers, estimation of tourist expenditures can be transformed into the resulting jobs and income of a given region. The basic equations of the input–output model are as follows:

$$\text{Tourist spending} = \text{Number of visitors} \times \text{Average spending per visitor}$$

$$\text{Economic impact} = \text{Number of visitors} \times \text{Average spending per visitor} \times \text{Regional multipliers}$$

Another more complicated and rigorous approach to estimate the income and jobs generated by tourism is the use of **multiplier analysis**. There are three types of multipliers:

1. **Output multiplier:** The ratio of change in total productive output of the total economy brought by the initial change in tourist expenditure

2. **Income multiplier:** The change in income, such as wages, salaries, and profits of the economy, resulting from the change in tourist expenditure

3. **Employment multiplier:** The change of job opportunities associated with the change in total tourist expenditure

Satellite account method
The process used to identify an overall estimate of tourism contribution to the state and national economies by utilizing data from a country's System of National Accounts.

Input–output model
A common approach for estimating the economic impacts of tourism by directly surveying tourists to obtain data on their spending habits.

Multiplier analysis
Procedure to estimate the additional impact generated in a tourist destination for every dollar spent on the tourist product itself.

The purpose of using multiplier analysis is to estimate the additional impact generated in a tourist destination for every dollar spent on the tourist product itself. A greater amount of local/regional resource utilization and lower proportion of imported goods that supply local consumption and production will result in a higher multiplier. Figure 6.5 provides a list of example questions that can be used in obtaining the necessary information for conducting an economic impact analysis.

The goal is to obtain information on total spending for the trip and then, using the information on the size of the party and the length of the trip, to convert the figures into per person per day so that the information can be compared over time and across market segments. In addition, there are often questions to determine the type of accommodations, attractions visited, where the respondent shopped and dined. This information is useful to the CVB in recruiting members, obtaining government funding, and communicating the value of the organization to the local economy.

6.4.2 Destination Image Studies

Destination choice is influenced by an individual's perceptions of alternative possibilities (i.e., cities, regions, or countries). Therefore, it is important for a destination that wants to attract visitors to promote a coherent image. *Destination image* refers to the impressions a person holds about a destination in which she or he does not reside. Images can be formed through contact or experience, or they can be developed in the absence of contact. Perceptions about destination image are formed through advertising and promotions, news accounts, discussions with friends or relatives, travel agents, and past experiences. Destinations cannot easily change their physical attributes, such as the landscape or climate, so they must build their images around unique attributes that provide them with some type of sustainable competitive advantage. The destination, including its attractions, should be designed to meet the needs of the target market. Therefore, the diagnosis of the destination's strengths and weaknesses on salient attributes, relative to competitive attractions, is critical in designing the tourism offerings and programs to market them.

---

1. How long did you stay in the Pioneer Valley?
   _____ days _____ nights

2. Where did you stay during your visit?
   (Please name the lodging facility)

   ☐ Hotel _____

   ☐ Family/friends _____

   ☐ Bed & Breakfast _____

   ☐ Campground_____

   ☐ Other: _____

3. How many people were in your party?
   Adults _____ Children _____

4. Approximately how much did you spend on the following:

   Accommodations $_____

   Food $_____

   Tourist Attractions $_____

   Shopping $_____

   Transportation $_____

   Other (please specify) $_____

FIGURE 6.5 • Economic impact sample questions.

How would you rate _____ on each of the following destination attributes?

	Poor				Excellent
Accommodations	1	2	3	4	5
Scenery	1	2	3	4	5
Shopping Facilities	1	2	3	4	5
Restaurants	1	2	3	4	5
Climate/Weather	1	2	3	4	5
Tourist Attractions	1	2	3	4	5
Historical Appeal	1	2	3	4	5
Safety and Security	1	2	3	4	5

FIGURE 6.6 • Destination image sample question.

Figure 6.6 provides an example of a question that could be included in a questionnaire used in a destination image study.

The example includes only eight attributes, but studies often include as many as 15 to 20 different attributes representing both tangible and intangible elements of the destination. Also, it is popular to put the attributes in the form of a statement (e.g., "San Antonio has many attractions" or "San Antonio has a good nightlife") and ask the respondent to provide his or her level of agreement on a scale ranging from "strongly agree" to "strongly disagree." Either way, it is possible to obtain respondents' perceptions of the destination on the attributes provided. The mean rating score for each attribute can provide the basic information regarding perceptions, or more sophisticated statistical methods like factor analysis and multidimensional scaling can be used to identify useful dimensions and create a perceptual map. The perceptual map can compare alternative destinations if the perceptions are gathered for them as well. These data are combined with the demographics and travel behaviors of the respondents to segment the market based on visitor profiles (e.g., seniors, families, etc.).

6.4.3 Conversion Studies

The purpose of the conversion study is to measure the effectiveness of the destination marketing organization's advertising and promotion. The most important performance measure is the number of inquiries that are converted to visitors. Inquiries come to convention and visitors bureaus through three main sources: telephone, website, and drop cards placed in magazines. The goal is to measure the conversion rate on each of the three methods of inquiry to determine the most effective means of reaching the target market. The most popular advertising and promotion pieces for conventions and visitors bureaus are the visitor's guide, magazine ads, and television ads, depending on the overall budget. In addition, there might be a meeting planner's guide, but many CVBs offer them only in electronic versions. This seems to be the preference for meeting planners because some of them deal with a large number of destinations and hotels, and they don't want to maintain large volumes of guides in hard copy form. Figure 6.7 provides a sample list of questions that can be used to measure the conversion rate for leisure travelers.

These questions obtain information on how respondents first became aware of the destination, if they decided to visit after receiving the promotion materials, the reason they didn't visit, and what other destinations they might have visited. In addition, there are questions about the purpose of the trip and how the visitors used the guide. Other questions that are important are the length of stay and the likelihood of visitation in the near future (return or first time). Finally, it should be noted that the information for all three types of studies can be part of one questionnaire: economic impact, destination image, and conversion. The questions for all three studies can be combined with questions about trip behaviors and visitor (or inquiry) profiles based on demographics and psychographics.

1. How did you first become interested in the Paradise Valley?
   ☐ Magazine ☐ Friends/Relatives
   ☐ Internet ☐ Newspapers
   ☐ Hotel/Restaurant brochures
   ☐ Other _____

2. After requesting information and receiving The Guide, did you visit the Paradise Valley?
   ☐ Yes (skip to # __) ☐ No

3. If not, what were your reasons for not visiting the Paradise Valley?
   ☐ Cost ☐ Alternative destination
   ☐ Distance ☐ Personal Reasons
   ☐ Other _____

4. Did you visit an alternative destination? (please list)
   _____
   _____
   (skip to # __)

5. For which of the following did you use The Guide? (check all that apply)
   ☐ Accommodations ☐ Restaurants
   ☐ Tourist attractions ☐ Shopping
   ☐ Maps ☐ Other:_____

6. What was the purpose of your trip to the Paradise Valley?
   ☐ Business ☐ Business and Leisure
   ☐ Leisure (vacation) ☐ Family/Friends
   ☐ Visiting Colleges ☐ Other:_____

FIGURE 6.7 • Conversion study sample questions.

6.5　ETHICAL ISSUES IN MARKETING RESEARCH

Research ethics
The code of behavior set by society and the research industry to define appropriate behavior for firms and individuals engaged in the research process.

As with most other areas in marketing, there is potential for unethical behavior in marketing research. Research ethics is the code of behavior set by society and the research industry to define appropriate behavior for firms and individuals. Three parties are involved in the marketing research process, and each has its own set of rights and obligations concerning ethics. The following is a brief description of the rights and obligations for respondents, research suppliers, and clients. Table 6.3 contains a summary of the obligations and rights of the research parties.

6.5.1　Rights and Obligations of the Respondents

Research clients make major decisions based on the information they obtain through surveys and other research methods. Therefore, it is incumbent on respondents to be truthful in their responses and their behavior when they choose to participate. Research suppliers count on this honesty, but the suppliers must be honest with respondents as well. Respondents have the right to privacy and should be allowed to refuse to participate. Also, research suppliers should honor any confidentiality

RESPONDENTS	SUPPLIERS	CLIENTS
Obligation to provide truthful responses	Obligation to maintain privacy of respondents	Obligation to reveal actual nature of the research
Right to privacy	Obligation to remain objective	Obligation to be honest when soliciting research proposals
Right to refuse to participate	Obligation to present results accurately	Obligation to have a real commitment to the research
Right to know true nature of the research	Obligation to base conclusions on actual results	

TABLE 6.3 • Rights and Obligations of Parties Involved in Marketing Research

agreements that they may make with respondents. Finally, respondents have the right to be informed about the true nature of the research. Respondents are often contacted under the guise of research when in reality it is merely a sales pitch. This type of deception is not acceptable behavior under normal ethical standards.

6.5.2   Rights and Obligations of the Research Suppliers

As just mentioned, research suppliers have an obligation to maintain the privacy and confidentiality of both their respondents and their clients. Research suppliers should not perform research for the sake of selling, and they should not sell their lists to other firms. These suppliers have an obligation to remain impartial and objective in performing their research. Also, the results should be presented accurately, without any attempt to misrepresent them. Similarly, conclusions should be based on the actual results, not misrepresented, or tailored, to meet the needs of the client.

6.5.3   Rights and Obligations of the Clients

Clients have an obligation to be open and forthright with research suppliers regarding the actual nature of the research. If clients send out a request for proposals (RFP), it should be for an actual project, not to obtain information for conducting their own research or for negotiating with other research suppliers. Clients should not misrepresent the research project as a pilot study that could lead to more projects in an attempt to decrease the cost. Finally, clients should have a sincere commitment to research and plan to use it properly. They should not put undue pressure on the research supplier to misrepresent results to suit the client's wishes.

In some cases, the client firm conducts research through an in-house research department. In this situation, the client and the research supplier are one and the same, and the firm is subject to the rights and obligations of both parties. This discussion is not meant to be complete; instead, it provides an overview of the most common areas for unethical behavior.

chapter review

SUMMARY OF CHAPTER OBJECTIVES

Marketing information systems should be designed to produce data that are useful to a hospitality manager. This information can be used as a basis for decisions; it should not, however, be used as the sole determining factor when making any decision. Two other factors also come into play when making a decision: experience and intuition. If all decisions could be based solely on information produced by marketing information systems, there would be no need for managers. Instead, machines could be used to tabulate the information and predict the correct answer. Managers, however, have far too many uncontrollable variables to contend with in gathering marketing information. For this reason a hospitality manager must view the situation by considering marketing information, previous experience in similar situations, and intuition as to what the future holds. Based on these three factors, a decision must be made, and the hospitality manager must accept the final responsibility for the decision.

A hospitality marketing information system is a structured organization of people and procedures designed to generate a flow of data from inside and outside the operation. It is used as a basis for marketing decisions. A marketing information system scans three subenvironments: the macroenvironment, the competitive environment, and the organizational environment. Marketing information systems involve both internally and externally generated marketing information, each with its own set of sources for information and its own methodology for obtaining necessary information.

The marketing research process is used to collect data to store in marketing information systems to be used in making marketing decisions. The basics of conducting marketing research are not difficult, but the specifics of designing, implementing, analyzing, and interpreting the results of a marketing research project are very demanding. It requires great skill to successfully manage a marketing research project. This chapter provided an overview of the research process, which involves five steps: (1) define the problem, (2) plan the research, (3) collect the data, (4) analyze the data, and (5) prepare the final report.

Management problems must be defined and converted to research problems that can be evaluated. After the research problems are defined, research objectives are established. Researchers can then choose the type of research to be performed: exploratory, descriptive, or causal. This decision is based on many factors, including the client's understanding of the nature of the problem, past research and experience, and the overall goal of the research. Next, the decision is made as to the method of data collection, and data collection forms are designed. Then a sampling plan is devised and implemented to ensure the reliability and validity of the research results. Finally, the data are analyzed using predetermined statistical methods, and the results are summarized in a final report.

The goal of marketing information systems is to collect information that can be useful in improving the quality of marketing decisions. The marketing research process is critical in this endeavor. Therefore, it is imperative that all parties involved in the research process adhere to the ethical standards set forth by society and the research industry. Each party to the process has certain rights and obligations that are crucial to the overall success of the marketing research process.

KEY TERMS AND CONCEPTS

Causal research
Census
Cross-sectional study
Descriptive analysis
Descriptive research
Experiments
Exploratory research
Focus group
Inferential analysis
Input–output model
Longitudinal study
Marketing information system (MIS)
Marketing research process
Multiplier analysis

Observation
Population
Primary data
Research design
Research ethics
Sample
Sampling error
Sampling unit
Satellite account method
Secondary data
Secondary data analysis
Surveys
Test marketing

QUESTIONS FOR REVIEW AND DISCUSSION

1. Why would it be useful for a hospitality organization to implement a marketing information system?

2. What do you consider the best sources for internal and external marketing information? Cite sources and discuss the advantages and disadvantages of each.

3. How do you differentiate between primary and secondary data, including their advantages and disadvantages?

4. What role should a marketing information system play in the management of a hospitality establishment?

5. Discuss the three types of research. Give an example of a situation in which you would use each one. Can you use more than one at a time? Explain.

6. What are the three methods of collecting data? Give an example of how each one would be used in the hospitality and tourism industry?

7. Compare and contrast the three types of surveys.

8. What are the two major types of data analysis? When should the decision be made as to which methods will be used for analyzing the data?

9. Who are the parties involved in the marketing research process? What are the rights and obligations of each party?

NOTES

[1] Alvin C. Burns and Ronald F. Bush, *Marketing Research*, 2nd ed. (Englewood Cliffs, NJ: Prentice Hall, 1998).

[2] David A. Aaker, J. Kumer, and George S. Day, *Marketing Research*, 8th ed. (New York: John Wiley & Sons, 2003); Carl McDaniel Jr. and Roger Gates, *Marketing Research Essentials*, 4th ed. (New York: John Wiley & Sons, 2003).

chapter review

CASE STUDY

The Biggest Loser Resort

You have been hired as the new development manager for "The Biggest Loser Resort" (BLR) chain and your first task is to perform a location analysis for the next property in the chain. Currently, there are four resorts in the chain, located in Chicago, Illinois; Ivins, Utah; Malibu, California; and Niagra, New York. The basic mission of BLR is to offer an affordable weight loss program that inspires and motivates participants to achieve their goals, resulting in a life-changing experience (you can view the entire mission statement at: http://www.biggestloserresort.com/).

The location must fit the brand, its mission, and make sense from a geographic perspective (i.e., fit with the other four properties). You can do research on the Internet, starting with an in-depth analysis of the current operations of the BLR chain to get an idea of the concept and the products and services offered at the current locations. Then, you need to choose a geographic location and an existing facility that would fit the business model. The preferred approach is to license an existing brand to change to the BLR brand name, or co-brand with an existing brand. The approach depends on the strength of the existing brand and the size of the operation. It is important to remember that both companies need to benefit from the relationship (e.g., hotels or spas with strong brand images can offer fitness facilities and programs without sharing revenues with BLR).

Case Study Questions and Issues

1. What geographic area did you choose, and why?

2. What resort or spa did you choose, and why? How will the resort or spa benefit from the BLR brand?

3. How will BLR benefit from forming an alliance with the resort or spa you chose?

CASE STUDY

Bel Air Motel

Bill Smith moved from Philadelphia, Pennsylvania, to take over as the general manager of the Bel Air Motel in California. Bill had been the assistant general manager of a large chain hotel in the downtown area of Philadelphia. He encountered problems with some of the employees and felt it would be a good idea to move to a more relaxed atmosphere. Bill had worked for the chain for 10 years, starting in the management training program and working his way up to his position as the assistant general manager.

The Bel Air Motel is one of the oldest properties in the area, but it has been renovated periodically over the years. The motel is owned by a group of independent investors and has 116 rooms with basic amenities. There is no restaurant or pool, but there are some restaurants in the local area. The motel's room rate is at the low end for the market, which consists mainly of upscale properties.

Upon starting his new position as general manager, Bill realized that there were major differences between working for a large chain and working at a small, independent motel. The chain hotels had sophisticated computer systems for reservations, sales, catering, and revenue management. In addition, customer information was gathered through surveys and comment cards. This provided managers with valuable information that could be used to make important decisions about rates and services. Unfortunately, the Bel Air Motel had a very simple reservations system and no additional information except for some historical figures on rate and occupancy. The average room rate was $125 and the occupancy rate was around 60 percent before Bill took over.

Bill understood the necessity of gathering more customer information and developed a comment card to be placed in every room. Customers were asked to complete the comment card and leave it in the room for housekeeping to collect. The purpose of the comment card was to determine how guests staying at the motel felt about the property and the services. Bill wanted to make sure the guests were satisfied. At the end of the first year, he received a total of 169 completed comment cards. The first question he looked at was the one dealing with customer satisfaction:

WHICH OF THE FOLLOWING BEST DESCRIBES YOUR EXPERIENCE AT THE BEL AIR MOTEL?	
The motel exceeded my expectations.	19.9%
The motel met my expectations.	55.9%
The motel failed to meet my expectations.	24.3%

The percentages indicate the guests' responses to the question. This year could serve as a benchmark for future years, but Bill was concerned that the motel failed to meet the expectations for approximately one-fourth of the guests. Next, he looked at the guests' ratings of the motel's facilities and services on a four-point scale (1 = poor, 2 = fair, 3 = good, and 4 = excellent).

HOTEL SERVICES	MEAN
Reservations	3.59
Front desk/check-in	3.55
Front desk/check-out	3.69
Front desk/guest service	3.41
GUEST ROOM	
Comfort	3.20
Bedroom lighting	2.88

HOTEL SERVICES	MEAN
Cleanliness	3.41
Furnishings	3.07
Adequacy of supplies	3.11
Heating/air-conditioning	3.12
Overall quality	3.07
Price/room rate	3.01

Case Questions and Issues

1. Is the response rate large enough for the comment cards to be representative of all the guests? How could the response rate be improved?

2. Are customers satisfied?

3. What are the major areas of concern, and how can they be improved?

4. What other information is necessary? How could you go about collecting that information?

case study

APPENDIX

Data Collection and Sampling

DESIGNING DATA COLLECTION FORMS. Data collection forms are necessary whether the research plan involves observation, surveys, or experiments. Surveys are most commonly used because much of the research being conducted is descriptive. Therefore, this section will focus on designing questionnaires to be used in surveys.

Questionnaires consist of questions designed to address the research objectives. The goal of the questionnaire is to standardize data collection by using questions that will elicit a consistent response from respondents. This is accomplished through the use of open-ended and closed-ended questions. An **open-ended question** does not provide the respondent with any options, categories, or scales to use in answering the question. These questions are valuable for obtaining information for exploratory research, or in instances when the researcher is not sure what the response might be. For example, a hotel chain could merely ask "what did you like least about your stay at our hotel?" Conversely, a **closed-ended question** provides the respondent with options from which to select a response. For example, a restaurant could ask a diner to rate the quality of the food on a 4-point scale ranging from poor, to fair, to good, to excellent. It is much easier to collect and analyze information that is in the form of closed-ended questions. The respondents' answers are consistent, and the data are in a form that is simple to record.

Open-ended questions are in the form of a basic question, but closed-ended questions can be in three different forms. The simplest form of closed-ended question is a **dichotomous question**, which contains two possible options. Examples of dichotomous questions would be questions with yes or no answers, or a categorical question such as gender with two possible responses, such as "male" and "female."

Another type of closed-ended question is the **multiple-category question**, which contains more than two options for the respondent. Demographic information, such as education and income, is often obtained using multiple-category questions. When framing the options for multiple-category questions, it is important for the researcher to make sure the options are *mutually exclusive* and *collectively exhaustive*. Options are said to be *mutually exclusive* if there is only one possible option for each respondent, and *collectively exhaustive* if there is at least one option that pertains to each respondent.

The final form of closed-ended question is the **scaled-response question**. This type of question involves a statement or question followed by a rating scale. One of the more popular scaled-response questions is the *Likert scale,* which has respondents indicate their level of agreement with a statement on a five-point scale, with 1 being "strongly disagree" and 5 being "strongly agree."

Open-ended question

Does not provide the respondent with any options, categories, or scales to use in answering the question.

Closed-ended question

Provides the respondent with options from which to select a response. It is much easier to collect and analyze information in this type of question. The respondents' answers are consistent and the data are in a form that is simple to record.

Dichotomous question

The simplest form of a closed-ended question is a dichotomous question, which contains two possible options. Examples include questions with "yes" or "no" answers or a categorical question such as gender with two possible responses, "male" and "female."

Multiple-category question

A multiple-category question contains more than two options for the respondent. Demographic information, such as education and income, is often obtained using this type of question.

Scaled-response question

This form of a closed-ended question involves a statement or question followed by a rating scale. One of the more popular scaled-response questions is the Likert scale, which has respondents indicate their level of agreement with a statement on a five-point scale, with 1 being "strongly disagree" and 5 being "strongly agree."

appendix

Surveys are used for a multitude of reasons, and it is difficult to establish rules that will apply in all situations. However, the following general guidelines apply to the construction of all survey instruments:

- Avoid talking down to the respondent or using technical language. Ask the questions using language that is familiar to and understandable by the respondent.
- Avoid long and wordy questions. These will tend to discourage the respondent and may reduce the number of respondents to a written survey.
- Avoid including more than one idea per question.
- Make certain that there is a legitimate reason for asking each question.
- Avoid putting any personal bias into the questions by using "leading" or "loaded" language.
- In closed-ended questions, provide a "don't know" or "no opinion" response where appropriate.
- All responses in a closed-ended question should be collectively exhaustive (i.e., all possibilities are included) and mutually exclusive (i.e., the answers don't overlap).
- Indicate very clearly in the directions the number of choices a respondent should check.
- Watch for words and phrases that have more than one meaning, as this can confuse the respondent.

The questionnaire should include three basic sections: opening questions, research questions, background questions. The opening questions are used to build a rapport and obtain information that is easy for the respondent to provide. This would include screening questions (e.g., Have you ever dined at this restaurant?) and purchase behavior questions (e.g., How often do you dine out? How much do you normally spend?). The research questions are more difficult to answer and normally require the respondent to rank or rate a brand. These provide the researcher with information for modeling and determining cause-and-effect relationships. Finally, the background questions are used for classifying the respondents and normally consist of demographic and psychographic variables. These tend to be more personal and should always come at the end of the questionnaire when the respondent is already highly involved in the process.

Probability sample
A sample chosen using a scientifically random method, where the chance of selecting any given population member can be calculated.

Simple random sample
A totally random process where each population member has an equal chance of being selected.

Systematic sample
A starting point is randomly chosen and then every *n*th member is selected for the sample.

SAMPLING. There are two basic types of samples: probability and nonprobability. A **probability sample** is more scientific, and a population member's chance of being selected can be calculated. This type of sample tends to be favored when the firm has some understanding of the problem, sampling errors are larger, and there is a high degree of variability in the population (i.e., it is heterogeneous). The most common probability sampling method is the **simple random sample**, where the process is totally random and each population member has an equal chance of being selected. With this method, there is little chance of selection bias or sampling error. Another popular probability method is the **systematic sample**, where a starting point is chosen arbitrarily and then every *n*th member is selected for the sample. This method is easier than random sampling, and it is often used with lists containing addresses and/or telephone numbers (e.g., the telephone directory). Normally, there is no reason to believe that any bias would occur due to the ordering of members in the list. For example, it would be

appendix

appendix

unusual for every 100th name on a list to share common characteristics such as age and income. A **stratified sample** is one in which the population is separated into different strata based on an important population characteristic, and a sample is taken from each stratum using a random or systematic process. For example, many firms want to include both customers and noncustomers in their samples but place more weight on customers' responses.

A **nonprobability sample** is based on judgment, and the selection process is very subjective. The chance of a member being selected cannot be calculated, but that does not mean that the sample won't be representative of the population. The representativeness of the sample will depend greatly on the judgment of the researcher. Nonprobability samples tend to be favored when the research is exploratory, there is more potential for nonsampling errors, and the population is homogeneous. The most basic method of nonprobability sampling is the **convenience sample** because the researcher chooses a sample of population members who, in his or her opinion, represent the target population. Often, professors use a class of students, or research firms intercept people at shopping malls. A **judgment sample** is slightly different in that the researcher makes a determination as to a subset of population members that will represent the population. This process is similar to the one used in choosing the members for a focus group. A **quota sample** is one of the most popular sampling methods. The sample is chosen to fill certain quotas that are predetermined by the researcher. This method is similar to stratified sampling, except that a convenience sample is used to fill the quotas and a probability technique is used to fill each stratum.

Stratified sample
The population is separated into different strata based on an important population characteristic and a sample is taken from each stratum using a random or systematic process.

Nonprobability sample
Nonprobability samples are based on judgment and the selection process is subjective.

Convenience sample
The most basic method of nonprobability sampling because the researcher chooses a sample of population members that, in his or her opinion, represent the target population (e.g., professors use a class of students, or research firms intercept people at shopping malls).

Judgment sample
The researcher makes a determination as to a subset of population members that will represent the population. This process is similar to the one used in choosing the members for a focus group.

Quota sample
Chosen to fill certain quotas that are predetermined by the researcher.

APPENDIX KEY TERMS

Closed-ended question
Convenience sample
Dichotomous question
Judgment sample
Multiple-category question
Nonprobability sample
Open-ended question

Probability sample
Quota sample
Scaled-response question
Simple random sample
Stratified sample
Systematic sample

APPENDIX QUESTIONS FOR REVIEW AND DISCUSSION

1. How are questionnaires organized? What are some of the guidelines that should be followed in developing questions?

2. What is the difference between a probability sample and a nonprobability sample? Which one is best? Explain your answer.

appendix

Pricing Strategy

Courtesy The Melting Pot.

Chapter Objectives

After studying this chapter, you should be able to:

1. Describe the traditional role of price in the marketing mix.

2. Explain the impact of pricing objectives, consumer price sensitivity, and environmental factors on pricing decisions.

3. Discuss the broad pricing strategies that can be used in hospitality and tourism.

4. Describe the various pricing techniques and procedures.

5. Explain the use of price to segment consumer markets.

6. Outline the role of price in revenue management.

7. Discuss legal and ethical issues surrounding pricing practices.

7.1 INTRODUCTION

Price is a component of the marketing mix and the vehicle used in free enterprise to allocate limited resources. The other three components of the marketing mix—promotion, product, and distribution—create value and appear on the firm's income statement as expenses. Conversely, price is the firm's tool for capturing value, and it affects the revenue section of the income statement. Price is the easiest of the marketing mix components to change, and it directly affects revenue. Therefore, firms should put a great deal of effort into formulating their pricing strategies. *Price* can be defined as the value given to a product or service by consumers.

Various names are associated with price, such as *fee, tuition*, and *premium*. The important thing to remember is the concept of exchange. In other words, the buyer and the seller have to be mutually satisfied for an exchange to take place, and this exchange does not have to include a monetary unit. The early system of exchange was referred to as **bartering**, where individuals or organizations exchanged goods and services with one another. Even nonprofit organizations are in the business of selling a sense of goodwill or charity in exchange for donors' contributions.

Pricing strategy integrates marketing and finance in an attempt to create an atmosphere of mutual satisfaction. The product or service attributes are combined with price to provide enough value to satisfy customers, while enabling the firm to cover costs and make an adequate profit. The rest of this chapter covers the process of strategic pricing, including the factors that influence pricing decisions.

Bartering
Individuals or organizations exchange goods and services with one another without the use of money.

7.2 FACTORS THAT AFFECT PRICING DECISIONS

The pricing decision remains a critical component of the marketing mix and the positioning of a product or service. Pricing is a continual process that requires a firm understanding of the market and its environments. The dynamic nature of the market and its environments creates a formidable challenge for even the most experienced managers. Therefore, it is best to take a systematic approach to pricing that includes establishing pricing objectives consistent with the overall objectives of the firm, assessing consumer price sensitivity, and monitoring the external environment.

7.2.1 Pricing Objectives

Most of the possible **pricing objectives** can be grouped into four major categories based on goals related to financial performance, volume, competition, and image. These objectives are consistent with the organizational objectives discussed in Chapter 5 and must be considered when setting prices. A brief summary of the categories follows:

Pricing objectives
Organizational objectives focused on financial performance, volume, competition, and image that are directly related to pricing decisions.

- *Financial performance objectives* focus on areas such as the firm's level of profitability, rates of return on sales and equity, and cash flow. Most large companies continually monitor these performance measures and find it easy to use these measures as benchmarks or objectives. It becomes relatively easy to see the role of price in these measures of firm performance.

- *Volume objectives* focus on sales and market share. These measures can be based either on the number of units sold or on the dollar amount of units sold. The sales measure looks at the firm individually, whereas the market share measure views the firm relative to the competition. Volume objectives are particularly common in the early stages of the product life cycle, when firms are willing to forgo profits in exchange for building long-term sales and market share. In addition, price competition stays strong in the maturity stage in an attempt to hold market share.

- *Competition objectives* focus on the nature of the competitive environment. A firm may want to maintain competitive parity with the market leader, widen the gap between itself and market followers, or simply survive. There is a good deal of head-to-head competition in the hospitality and tourism industry. For example, airline companies match each other's price changes so closely that the industry is often under investigation for price collusion.

- *Image objectives* focus on the firm's overall positioning strategy. A firm's position in the market is a direct result of its price–quality relationship as perceived by consumers. The hotel market can be segmented by price into economy, midmarket, and premium categories. Also, airline companies offer bereavement fares for emergency travel, and hotels offer discounts for guests with family members in the hospital. These discounts enhance the image of the firm.

7.2.2 Consumer Price Sensitivity

An important factor in setting price is **consumer price sensitivity**, or how consumers react to changes in price. Many situational factors affect a consumer's price sensitivity, and these factors can actually vary from one purchase decision to another. For example, a married couple may be less price-sensitive when choosing a restaurant for a special occasion than they would be if they were having a normal meal after work. The following sections summarize the most common effects on consumer price sensitivity.[1]

Consumer price sensitivity
The degree to which a change in price will affect a consumer's purchase decision.

7.2.2.1 PRICE–QUALITY EFFECT.   In many situations, consumers use price as an indicator of a product's quality, especially when they do not have much experience with the product category. In this case, consumers will be less sensitive to a product's price to the extent that they believe higher prices signify higher quality. For example, overseas travelers often use price as a gauge of quality because they lack familiarity with the travel products in foreign countries. This pertains to all components of the travel product, such as hotels, restaurants, car rentals, and tourist attractions. This lack of information is one of the main reasons that consumers would use price as a signal of quality, along with the perceived risk of making a bad choice and the belief that quality differences exist between brands.

7.2.2.2 UNIQUE VALUE EFFECT.   Consumers will be less price-sensitive when a product is unique and does not have close substitutes. If a firm successfully differentiates its product from those of its competitors, it can charge a higher price. Consumers must remain aware of the differentiation and convinced of its value in order to pay the higher price. In essence, the firm's strategy is to reduce the effect of substitutes, thereby eliminating the consumer's reference value for the product. Resorts and health spas use this strategy by marketing themselves as one-of-a-kind properties. Similarly, many fine-dining restaurants use this approach and differentiate themselves on attributes such as the chef, the atmosphere, and/or the menu. Airline and car rental companies would have a more difficult time using this strategy because of the homogeneity of the products.

7.2.2.3 PERCEIVED-SUBSTITUTES EFFECT.   Consumers become more price-sensitive when comparing a product's higher price with the lower prices of perceived substitutes for the product. Consumers must be aware of the other products and actually perceive them as substitutes. The prices for the substitutes help consumers form a reference price, or a reasonable price range, for the product. There are many perceived substitutes for products such as fast food, airline travel, car rentals, and hotel rooms. When there are a number of substitutes that consumers are aware of, there tends to be a downward pressure on price, resulting in a relatively narrow acceptable range for prices. For example, there are no significant price differences between products in fast-food restaurants or airline tickets for a popular route (e.g., New York to Chicago).

7.2.2.4 DIFFICULT-COMPARISON EFFECT.   The difficult-comparison effect is closely related to the perceived-substitutes effect. Consumers may be aware of substitutes for a product, but they will tend to become less price-sensitive as it becomes more difficult to compare brands. Therefore, many firms try to differentiate themselves from the competition on certain attributes that are difficult to compare. For example, bars may serve drinks in different quantities, or resorts may package products in an attempt to make direct comparisons more difficult. However, rather than spend the time and effort to make comparisons, many consumers are content simply to choose a brand that they perceive as satisfactory. Franchises benefit from this phenomenon because they focus on providing consistent products and services under a recognizable brand name. Even though they have not made direct comparisons or familiarized themselves with all of the alternatives, consumers will feel safe in choosing one of these well-known brands.

7.2.2.5 SHARED-COST EFFECT.

Consumers will be less sensitive to price if another organization or individual is sharing in the cost of a product. The smaller the portion of the price paid by the consumer, the less sensitive the individual is to price. This sharing could be in the form of a tax deduction, a business reimbursement, or some type of sales promotion (e.g., coupon or rebate). When business travelers stay in hotels, eat at restaurants, or rent cars, they tend to be less sensitive to price because their firms normally pay for most of their travel expenses. Hospitality and tourism firms that target business travelers often charge higher relative prices for their products. One exception is hotels, where business travelers usually pay lower prices than individual travelers, due to the overall volume of the business segment.

7.2.2.6 TOTAL EXPENDITURE EFFECT.

The larger the amount of the total expenditure, the more price-sensitive consumers will tend to be. This amount can be measured either in absolute terms or as a percentage of income. For example, a consumer booking a cruise at a price of $5,000 will be more sensitive to price than if he or she were eating a meal in a restaurant. The cost of the cruise is a relatively large travel expenditure, whereas the cost of a meal pales in comparison. However, a consumer with an income of $500,000 a year would normally not be as price-sensitive regarding the cruise as one with an income of $50,000 a year. Also, consumers with higher incomes place a greater value on their time and may decide to accept higher prices without evaluating alternative products.

7.2.2.7 END-BENEFIT EFFECT.

A product may represent only one component of the purchases necessary to attain a desired benefit. The end-benefit effect consists of two parts: derived demand and the share of total cost. *Derived demand* refers to the relationship between the desired end benefit and the consumer's price sensitivity for something that contributes to that end benefit. This is most popular in industrial markets where firms purchase products to resell to other consumers. The more price-sensitive the firm's consumers are, the more price-sensitive the firm will be in purchasing components of the end benefit. For example, tour operators determine the type of hotel or car rental to be included in a package based on the price sensitivity of the target segment.

Consumers are willing to pay high prices for spa treatments in luxury hotels when the perceived quality is high.

Pozmyakov/Shutterstock

In the retail market, consumers tend to be more price-sensitive when the price of a component represents a larger portion of the total cost. Consumers would be less sensitive to beverage or dessert prices at an upscale restaurant where dinner for two can cost $100 or more. Similarly, a consumer may not be as price-sensitive to hotel parking rates when spending $300 a night in a downtown hotel. The use of packages, or bundles, by resorts and tourist attractions attempts to extract as much consumer surplus as possible by "backing in" to the consumer's value for the end benefit.

7.2.3 Environmental Factors

As discussed in depth in Chapter 2, management must keep abreast of the developments in the external environment. Even though these developments cannot be controlled, they can affect pricing decisions because they affect a firm's costs, the demand for its products, and the competition. The components of the external environment include the economic environment, the social environment, the political environment, the technological environment, and the competitive environment.

7.2.3.1 ECONOMIC ENVIRONMENT.   Constant changes occur in the state of the economy as measured by indicators such as business growth, inflation, consumer spending, unemployment rates, and interest rates. If firms are to compete and earn an acceptable profit, their pricing strategies should reflect changes in the economy. Firms that compete in international markets must consider the state of the economy in the foreign markets as well as the domestic market. Foreign exchange rates can affect a firm's income statement drastically and influence the future of the firm. Prices alter in accordance with changes in income and consumer spending, as well as with variations in a firm's costs resulting from changes in the economy.

7.2.3.2 SOCIAL ENVIRONMENT.   Consumers' tastes often change over time, and firms that do not adapt go out of business. Changes in cultures and subcultures throughout the world are affecting many societies. Different cultures have different spending patterns and saving practices. For example, many Asians tend to save more of their incomes than other nationalities do, but they also tend to purchase name brands that are associated with high quality. Therefore, the Asian market is less price-sensitive than some of its counterparts. As cultures mesh, they influence each other's eating habits. For example, consumers in the United States are eating more sushi and drinking more tea than in the past.

7.2.3.3 POLITICAL ENVIRONMENT.   All levels of government have a tremendous impact on the operation of hospitality and tourism firms throughout the country. Changes in minimum-wage laws affect the costs of restaurants, and changes in tax laws related to business expenses affect the demand in restaurants. Managers must consider both of these areas when setting menu prices. Similarly, hotels must consider the impact of hotel taxes on consumers when setting their prices. For example, hotels in New York City were very concerned about the impact on group and convention business when local hotel taxes were raised. At one point, the total taxes on guest rooms added up to more than 21 percent. In response, the city lowered hotel taxes to make New York City a more attractive destination for group business. In addition, governments impose many fees on businesses, and firms operating in international markets must contend with additional fees and tariffs.

7.2.3.4 TECHNOLOGICAL ENVIRONMENT.   Another area of concern for managers is keeping up with advances in technology. Many of the new technologies in the hospitality and tourism industry are intended to improve the efficiency of firms, thereby reducing costs. For example, when food servers use handheld terminals to place orders, they no longer have to enter the kitchen or move to a stationary terminal in another location. These new point-of-sale (POS) systems also enable firms to track costs and demand for particular food items. This information is invaluable in setting prices. Similarly, hotels and airlines use sophisticated systems to capture costs and demand that help them maximize revenues through price setting.

7.2.3.5 COMPETITIVE ENVIRONMENT. Finally, managers must know what occurs in the competitive environment. New firms entering the market will change overall supply, thereby changing the market structure and putting downward pressure on prices. Competitors also engage in promotional campaigns offering price discounts or free merchandise that will affect consumers' perceptions of value. An example is the airline industry, which is notorious for its short-term price wars in a battle for market share.

7.3 BROAD PRICING STRATEGIES

After a firm's pricing objectives are set, managers must identify the role that price will serve in the product's overall marketing strategy. Prices can be (1) set high to restrict the firm's market to a limited segment of buyers, as in luxury hotels and fine-dining restaurants (skim pricing); (2) set low to attract buyers, as in economy hotels and fast-food restaurants (penetration pricing); or (3) kept neutral to emphasize other aspects of marketing, as in midscale hotels and theme restaurants (neutral pricing).[2] Table 7.1 illustrates these strategies based on the relationship between price and economic value for the middle market of consumers. Economic value can be defined as the sum of a product's reference value (i.e., the cost of the competing product that the consumer perceives as the closest substitute) and a product's differentiation value (i.e., the value to the consumer, both positive and negative, of any differences between a firm's offering and the reference product).

7.3.1 Skim Pricing

A skim pricing strategy involves setting high prices relative to the product or service's economic value to capture high profit margins. An exclusive segment of consumers places a high value on a product's differentiating attributes. Skim pricing is a preferred strategy when selling to the exclusive, price-insensitive market, and it results in higher profits than selling to the mass market at a lower price. For example, luxury hotels and resorts market hotel rooms with many amenities such as valet parking, laundry service, and golf. Most consumers are not willing to pay the higher prices associated with this level of service, but there is a smaller segment of consumers that places a high value on the additional amenities and will pay the higher prices. Similarly, upscale and fine-dining restaurants charge higher prices based on the menu, the ambience, the location, and the restaurant's reputation. In addition, many of the restaurants in this market segment offer valet parking.

Many service firms have limited capacity, and it may be necessary to maximize profits by managing supply and demand through higher prices. Skim pricing also tends to be used by firms whose variable costs represent a large portion of total costs and the product's price. There is little incentive to decrease cost per unit by increasing volume under this cost structure. From a competitive standpoint, skim pricing works best when a firm's product remains unique or is superior to competitive products in perceived quality. Once again, restaurants with good reputations, exclusive resorts, and airlines with limited business and first-class seating (especially on international flights) practice skim pricing.

Economic value
The sum of a product's reference value and a product's differentiation value.

Reference value
The cost of the competing product that the consumer perceives as the closest substitute.

Differentiation value
The value to the consumer (both positive and negative) of any differences between a firm's offering and the reference product.

Skim pricing
The practice of setting a high price relative to a product's perceived economic value.

PERCEIVED ECONOMIC VALUE	RELATIVE PRICE	
	LOW	HIGH
LOW	Neutral Pricing	Skim Pricing
HIGH	Penetration Pricing	Neutral

TABLE 7.1 • **Strategies Based on Price and Economic Value**

Courtesy Mobile Bay CVB.

Luxury hotels and resorts can add differentiation value through amenities such as golf courses.

7.3.2   Penetration Pricing

Penetration pricing involves setting low prices relative to the product's economic value. This strategy works best on price-sensitive consumers who are willing to change product or service providers to obtain a better price. Firms using this strategy choose to have lower profit margins in an attempt to gain high sales volumes and market shares. Penetration pricing stays common among economy hotels that market to consumers who view the product as merely a place to sleep and have no need for additional amenities. However, firms must have the necessary capacity to accommodate the large volume in order to use this pricing strategy.

Penetration pricing
The practice of setting a low price relative to a product's perceived economic value.

   Most of the costs of providing the rooms in economy hotels are fixed. Normally, an economy hotel does not have a restaurant with room service or a concierge to help guests with travel plans. Similarly, quick-service restaurants do not have chefs, and food costs are relatively low. In both cases, the furniture and decor are fairly basic. The higher volume generated by the lower prices is expected to result in economies of scale and a lower cost per unit of providing the service. From a competitive standpoint, penetration pricing works best when a firm has a significant cost advantage over its competitors or when the firm is small and not considered a threat by its competitors. Charter airlines and small commuter airlines are examples of firms that can adopt a penetration pricing strategy and are not considered a threat by larger airline companies.

7.3.3   Neutral Pricing

A neutral pricing strategy involves setting prices at a moderate level relative to the product's economic value. In other words, the firm makes a strategic decision to use attributes other than price to gain a competitive advantage (i.e., attributes related to product, promotion, and/or distribution). Another reason firms use this strategy is to maintain a product line that includes product offerings at different price levels. For example, many hotel chains have brands across all price categories such as budget/economy, midpriced, upscale, and luxury. Therefore, one or more of their offerings will occupy the average price range with the basic amenities (i.e., low economic value) for full-service hotels. Franchising and the proliferation of chains in the hospitality industry often lead to homogeneous offerings with little differentiation and standard pricing across competitors in the same market segment.

Neutral pricing
The practice of setting a price consistent with a product's perceived economic value.

A neutral strategy can be used by default, when a firm cannot use skim pricing or penetration pricing because of its cost structure or the market conditions. However, this strategy has become more popular with the growth in the value segment of consumers. In the hotel industry, many consumers do not want to pay high prices, but they do want some amenities such as restaurants and pools. Also, the Internet has simplified the information search process for consumers and it allows them to make quick price comparisons. For example, online travel agents obtain inventory from various companies and manage it based on the overall supply and demand for the product category and the market. Finally, a high price can actually be a neutral price when product value justifies the price to most potential consumers.

7.4 PRICING TECHNIQUES AND PROCEDURES

When management establishes prices, three approaches can be used, either individually or in combination with one another: cost-oriented pricing, demand-oriented pricing, and competitive pricing.

7.4.1 Cost-Oriented Pricing

Cost-oriented pricing
Basing pricing decisions on the cost of providing a product or service.

As the name implies, **cost-oriented pricing** uses a firm's cost to provide a product or service as a basis for pricing. In general, firms want to set a price high enough to cover costs and make a profit. Two types of costs can be considered: fixed costs and variable costs. *Fixed costs* are those incurred by a company to remain in business, and they do not vary with changes in sales volume. For example, restaurants must invest in a building, kitchen equipment, and tables before they begin to serve customers. *Variable costs* are the costs associated with doing business, and they vary with changes in sales volume. For example, restaurants incur costs for food, labor, and cleaning that are directly related to the level of sales.

Break-even analysis
Uses the break-even point (BEP) to examine the relationships between costs, sales, and profits.

Break-even analysis can be used to examine the relationships between costs, sales, and profits. The break-even point (BEP) is the point where total revenue and total cost are equal. In other words, the BEP in units would be the number of units that must be sold at a given contribution margin (price-variable cost) to cover the firm's total fixed costs:

$$\text{BEP}_{\text{units}} = \frac{\text{Total fixed costs}}{(\text{Selling price} - \text{Variable cost})}$$

The break-even point in dollars can be calculated by multiplying the break-even point in units by the selling price per unit. Break-even analysis is a seemingly easy method for analyzing potential pricing strategies, but one must be careful to use only costs that are relevant to the decision so that the results are accurate.

Figure 7.1 illustrates the relationships between costs, sales, and profits. As mentioned before, fixed costs are incurred regardless of sales. Therefore, they remain constant with changes in sales volume and are represented by a horizontal line. The total costs line intersects the fixed costs line where it begins on the vertical axis and increases with volume to account for variable costs. The total revenue line begins at the origin and increases with volume. The break-even point in units is the point where the total revenue line intersects the total costs line. When firms operate at volumes less than the break-even point, losses are incurred because total revenue is not enough to cover the total cost of producing and marketing the product. When volume exceeds the break-even point, firms will make a profit because total revenue exceeds total cost.

For example, suppose a family purchases a large home and renovates it for use as a bed-and-breakfast. The total fixed costs would be the $300,000 purchase price plus the $100,000 spent on renovations, or a total of $400,000. The owners estimate the variable costs to clean the rooms, restock supplies, and feed the guests at approximately $25 per day. If the owners were to charge guests $75 per night to stay at the bed-and-breakfast, the break-even point in units would be 8,000 room nights [400,000/(75 − 25)]. If there were a total of 20 rooms and the occupancy of

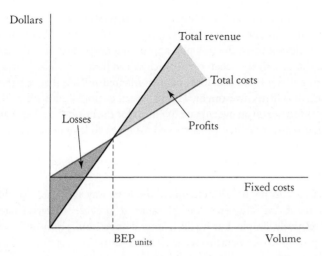

Dollars

Total revenue

Total costs

Losses

Profits

Fixed costs

BEP_{units}

Volume

FIGURE 7.1 • **Break-even analysis.**

those rooms averaged at 50 percent throughout the year, it would take 800 nights (a little over two years) to recoup their original investment. However, it is more likely that the purchase was financed over time, and the owners receive tax credits on the interest, expenses, and depreciation. Therefore, assuming the owners did not take salaries or hire additional workers, it is more likely that the yearly fixed costs are in the neighborhood of $30,000. The new break-even point would be 600 room nights [30,000/(75 − 25)], which would represent 60 days at an average occupancy rate of 50 percent.

This example illustrates the benefit of using break-even analysis for setting the prices for new products. However, break-even analysis does not account for the price sensitivity of consumers or the competition. In addition, it is very important that the costs used in the analysis are accurate. Any changes in the contribution margin or fixed costs can have a significant impact on the break-even point. For instance, if the owners overestimated the price, and consumers are only willing to pay $50 a night, then the break-even point would change to 1,200 nights, or double the original estimate. Finally, the break-even formula can be easily adjusted to account for a desired amount of profit. The desired amount of profit would be added to the numerator (total fixed costs) and would represent the additional number of units that would need to be sold at the current contribution margin to cover the desired amount.

Cost-plus pricing is the most widely used approach to pricing in the industry. The price for a product or service is determined by adding a desired markup to the cost of producing and marketing the item. The markup is in the form of a percentage, and the price is set using the following equation:

$$\text{Price} = \text{ATC} + m(\text{ATC})$$

where

$$\text{ATC} = \text{the average total cost per unit and}$$
$$m = \text{the markup percentage} / 100\%$$

The average total cost (ATC) per unit is calculated by adding the variable cost per unit to the fixed cost per unit. The fixed cost per unit is simply the total fixed costs divided by the number of units sold. For example, suppose a hotel manager has an ATC of $35 for turning a room and would like to have a 200 percent markup, which is reasonable for a full-service hotel. The selling price, or room rate, would be calculated as follows:

$$\text{Price} = \$35 + [(200 / 100) \times \$35] = \$105$$

This approach is popular because it is simple and focuses on covering costs and making a profit. However, management must have a good understanding of the firm's costs in order to price

Cost-plus pricing
Determining the price for a product or service by adding a desired markup to the cost of producing and marketing the item.

effectively. Some costs are truly fixed, but other costs may be semi-fixed. Semi-fixed costs are fixed over a certain range of sales but vary when sales go outside that range. In addition to the problem of determining the relevant costs, the cost-plus approach ignores consumer demand and the competition. This may cause a firm to charge too much or too little.

Target-return pricing

Setting a price to yield a target rate of return on a firm's investment.

Target-return pricing is another form of cost-oriented pricing that sets the price to yield a target rate of return on a firm's investment. This approach is more sophisticated than the cost-plus approach because it focuses on an overall rate of return for the business rather than a desired profit per unit. The target-return price can be calculated using the following equation:

$$\text{Price} = \text{ATC} + (\text{desired dollar return} / \text{unit sales})$$

The average total cost per unit is determined the same way as in the cost-plus approach, and it is increased by the dollar return per unit necessary to provide the target rate of return. This approach is also relatively simple, but it still ignores competitors' prices and consumer demand. For example, suppose someone wants to sell souvenir T-shirts in a tourist area of a popular destination such as the French Quarter in New Orleans. If the person wants to make $30,000 a year, assuming the average total cost is $6.00 (cost per unit of T-shirts, cart rental, and license/permit) and she or he sells an average of 20 shirts per day, the price would be calculated as follows:

$$\text{Price} = \$6.00 + [\$30,000 / (20 \times 365)]$$
$$= \$6.00 + (\$30,000 / 7,300)$$
$$= \$6.00 + \$4.11 = \$10.11, \text{ or approximately } \$10.00$$

The 20 shirts per day is an average, assuming some seasonality and variations due to weather. However, it is important to have accurate estimates for costs and sales in order to price effectively. In addition, the price should be compared with the competitors' prices in the area to make sure it is reasonable.

7.4.2 Demand-Oriented Pricing

Demand-oriented pricing

Approaches to pricing that use consumer perceptions of value as a basis for setting prices.

Demand-oriented pricing approaches use consumer perceptions of value as a basis for setting prices. The goal of this pricing approach is to set prices to capture more value, not to maximize volume. A price is charged that will allow the firm to extract the most consumer surplus from the market based on the reservation price, or the maximum price that a consumer is willing to pay for a product or service. This price can be difficult to determine unless management has a firm grasp of the price sensitivity of consumers. Economists measure price sensitivity using the price elasticity of demand, or the percentage change in quantity demanded divided by the percentage change in price. Assuming an initial price of P_1 and an initial quantity of Q_1, the price elasticity of demand (ε_p) for a change in price from P_1 to P_2 can be calculated by:

Reservation price

The maximum price that a consumer is willing to pay for a product or service.

Price elasticity of demand

A measure of the percentage change in demand for a product resulting from a percentage change in price.

$$\varepsilon_p = \frac{(Q_2 - Q_1)/Q_1}{(P_2 - P_1)/P_1}$$

The price elasticity of demand is usually negative because price increases tend to result in decreases in quantity demanded. This inverse relationship between price and quantity demanded, referred to as the law of demand, is representative of most products and services. However, the demand for products and services can demonstrate varying degrees of elasticity (see Figure 7.2). The demand for products is said to be *elastic* ($\varepsilon_p > 1$) if a percentage change in price results in a greater percentage change in quantity demanded. Conversely, the demand for products is said to be *inelastic* ($\varepsilon_p < 1$) if a percentage change in price results in a smaller percentage change in quantity demanded. *Unitary elasticity* ($\varepsilon_p = 1$) occurs when a percentage change in price results in an equal percentage change in quantity demanded. The absolute value of the price elasticity of demand is used to determine the type of demand.

Law of demand

The inverse relationship between price and quantity demanded that exists for most products and services.

In a market with elastic demand, consumers are price-sensitive, and any changes in price will cause total revenue to change in the opposite direction. Therefore, firms tend to focus on ways to

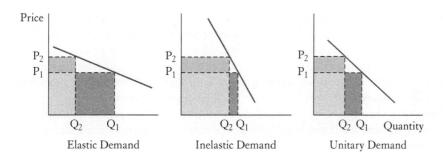

FIGURE 7.2 • Price elasticity of demand.

Elastic Demand   Inelastic Demand   Unitary Demand

decrease price in an attempt to increase the quantity demanded and total revenue. In a market with inelastic demand, consumers are not sensitive to price changes, and total revenue will change in the same direction. In this situation, firms tend to focus on raising prices and total revenues, even with a decrease in quantity demanded. In markets with unitary demand, price changes have no effect on total revenue and firms should base pricing decisions on other factors, such as cost. For example, suppose a theme park decreases its price of admission from $50 to $45 in an attempt to increase the number of visitors. After initiating the price change, the park observes an increase in the average daily attendance at the park from 10,000 to 12,500 people. The price elasticity of demand for this example would be calculated as follows:

$$\varepsilon_p = \frac{(12,500 - 10,000)/10,000}{(45 - 50)/50} = \frac{.25}{.10} = 1.5$$

This indicates that the demand for theme park visitation is elastic. In other words, theme park visitors are price-sensitive and the percentage change in quantity demanded exceeds the percentage change in price. The total revenue before the price change was $500,000 and after the change $562,500, representing an increase of $62,500.

Some popular demand-oriented pricing approaches are based on consumer perceptions of value. These **psychological pricing** practices have been proven to be successful based on their ability to influence consumer perceptions of price. **Prestige pricing** is used by firms that have products with strong price–quality relationships in markets with inelastic demand. These firms set high prices and try to build value through other quality-related attributes such as service and atmosphere. This approach is common among five-star hotels and fine-dining restaurants. **Odd/even pricing** involves setting prices just below even dollar amounts to give the perception that the product is less expensive. For example, car rental agencies set prices such as $79.95 rather than $80, and hotels use prices such as $99 instead of $100. Also, many menu items are priced with odd endings such as $5.99 or $10.95. Theory has it that people read and process prices from left to right, rounding to the lower number.

Price lining refers to the practice of having a limited number of products available at different price levels based on quality. Demand at each price point is assumed to be elastic, whereas demand between price points is assumed to be inelastic. The products at each price level are targeting a different market segment. For example, rental car companies have economy, midsize, full-size, and luxury categories.

Psychological pricing
Setting prices based on consumer perceptions of value.

Prestige pricing
Setting relatively high prices based on quality-related attributes valued by a particular segment of consumers.

Odd/even pricing
Setting prices just below even dollar amounts to give the perception that the product is less expensive.

Price lining
Refers to the practice of having a limited number of products available at different price levels based on quality.

7.4.3 Competitive Pricing

As the name implies, **competitive pricing** places emphasis on price in relation to direct competition. Some firms allow others to establish prices and then position themselves accordingly—at, below, or above the competition. This method ensures that the price charged for products and services will be within the same range as prices for competitive products. This method, however, has several drawbacks. First, consider the case of two similar firms. One is new and the other has been operating for several years. On the one hand, the new establishment is likely to have higher fixed costs such as a mortgage with a high-interest rate that must be paid each month. On the

Competitive pricing
Setting prices within the same range as prices for competitive products in the immediate geographic area.

other hand, the established firm might have a much lower mortgage payment each month and fewer costs. Because of these differences, the established firm would have lower fixed operating expenses and could charge lower prices, even if all other expenses were equal. Second, other expenses might also vary among different firms. Labor costs might be higher or lower depending on the skill level of the personnel, their length of service in the operation, and numerous other factors that may come into play. For this reason, it is extremely risky for managers to rely on the prices of a direct competitor when setting their own prices. Each operation is unique and has its own unique cost and profit structure. Although management does need to monitor the competition, prices should never be based solely on prices charged by a competitor.

7.5 SEGMENTED PRICING

Segmented pricing

Varying prices across market segments based on certain characteristics of consumers or the buying situation.

The importance of price varies among consumers, and firms often use segmented pricing as a means for segmenting markets. Then a firm can choose to target one or more of these markets with specific marketing strategies (e.g., discounts) tailored to each market segment. The appropriate strategy depends on the firm's costs, the consumers' price sensitivities, and the competition. Several tactics can be used to segment markets on the basis of price.[3] Table 7.2 provides a summary of segmented pricing examples across the major segments of the hospitality and travel industry.

7.5.1 Segmenting by Buyer Identification

One method that can be used to segment by price is to base the price on some form of buyer identification. That is, in order to obtain a discounted price, consumers must belong to a group of people that share similar characteristics. For example, hotels and motels have many discounted rates available for consumers belonging to groups such as the American Automobile Association (AAA) or the American Association of Retired Persons (AARP). Another variation is for consumers to save coupons that can be presented at a later date for a discount. Many restaurants put

SEGMENTATION STRATEGY	LODGING	FOOD SERVICE	TRAVEL	LEISURE
Buyer Identification	Business vs. leisure	Seniors and children	Seniors, students	Golf memberships for ladies, children, seniors
Purchase Location	City, suburban, airport, resort	Mall, airport, corporate dining	Online vs. calling or using a travel agent	Theme parks onsite vs. off-site
Time of Purchase	Weekend vs. weekday	Peak hours vs. early-bird (before 6:00 P.M.)	Peak business travel vs. leisure	Theme parks and golf courses with twilight discounts
Purchase Volume	Meetings and corporate contracts vs. transient	Banquets vs. restaurants in hotels	Airlines and rental car companies that offer corporate rates	Golf course discounts for tournaments
Product Design	Concierge or business level	Corporate dining facilities often have fine dining and cafeterias	Southwest Airlines "business select" and airline first-class seats	Country clubs offer social memberships and full memberships
Product Bundling	Overnight stay with champagne brunch and/or theater tickets	"Value" meals or combos (e.g., meal deal at Subway)	Cruise lines offer airline tickets and online travel agents package hotels, airlines, and rental cars	Grouping museum admissions (e.g., Ripley's Believe It Or Not and Guinness World Records)

TABLE 7.2 • Segmented Pricing Examples across Industry Segments

coupons in newspapers or direct-mail pieces that must be saved and brought to the establishment to get a discount within a certain time period. However, only a particular type of price-sensitive consumer will take the time to save, file, and redeem coupons for price discounts.

7.5.2   Segmenting by Purchase Location

It is possible to segment consumers based on where they purchase a product or service. Some restaurant chains will vary their prices in different geographic locations to account for differences in purchasing power and standard of living. For example, fast-food restaurants often charge more for menu items in large cities, food courts, and major highway locations than in suburban and rural locations. Also, hotel, restaurant, and car rental chains charge different prices in international markets based on a country's standard of living. Finally, a general practice by theme parks is to charge more for tickets purchased at the gate and less for tickets purchased at nearby locations (e.g., hotels and supermarkets) or through various organizations (e.g., government agencies and AAA).

7.5.3   Segmenting by Time of Purchase

Service firms tend to notice certain purchasing patterns based on the time of day, week, month, or year. Unfortunately, it is not always possible to meet the demand during these peak periods. One way to smooth the demand is to offer discounted prices at off-peak times. Restaurants offer early-bird specials for patrons who are willing to eat earlier in the evening, airlines offer supersaver rates for consumers who are willing to travel at off-peak times, and hotels offer lower rates for weekends and slower seasons throughout the year. This results in a shift in demand from peak times to off-peak times by the most price-sensitive consumers. Dynamic pricing is the most recent term used to describe the practice of continually changing prices based on market conditions (e.g., supply and demand). In theory, each customer will be charged the price he or she is willing to pay.

Dynamic pricing
Continually changing prices based on market conditions.

7.5.4   Segmenting by Purchase Volume

One of the most common forms of price segmentation is to vary price based on the quantity purchased, offering discounts for larger orders. The majority of firms, both small and large, will negotiate price discounts for larger volume orders. Hospitality and tourism firms will normally start discounting prices for groups of 10 or more people. In particular, hotel salespeople are responsible for filling the hotel with groups by offering discounts that tend to increase with the size of the group. Hotels and restaurants use the same tactics to sell catering functions such as weddings and banquets.

7.5.5   Segmenting by Product Design

Another form of price segmentation is based on the actual product or service. It may be possible to segment consumers by offering simple variations of a firm's product or service that appeal to the different segments. For example, airlines found that they could charge substantially more for first-class seating by widening the seats slightly and providing a little more service. Similarly, hotels offer suites and concierge floors that are slightly larger and/or provide some additional services. None of these variations by airlines or hotels has a significant impact on the cost of providing the service, but the firms are able to charge significantly higher prices to a small segment of the market that values the additional amenities and services.

7.5.6   Segmenting by Product Bundling

The last form of price segmentation involves packaging products and services into price bundles. Firms offer several products to consumers at a packaged price that is lower than the cost of purchasing the products separately. Fast-food restaurants offer bundled meals that include a sandwich,

Some hotels and motels offer discounted rates to consumers belonging to groups such as the American Automobile Association.

an order of french fries, and a soft drink. They also allow consumers to increase the size of the components for a small amount more. An alternative form of product bundling is to offer premiums, or free merchandise, with the purchase. Many fast-food restaurants put free game pieces and pull-tabs on their packaging and give children free toys with a child's meal.

These are some of the basic tactics that can be used to segment markets on the basis of price. The various tactics can be used alone or in combination with one another to achieve a firm's desired goals. Today's consumers can obtain information about competitive products and services very easily, resulting in a large, value-conscious market. Firms will need to find ways to segment the price-sensitive consumers from the quality-oriented consumers so that they can extract the most consumer surplus and revenue from the marketplace.

7.6 REVENUE MANAGEMENT

Revenue management involves combining people and systems in an attempt to maximize revenue by coordinating the processes of pricing and inventory management. *Pricing* is the process of determining the value of products and services that will result in the maximum total revenue for the firm. In reality, hospitality and tourism firms offer many different products and must determine the appropriate price points based on customer demand and competition. *Inventory management* is the process of determining how much of a product or service should be offered at each price point. For example, hotels allocate a certain number of guest rooms for groups and try to fill the quota by setting a price that will extract the most revenue from the market.

One of the challenges of revenue management is that price sensitivity varies from customer to customer. Market segmentation allows hospitality and tourism firms to group customers into market segments that share certain characteristics such as price sensitivity. In a perfect world, a firm would maximize its revenue by selling its products and services to customers at the highest price each customer is willing to pay for the product or service. Therefore, the goal of revenue management is to "sell the right product to the right customer at the right time for the right price."

This concept of revenue management is particularly important in service industries because of the intangible nature of the product. Hospitality and tourism firms such as hotels and airlines have limited capacities and resources. This situation, combined with the fact that the product is perishable and revenue cannot be inventoried, leaves firms in a difficult position. Unused capacity for service firms is lost forever. For example, airlines cannot recoup the revenue lost by having unoccupied seats on a flight, hotels cannot make up for unsold rooms, and car rental companies cannot compensate for cars sitting on the lot.

This phenomenon often leads to overbooking by hotels and airlines, because the firms do not want to have unused capacity due to cancellations or no-shows. In some cases, revenue can be recouped through requiring deposits or charging penalties, but there are limits to the effectiveness of these practices. For example, charging a group a penalty for not picking up its entire room block could cause the group to discontinue using your hotel or brand in the future.

7.6.1 Establishing a Pricing Structure

Revenue per available room (REVPAR) provides a better indication of a hotel's capacity utilization than average daily rate (ADR). The ADR is calculated using total revenue, occupancy rate, and the number of available rooms.

$$\text{Total revenue} = \text{Sum of (room} \times \text{price) for all rooms sold}$$

$$\text{Number of rooms sold} = \text{Occupancy rate} \times \text{Available rooms}$$

$$\text{Average daily rate} = \text{Total revenue} / \text{Number of rooms sold}$$

The ADR and the average occupancy rate can be used to estimate long-term revenues (monthly, quarterly, or annually) for hotels and other lodging facilities. Airlines perform the same type of analysis using revenue per available seat and average fare based on the number of seats sold. However, there are many factors—such as seasonality, business cycles, and economic trends—that can affect future performance. This makes it difficult to get accurate estimates for use in strategic pricing, but firms need to determine how much inventory to make available at each price point in an effort to maximize revenue.

The following is a simplified example to illustrate the decision facing an airline trying to maximize revenue. Only two possible prices exist: a discounted fare and the full fare. The airline must decide whether to sell a seat at the discounted fare ($200) or take the chance that the seat can be sold at a later date at full fare ($500). The decision tree that appears in Figure 7.3 outlines the options facing the airline.

Revenue management

Involves combining people and systems in an attempt to maximize revenue by coordinating the processes of pricing and inventory management.

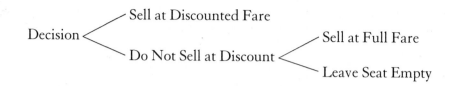

Decision

Sell at Discounted Fare

Do Not Sell at Discount

Sell at Full Fare

Leave Seat Empty

FIGURE 7.3 • **Decision tree for airline revenue.**

If the airline sells now at the discounted fare, there is guaranteed revenue of $200. If the airline decides not to sell at the discounted fare, the two possible outcomes are to sell at the full fare or to have the seat remain empty. If the seat does not get sold, there is zero revenue. Therefore, the final decision is based on the expected value of each option based on the probability that the seat will be sold at a later date for full fare. If there is a 50 percent chance of selling the seat for full fare, the expected value of waiting would be:

$$.50(\$500) + .50(\$0) = \$250$$

Because the expected value of waiting ($250) exceeds the expected value of selling at the discounted fare (1.0 × $200 = $200), then the airline should wait. In this case, as long as the probability of selling at a later date for full fare is greater than 40 percent (200/500), the airline is better off waiting. The estimated probability is based on past experience. In reality, this decision is much more complicated.

A firm's pricing structure gets established based on a careful analysis of customers, the firm's business, and the market for its products and services. First, the customer analysis should include an examination of customer market segments and their shared characteristics. It is important to know what attributes are used by the customers to make decisions (e.g., rate/price, location, convenience, service quality). In addition, it is useful to know the price sensitivity of the market segment and what distribution channels are used to buy the firm's services. Second, the firm should take an objective look at the quality of its product–service mix, its marketing programs, and the results of past pricing actions. Finally, the firm should examine the demand for its product and its competitive position (i.e., strengths and weaknesses relative to the competition).

7.6.2 Yield Management

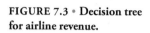

Yield management
Using a model to maximize the revenue, or yield, obtained from a service operation, given limited capacity and uneven demand.

Yield management is a technique used to maximize the revenue, or yield, obtained from a service operation, given limited capacity and uneven demand. This technique was first used by airline companies and then adopted by lodging and cruise firms. Within the hospitality and tourism industry, yield management has come into more widespread use with the expansion of computerized property management systems. In its most basic form, yield management uses a firm's historical data to predict the demand for future reservations, with the goal of setting prices that will maximize the firm's revenue and profit. Whereas yield management is focused more on maximizing income from customers who are more price inelastic (i.e., less price-sensitive), revenue management focuses on maximizing occupancy (seats sold) as well. Therefore, yield management and dynamic pricing are practices covered under the umbrella of revenue management. In fact, many people use the terms interchangeably because of the subtle differences between them. Dynamic pricing is the more recent term being used, especially in the context of selling tickets for sporting events.

Yield management is widely used within the hospitality and tourism industry for several reasons:

- **Perishable inventory.** As discussed in Chapter 2, hospitality and tourism services are highly perishable. If a hotel room is not occupied one evening or an airline flies with empty seats, the potential revenue for those services cannot be captured at a later date. In other words, there are no inventories for services.

- **Fluctuating demand.** Most hospitality and tourism firms experience demand that rises and falls within a day, week, month, or year. During high-demand periods, services are sold at or near full price. During the low-demand or nonpeak periods, capacity remains unused.

- **Ability to segment customers.** Firms must segment customers based on price, as discussed earlier in this chapter, and offer a discounted price to a selective group of customers.

- **Low variable costs.** Hospitality and tourism firms often have a large ratio of fixed to variable costs, which would favor a high-volume strategy. The marginal cost of serving an additional customer is minimal as long as there is excess capacity.

7.6.3 Selective Discounting

One of the cornerstones of yield management is the ability to offer discounts to only a selected group of customers. Rather than offer one price for a given time period, either peak or nonpeak, firms can distinguish between consumers. This minimizes the effect of lost revenue resulting from consumers who are willing to pay full price being able to pay the discounted price. To accomplish this, service firms normally place restrictions on the discounted price so that consumers must sacrifice something in return for the discount. For example, airline companies require passengers to book in advance (up to 21 days), stay over Saturday night, and accept a no-cancellation policy to obtain the discounted fare. Similarly, hotels require guests to stay over weekends, during nonpeak seasons, or for a minimum number of nights.

7.6.4 Historical Booking Analysis

One of the major problems facing service firms using yield management systems is the determination of the amount of capacity to make available at the discounted rate. As mentioned earlier, yield management makes use of historical data in predicting future trends. A curve is constructed using data from the same period the previous year, and adjusting for recent trends seen in the most recent periods. Figure 7.4 illustrates a typical pattern for a large conference hotel. The solid line represents the historical pattern for room sales prior to the date in question. In general, the hotel would determine a comfort zone or construct a confidence interval around the actual occupancy rate. If prior sales are within this interval, then the hotel continues to use its current discounting policy. If the occupancy rate exceeds the upper level, then the hotel will temporarily reduce the number of discounted rooms and rates. If the occupancy rate falls below the lower level, then the hotel will offer more discounted rooms and rates until the occupancy rate is brought back within the predicted interval.

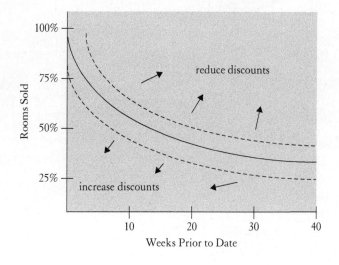

FIGURE 7.4 • Booking pattern curve for a conference hotel.

7.6.5 Yield Management Equation

As stated earlier, the goal of yield management is to maximize the revenue, or yield, from a service operation. The following equation is a simplified version of the calculation used in actual programs.

$$\text{Maximize} \left[\frac{\text{Actual revenue}}{\text{Potential revenue}} \right]$$

The potential revenue for a hotel would be the number of total rooms available for sale multiplied by the rack rate (published price) for those rooms. For instance, if a hotel had 200 rooms that all had a rack rate of $100, the potential room revenue for that hotel would be $20,000 per night. However, if the hotel had an occupancy rate of 70 percent and an average room rate of $80, then the actual revenue would be $11,200 [(0.7 × 200) × 80]. The yield in this case would be 0.56 (11,200/20,000). The goal is to maximize this figure or to get it as close to 1.0 as possible. What if this hotel offered more discounts and had an occupancy rate of 80 percent and an average room rate of $75? The actual revenue would have been $12,000 [(0.8 × 200) × 75], or a yield of 0.6(12,000/20,000). As you can see, the potential revenue remains the same, but the actual revenue will change, depending on the level of discounts and the price sensitivity of consumers.

This example is simplified to demonstrate the basic use of yield management. In reality, hotels have different rooms with different rack rates, and many different market segments, including business, pleasure, or transient, and various group markets. Each of these major segments can be divided into smaller subsets. For instance, the group market can be segmented into association, corporate, and incentive travel. Hotels have created positions and, in some cases, departments that are responsible for revenue management. These individuals perform historical booking analysis and confer with the hotel's executive committee to determine discounting policies.

Another area that needs to be considered in determining a hotel's discounting policy is the additional revenue, other than room revenue, that is generated from guests. For example, hotels can earn additional revenue from the restaurant, bar, fitness center, parking, laundry services, room service, corporate services such as faxing and shipping, and catering for groups. Rather than analyze each guest, hotels look at the major market segments and calculate a multiplier that can be used to adjust room revenue for additional revenue potential. This is important because hotels must maximize the revenue they receive from all sources. For instance, it would be a mistake to

Hotels earn additional revenue through various on-site services, including the bar.

Courtesy of Foxwoods Resort Casino.

sell the room to a transient guest who paid $10 more a night than a business traveler if the business traveler is likely to spend more than $10 a day for additional services. Similarly, turning down a group because of high demand among transient customers may result in a loss of revenue from catering services that would have been purchased by the group. However, in peak demand seasons, such as fall in New England, hotels can charge considerably more to transient customers than to groups, and it would be a mistake to book a group well in advance and forgo this additional revenue.

Yield management has had a major impact on the hospitality and tourism industry. Advances in computer technology have improved the ability to estimate demand and revenue. In addition, it has become easier to segment markets and employ selective discounting through vehicles such as the Internet. In the future, yield management programs will become more affordable for smaller operations. In fact, yield management systems can be developed using ordinary spreadsheet software. Finally, companies are working on resource management models that will analyze the revenue contribution from all sources in the hotel, rather than focusing only on guest rooms.

7.7 PRICING LAW AND ETHICS

Pricing practices are normally illegal if they are found to be anticompetitive or if they take unfair advantage of consumers. However, ethical standards are not as clear as legal standards developed through case law. Many people feel that although it is legal to maximize profits through pricing, it may not always be ethical. First, we will discuss the legal issues surrounding pricing decisions, and then we will present a typology that can be used for considering the ethical constraints on pricing.

7.7.1 Legal Issues in Pricing

The federal government has sought to ensure fair price competition since it passed the Sherman Act in 1890, followed by the Clayton Act in 1914. These two pieces of antitrust legislation were enacted in response to growing concerns for small businesses with the advent of large corporations competing on a national level. Most of the laws are open to interpretation and often difficult to enforce, especially in regard to services. The Robinson-Patman Act, passed in 1936 to strengthen the Clayton Act, targeted unfair pricing practices. Most laws focus on goods or commodities, for which grade and quality can be easily determined, whereas services vary greatly. Therefore, the government has devoted most of its resources to monitoring the pricing of tangible products. Pricing practices that are potentially illegal fall into four groups: explicit agreements, nonexplicit agreements, price discrimination, and tie-in sales.[4]

7.7.1.1 EXPLICIT AGREEMENTS. *Explicit agreements* are formal agreements among firms to set the same prices or to use the same formula in setting prices. This practice of price fixing is generally regarded as illegal and will be enforced. It is illegal for competitive hotels to discuss prices, even if they are accommodating guests for the same conference. For example, a Marriott and a Sheraton have formed a hotel "connection" in Springfield, Massachusetts, to compete for meetings requiring more rooms than either hotel contains. The two hotels are physically connected, and they operate as two wings of one hotel for larger conferences. Guests can charge meals and other services from either hotel to their rooms. However, each hotel must negotiate price separately with the meeting planner without any contact, or it would be illegal.

7.7.1.2 NONEXPLICIT AGREEMENTS. *Nonexplicit agreements* take the form of concerted actions by competitors that are not formal but represent some level of collusion. The courts look for a pattern of uniform business conduct, or *conscious parallelism*. It is not enough for competitive firms to exhibit parallel behavior; they must also be found guilty of making a conscious effort to engage in that behavior. Airline companies have been investigated, and prosecuted, for this behavior in the past. Even today, it is not uncommon to be quoted identical fares on competitive airlines for the same routes. As with explicit agreements, it is unlawful for firms to exchange price information if it is intended to affect prices or if it identifies specific customers. Convention and visitors bureaus are able to provide aggregate price information on hotel rates in their regions, so long as they do not identify the rates for specific customers, including groups for meetings and conventions.

7.7.1.3 PRICE DISCRIMINATION. Firms are forbidden from charging purchasers different prices for commodities of like grade and quality in an attempt to substantially lessen competition. Two legal defenses exist for discriminatory prices: cost justification and meeting competition. The *cost justification defense* allows firms to charge different prices when the costs of providing the product differ between purchasers. The *meeting competition defense* allows firms to charge different prices to meet the lower price of a competitor. As mentioned earlier, it is difficult to use these criteria to evaluate the pricing practices of service firms. Every service experience is different and, with the consumer being part of the production process, firms could argue that the cost of providing the service differs between purchasers. There is a fine line when it comes to the price-segmentation techniques applied in the yield-management programs used by hotels and airline companies, but services have remained largely untouched by the price discrimination laws, as stated in the Robinson-Patman Act.

7.7.1.4 TIE-IN SALES. This is the practice of sellers requiring that, as a condition of purchasing one product, customers must buy other products exclusively from the seller. Tying arrangements were deemed unlawful according to the Clayton Act if the arrangements were meant to substantially lessen competition. The courts have been lenient in allowing tying arrangements that are voluntary or result in pro-competitive benefits. For instance, courts have allowed franchisors, such as McDonald's, to require franchisees to purchase products from them that are necessary to maintain standards of performance and a consistent image.

7.7.2 Ethical Issues in Pricing

Ethical standards are much more difficult to evaluate and uphold than legal standards in the area of pricing. People's views regarding ethics can be as diverse as their cultural or socioeconomic backgrounds. At one end of the continuum, there is a view that so long as a practice is legal, it is ethical to charge a price that will result in maximal profit. At the other end, there is a view that individuals and firms should not exploit one another for personal gain and that societal benefits should be stressed over those of any one entity. Table 7.3 illustrates the levels constituting the continuum, from the legal perspective to the societal perspective.

Level 1 assumes that all exchanges are voluntary and it is the responsibility of the buyer to obtain as much information as necessary to make a good decision. The legal principle of *caveat*

PRICING POLICY	LEVEL OF ETHICAL RESTRAINT				
	LOW ⟵			⟶ HIGH	
	LEVEL 1	LEVEL 2	LEVEL 3	LEVEL 4	LEVEL 5
Price is paid voluntarily	X	X	X	X	X
Price is based on equal information		X	X	X	X
Price is not exploiting buyers' essential needs			X	X	X
Price is justified by costs				X	X
Price provides equal access to goods regardless of one's ability to cover costs					X

TABLE 7.3 • **Pricing Ethics**

emptor, or let the buyer beware, is the cornerstone of a capitalist economy. This principle enables firms to compete and results in a larger variety of products offered at lower prices. However, services cannot be physically held or evaluated until after they are purchased and consumed. This, along with the high level of variability associated with services, provides a high degree of risk and uncertainty for consumers in purchasing hospitality and tourism products.

Level 2 suggests that consumers should not be exposed to making purchases under conditions of asymmetric information. That is, the seller should be required to disclose pertinent information to buyers so that they are not at a disadvantage. For example, airline companies are required to disclose any restrictions placed on tickets for air travel, such as the fact that supersaver rates are nonrefundable. Similarly, hotels must disclose room cancellation policies to would-be guests.

Level 3 imposes an additional restriction that sellers cannot earn excessive profits by charging artificially high prices for essential products. The best example of this practice would be when pharmaceutical companies charge high prices for life-saving drugs that are unaffordable for those without insurance or people with lower incomes. For example, airline companies and hotels offer discounted prices for certain consumers who must travel and find lodging away from home because of emergencies (e.g., funerals, family illnesses, accidents).

Level 4 condemns the practice of segmented pricing even when the product is nonessential. It states that prices should not be segmented based on value, and firms should not take advantage of consumers during periods where there are shortages, even for nonessential products. Hotels engage in questionable practices when they charge higher than normal rates during periods of high demand such as college graduations and special events. They often require minimum stays and charge a price above the published rate (rack rate). Additionally, some restaurants use different menus with higher prices for holidays and other special events.

Level 5 would seem extreme to most people because it is not consistent with free markets in a capitalist economy. Instead, this ethical restraint resembles a standard that one would find in a socialist society. It suggests that every member of the community or society should share with others to ensure a minimum standard of living. This standard would be more applicable to underdeveloped countries or to communities where the members are committed to a societal goal (such as religious communities). This ethical restraint would normally result in less variety of products and services of lower quality. For example, institutional food service operations in K–12 schools often offer subsidies for children from lower-income families.

In closing, one's approach to the world would certainly affect one's belief about the appropriate level of ethical restraint. Obviously, a trade-off exists between what is best for an individual and what is best for society. The more levels of restraint imposed, the smaller the gap between the higher and lower incomes in a society. There is not as much incentive for people to invest, resulting in a lower overall standard of living. Therefore, the correct level of restraint is probably somewhere between levels 1 and 5 as determined by the respective society.

chapter review

SUMMARY OF CHAPTER OBJECTIVES

Price remains an important component of the marketing mix because it directly affects the revenue of a firm. Price is also a critical element in segmenting markets and positioning a firm's products and services. As such, firms must consider all the factors that affect price, such as the objectives of the firm, the consumers' price sensitivity, and the external environment. Government regulations, trends in demographics and purchasing patterns, economic conditions, technological advances, and changes in the competitive environment all have an impact on prices.

Consumers' perceptions of value are the basis for making pricing decisions. After all, price must be an accurate representation of the value that a consumer places on a product or service, or an exchange would not occur. The three broad pricing strategies—price skimming, price penetration, and neutral pricing—are based on the relationship between price and economic value. Firms attempt to differentiate their products from one another, and then focus on those segments of the population that value their product–service mixes. Price segmentation should concentrate on those attributes that are valued differently by various segments of the population.

The most common pricing techniques are the cost-oriented, demand-oriented, and competitive pricing approaches. Cost-oriented approaches base pricing decisions on the cost of providing the product, starting with the break-even point and then adding a markup or target return. Demand-oriented approaches focus on consumer price sensitivity and market demand, including certain psychological tactics. Competitive pricing involves setting prices in relation to a firm's competition. The firm must choose to price at, below, or above the competition. Revenue management is the practice of changing prices based on market conditions and the price consumers are willing to pay.

Finally, legal and ethical issues surround product pricing. Laws exist to protect consumers and ensure fair competition. Firms cannot collude to fix prices and take advantage of consumers and other competitors. In addition to the legal standards, firms must often deal with ethical standards imposed by society. These standards will vary somewhere between "let the buyer beware" in a pure capitalist economy and a socialist economy, which restricts profits for personal gain.

KEY TERMS AND CONCEPTS

Bartering
Break-even analysis
Competitive pricing
Consumer price sensitivity
Cost-oriented pricing
Cost-plus pricing
Demand-oriented pricing
Differentiation value
Dynamic pricing
Economic value
Law of demand
Neutral pricing
Odd/even pricing

Penetration pricing
Prestige pricing
Price elasticity of demand
Price lining
Pricing objectives
Psychological pricing
Reference value
Reservation price
Revenue management
Segmented pricing
Skim pricing
Target-return pricing
Yield management

QUESTIONS FOR REVIEW AND DISCUSSION

1   What is price? What are some of the major factors that affect pricing decisions?

2   What are the major pricing objectives discussed in this chapter?

3   What are the most common effects on consumer price sensitivity?

4 What are the three broad pricing strategies? When is it appropriate to use each strategy?

5 What are the advantages and disadvantages of using break-even analysis?

6 What is economic value? Give an example of how you would determine the economic value for a particular hospitality service.

7 Discuss some of the price-segmentation strategies that can be used by hospitality and tourism firms.

8 What are the three major pricing techniques? Can you use more than one? Explain.

9 What is revenue management? How are dynamic pricing, yield management, and revenue management related?

10 What are some of the legal and ethical issues surrounding pricing decisions?

11 Internet exercise: Online travel agents normally have access to the same hotel and airline rates. The purpose of this exercise is to compare the prices between two online travel agents for the same products, and determine if there is a discount relative to purchasing the products directly from the suppliers.

   a Go to Expedia.com and Travelocity.com and compare the rates for a trip from your airport to Orlando, Florida. Look at the same hotel and airline, both separately (hotel only and flight only) for a 5-night trip that is approximately 6 months away (use the same dates for both online travel agents). Is there a difference in the prices?

   b Go to the individual suppliers (e.g., Sheraton Hotels and Delta Airlines) and get the prices for the same dates. Is there a difference between the online travel agents and the suppliers?

   c Compare the package price (Flight + Hotel) for the same trip between the online travel agents. Is there a difference? Is the savings significant compared to purchasing the products separately from the travel agent or the suppliers?

   d What concepts in the chapter can be used to describe the pricing strategies for the online travel agents?

NOTES

[1] Thomas T. Nagle and Reed K. Holden, *The Strategy and Tactics of Pricing: A Guide to Profitable Decision Making*, 3rd ed. (Englewood Cliffs, NJ: Prentice-Hall, 1995), pp. 77–94.

[2] Ibid., pp. 152–61.

[3] Thomas T. Nagle, "Economic Foundations for Pricing," *Journal of Business* 57, 1, Part 2 (1984), pp. S3–S26.

[4] Nagle and Holden, pp. 366–381.

chapter review

INTERNET CASE STUDY

Airline Pricing

The practice of yield management used by hospitality firms and sports operations was started in the airline industry. All industries use the same basic premise. However, given the nature of the airline industry, it is easiest to see the concept being used as an outside observer. Online travel sites such as Expedia, Travelocity, Orbitz, and Kayak provide instant comparisons for most of the major airlines for domestic and international routes on given dates.

Choose a pair of cities in the United States and compare the one-way and roundtrip airfares using Kayak.com for a set of dates originating at the following times: 1 month ahead, 10 days ahead, 5 days ahead, and 1 day ahead. Compare an overnight stay, a 5-day stay, and a 10-day stay for the roundtrip ticket. Construct a simple booking curve for the one-way and roundtrip prices using the "lead time" (i.e., how far in advance the ticket is booked) and the price for three different airlines in each chart.

Case Study Questions and Issues

1. Is there any noticeable pattern based on how far in advance the ticket is booked? Does the roundtrip price change based on the length of stay?

2. Are there any differences between the airlines? If so, what are some possible explanations? Are the differences consistent over the different time periods?

3. Do you think the results would be similar for any given combination of cities (e.g., large or small, domestic or international, distance between, etc.)? Explain your answer.

4. Now compare your results from Kayak.com with one other travel site that was previously given (i.e., Expedia, Travelocity, Orbitz). Is there any difference? How would you explain it?

5. Is it "fair" for airlines to charge different customers different prices for air travel on the same airline, in the same class seat, on the same date and time (i.e., the same flight)? Why or why not?

case study

CASE STUDY

The Pasta Shack

The Pasta Shack, an Italian restaurant in Orlando, Florida, near the major tourist attractions, has noticed a recent decline in sales. The owner and his managers decided to have a meeting to come up with some strategies to reverse this trend. One of the managers used to work for an independent restaurant in a suburban neighborhood in Chicago and suggested a strategy used successfully by his former restaurant: offering an early-bird menu to customers who order before 6:00 P.M. The idea is to provide a limited number of entrees at a discounted price.

The regular price of the entrees placed on the early-bird menu was $10.95 and included a salad. The new price for the specials would be $8.95. After the first two weeks of offering the specials, the daily average number of covers increased from 50 to 58 during the 4 to 6 P.M. time period. However, the daily average number of covers after 6 P.M. decreased from 75 to 70, due to some cannibalization of current customers. Assume that $8.95 is the average price per person from 4 to 6 P.M. and $10.95 is the average price per person after 6 P.M. when answering the following questions.

Case Study Questions and Issues

1. What was the effect of the price change on total revenues during the early-bird time period?

2. Using the concepts presented in the chapter, how would you explain this change?

3. Is the new strategy successful? Explain your answer.

4. What could be the cause for the initial decline in sales?

5. Are there any additional costs associated with the new strategy?

6. How could you increase the profitability associated with the early-bird strategy?

Developing New Products and Services

Courtesy of Pacific Edge Hotel, A Joie de Vivre Hotel, Laguna Beach, California.

Chapter Objectives

After studying this chapter, you should be able to:

1. Explain the importance of developing product lines.

2. Describe the two types of planning strategies for developing new products and services.

3. Outline the roles of new product committees, new product departments, product managers, and venture teams.

4. Describe the new product development process.

5. Explain the marketing roles of brands, brand names, and trademarks.

6. Apply product development and branding concepts to tourism destinations.

8.1   INTRODUCTION

No matter how successful a hospitality or tourism concept is, if the company associated with the concept does not evolve and change, then it will be left behind. If we were to consider the top 100 companies in the lodging and food service sectors, we would find that each year, some companies drop off the list and get replaced by new ones. Corporations such as Marriott International, Carnival Cruise Lines, Hilton, Starbucks, and Disney continue to lead the industry because they have been very successful in developing products and services that enhance their market position. However, it has become increasingly difficult for hospitality firms to expand sales and market share simply by adding new units. Today, growth must be accomplished within existing units by developing and implementing a superior product–service mix or by opening new units in untapped markets that may require a good deal of research and effort. For example, many firms have expanded their product–service mix offerings into international markets.

To further illustrate this point, consider the following examples. Because the number of great potential locations for restaurants has been reduced through market saturation, the leading companies have taken innovative steps to increase sales and grow their respective companies. First, they have sought new locations and venues to sell their product–service mix. For example, Pizza Hut, through an agreement with Marriott International, began selling a scaled-down version of its product–service mix in selected Marriott hotels. This scaled-down version, or kiosk style of operation, offers a limited menu with no seating within the immediate kiosk facility. In addition, Pizza Hut participates in some of the noncommercial food service accounts operated by contract food service companies such as Aramark. This allowed Pizza Hut to reach new markets—ones that it had not previously reached. The result has been increased sales and increased consumer satisfaction. This is a **win-win relationship** for both Pizza Hut and its partners. Win-win relationships are defined as situations in which both parties benefit, without one being a winner and the other a loser. When companies attempt to negotiate win-win agreements, they seek long-term relationships that over time benefit both organizations.

> **Win-win relationship**
> A situation that results when both parties are satisfied at the end of a negotiation.

A second example of using product–service mix development to increase sales would be fast-food restaurants that introduce new products on a regular basis. These companies routinely introduce new products or a bundle of products that are available for a limited time. The goal is to increase patronage and market share by taking customers away from the competition. A second goal is to increase brand loyalty, or the repeated purchasing of a firm's brand over time. These limited-time offerings are often a bundling of several products with a reduced price and/or increased portion size to convey a high level of perceived value to the consumer. Companies often call such bundling "value meals," "meal deals," or a similar term to convey better value.

The third example is best illustrated by the manner in which theme parks extend the life of their product–service mix life cycle by engaging in product–service mix development. Each year, thrill seekers want to try the newest and greatest rides at the many theme parks around the country. Among the leaders in this market are Disney, Six Flags, and Paramount. Each of these companies develops new rides each year in an effort to attract consumers to their respective parks. Having the latest, largest, or greatest of these thrill-type rides can have a very positive impact on theme park attendance, sales, and profitability.

Finally, product–service mix development includes additions to and enhancements of the service elements. For example, several restaurant chains, such as Outback™ and Chili's™, have increased sales by encouraging customers to purchase meals via a drive-up or take-away service. This added service allows them to increase unit sales without adding seats in their restaurants. Slight additions to staffing levels allow them to provide this service profitably.

There are two basic approaches to product development: **innovation** and follow-the-leader. With the innovation approach, the product developers are the risk takers, always seeking to be the first in the market with a new product or service. The leader, or innovator, will benefit from being the first to market with a new product or concept. Customers may associate the innovation with the leader or become loyal to that brand. For example, it is not unusual to hear customers at Burger King order a Happy Meal (a McDonald's product).[1] However, given the ease with which hospitality products and services can be duplicated, those who subscribe to the follow-the-leader approach can introduce their competing products and services soon after the market leader introduces its own products and services.

> **Innovation**
> The process of converting new ideas into products and services that offer value to consumers.

8.1.1 The Importance of Product Lines

Product line
A firm's portfolio of products and services.

For the continued success of a hospitality or tourism firm, it is important to have a product line, or portfolio of products and services. Few firms can survive and sustain long-term growth with only one or two products or services, because of the high risk associated with the lack of diversification. In addition to diversifying a firm's operating risk, there are several other reasons for developing new product lines, discussed in the following sections.

8.1.1.1 GROWTH OPPORTUNITIES FOR THE BUSINESS. When a company limits itself to one product or a limited number of products, it holds back the firm's growth potential. Consider a firm such as Baskin-Robbins. It was quite successful selling ice cream, but when consumer tastes shifted toward lower-fat and healthier items, the firm developed and offered new products such as frozen yogurt that met this demand.[2] This allowed Baskin-Robbins to appeal to more consumers and increase sales. McDonald's is another good example of a firm that expanded its product line to attract additional business. In addition to the hamburgers, french fries, and children's fare, it added salads and other menu items that are targeted toward adults. In recent years, McDonald's has enhanced its coffee products in an attempt to compete successfully against Starbucks and Dunkin' Donuts.

8.1.1.2 EFFICIENT AND EFFECTIVE USE OF COMPANY RESOURCES. As more products are developed or as a firm works on additional brands, it can make better use of corporate resources. For example, Choice Hotels International operates and franchises several brands of lodging products, including such brands as Clarion Hotels and Suites, Clarion, Quality Inns and Suites, Comfort Inns and Suites, Cambria, MainStay Suites, and Sleep Inns. Marriott International uses a similar strategy, offering traditional Marriott Hotels and Resorts, as well as J. W. Marriott Hotels and Resorts, Courtyard, Residence Inns, Fairfield Inns, Renaissance Hotels and Resorts, TownPlace Suites, SpringHill Suites, and Marriott Vacation Club. Operating multiple brands allows Choice Hotels International and Marriott International to make better use of corporate resources by segmenting the market and tailoring their offerings to the various segments using separate marketing programs.

8.1.1.3 INCREASING COMPANY MARKET SHARE AND IMPORTANCE OF THE COMPANY WITHIN THE OVERALL MARKET. When multiple products or brands are made available to the public, sales will increase and overall market share will also increase. This affords the firm a stronger position in the market and increases the importance of the firm.

8.1.1.4 DIVERSIFYING A FIRM'S BUSINESS RISK. Without a steady flow of new products and services, a hospitality or tourism firm could have serious problems if the sales of existing

The sunburst logo is consistent across all of the brands in the Days Inn product line.

product–service mix start to decline. However, increased sales from new products and services can counteract poor sales from the current ones. The larger the portfolio of products and product lines, the smaller the firm's business risk.

8.2 PLANNING FOR NEW PRODUCTS

It is critical for firms to take a systematic approach to developing and marketing new products and services. The potential rewards are high for successful new products or services, but the potential risks of failure are equally high. A firm must do a thorough analysis of a new product idea to determine if it is compatible with the firm's goals, if the firm has the necessary resources, and if the environment is favorable. Marketing plans should contain information regarding new product development, as well as the goals and strategies for existing products. As with strategies for existing products, strategies for new products can be either reactive strategies or proactive strategies.[3] **Reactive strategies** are developed as a response to a competitor's action, whereas **proactive strategies** are initiated as a preemptive effort to gain a competitive advantage.

8.2.1 Reactive Strategies for New Product Development

A **defensive strategy** is used to counter the effects on an existing product from a competitor's new product. Initially, this strategy involves minor changes in a firm's marketing mix such as advertising, packaging, and/or pricing. This will negate some of the impact from the competitive product until more information can be obtained and substantive changes made, if necessary. These changes could involve the development of a new product or service, or some major modifications to the current product–service mix. Normally, when new restaurants open, the other local restaurants counter with increased promotions and/or discounts. Similarly, when small airlines have tried to start a new service in niche markets, the larger airlines serving those same markets have retaliated with price cuts and promotions for their routes in those markets. The goal of the larger airlines is to prevent the smaller airline from gaining market share and profitability.

An **imitative strategy** involves copying a new product or service before it can have a large impact in the market. This strategy is particularly appealing when the product or service is not unique or when it can be easily duplicated. This strategy is heavily relied on in the fast-food industry. Every time McDonald's launches a successful new product, Burger King and some of the other competitors are quick to respond with similar offerings and prices. This practice is also popular for other hospitality and travel products. For example, the airline industry saw this happen after American Airlines introduced the first loyalty program in 1981. It was quickly copied by most of the other major airlines after it was met with success. More recently, most major airlines in the United States decided to offer "economy plus" seating with extra legroom at an additional price—a concept first started in 1991 by EVA Air from Taiwan.

An adapted version of the imitative strategy is the **second but better strategy**. Once again, firms respond to competitors' new products; however, the firm's primary goal in this case is to improve on the initial product. Marriott International's introduction of its Courtyard division and extended-stay properties was eventually followed by competitors with similar products. For example, both Wyndham Hotels and Hilton introduced a line of garden hotels that are targeted at business travelers with modest budgets and a dislike for large hotels. These new product lines or brands will compete directly with Marriott International's Courtyard brand, but their ultimate goal is to be better. This strategy is more common for products or services that require a large investment and a longer period of time to develop. For example, Avis rental car company used the slogan "We try harder" for 50 years. The slogan was first introduced in 1962 to highlight its position as number 2 in the rental car industry and the fact that it offered superior customer service than its number 1 competitor, Hertz.

The final reactive strategy is referred to as a **responsive strategy**. Firms are responsive in that they react to the demands of customers. These new products are truly market-driven. Hotels often modify their offerings and design new properties based on the observed behavior of their guests. The way guests tend to rearrange a room, common complaints, and frequency of use of amenities

Reactive strategies
Strategies that respond to changes in the marketplace.

Proactive strategies
Strategies that anticipate changes in the marketplace.

Defensive strategy
A reactive strategy that is used to counter the effects on an existing product from a competitor's new product.

Imitative strategy
A reactive strategy that involves copying a new product or service before it can have a large impact in the market.

Second but better strategy
An adapted version of the imitative strategy where the firm's primary goal is to improve on the competitor's product.

Responsive strategy
A reactive strategy where firms adapt to the demands of customers.

Courtesy of Wyndham Worldwide.

Hotels design their facilities to appeal to their specific target markets.

and services are all factors that affect the design of hotel products. A recent response to guests' changing demands has been the addition of spa services at many hotels. Previously, spa services were normally offered only at resorts.

8.2.2 Proactive Strategies for New Product Development

Research and development strategy

A proactive strategy where firms conduct research to aid in the design and development of new products or services.

Another approach to developing new products is to be proactive and initiate change, rather than react to it. A popular proactive strategy used by manufacturing firms is a **research and development strategy**. Service firms also do research in an attempt to design and develop new service concepts. Hospitality and tourism firms are continually searching for new ways to improve facility designs and computer systems for reservations and resource management. Marriott International developed proprietary computer systems for conducting business, whereas many other firms choose to use systems developed by outside vendors.

Customer-oriented strategy

A proactive strategy that focuses on the wants and needs of current and prospective customers.

Another proactive tactic used by service firms is a **customer-oriented strategy**. This strategy embraces the marketing concept and the notion that it is important to determine customer wants and needs and then design products and services to meet those needs. Most hotels and restaurants use marketing research, comment cards, and other methods to gather information from consumers. Firms such as Ritz-Carlton Hotels take a comprehensive approach to gather information on service quality and satisfaction. Ritz-Carlton has received the Malcolm Baldrige National Quality Award as a result of its efforts to meet customer needs. The hotel firm obtained feedback from customers, employees, and suppliers in an attempt to completely understand the process of delivering high-quality service to its customers.

Firms that are innovative and tend to be leaders in their respective industries try to create an entrepreneurial strategy for their employees. These firms are looking for new ideas that are generated internally through means other than research and development. Employees are a great source for ideas on improving existing products and services and developing new ones. After all, what employee does not have an opinion about how to improve his or her firm's products or services? Rather than have this be a negative influence on the organization, some firms choose to encourage employees to share their ideas and opinions. As a result, some of the new service concepts become separate operating divisions or separate components of current operations.

Another way to add products or services to a firm's portfolio is through mergers or acquisitions. A firm can acquire the rights to new products or services by entering into a legal arrangement with another firm, thereby combining the two firms' products and services. Acquisitions are plentiful in the hospitality and tourism industry. At one time, PepsiCo developed a major presence in the hospitality industry through its acquisitions of brands such as Pizza Hut, Taco Bell, and KFC. The advantage is that the individual firms do not have to diversify their offerings because the diversification has occurred at the corporate level. Later, PepsiCo reassessed this strategy and divested itself of these brands, which were acquired by Yum! Brands.

Finally, some firms choose to form alliances for a specific goal or purpose instead of combining ownership. Alliances are designed to take advantage of synergies that exist between companies by pooling resources such as marketing, research, and distribution. Many airlines, hotels, and car rental agencies have formed strategic alliances to help promote and sell their products and services. The firms benefit from cooperative advertising and shared databases, among many other areas. For example, United Airlines Mileage Plus members earn free miles that can be redeemed with lodging companies Marriott, Carlson Hotels Worldwide, Starwood, Hilton, Omni, Wyndham, and Choice Hotels, as well as rental car partners Hertz, Alamo, Budget, Avis, Dollar, and National. Alliances have been used most effectively by airlines. One of the best known of these alliances is the Star Alliance that, as of March 2016 includes 28 airlines operating in more than 190 countries. Aimed primarily at business travelers, the Star Alliance allows airlines to share information about travelers, as well as allowing travelers to have better access to route information and reservations among the airlines that are members of the alliance. Product development is a highly complex issue. It requires critical thinking and careful planning. The next section addresses issues related to how companies organize for product development and how it is conducted.

Entrepreneurial strategy
A proactive strategy where firms generate new ideas internally through means other than research and development.

Acquisitions
A firm can acquire the rights to new products or services by entering into a legal arrangement with another firm, thereby combining the two firms' products and services.

Alliances
Firms pool resources for a specific goal or purpose instead of combining ownership.

8.3 ORGANIZING FOR NEW PRODUCT PLANNING

Firms use a variety of organizational structures to develop new products and services. No one way is best, and each has inherent advantages and disadvantages. The primary organizational structures are new product committees, new product departments, product managers, and venture teams. Each of these structures is explained in the following paragraphs.

8.3.1 New Product Committees

A new product committee consists of individuals representing cross-functional areas of the firm. Usually, representatives provide input from operations, marketing, finance, and accounting. Committee members are charged with the responsibility of reviewing new product ideas and with determining the impact that new products will have on each of their respective areas. The process of using new product committees is often slow, and members normally have their own day-to-day responsibilities within their respective functional areas of the firm. Although these committees typically make decisions about which new products or services to offer, they do not develop the actual products or services.

8.3.2 New Product Departments

Some firms establish a full-time new product department. This addresses the problem of product development being a part-time responsibility of members of the product development department. It is still very important for members of the product development department to solicit input from all cross-functional areas of the firm.

8.3.3 Product Managers

Some firms appoint product managers, or brand managers, to assume complete responsibility for determining marketing objectives and marketing strategies for a specific brand. Included in these responsibilities is product development as it relates to that brand. For example, suppose that someone was responsible for the brand Holiday Inn Express. In the role of a marketing manager, the individual would be responsible for all elements of the marketing mix: the product–service mix, the presentation mix, the communications mix, and the distribution mix. The marketing manager would also have the responsibility of establishing and implementing marketing strategies for the brand. Among the additional responsibilities of this role is being involved in product development.

8.3.4 Venture Teams

Venture teams are similar to new product committees, but they are formed to complete a specific product assignment. Venture teams bring together expertise from operations, marketing, accounting and finance, and, if necessary, architecture and construction. The venture team is charged with new product planning, development, and implementation. Unlike new product committees, which normally only review and make decisions about whether new products should be developed further, the venture team is expected to stay on the project through the entire new product development process.

8.4 NEW PRODUCT DEVELOPMENT PROCESS

Developing new products and services is time-consuming and risky, but it is essential to the continued long-term success of a firm. Many methodologies can be used to develop products and services. In this section, we will explore the steps in new product development within the hospitality and tourism industry (see Figure 8.1). Many firms, especially food service firms, use this process when developing new products and services. The examples used in this section relate to how new menu items are developed by food service firms. Comparable product development processes are used in the development of lodging products and other types of products and services within the hospitality and tourism industry. Similar techniques are used to develop new services and elements of the total customer experience. The stages of the product development process are (1) idea generation, (2) product screening, (3) concept testing, (4) business analysis and test marketing, and (5) market introduction.

8.4.1 Idea Generation

Idea generation
The process of generating new ideas for products and services from internal and external sources.

New product ideas should take advantage of opportunities and trends in the dynamic marketplace, while matching the firm's strengths and overall mission. Ideas for new products can be generated internally as an assigned function for research and development groups, or as a result of brainstorming by the structures covered in the previous section—a process called idea generation.

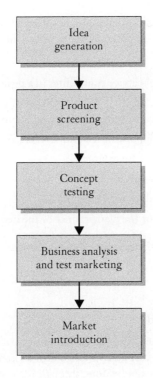

FIGURE 8.1 • New product development process.

Other internal sources for ideas include salespeople and other employees. Many of the employees in a service firm are in customer contact positions. This enables them to get direct feedback concerning problems and to detect problem areas as they perform their normal job functions. This type of information is invaluable in improving customer satisfaction with service enhancements and new services.

Some of the external sources for new product ideas are competitors, suppliers, trade shows, and trade magazines. A firm can produce new product ideas from following the actions of competitors and reading about new developments in trade magazines. These new developments are also the focus of companies attending trade shows, whether they are direct competitors or simply similar firms in other markets. Finally, suppliers can sometimes have a keen insight into a firm's operations. They deal with many different firms and often generate ideas for improvement based on their own developments.

Firms should seek ideas from all potential sources. For example, menu items should be sought that expand, extend, or enhance the current menu. Today, new menu item development appears to be most active in breakfast foods, light and healthy menu items, new tastes in foods such as regional cuisine, foods that cannot be easily prepared at home, foods that lend themselves to take-out, and food that is delivered.

8.4.2 Product Screening

After ideas have been generated, the focus should turn toward **product screening**—evaluating the list of potential products to select the ones with the greatest potential for success. Managers should perform both qualitative and quantitative analyses to evaluate new product ideas. The *qualitative* standards involve answering the following questions:

- To what extent will the product increase sales and profits?
- Will the product attract new customers, and to what extent will it cannibalize from the sales of current products?
- What price would consumers pay for the product?
- Do we have the expertise and capacity to produce this product within our units?
- Does the competition offer a similar product? If so, how can we differentiate our product?

Product screening
Screening the list of potential products or services to select the ones with the greatest opportunity for success.

The *quantitative* analysis involves developing a weighted scoring for each new product idea to determine those with the greatest potential for success. The scoring is normally based on the following criteria:

- How the potential product or service contributes in a positive way to the image of the product and the company
- How the potential product contributes to achieving the overall company goals
- The strengths, weaknesses, opportunities, and threats (SWOT) that the firm faces
- Impact on current and potential customers
- Voids in the current product–service mix
- Equipment necessary to produce the new item
- Potential sources of supply for the new product or the necessary ingredients

When the two types of analysis are completed, new product ideas with the most potential are selected for further development.

8.4.3 Concept Testing

Concept testing
A written or oral description and/or a visual representation of a new product or service is tested on consumers in the target market.

After new product ideas are screened, the ones that show signs of promise are subjected to concept testing. At this stage, a written or oral description and/or a visual representation is shown to consumers in the target market. This can be done through focus groups or using a more extensive marketing research data collection method. The consumers are asked a series of questions regarding the concept and its value in relation to competitors' products. The results of this analysis are used to refine the new product's design and assess its market potential. At this point, only products with a high probability of success are moved forward because the resources necessary to proceed begin to escalate.

At this stage in the menu design process, the products are typically tested further in corporate test kitchens. The emphasis is on recipe development to refine the product so that it can be consistently produced. Standards are established for portions, preparation, holding times, and presentation. If the development plan proceeds according to schedule, the product is tested in a few units. At this point of development, focus groups representing individuals from the target markets evaluate the product. The focus groups, led by a skilled facilitator, assess the product's potential impact by conducting taste tests and soliciting consumer feedback about the product, price, appearance, and other attributes. If this process continues to be successful, the product is then ready to undergo limited test marketing in more units.

8.4.4 Business Analysis and Test Marketing

The information obtained from potential consumers, representing the target market, in the concept testing stage is used in a business analysis to evaluate the business potential of the new product. Consumer responses are used to estimate potential sales and market share so that costs can be allocated and potential profitability assessed. It is important to run more than one scenario (e.g., best case, worst case, and most likely case) for different market conditions. If the figures are promising, then the new product is prepared for test marketing.

Test marketing
The limited introduction of a new product or service in select locations.

Test marketing is the limited introduction of a new product in selected locations. It is necessary to extend the testing period long enough to view consumers' true purchase patterns, including repurchase (approximately 3 to 12 months). During the test-market period, the product is evaluated based on (1) consumer feedback concerning quality, price, and various forms of sales promotion and advertising; (2) sales figures during various days of the week and times of day; and (3) the financial contribution that the new item has made.

Locations chosen for test-markets should possess some common characteristics. First, the city or location should be similar to the planned market for the final product. It should have the same forms of media, the same demographic and psychographic backgrounds for potential customers, and the same or similar competitors. Second, the city or location should be somewhat isolated and of manageable size. There should not be any influence by competitors or media from neighboring locations. The most important point to remember when conducting test marketing is to make sure the test-market locations are representative of the planned market to ensure the reliability and validity of the results.

8.4.5 Market Introduction

The final stage in the new product development process is **market introduction**—introducing the new product to the entire market, or rolling it out, market by market. New products that demonstrate favorable business projections and test-market results are given the green light by management. It is very costly to launch a new product because of the advertising campaigns and sales promotions, the employee training, and any required changes to the facility. At first, there are negative profits due to fixed start-up costs and inventories, and little revenue. It may take a good deal of time for the new product to be accepted and build market share. During this period, the firm must monitor the results and make any necessary changes in marketing strategy. Once the product is successfully launched, it is monitored and managed through the rest of its product life cycle.

Market introduction
A new product or service is made available for sale in the marketplace with an associated marketing program.

8.5 IDENTIFYING PRODUCTS AND SERVICES

Hospitality and tourism firms may offer more than one service or product line that is targeted at different market segments. It is often necessary to distinguish these offerings from one another if they are to hold different positions in the marketplace. Therefore, branding is a critical component of the marketing strategy for hospitality and tourism firms. The following section defines the terms related to branding and their use in the positioning of products. Brands are a very powerful marketing tool, and if properly managed, they have the potential of increasing sales, increasing profitability, and increasing customer satisfaction. Definitions of important terms follow:

- **Brand.** A **brand** is the name, sign, symbol, design, or any combination of these items that is used to identify the product and establish an identity that is separate and unique from competitors. Consider the impact that various brands have within the hospitality and tourism industry. Is there any brand more recognizable than the golden arches of McDonald's or the green circle of Starbucks Coffee?

- **Brand name.** The **brand name** is the part of the brand consisting of the words or letters that can be used to identify the firm.

- **Brand mark.** A **brand mark** is the symbol or logo design that is used to identify the product. Consider the stylized *M* and *H* that represent Marriott International and Hilton, respectively. When we see this brand symbol on the side of the hotel, we instantly know which brand the hotel represents.

- **Trademark.** A **trademark** is a brand that has been given legal protection and is restricted for exclusive use by the owner of the trademark.

Here is an example that illustrates the importance of branding and its impact on sales and customer satisfaction: In a university dining services operation, one of the venues available on campus was an unbranded pizza operation. It was successful and turned a reasonable profit for dining services and the university. Students could purchase pizzas from the operation à la carte or use part of their meal plan as a credit toward the cost of a pizza. As any professional manager would do, the dining services director of the university was seeking ways to increase student satisfaction with the dining services operations and also increase profitability for the university. One of the options considered was replacing the unbranded pizza operation with a regional or national brand pizza operation. After surveying the student body to determine preference, it was decided that Pizza Hut

Brand
The name, sign, symbol, design, or any combination of these items that is used to identify a product or service in an attempt to establish an identity that is separate and unique from competitors' offerings.

Brand name
A part of the brand consisting of the words or letters that can be used to identify the firm.

Brand mark
The symbol or logo design used to identify the product or service.

Trademark
A brand that has been given legal protection and is protected for exclusive use by the owner of the trademark.

was the most popular choice among the students. Working with the corporate office of the contract food service company, which had previously negotiated with Pizza Hut for franchises at other universities, they were able to secure a franchise and open the Pizza Hut. In the first year that the Pizza Hut was in operation, sales increased nearly 30 percent. This increased revenue more than offset the franchise fee and other types of royalties that the management services company paid to Pizza Hut, Inc. The results of surveys administered to the students indicated that customer satisfaction had also increased. This is one example of the impact that brands can have.

8.5.1 Characteristics of Effective Branding

Marketers, especially in other fields, have long studied the use of brand names and have established criteria that are believed to make brand names more effective. Within the hospitality and tourism industry, these criteria are not always closely followed. Instead, the names of families or the founders have been used as the basis for the brand name. Consider that McDonald was the family name of the two brothers who first opened a hamburger restaurant in California. J. W. Marriott Sr. opened his first restaurant, a Hot Shoppe, in Washington, DC. Conrad Hilton opened his first hotel in Texas.

Marketing managers recommend that the following criteria be used to establish brand names:

- **Easy to pronounce, recognize, and remember.** Some of the leading brands are the ones that are easiest to remember. Examples are USAir, Red Lobster, and National Car Rental.

- **Describes the benefits of the product or service.** It is a bonus for advertising and promoting a brand if the name describes the product's benefits. Examples are Comfort Inn, Residence Inn, and Friendly's Restaurants.

- **Can be translated into foreign languages.** Many firms have been shortsighted in choosing brand names, overlooking name-related problems that could occur if they expand into foreign markets. Examples of good brand names include Marriott International, Hertz, McDonald's, and United Airlines. An example of a brand name that didn't translate well was KFC in Montreal where they require the French equivalent of an English name—the equivalent of "Kentucky Fried Chicken" is "Poulet Frit Kentucky" or PFK. In many countries, there are limits on the number of foreign languages that can be used in advertising and brand names. The most restrictive country is France.

- **Distinctive and capable of legal protection.** Some brands are distinctive and easy to remember. It is also important to consider the possibility of becoming a chain or franchise and to choose a brand name that can be registered. Some examples are Wyndham Hotels, Avis, and Delta Airlines. Marriott International has been among the most successful companies when it comes to developing successful brands. The firm has a long history of effective branding, while at the same time leveraging the Marriott name when new brands are created.

8.5.2 The Use of Co-Branding

Co-branding
Using multiple brand names to promote and/or sell a single product, service, event, or cause.

Often, two or more companies form a partnership or alliance to work together in promoting their individual brands. The term co-branding is used to refer to this practice of using multiple brand names to promote and/or sell a single product, service, event, or cause. The main goal of co-branding is for organizations to join forces by leveraging each other's reputation and creating a marketing synergy. The strategy tends to be successful if the brand awareness and perceived brand quality of the constituent brands is high (e.g., Bulgari and Ritz-Carlton), and there is an adequate level of compatibility and brand fit between the brands. However, there is also the potential for a "spill-over" effect when one of the constituents has a higher level of brand awareness and/or perceived brand quality than the other constituent. For example, if a regional airline was to offer its frequent flyers a credit card through Citibank (e.g., MasterCard or Visa), it would instantly lend credibility to the airline and probably increase consumer perceptions of reliability and quality.

Courtesy Allied Domenq OSR

Courtesy Hyatt Hotels Corporation

Some brands are recognized worldwide.

Basically, there are two types of co-branding: ingredient co-branding and composite co-branding. *Ingredient co-branding* involves using a popular brand as an element or component of another product or service. This is common in restaurants when a chain such as TGI Fridays or Chili's uses popular products such as Jack Daniel's or Tabasco in its recipes and advertises them using the brand name, trademark, and/or company logo. *Composite co-branding* involves using two popular brands in a way that they can collectively offer a distinct product or service that could not be offered otherwise. This can be in the form of brands from the same company such as YUM! Corporation combining KFC and Taco Bell in one building, or brands from different companies to form a joint venture or multiple sponsorships, like when banks and credit card companies form partnerships or alliances with hotels and airlines.

There are several advantages associated with a successful co-branding partnership. Some of the more likely benefits are:

- Brand entry into new markets
- Financial benefits such as increased income and shared costs/expenses that result in lower risk
- Potential for package deals and promotions
- "Spill-over" effect from high perceived quality and brand personality of the partner brand

However, that is not to say that there aren't also possible risks, or disadvantages, associated with co-branding. Some of the more common risks are:

- Overexposure of one or both brands in the marketplace
- Changes in financial status, corporate ownership, and/or corporate strategy of either (or both) partner have an effect on the other
- Negative "spill-over" effect from the other brand based on its perceptions by consumers and the general public
- Dilution of the brand because of its association with a new product or service

8.6 DESTINATION PRODUCT DEVELOPMENT

Regional tourism products are developed by three different types of organizations: (1) individual service providers such as amusement parks, (2) tour operators and travel agents, and (3) destination marketing organizations. *Destination marketing organizations (DMOs)* promote a number of different products, including convention centers, hotels, attractions, and events. In addition, DMOs promote transportation services and vendors/suppliers for meetings and events. Once again, the primary target markets for these products are the groups that hold meetings and leisure tour travel groups. The needs of the individual traveler are handled through mass communications, the DMOs' websites, and the visitors' information centers located throughout the tourist areas. Destination marketing organizations recognize the economic impact of bringing groups to the destination and focus a great deal of effort on acquiring this business. The main goal of the DMO is to increase visitor arrivals, resulting in an increase in hotel tax revenue and the additional spending on attractions, food, shopping, and transportation.

A large portion of the money received from hotel taxes is normally given to the convention and visitors bureau (CVB) to use in promoting the destination. The CVB must create promotional materials—for example, event planning guides and visitor guides—that are distributed to organizations and individuals who make inquiries to the CVB by telephone, through the website, or via direct-mail placements (i.e., drop cards) in magazines. Other support materials include signs and maps that are used by visitors to navigate the destination and its tourist areas. Finally, the CVB needs to hire full- and part-time employees to handle inquiries, sell to groups, staff visitor centers, recruit members, and take care of administration. One area that many destinations overlook, to their detriment, is the investment in infrastructure. This is a major part of product development, and funds should be allocated to improve the destination's accessibility. For example, countries such as Vietnam and Cambodia have nice beaches but the infrastructure in these countries prevents them from competing with other Southeast Asian destinations such as Singapore and Thailand.

The first task in the product development process for the DMO is to take an inventory of all of the various elements (e.g., accommodations, attractions, events, etc.) that are available at the destination and determine the best way to market them in an attempt to create a **unique destination proposition (UDP)**. The second task is to combine the various elements to create packages that will appeal to the various target markets. The last task is to develop marketing programs that will be used to meet the needs of the potential visitors, including the communications plan. The overall goal of the product development process is to achieve an effective allocation of available resources to ensure economic sustainability. The following is a discussion of the common destination attributes that combine to form the product and are used by visitors to form their overall perceptions of the destination.

Unique destination proposition (UDP)

A statement to describe the unique elements that are available at the destination in an attempt to differentiate it from other destinations.

8.6.1 Destination Attributes

Destinations are a combination of tangible and intangible elements, or attributes, that define the location. Tangible elements consist of accommodations, restaurants, transportation, and shopping facilities. The visitors' perceptions of competing destinations are based on the number and quality of these tangible attributes. It is necessary to determine the weight, or importance, that visitors place on each of these attributes when positioning the destination using product development and marketing communications. However, it is difficult to make physical changes without an influx of capital from public and/or private sources. For example, international destinations that host the Olympic Games invest a great deal of time and resources in improving the destination's infrastructure and providing an adequate level of tangible elements such as hotels and sports venues.

Other tangible elements include a destination's parks and historic sites. The United States has a national parks system and heritage sites such as battlefields, missions, and museums. Tourists visit places such as the Grand Canyon in the United States and the pyramids in Egypt because of the natural beauty of these tangible elements. Paris and London are popular destinations because of the numerous historic sites and the overall scenery. Finally, the climate in the destination also influences visitors. Many travelers seek out sunny climates, such as those of Florida, California, and Arizona. Others prefer ski vacations in the snowy mountains of Colorado, Utah, and Vermont. However, natural disasters such as hurricanes, tornadoes, and earthquakes can limit a destination's peak season.

The other set of elements that are used by visitors to evaluate a destination are the intangibles. The intangibles are important because they can distinguish one destination from another, even if the destinations enjoy the same number and quality of tangible elements. Perceptions are everything in marketing, and DMOs must determine the visitors' perceptions of the overall appeal of the destination. Some areas of concern are crime, safety and security, crowdedness, friendliness, and cleanliness. It is often difficult to overcome negative perceptions regarding these attributes because they are developed over time and can be based on information from reliable sources such as friends and relatives who visited the destination. In addition, the media are influential based on how they cover certain news and events. That is why it is critical for DMOs to have a good relationship with the local and national media. Finally, there are other intangible elements—nightlife, adventure, and rest and relaxation, for example—that can help define a tourist destination.

The final decision to visit a destination is based on the visitor's overall perception of the destination, including the level of each of the tangible and intangible attributes, and his or her perception of the cost or value associated with the destination. This is similar to the decision-making process that consumers go through for other product and service purchases. First, there is need recognition, then some degree of information search, an evaluation of alternatives, and a final

Destination brand advertisement.

purchase decision. Tourism and travel are services and cannot be fully evaluated before purchased, or inventoried like tangible products. Therefore, there is a high potential for cognitive dissonance after the purchase, and before the actual consumption of the service. For example, many travelers purchase cruises and vacation packages several months in advance and must wait to enjoy the trip. In the meantime, they are exposed to advertisements, word-of-mouth, and news stories.

8.6.2 Destination Branding

The goal of destination branding is to capture the distinct elements of the destination in the brand and communicating them through its components such as identity, personality, and image. This is accomplished by combining all the attributes associated with the brand to form an identity that is unique and that differentiates the destination from the competition. Destination marketing organizations can start by conducting consumer research to determine the visitors' perceptions of the destination in terms of the destination's features and brand benefits. The following destination brand benefit pyramid is used by many organizations to conduct this task.[4]

Destination branding
Process of capturing the distinct elements of the destination and communicating them through components such as identity, personality, and image.

Level 1—What are the tangible, verifiable, objective, measurable characteristics of this destination?

Level 2—What benefits to the tourist result from this destination's features?

Level 3—What psychological rewards or emotional benefits do tourists receive by visiting this destination?

Level 4—What does value mean for the typical repeat tourist?

Level 5—What is the essential nature and character of the destination brand?

In summary, these questions help determine the key attributes or features that are associated with a destination, how these features benefit potential tourists or visitors, what value tourists and visitors place on travel to the destination, and the overall brand character or essence. For example, an appealing print advertisement was used to launch a new San Antonio brand with the theme "Deep in the Heart."

The advantages of branding a destination are that it provides a means of communicating the destination's unique proposition, or identity, to potential visitors and it differentiates the destination from those of the competitors. Destination branding also helps organizations create a theme and a consistent message that can be communicated to the target markets using a combination of the brand's name, symbol, and logo. However, there are several reasons why branding destinations is difficult.[5]

1. Destinations are more multidimensional than most other products and services.

2. The market interests of the diverse group of stakeholders are heterogeneous.

3. Politics are involved in determining who will decide the brand theme and how the decision maker will be accountable.

4. Destination marketing organizations lack direct control of the delivery of the brand promise by the local tourism community.

5. It is difficult to measure and monitor the brand loyalty of the visitors to a destination.

6. The scale and consistency of funding for destination marketing varies over the destination's life cycle.

SUMMARY OF CHAPTER OBJECTIVES

This chapter introduced the concept of product lines and how companies attempt to manage these product lines to achieve long-term customer satisfaction and financial success. The methods that companies use to develop new products and services—including the actual development process, branding, and the organizing of employees—were explored. Without a consistent flow of new products and services, few companies will achieve long-term success. New products are important to companies for the following reasons: (1) growth opportunities for the business, (2) efficient and effective use of company resources, (3) increasing market share and importance of the company within the market, and (4) exploiting and extending the product–service mix life cycle.

New product development strategies can be either reactive or proactive. The strategy employed depends on a firm's resources and market position. Some firms have chosen to be innovators and leaders in the market, whereas other firms are more comfortable in the follower role and tend to be more reactive than proactive. It is important to note that there are many success stories to support the use of both strategies.

Firms use many organizational structures to develop new products and services, the most common of which are new product committees, new product departments, product managers, and venture teams. The firm should provide an atmosphere conducive to the development of new ideas and support its progression through the development process.

The process used by many firms to develop new products includes the following steps: (1) idea generation, (2) product screening, (3) concept testing, (4) business analysis and test marketing, and (5) market introduction. Ideas can be generated through formal channels within the firm or through external sources such as competitors and customers. Ideas with good potential are screened, tested, and analyzed until management feels it is ready for market introduction.

The significance of brands within the hospitality and tourism industry was explored. The important concepts of brands, brand names, brand marks, and trademarks were defined and discussed. Also, the characteristics of effective branding were presented. Finally, the use of the new product development process and branding by tourism destinations was discussed.

KEY TERMS AND CONCEPTS

Acquisitions
Alliances
Brand
Brand name
Brand mark
Co-branding
Concept testing
Customer-oriented strategy
Defensive strategy
Destination branding
Entrepreneurial strategy
Idea generation
Imitative strategy

Innovation
Market introduction
Proactive strategies
Product line
Product screening
Reactive strategies
Research and development strategy
Responsive strategy
Second but better strategy
Test marketing
Trademark
Unique destination proposition (UDP)
Win-win relationship

QUESTIONS FOR REVIEW AND DISCUSSION

1 **What is a product line?**

2 **What is the best type of new product development strategy: reactive or proactive? Explain your answer.**

3 **What are the four reasons it is important to develop and extend product lines within a business?**

4 **What steps are used to develop new products and services?**

5 **What is a strategic alliance? Why do you think a company would enter a strategic alliance? What are the pros and cons of entering a strategic alliance? What impact do you think strategic alliances have had on the airline industry?**

6 **How are qualitative and quantitative analyses used in assessing potential new products and services?**

7 **Define and cite two examples for each of the following: brand, brand name, brand mark, and trademark.**

8 **What are the characteristics of effective branding? Do you agree or disagree with these criteria? Can you cite examples of successful brands that do not meet these criteria? Why do you believe these brands are successful?**

9 **What are some of the advantages and disadvantages associated with co-branding?**

10 **Is the product development process different for tourism destinations than hospitality firms like hotels and restaurants? Explain your answer.**

NOTES

[1] Jennifer Waters, "R&I Special Report, Burger King," *Restaurants and Institutions* (October 1, 1998), p. 54.

[2] Michola Zaklin, "Baskin-Robbins Scoops Up Healthier Fare," *Adweek's Marketing Week* (June 4, 1990), pp. 30–31.

[3] Glen L. Urban and John R. Hauser, *Design and Marketing of New Products*, 2nd ed. (Englewood Cliffs, NJ: Prentice Hall, 1993).

[4] Steven Pike, "Tourism Destination Branding Complexity," *The Journal of Product and Brand Management*, 14 (4/5), (2005): 258–259.

[5] Ibid.

chapter review

CASE STUDY

Product Development Dilemma at Rocco's

You are employed as the vice president of marketing for Jiffy Foods, Inc., a regional food service company that operates 40 restaurants in the fast-food or quick-service segment. The restaurants that Jiffy Foods operates are a single brand called Rocco's. The restaurants offer a menu that is fairly typical of a fast-food chain—burgers, french fries, milk shakes, chicken tenders, and the like. In the last year, Rocco's has started offering prepackaged salads, but it has not done any other menu development. The restaurant's founder recently retired and turned over day-to-day management of the chain to the company president, James ("Jim") O'Connor. The founder indicated that the menu development and promotions that are done by the national chains "would not be profitable for a 40-unit chain like Rocco's. The national chains have the advertising clout to support promotions for special product offerings. We do not. We should stick to the basics: good food, clean restaurants, and friendly staff. That is what has worked in the past, and it will work in the future."

In the quick-service market, the brand is a small player, competing against the national chain companies such as McDonald's, Burger King, and Wendy's, as well as many other regional chains. During the last 18 months, sales at Rocco's have been flat—there has been no increase in sales, despite the fact that prices were increased 2.5 percent a few months ago. The mix of sales is much the same as it was 5 years ago. The prepackaged salads that were introduced last year have not sold well. All the salad offerings combined make up only 2 percent of total sales.

Earlier today, Jim O'Connor dropped by your office in a very frustrated mood. The two of you had a very intense and animated conversation about how the products and services offered by Rocco's were very traditional and not exciting to the targeted consumers. The national chains are always offering new or modified products and services that are promoted for a limited period of time at a special promotional price. Jim felt that the competitors' promotions were hurting Rocco's and wanted you to do something about it. You were quick to point out that the marketing strategy of "staying the course" had been very successful in the past. In fact, the company founder had used this approach for more than 25 years. Ideas for new products generally came from the managers of the 40 restaurants or the customers who patronized the restaurants. Rocco's did not maintain any product development structure or organization. As the vice president of marketing, your primary responsibilities centered on developing, implementing, and evaluating promotional campaigns; selecting sites for new stores; and working with the advertising agency to develop and evaluate campaigns.

As your meeting with the president concluded, he said, "It's Friday. I want you to think over the weekend about the way we develop new products and services. We need to do a better job. Maybe we should think about a different way of doing things. What we're doing is not producing the results we want, and we need to increase our sales. Let's meet on Monday morning to talk further. I want to see your preliminary plan when we meet on Monday."

Case Study Questions and Issues

1. What should you tell the president when you meet on Monday? What action steps should you recommend? Why?

2. Should Rocco's develop a more structured approach to product development? Why or why not? If yes, what structure would you recommend and why? If no, why not?

3. Are there any specific structures or ideas that you might adapt from what the national chains do?

4. What type of product development strategy should Rocco's use—defensive, imitative, or responsive? Why?

CASE STUDY

The Development of Seasons 52

Darden is one of the world's largest full-service restaurant companies. The Darden family of restaurants features some of the most recognizable and successful brands in full-service dining. Some of the popular chains include Red Lobster, Olive Garden, and LongHorn Steakhouse. A key to Darden's success has been the ability to develop new restaurant brands. One of the latest additions to the Darden family is Seasons 52—a fresh grill and wine bar that offers a seasonally inspired menu using local ingredients. All entrees are less than 475 calories and the average check per person is around $40. The idea for Seasons 52 was generated in 2003; today there are 17 locations in 13 different states in the United States.

The Seasons 52 architectural style is clean and contemporary, accentuated by the use of autumn ledgestone, earth tone colors, and designer lighting. The interior has a casually sophisticated ambiance, with soft lighting, contemporary art, as well as stone and warm wood accents. The menu is inspired by the seasons and the fresh appeal of the farmer's market. Every week of the year the restaurant strives to feature the freshest ingredients at their peak of ripeness and maximum flavor profile, changing to take advantage of each season's bounty and continually enticing guests to return and experience what's new. Four significant menu changes are made each year to reflect the four seasons. Initial market research indicated that food prepared with fresh seasonal ingredients would be especially appealing to adults.

Case Study Questions and Issues

1. Explain how the Seasons 52 restaurant concept would have progressed through the new product development process. You can research the restaurant on the Internet to get specific details.

2. How is Seasons 52 different from other upmarket restaurants?

3. How would you evaluate Seasons 52 as a brand name?

4. Can you think of any possible co-branding opportunities?

case study

Managing Products and Services

Courtesy of The Breakers, Palm Beach, Florida.

Chapter Objectives

After studying this chapter, you should be able to:

1. Identify the three levels of a product and how they are used to differentiate the product–service mix.

2. Describe the four stages of the product life cycle and their effects on marketing activities.

3. Discuss strategies for using the product life cycle for hospitality firms and tourist destinations.

4. Use resource allocation models and explain the relationship between resource allocation models and the product life cycle.

5. Define service quality, its relationship to customer satisfaction, and the service recovery process.

6. Discuss the techniques used to measure customer satisfaction.

Product levels

The varying levels of goods and services that combine to form the final product.

Product life cycle

A theory that describes how a product progresses from its infancy as a new product to its eventual decline.

Resource allocation models

Models used by firms to determine the most effective use of company resources within their product portfolios.

Core product

The most basic form of the product represented by the main benefit sought by consumers to fulfill their needs.

Peripheral services

Additional goods and services that expand the core offering and can be used to obtain a competitive advantage.

Facilitating products

Services that enable the customer to consume the core product by making it available where and when the customer wants it.

Supporting products

Additional goods and services that can be bundled with the core service in an attempt to increase the overall utility or value for consumers.

9.1 INTRODUCTION

Developing a sound marketing strategy is a cornerstone of successful marketing. When a company is successful and its marketing programs are the benchmarks among its competitors, it is often the result of a sound and well-developed marketing strategy. This chapter examines the key aspects of managing the product–service mix. The first area concerns the **product levels** and their importance in differentiating the product. The second area is the **product life cycle**. This advances the concept that all products and services progress through a life cycle, much as people do. The concept of the product life cycle is that different marketing strategies are best used at different stages in the life cycle. The third area involves the **resource allocation models** used by firms to determine the most effective use of company resources within their product portfolios. Most firms have a limited amount of resources, and it is necessary to prioritize their expenditures based on potential returns and company goals.

Finally, this chapter examines the various issues surrounding managing services. The characteristics that distinguish services from goods create different challenges for managers. It is important to manage supply and demand in service industries because of the inability to maintain inventories for intangible products. Basically, there are four product levels: the core product, the facilitating products, the supporting products, and the augmented product. The **core product** is the basic form of the product. In other words, it is the main benefit sought by customers in an attempt to satisfy their needs as recognized by the gap between the ideal state and actual state. For example, for a restaurant, the core product is the food that will resolve the consumer's state of hunger.

As one can see, there are many ways that this need can be satisfied. Similarly, consumers in the lodging industry are looking for guest rooms with a shower. Two of the other product levels can be referred to as **peripheral services**. These services expand the core offering and can be used to obtain a competitive advantage. Peripheral services must meet or exceed customer expectations if customers are to be satisfied. The **facilitating products** are services that enable the customer to consume the core product. They must be present to make the product available where and when the customer wants it. Hotels have front desks and reservations departments, and restaurants have hosts or hostesses and wait staff. **Supporting products** are additional goods and services that can be bundled with the core service in an attempt to increase the overall utility or value for consumers. Examples of supporting products within the hotel industry include concierge service, multilingual staff, 24-hour room service, and complimentary newspapers for business travelers.

Courtesy of Wyndham Worldwide.

Supporting services such as a hotel gym add value for guests.

The **augmented product** is the core product and peripheral services that combine to form the package of benefits offered by a product or service. In addition, it includes how the service is delivered. In other words, the augmented product encompasses everything surrounding the service and its delivery, including intangible attributes such as accessibility and atmosphere. For example, Las Vegas hotels and casinos have augmented the core product to include extravagant design, in an attempt to attract visitors and gain a competitive advantage over other hotels and casinos. The basic hotel service is augmented with casinos, shows, high-quality restaurants, and incredible atmospheres. Also, the hotels make themselves very accessible, with good deals and special packages.

> **Augmented product**
> The core product and peripheral services that combine to form the overall package of benefits offered by a product or service.

9.2   PRODUCT LIFE CYCLE

The product life cycle theory describes how a product progresses from its infancy as a new product in development through a growth phase to a maturity phase and then eventually into decline. Each stage of the product life cycle will be discussed in detail, followed by a discussion of the uses of the theory. Figure 9.1 illustrates the general shape of a typical product life cycle and its four stages.

9.2.1   Introduction Stage

The first stage of the product life cycle is called the **introduction stage**. At this point, the product has been through the new product development process presented in Chapter 8. It has survived analysis and testing, and it was deemed worthy of market introduction. The product represents a new concept, so there are no competitors offering the same product, and if it is unique, there aren't even similar products in the market. Therefore, the goals for the firm are to develop product awareness and stimulate trial and adoption. To accomplish these goals, the firm must make a sizable investment even though sales will initially be low, leading to negative profits. The investment is in the form of capital expenditures on facilities and inventories, and a promotional campaign to attract customers. However, even though the cost per unit of manufacturing the product or providing the service is high, it is often necessary to offer discounts and other promotions to induce potential customers to try it. The pricing decision is usually based on the estimated costs and demand for the product because there are no direct competitors. During the introductory phase, customers tend to be innovators who are willing to take risks to try new products and services. The distribution of the product is selective in an attempt to build a customer base before adding new units or distributors.

> **Introduction stage**
> The first stage of the product life cycle involving the launch of new products and services.

9.2.2   Growth Stage

If the firm is able to accomplish its goals in the introductory stage and the product builds an adequate customer base, the product will move into a growth stage. The **growth stage** is evidenced by rapidly rising sales and profits, and a decreasing cost per unit for providing the product

> **Growth stage**
> The second stage of the product life cycle represented by rapidly rising sales and profits as the cost per unit decreases for providing the product or service.

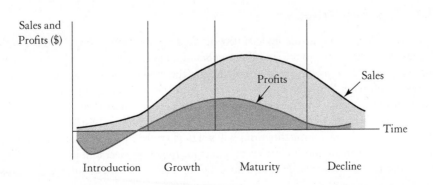

FIGURE 9.1 • The product life cycle.

or service. This positive outlook attracts competitors who are willing to take the risk because of customer acceptance and increasing profit margins. In this stage, the profits being generated by the product allow the firm to consider product extensions, new markets, and organizational expansion in the form of additional properties or units. Minor changes may be made in the unit design and concept, but normally the owners attempt to standardize the physical plant, thereby reducing developmental costs. The owners' rationalization is that if the original unit is successful, additional units will also be successful.

During the growth stage, the organization typically expands its distribution by adding new units. These units are often located in clusters within geographic regions. It is during the growth stage that the second group of consumers, known as *early adopters,* begins to enter the market as they obtain feedback from the innovators. The increase in competitors during this stage and the need to build market share put downward pressure on price. The use of the intensive distribution strategy helps the firm build its customer base and market share by creating more awareness and interest in the product. The goal is that the firm penetrates the market and develops loyal customers, while gradually reducing the amount of sales promotions and discounts. Instead, more emphasis can be placed on other forms of promotion, such as personal selling and advertising.

9.2.3 Maturity Stage

Maturity stage
The third stage of the product life cycle where the organization has expanded as much as the market will allow, and volume, measured in annual gross sales, levels off.

If an organization is able to achieve the desired success in the growth stage, it will eventually move to the maturity stage. At this point, the organization has expanded as much as the market will allow, and volume, measured in annual gross sales, will level off. Companies in this stage of the product life cycle find that the market is often saturated and competition is increasing from alternative options. Industry profits tend to peak near the end of the growth stage as the product moves into maturity. However, there are still high profits due to the large volume and the beginning of a decline in the number of competitors. In other words, the weaker competitors leave as the market reaches equilibrium and stronger competitors are left to battle for market share. A common strategy is for firms to standardize products and remove some of the less-valued attributes. This streamlining will enable the firm to take advantage of the economies of scale associated with higher volume, thereby widening the profit margin. There may also be changes in consumer preference as the consumer turns toward newer and more innovative concepts.

Economies of scale
Cost efficiencies derived from operating at higher volumes.

The advertising and promotions during this stage focus on differentiating the product, although it can be difficult because the core products tend to be very similar. This product homogeneity increases the consumer's price sensitivity and firms are forced to meet their competition and price at the market. At this point, the market may fragment into more segments with different needs and price sensitivities. For example, most hotel chains offer more than one brand in an attempt to attract consumers from various market segments (e.g., limited service, full service, upscale, and luxury). In this stage, the distribution of the product becomes even more intensive to ensure consumer convenience and accessibility. This expansion can be developed internally, or it can be the result of mergers and acquisitions. Also, the product adoption cycle has progressed to the point of including the majority segment of consumers, leaving little room for growth in the sales for the product category. As a result, individual brands can increase sales only at the expense of their competitors, rather than rely on new consumers in the market.

9.2.4 Decline Stage

Decline stage
The last stage in the product life cycle when industry sales and profits decline more rapidly, and the number of competitors gets reduced to only those with strong positions.

The last stage in the product life cycle is decline. During the decline stage, industry sales and profits are dropping more rapidly, and the number of competitors is reduced to those with very strong positions. The only new consumers entering the market are the laggards, and prices are often cut even further. Firms have progressed through the experience curve and the cost per unit has been driven down with accumulated volume. The product consists of the core product and only those peripheral services that are of real value to the consumer. Distribution is selective as weaker outlets are closed. Hospitality firms will sell or close their properties in markets that aren't performing well in an attempt to free up resources for the more successful properties. The major objective during the decline stage is to reduce overall marketing expenditures and increase cash flow (i.e., milk the brand). The decrease in marketing expenditures comes in the form of reduced customer service, reduced quality and variety, reduced distribution, and reduced promotion and advertising. Firms are left with a group of loyal customers that may or may not be large enough to continue with a profitable operation.

9.3   DEVELOPING STRATEGIES USING THE PRODUCT LIFE CYCLE

A number of strategies have been used for the various stages in the product life cycle. To develop strategies, however, management must first analyze the life cycle. This can be done in a seven-step process:

1. **Compile historical data.**   It is imperative that hospitality firms compile historical sales data. Ideally, the data should be available for the entire history of the organization. The specific type of data needed include sales volume (in units), prices, total sales revenue, costs, and profits.

2. **Identify competitive trends.**   Recent activities of major competitors should be monitored closely to determine changes in market share and position, as well as changes in quality of the product–service mix. Additionally, the other elements of the marketing mix should be monitored for significant changes.

3. **Determine changes in product–service mix.**   The marketplace must be monitored to learn about new products and services that other hospitality organizations are introducing, as well as to anticipate the potential effects on your operation.

4. **Study the product life cycles of similar products.**   It is helpful to study the life cycle of similar products or services to determine whether a pattern exists. Rarely is a product or service so new and unusual that it is not possible to compare it with a previous one.

5. **Project sales.**   Based on the data collected, sales for a 2- to 3-year period should be projected. Applying computerized statistical techniques may be particularly beneficial at this stage. Specialized software packages are available that will allow a marketing manager to develop sophisticated sales forecasts. However, for many business decisions, the statistical procedures and techniques that are part of spreadsheet software, such as Microsoft Excel, will suffice. The software will permit the development of multiple scenarios or what-if scenarios by altering the levels of the decision variables. In addition to projecting sales, management should examine key financial ratios and other indicators of financial performance.

6. **Locate the current position on the life cycle.**   Based on the historical data as well as the projections, it should now be possible to locate the product's position on the life cycle. This position is used to determine the most appropriate baseline marketing strategies.

7. **Develop strategies.**   Once the position is located on the product life cycle, strategy formulation begins. Table 9.1 illustrates the characteristics and strategies that apply to different stages in the product life cycle. These strategies should not be viewed as being absolutely firm, but they do represent the most widely accepted ideas in the marketing community.

9.3.1   Strategies for Extending the Product Life Cycle

One of the marketing manager's goals is to extend the product life cycle as long as possible. By doing this, cash flow can be extended and greater long-term profitability will result. There are several strategies that can be used to accomplish this.

9.3.1.1 INCREASING SALES TO EXISTING CUSTOMERS.   During the maturity stage of the product life cycle, the rate of sales growth begins to decrease and eventually levels off because most

	STAGE I INTRODUCTION	STAGE II GROWTH	STAGE III MATURITY	STAGE IV DECLINE
CHARACTERISTICS				
SALES	Low	Rapidly rising	Peak	Declining
PROFITS	Negative	Positive and increasing	High, starting to decline	Declining
CASH FLOW	Negligible	Moderate	High	Low
CUSTOMERS	Innovators and some early adopters	Remaining early adopters and some early majority	Remaining early majority and late majority	Laggards
COMPETITORS	Few increasing in number and strength	Many	Declining in number	
STRATEGIES				
MARKETING OBJECTIVE	Create trial and awareness	Increase sales and maximize market share	Increase profits and maintain market share	Decrease market expenditures and maximize short-term profits
PRODUCT	Core product with some basic peripheral services	Minor product changes and extensions	Add attributes with positive differentiation	Core product and key attributes
DISTRIBUTION	Selective	Becoming intensive	Intensive	Selective
PRICE	Set initial price based on costs and estimated demand	Price to penetrate market based on actual demand	Lower price to increase market share	Reduce price to maintain volume
PROMOTION	Create trial and awareness through sales promotions	Build awareness and interest and reduce sales promotions	Use to differentiate among major competitors	Reduce expenditures and focus on loyal customers

TABLE 9.1 • Characteristics and Strategies for Stages of the Product Life Cycle

of the potential users of the product have either been converted or left the market. Under normal circumstances, it becomes very difficult and expensive to identify potential new customers and convert them into buyers. One way to increase sales and market share under these circumstances is to sell more to existing customers. There are basically two alternatives: encourage the customers to purchase more on each occasion, or encourage the customers to purchase more frequently. In order to get a consumer to purchase more, some hotels periodically offer one "free" night if the consumer purchases two or three nights. Similarly, restaurants train waiters to "upsell" customers by suggesting more expensive entrees, appetizers, wine, and dessert. Another common method of increasing sales to existing customers is the use of product bundling. Internet travel agents (e.g., Expedia and Travelocity) form relationships with hotels, airlines, rental car companies, and tourist attractions to offer vacation packages. Finally, hospitality and tourism firms get customers to purchase more frequently with loyalty programs that reward heavy users with free products and services in exchange for points.

9.3.1.2 INCREASING THE NUMBER OF USERS. Another strategy used to extend the product life cycle is to seek new users of the product. The goal is to increase the size of the overall market by identifying those who have not previously purchased the products or services. Several quick-service restaurant chains have used this strategy very successfully. As the number of primary locations for new stores decreased, these chains have sought additional locations where they might attract new customers, such as kiosk locations within stores, shopping malls, and gas stations along the highways. By expanding the definition of so-called suitable location, they have been able to increase the number of purchasers, increase sales, and extend the product life cycle. Another example of this strategy is when hotels sell memberships to local residents for their pools and fitness centers in order to increase revenue by increasing the customer base.

9.3.1.3 FINDING NEW USES.   Within the realm of product marketing, one of the ways product life cycles can be extended is to find new uses for products. In some cases, new uses for products are discovered and marketed by the firm. However, in other instances, they are the result of market feedback. For example, many restaurants realize that it is relatively easy to run a catering operation out of the same facility that is used to serve regular customers. The catering operation uses the same equipment and adds little to the fixed costs of operating the restaurant, but it brings in additional revenue that can enhance the firm's overall financial condition. Similarly, hotels are able to generate additional revenue by allowing the general public to use facilities such as fitness centers, spas, and golf courses.

9.3.2   Criticisms of the Product Life Cycle

As with most concepts or theories, the product life cycle has its supporters and its opponents. There has been a good deal of debate over the applicability and usefulness of the concept in the real world. Whether you agree or disagree with the use of the product life cycle, it is important to view it solely as a tool. Complete reliance on the product life cycle as the basis for marketing management decisions would be unwise. The main argument against using the product life cycle concept is that few products or services actually conform to the shape of the curve illustrated in Figure 9.1. Rather, the curve may rise and fall in any number of patterns, each unique to the product or service itself. If managers believe that a product follows the normal life cycle curve, the product's demise may become a self-fulfilling prophecy. As industry sales begin to decline, a firm may decide to reduce distribution and marketing expenditures in conformance with the recommendations for decline stage strategy. This may lead to the premature decline of the product with substantial consequences.

Opponents of the produce life cycle concept also claim that it is often difficult to determine the exact stage in which a product lies. There are clearly no indicators to mark the transition from one stage to another. It is possible that changes in industry sales or firm sales could be the result of temporary conditions, and it may be possible to rejuvenate the product and extend the product life cycle. A product could remain in the maturity stage indefinitely if management is able to continually reinvent it. The product life cycle is more of a descriptive tool than a prescriptive tool. It cannot be used to forecast changes, because of the various shapes and time frames associated with different products and industries.

Also, opponents of the product life cycle concept indicate that some marketing managers place too much faith in it. These individuals focus too much attention on the product life cycle and forget about all the other environmental factors that can influence the success of a product or service. This marketing myopia or narrow-mindedness can cause firms to miss opportunities and not take risks that could be advantageous in the long run.

Finally, the product life cycle can put too much emphasis on the development of new products to the detriment of existing products. Managers are painfully aware that as products reach decline, they will be responsible for finding ways to replace the lost revenues.

9.3.3   Tourist Area Life Cycle

Several decades ago, Richard W. Butler introduced the concept of a **tourist area life cycle (TALC)**, which is similar to the product life cycle.[1] Like products, tourist destinations have a finite life and evolve through several stages of development, from introduction (exploration and involvement) to growth (development), maturity (consolidation), and finally decline (stagnation and poststagnation). However, just as with products, once a destination reaches maturity (stagnation) it can extend this stage by going through some changes and rejuvenating itself. This could involve adding more tourist attractions or accommodations, or targeting a new market. For example, many cities along the beaches in the southern United States followed Fort Lauderdale, Florida, and targeted the spring break crowd from universities and colleges. Each stage of development has its

Tourist area life cycle (TALC)
The evolutionary stages for tourist destinations that illustrate their rise and decline, from the initial exploration by tourists to eventual stagnation.

own set of opportunities and threats for the local area. Figure 9.2 provides a graphical representation of the tourist area life cycle (TALC).

9.3.3.1 EXPLORATION.

Exploration stage
The first stage in the tourist area life cycle when a small number of adventurous tourists visit sites with limited public facilities.

During the exploration stage, there are a small number of adventurous tourists visiting sites with limited public facilities. The visitors are initially attracted to the destination because of some natural physical feature. At this point, the destination attracts only a very specific type of visitor. The exploration stage of the tourist area life cycle is when the more adventurous travelers find destinations that aren't frequented by the masses. These travelers are normally looking for places that haven't become major tourism destinations. The new destinations don't have the infrastructures or the commercial enterprises that are found in the more established tourism destinations. One of the major appeals of the new destinations is the ability to interact with the resident populations and experience the local environment. These early tourists are welcomed by the host population, and some of the tourists decide to become residents. For example, Walt Disney World was started as a small theme park in a remote area around Orlando, Florida, in 1971. After visiting the park, tourists began to move to Orlando, and the city started to grow.

9.3.3.2 INVOLVEMENT.

Involvement stage
The second stage in the tourist area life cycle occurs when there is limited interaction between tourists and the local community, resulting in only basic services.

As the destination moves into the involvement stage, there is limited interaction between tourists and the local community, resulting in only basic services. Increased advertising induces a pattern of seasonal variation and a definite market area begins to emerge. The involvement stage of the tourist area life cycle sees an increase in the number of tourists based on the word of mouth generated by the adventurous travelers. The number of tourism support businesses begins to increase, but most of the accommodations and restaurants are still owned and operated by local residents. There is not much planning for the regional development during this stage, often leading to the creation of a tourism organization to address the needs of the region. The local residents have more interaction with visitors that may enlighten them about the opportunities that exist for education, politics, and economic development. During this stage, there is an increase in the use of technology, and improvements are made to the local establishments.

9.3.3.3 DEVELOPMENT.

Development stage
The third stage in the tourist area life cycle occurs when there is continued growth in the number of visitor arrivals.

The development stage is the last stage where there is continued growth in the number of visitor arrivals. There is a noticeable development of additional tourist facilities and increased promotional efforts. The destination experiences a shift in control of the tourist trade to outsiders, and the number of tourists at peak periods outnumbers the local residents. This results in some antagonism toward tourists. As this stage progresses, the interaction between tourists and local residents becomes less personal and more businesslike. For example, many support businesses such as hotels, restaurants, and other retail establishments emerged in

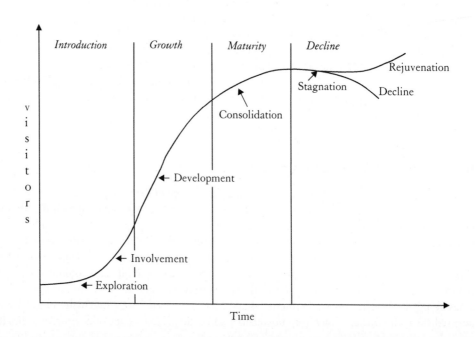

FIGURE 9.2 • The tourist area life cycle (TALC).

the Orlando area due to the success of Walt Disney World. Also, contractors moved to the area and a convention and visitors bureau was formed.

9.3.3.4 CONSOLIDATION. When the growth rate of visitor arrivals begins to decrease, the destination enters a consolidation stage. Tourism has become a major component of the local economy, and a well-delineated business district has begun to take shape. Some of the facilities are outdated and the destination tries to extend the tourist season. The consolidation stage of the tourist area life cycle is characterized by a shift from local control of businesses to more outside ownership and larger establishments. This causes the local economy to become more dependent on large corporations with a lack of empathy for the local population. More of the businesses are franchised and more people migrate to the area because labor is needed to support the increase in tourism. This results in more conflicts between the original residents and the new residents. In addition, the area becomes more crowded, and there are other negative impacts, like an increase in crime and pollution. Finally, there is an economic divide between the people who prosper as a result of the increased tourism and those who are directly involved. For example, the main industry for the island of Hilton Head, South Carolina, converted from logging to tourism in the mid-1900s. However, many of the original residents couldn't afford the increase in taxes brought about by the increase in real estate prices. As a result, many of the residents lost their homes, or had to sell and leave the island where they were born and raised. Others were able to remain, but the cost of food and other basic necessities continued to rise, and the island's new residents had higher incomes and more luxurious lifestyles.

9.3.3.5 STAGNATION. This leads to the stagnation stage, where peak numbers of tourists and capacity levels are reached. The destination has a well-established image, but it is no longer popular and the lodging facilities begin to erode and turn over to new owners. The stagnation stage in the tourist area life cycle is characterized by an abundance of tourism facilities and services. The market becomes saturated, and tourists' experience becomes less satisfying. In some cases, the negative impacts of tourism outweigh the benefits associated with the increase in visitation, and the local population loses its enthusiasm for entertaining tourists. The adventurous travelers who discovered the area are disillusioned by the commercialization and look for new destinations. Some of the less efficient firms go out of business, and the area is left with large franchises and chain operations.

A destination can attempt to avoid or postpone a decline during stagnation by finding a way to rejuvenate the area. This could include the addition of new attractions or focusing on a niche market. For example, the introduction of Walt Disney World rejuvenated the area when Cypress Gardens (an original attraction outside Orlando) started to show a decline in visitors. More recently, it has become popular for destinations facing a lack of growth (or even decline) in the numbers of visitors to add casinos, or integrated resorts, as a strategy for rejuvenation.

> **Consolidation stage**
> The fourth stage of the tourist area life cycle occurs when tourism has become a major component of the local economy, and a well-delineated business district has begun to take shape.

> **Stagnation stage**
> The last stage of the tourist area life cycle occurs when peak numbers of tourists and capacity levels are reached, and the infrastructure and facilities start to erode.

9.4 RESOURCE ALLOCATION MODELS AND APPLICATIONS

This section presents two other concepts that should be discussed to provide a thorough understanding of product management. All the concepts discussed thus far are all interrelated in that they are based on the management of the marketing mix and the positioning of products in the marketplace. Firms change their product–service mixes over time to reflect changes in consumers' tastes and lifestyles. The two concepts in this section address the question of resource allocation as it relates to the firm's image and its mix of products and services.

9.4.1 Resource Allocation Models

It is important for firms to view themselves as a portfolio of products that both provide funds and need funds. Within the portfolio, some brands or items are in industries or categories that show strong potential for future growth, whereas others don't show the same potential. In addition,

Strategic business units (SBUs)
Brands or units that have their own sets of market conditions and competitors.

Boston Consulting Group (BCG) matrix
A 2 × 2 resource allocation matrix consisting of four quadrants based on two axes representing relative market share and the market growth rate.

some of the brands or items have strong positions in their industries or categories, and others do not. These brands or items can be referred to as strategic business units (SBUs) because each is viewed as a separate entity with its own set of market conditions and competitors. All of a firm's SBUs will affect a firm's cash flow by providing a source of funds through revenues and using funds in the form of expenses to produce the product and compete in the marketplace.

A few variations of resource allocation models are similar in their matrix approaches. The cells within the matrix are classified using the SBUs' ability to act as a source of funds (e.g., relative market share or competitive position) and its need for funds based on future growth potential (e.g., market growth rate or industry attractiveness). This process of plotting SBUs and determining the best sources and uses for funds will aid an organization in allocating its finite resources. The resource allocation process will be explained using the Boston Consulting Group (BCG) matrix because it is the most common, straightforward resource allocation model in marketing.

Howard Johnson Hotels' expansion into the middle market for full-service hotels created a new strategic business unit.

Courtesy of Wyndham Worldwide.

The BCG matrix is illustrated in Figure 9.3 with four cells based on two axes. The horizontal axis is labeled *relative market share* and can be viewed as a proxy for competitive position. Relative market share refers to a firm's market share relative to its largest competitor. The vertical axis is labeled *market growth rate* and can be viewed as a proxy for industry attractiveness or future growth potential. The market growth rate is usually based on average annual growth rate over the last few years, depending on the age of the industry or category. There are two levels, high and low, for each axis, resulting in four cells. The ensuing discussion will explain the characteristics and marketing objectives associated with each of the four cells.

9.4.1.1 QUESTION MARKS. The SBUs in the question marks category contain products and services that have low relative market shares in industries or categories with high market growth rates. This is a critical category for managers because question marks can either improve their market share or the growth rate in the industry could decline. At this point, these SBUs require a good deal of cash to increase sales and build market share. However, with limited available resources, not all question marks can be completely funded, and choices have to be made. If a question mark does not receive adequate funding, it is almost certain that its business position will not improve. Most question marks provide little or no positive cash flow and must be supported for growth or eliminated from the portfolio. Strategic business units in this category are often represented with relatively new products in new markets, creating a risky environment.

9.4.1.2 STARS. The SBUs that are considered stars contain products with high relative market shares in industries or categories with high market growth rates. This is the second-best category for producing positive cash flows, and the objective is to build these products. The SBUs' strong business positions and high market shares provide good returns and become strong sources of funds for the firm. However, they are in industries or categories that are experiencing high market growth rates. This will attract many competitors and require a high level of marketing expenditures in order for an SBU to compete and maintain its business position. Therefore, these SBUs are normally self-sustaining in that they don't require funds from other sources, but they aren't able to supply much in the way of excess funds for other SBUs.

9.4.1.3 CASH COWS. The SBUs in the category of cash cows contain products with high relative market shares in industries or categories with low market growth rates. Products or divisions

Relative market share
Refers to a firm's market share relative to its largest competitor.

Market growth rate
The average annual growth rate over a specified time period that can be viewed as a proxy for industry attractiveness, or future growth potential.

Question marks
Products and services that have low relative market shares in industries with high market growth rates.

Stars
Products and services with high relative market shares in industries that show good potential for future growth.

Cash cows
Products and services with the best opportunity for positive cash flow: they have high relative market shares in industries with low market growth rates.

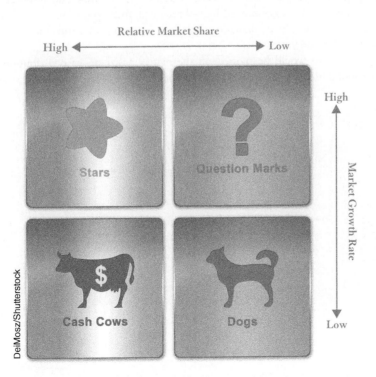

Relative Market Share

High ⟷ Low

High

Market Growth Rate

Low

Stars

Question Marks

Cash Cows

Dogs

DeiMosz/Shutterstock

FIGURE 9.3 • The Boston Consulting Group Matrix.

that are cash cows are the best source for positive cash flows because they have strong sales in established markets. There is not much growth potential, and the risk of new competitors is low. Cash cows are used as sources of funds for the SBUs in the other categories, especially question marks. However, it is important that as much of the cash flow as necessary to maintain or hold the market shares for cash cows is kept within the division or SBU. They are the foundation of the firm's portfolio, making it possible to develop new products and take chances with other existing products.

9.4.1.4 DOGS. The SBUs that are considered dogs contain products with low relative market shares in industries or categories with low market growth rates. Dogs are the least attractive category in the matrix. They generate low or negative cash flows because of their poor business positions and the low rate of growth in their markets. These SBUs are drains on the firm's resources and should be phased out or divested. Marketing expenditures should be decreased unless there is some potential for repositioning the product. Most firms will try to sell these divisions and products to companies that are better equipped to market them while they are still viable.

9.4.2 Menu Sales Mix Analysis

Numerous methods can be used to evaluate menu effectiveness. The selection of one method over another is usually a function of time and money. The simplest method used to evaluate menu effectiveness is to count the number of times that each item is sold. This method is commonly referred to as **menu sales mix analysis**. In most food service operations today, this information is readily available from the detailed tape printout and spreadsheet files produced by **point-of-sale (POS) systems**. Based on this information, management can add or delete menu items or change the merchandising focus of the menu. Another common approach is a comparison with menu census data. Menu census data allow management to compare sales figures and sales trends with regional and national data.

A more sophisticated approach, referred to as **menu engineering**, would be to perform an in-depth analysis of the menu items, including their sales and costs. In the case of a menu, each item is treated as its own strategic business unit. The two axes are item contribution margin in dollars and the number sold of each item. Items with larger contribution margins would be considered good growth prospects that warrant more marketing effort and resources. Items with larger sales figures would be considered high-share items and a good source of revenue. The axes would be divided to form four quadrants using the average contribution margin and the average number sold (see Figure 9.4).

Each menu item would be plotted on the matrix based on its contribution margin and the number sold during the time period in question. Based on these two criteria, menu items are

Dogs
Products and services with low relative market share in industries with low market growth rates that incur negative cash flows and show little promise for future growth.

Menu sales mix analysis
The simplest method used to evaluate menu effectiveness by counting the number of times each item is sold.

Point-of-sale (POS) systems
A computerized system for recording sales and transactions.

Menu engineering
Analysis of menu items based on cost, volume, and profitability.

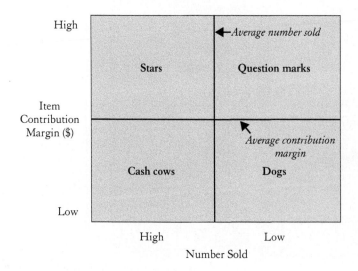

FIGURE 9.4 • Sales mix analysis matrix.

classified as dogs, question marks, stars, or cash cows. Each quadrant has some baseline strategies that can be used for the menu items that are positioned in it. Once again, this is similar to the Boston Consulting Group's growth-share matrix. There are other variations of this methodology, but this one was chosen because it is consistent with the approach used in product management. The important thing to remember is that any approach should take into account food costs, food prices, and sales volume. In this case, the contribution margin is the difference between menu price and food cost.

The menu items classified as *dogs* have low sales volumes and low contribution margins. They don't warrant much attention and should be placed in less desirable locations on the menu. In an attempt to increase the contribution margin, management can consider raising the prices on these items and/or lowering the food costs of preparing the items. In the long run, management should consider finding a substitute for any "dog" item. The substitute could be an item that is already on the menu that can be promoted, or a new item that can be added to the menu to take its place. If the contribution margin cannot be improved, then the item may need to be removed from the menu.

The menu items classified as *question marks* have low sales volumes and high contribution margins. They have the potential for growth and should receive management's attention. Given the high contribution margin, an increase in sales volume would greatly benefit the restaurant. "Question mark" items should be placed in prime locations on the menu and be strongly promoted. For example, waiters could be instructed to focus on them in their suggestive selling, and the items could be highlighted on table tents and other in-store promotions. Other strategies that could be employed include making one a signature item, or offering special deals to create awareness and trial.

The menu items classified as *stars* have high sales volumes and high contribution margins. They should occupy prime locations on the menu and be a major focus of promotional efforts. These menu items should be promoted through in-store displays and suggestive-selling efforts. It is important to maintain current levels of quality and price. Any significant changes could hurt the sales of these items, which would impact greatly on the profitability of the restaurant. "Star" menu items are often signature items for restaurants and should be carefully managed until newer items (i.e., question marks) can be phased in.

The menu items classified as *cash cows* have high sales volumes and low contribution margins. They tend to be menu items that have been around for a while, and in many cases, they are used as loss leaders because they attract customers and are often signature items (e.g., Burger King's Whopper). Management should experiment with price increases or ways to decrease food costs. However, if customers are sensitive to changes in price, it is advisable to focus more on costs. For example, management could decide to substitute less expensive ingredients or serve smaller portions, thereby increasing the contribution margin. In the long run, it is possible to find different items that are similar and offer larger contribution margins. Over time, "cash cow" menu items can be moved to less prominent locations on the menu.

9.4.3   Resource Allocation Models and the Product Life Cycle

There is a relationship between resource allocation models, such as the BCG matrix, and the product life cycle. The two dimensions in the product life cycle are *time* and *annual sales*. The stages are based on the rate of sales growth over time. The two dimensions in resource allocation models are *competitive position or market share* and *industry attractiveness or market growth rate*. The underlying premise of the resource allocation models is that products evolve from question marks into stars and then into cash cows. When the market stops growing and/or the product loses market share, it will move into the dog category, where it is eventually divested. This is similar to a product's movement from introduction (question mark) through a growth stage (star) to maturity (cash cow) and eventually into decline (dog). In addition to the similarities in evolution or movement through the matrix, the two concepts share similar characteristics and strategies. Question marks are often new products, like those found in the introduction stage having negative cash flows but good growth potential. Stars experience rapid growth and start to realize positive cash flows, like products in the growth stage. Cash cows have large sales volumes and market shares, resulting in large cash flows, like the products that survive the maturity stage. Finally, dogs have low market shares and decreasing cash flows, just like products in the decline stage.

Marketing strategies are also similar. Marketing expenditures are greatest for question marks and stars, like products in the introduction and growth stages. Money is spent selectively to hold market share during the maturity phase and for cash cows, whereas marketing expenditures are very low for dogs and products in decline. Finally, both concepts can overemphasize the importance of new product development to the detriment of existing products. Many companies have survived with cash cows and products in the maturity stage over a long period of time. Many local or regional food chains, airlines, and large hotel chains such as Sheraton and Holiday Inn have survived with minor product extensions over their respective life cycles.

9.5 MANAGING IN THE SERVICE ENVIRONMENT

As discussed in Chapter 1, certain characteristics are associated with services that distinguish them from tangible products. Most of these characteristics stem from the fact that services are intangible. In other words, services cannot be held, inspected before purchase, or inventoried. As a result, the consumer is actually part of the production process, making it difficult to maintain the consistency and efficiency that a firm can experience in the manufacture of tangible products. Managing supply and demand in a service organization such as a hotel or restaurant is very difficult. Demand for services comes in waves and often is not as consistent as one would like. The demand may be seasonal, as with a resort hotel, or it may vary by time of day, as with restaurants. It might also fluctuate by day of the week, as is the case with business-oriented hotels that are busy Monday through Thursday but quite slow on Friday through Sunday. Managing the shifting demand and the corresponding supply is perhaps one of management's greatest challenges.

Two calculations can be used to evaluate the extent to which the supply and demand are being successfully managed: asset revenue generating efficiency and revenue per available room. **Asset revenue generating efficiency (ARGE)** evaluates the relationship between actual revenue and maximum potential revenue. For example, within a hotel operation, ARGE takes into account the occupancy percentage and the average daily rate to determine the extent to which the revenue potential is being realized. Suppose that a hotel has 400 available rooms each day with a rack rate of $100. If all of the rooms were sold each day at the maximum rate that can be charged for each room (i.e., the published rack rate), the maximum daily revenue would be $40,000. However, it is rare that a hotel would be able to do this consistently. Assume that in one month, the hotel achieved a 68 percent occupancy rate and had an average daily rate of $75. This means that, on average, 272 rooms were sold at an average daily room rate of $75, resulting in total revenue of $20,400. When the total daily revenue is divided by the maximum potential daily revenue of $40,000, the result is an ARGE of 51 percent [(20,400/40,000) × 100]. The ARGE is useful as an evaluation tool for sales and marketing personnel because it measures performance against potential revenue at full capacity.

Revenue per available room (REVPAR) is calculated by multiplying the average daily rate by the occupancy percentage. For example, if a hotel has an average daily rate of $85 and is running an occupancy percentage of 75 percent, then the REVPAR would be $85 × 0.75 = $63.75. This figure, like ARGE, accounts for the amount of unused capacity. An alternative calculation would be to multiply the average daily rate by the number of occupied rooms to get the total room revenue, and then divide total room revenue by the total number of rooms in the hotel to get the REVPAR. The main difference between ARGE and REVPAR is that REVPAR does not compare actual revenue to maximum potential revenue. However, REVPAR does give a measure that can be tracked over time to assess the hotel's performance. Higher values of REVPAR would denote more effective use of available resources. One of the major issues facing service industries such as hospitality and tourism is the inability to inventory the product. Unused capacity is lost forever when there are empty hotel rooms, tables in restaurants, or seats on airplanes. The following strategies can be used to manage supply and demand:

- **Modify price.** Prices can be used to transfer demand from peak periods to nonpeak periods. Firms can raise prices during peak demand periods in an effort to shift demand to nonpeak periods.

Asset revenue generating efficiency (ARGE)
A measure of the relationship between actual revenue and maximum potential revenue.

Revenue per available room (REVPAR)
An efficiency measure used by hotels to evaluate revenue based on capacity and occupancy rate.

- **Develop programs to boost nonpeak demand periods.**   Add services and amenities to make the nonpeak period more attractive.

- **Shift demand through reservations.**   Using a reservation system allows a firm to manage its capacity and avoid customer dissatisfaction derived from waiting.

- **Increase personnel efficiency.**   Use part-time employees and cross-training employees to perform two or more jobs.

- **Increase consumer involvement in self-service aspects of the service delivery system.**   Service firms are able to decrease labor costs and increase supply by having consumers become more involved in the service delivery process.

9.5.1   Customer Satisfaction and Service Quality

Customer satisfaction occurs when a firm's service, as perceived by customers, meets or exceeds expectations. Firms that can consistently meet or exceed customer expectations will develop good reputations and high-quality images. Service quality is a perception resulting from attitudes formed by customers' long-term, overall evaluations of performance.[2] Maintaining high-quality service in the hospitality and tourism industry remains difficult because of the variability in service delivery. Service quality is affected by all the individuals who have contact with customers. Therefore, it is important to understand the entire process of service delivery that leads to consumer perceptions of quality. Improving customer service should be a top priority of all managers working in the hospitality and tourism industry.

The service quality process is the product of the expectations and perceptions of a firm's management, its employees, and the customers it serves.[3] Whenever there are differences in expectations or perceptions between the people involved in the delivery and the consumption of services, a potential for a gap in service quality exists. Firms should diagnose any service quality gaps because there is a direct relationship between service quality and customer satisfaction. Simply stated, when customers are satisfied, they are much more likely to purchase from the service provider again. Over time, if they remain satisfied, they become loyal customers. The service gap is the gap that exists when there is a difference between customers' expectations of a service and their perceptions of the actual service once it is consumed. When this difference occurs, it is the result of one or more gaps that occur in the service quality process.

Customer satisfaction
Occurs when a firm's service, as perceived by customers, meets or exceeds their expectations.

Service quality
A perception resulting from attitudes formed by customers' long-term overall evaluations of performance.

Service gap
The gap that exists when there is a difference between customers' expectations of a service and their perceptions of the actual service once it is consumed.

Courtesy of Shutterstock

Satisfied customers are repeat customers, one of the goals of managing service quality.

Knowledge gap
Occurs when management's perception of what consumers expect is different from the consumers' actual expectations.

Standards gap
The discrepancy that can occur between management's perception of what customers expect and how they design the service delivery process to meet those expectations.

Service blueprint
A flowchart that details the delivery points of contact with customers.

Delivery gap
Occurs when there is a difference between the service delivery specifications and the actual service delivery.

The first potential gap is referred to as the **knowledge gap**, which occurs when management's perception of what consumers expect is different from the consumers' actual expectations. This gap may lead to other gaps in the service quality process, and it is usually the result of a failure in the firm's research program or organizational structure. Firms need to obtain feedback from customers and employees that can be used to design services that will appeal to customers. If the current service offering is not satisfying customers, then the firm should know from its customer surveys or from its employees who are able to provide valuable information that they obtain from customers, either voluntarily or involuntarily.

The second potential gap is referred to as the **standards gap**, which refers to the discrepancy that can occur between management's perception of what customers expect and how the service delivery process is designed to meet those expectations. Management establishes the specifications to provide the desired service at the desired level of quality. Therefore, even if management remains accurate in its perception of customer expectations, a gap could still exist in service because the delivery process does not accomplish the goals of the firm. For example, management may have correctly determined the amount of time that customers are willing to wait to check in to a hotel, but they may not schedule enough front-desk clerks to meet the customers' expectations. This could result from a lack of commitment on the part of management or the result of management trying to reduce the firm's operating costs. One of the techniques used by management is to develop a **service blueprint**—a flowchart that details the delivery process, including the points of contact with customers. Figure 9.5 is an example of a service blueprint for the check-in process at a typical hotel. You have elements that the guest doesn't see such as the entry of the reservation in the property management system (PMS) and the food preparation for room service, as well as elements that involve customer contact with employees such as the checking-in and checking-out processes. This will help to uncover any shortcomings in the delivery process that may lead to a gap in service quality. Management should document each step in the process to identify areas for improvement.

The third potential gap is referred to as the **delivery gap**, which occurs when there is a difference between the service delivery specifications and the actual service delivery. Management may have correctly assessed customer expectations and developed specifications that will meet these expectations, but employees may not deliver the service properly. For example, a restaurant

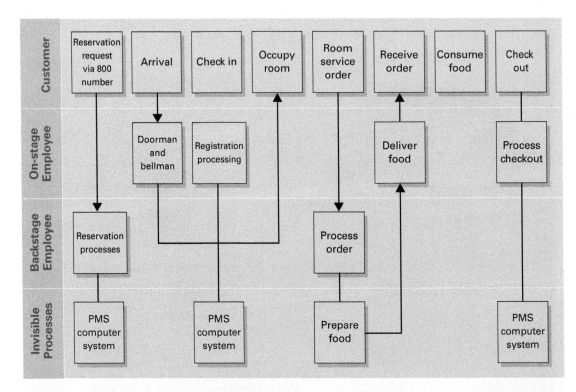

FIGURE 9.5 • Service blueprint for a hotel check-in.

may specify that the wait staff should approach customers within 2 minutes of seating. However, the wait staff may stand around discussing their plans for later in the evening and ignore the specifications. Firms must find ways to create an atmosphere for employees that ensures their willingness to perform the job tasks as desired by management. Employee selection and training are critical in this process, as are the rewards and recognition provided for good performance.

The fourth potential gap is referred to as the communications gap, which occurs when there is a difference between the service delivered and the service promised through the firm's external communications with customers. Many firms have a tendency to promise more than they can deliver in an attempt to persuade customers. For instance, advertisements for hospitality and tourism firms lead customers to believe that in the event of a problem or mishap, the firms will do whatever they can to satisfy customers. Making promises to consumers that cannot be delivered is a big mistake that service providers often make. It results in service performance levels that are below consumer expectations, leading to dissatisfaction. Each individual consumer makes purchase decisions and has established, based on past experiences, a set of expectations for the performance of a product or service.

Anyone who travels on a regular basis can provide stories related to experiences with airlines, hotels, and restaurants. Ironically, firms that advertise 100 percent satisfaction guarantees are banking on the fact that most customers will not complain or force the issue. In other cases, firms simply neglect to inform customers about procedures or policies that would affect their expectations. For example, a good waitress or waiter will make sure that customers know that a dish is spicy or that a certain entree will take longer to properly prepare, so that customers can make informed decisions and are less likely to become dissatisfied, because the actual performance will more closely match consumer expectations.

If any of the first four gaps occur, then the service gap will occur because the actual service will not meet the customer's expectations. Comment cards and guest surveys will often uncover a service gap, but they may lack the detail needed to evaluate the other potential gaps. Therefore, firms should have a mechanism in place to obtain feedback from customers and employees that can be used to examine the entire service quality process. If services do not meet customers' expectations of quality, then the customers become dissatisfied and will likely not return. Also, they will convey these negative experiences to their friends and colleagues, creating negative word-of-mouth impressions.

9.5.2   Managing Service Quality

To provide high-quality service, all members of the staff, from the highest to the lowest level on the organizational chart, must view the guest as the highest priority. Delivering high-quality service is based on an attitude of serving customers. Developing an attitude that places the customer as the highest priority for the business remains critical. Without satisfied customers and repeat patronage, the business will not succeed in the long term. Firms that use a customer orientation become more successful at providing products and services that meet customers' needs and expectations. In contrast, firms that assume they know what is best for the customer are more likely to fail. Therefore, it is important for firms to develop long-term relationships with customers and convey the firms' missions and objectives to its employees.

9.5.2.1 RELATIONSHIP MARKETING.   All progressive companies devote marketing resources to attract and retain new customers. Relationship marketing is based on the proposition that it is important to focus on customer loyalty and retention as well as customer acquisition. It is short-sighted to think that merely attracting new customers will keep the business headed in a successful direction. Rather, an equal amount of attention and resources should be devoted to keeping the customer base that already exists. In times of slow market growth and increasing competition, it will be less expensive to maintain an existing customer base than to seek new customers. One way to visualize the process of relationship marketing is to visualize a bucket, into which new customers are placed. At the same time, as customers switch or defect to another provider, they leak out of the bottom of the bucket. Relationship marketing is built on the proposition that it is easier and cheaper to keep existing customers than to spend the resources necessary to always be gaining new customers.

Communications gap
Occurs when there is a difference between the service delivered and the service promised.

Consumer expectations
Each consumer forms a set of expectations for the performance of a product or service based on past experiences and other internal and external sources.

Relationship marketing
Marketing based on the proposition that it is important to focus on customer loyalty and retention as well as customer acquisition.

Relationship marketing involves attracting, developing, and retaining customer relationships.[4] This long-term view toward the customer must be seen as being equal in importance to attracting new customers. Many firms make the mistake of focusing on new customers at the expense of existing customers, and the level of service quality diminishes. For example, hotel sales managers are expected to develop new accounts with corporate and association groups. Sometimes they spend so much time trying to get these new accounts that they neglect some of their existing accounts. This lack of attention may cost the hotel the group's future business because they took the customer for granted. Service firms should build relationships and maintain them. A relationship marketing approach is highly desirable when the following conditions are met:

- A customer has an ongoing or periodic desire for the service.
- The service customer controls the selection of the service organization.
- Alternative service providers make it easy for customers to switch.

All three of these conditions are present in the hospitality and tourism industry. Many firms offer special prices and additional services to highly desirable customers in an attempt to build long-term relationships. These practices are most commonly used with business accounts and frequent users. For example, hotels provide contract rates for corporations that supply a high volume of annual business. Airlines receive one of the lowest rates possible in hotels near airports because they have flight crews who need guest rooms on a daily basis. Also, airlines build relationships with frequent flyers by providing them with additional services such as preboarding before regular flyers, free upgrades, free flights, and airport clubs where they can rest or conduct business away from crowded lounges at departure gates.

The growth and success of relationship marketing has been aided by the advancement in software used to track and monitor customer engagement and purchase behavior. Software can be used to keep track of customer purchasing patterns, preferences, and likes and dislikes. A terrific example of relationship management in practice is Amazon.com. When a user establishes an account, the website behavior and purchases are carefully tracked. These data are then analyzed and used to promote additional products that the customer may find attractive. Amazon.com was among the first companies to take maximum advantage of the power of software to track customer behavior and use this knowledge to provide a more personalized shopping experience for customers. Such data can be used to cross-sell additional products or services, develop e-mail promotions and other forms of direct marketing, or create a more personalized experience for customers.

Researchers have advanced the theory that if customer retention increases through successful relationship marketing, profitability will increase. Several positive financial factors are associated with successful relationship marketing:

- The cost of acquiring a customer occurs only once. Therefore, the longer the relationship, the lower the ongoing or amortized cost.
- Customer retention costs decrease over time, especially as a percentage of sales.
- Long-term customers are less likely to switch, may also be less price-sensitive, and provide positive word-of-mouth referrals.
- Long-term customers will purchase ancillary products and services, often at higher margins.
- Long-term customers require less education about the firm's processes.
- Long-term customers tend to be satisfied, making the jobs of service providers easier and more satisfying.

9.5.2.2 INTERNAL MARKETING. In addition to focusing efforts on consumers, firms can achieve higher levels of service quality by marketing to their employees. Internal marketing encompasses all activities used by a firm in an effort to improve the marketing effectiveness of its employees. Efforts should be made to communicate with all employees, especially those in boundary-spanning roles who come in contact with customers. The ability to deliver consistent, high-quality service depends on the organization's ability to recruit, train, retain, and motivate dedicated service personnel.

First, service firms need to select and hire employees who are willing and able to provide high-quality service. There are many people in the job market, and firms need to create attractive

Internal marketing
Encompasses all marketing activities used by a firm in an effort to improve the effectiveness of its employees.

positions that appeal to highly motivated individuals. There is a range of potential services that an employee can provide—from the minimum necessary to retain the position and not be penalized to the maximum possible service. This variability in the level of possible service is referred to as discretionary effort. For example, if an airline passenger leaves a carry-on item on a flight, the airline's personnel have some discretion as to the level of service they will provide. They can take their time and forward the item to the traveler's next destination, or they can try to deliver it to the traveler before he or she boards the next plane or leaves the airport.

Second, service firms should provide employees with adequate training so they possess the skills that are required in performing their job tasks. In addition, the firm should communicate with employees so they are aware of changes within the organization as well as upcoming events. If service personnel are well trained and they understand what management expects, the environment is right for success. Firms can use both internal communications, such as newsletters and e-mail, and external communications, such as advertising and public relations, to convey their expectations to employees. An advertisement can be used to create and manage consumer perceptions and expectations, but the ad can be used to educate employees as well. One of the major airlines aired a commercial on television that showed an athletic employee running through the airport to catch a traveler who left his briefcase at the check-in counter. This commercial served two purposes: (1) It let customers know that the airline provided high-quality service and (2) it gave employees an idea of the firm's service expectations.

Finally, firms need to provide employees with rewards and recognition when they perform at a high level of discretionary effort. This motivates service providers to continue performing at high levels and to remain loyal to the firm. Retaining good employees is important in providing high-quality service, and it reduces the costs associated with turnover. It takes a great deal of time and effort to hire and train good employees. Firms can use extrinsic rewards such as salary increases and bonuses or intrinsic rewards such as recognition and job satisfaction to motivate employees. Many firms recognize "employees of the month" by honoring them with plaques displayed where customers can see them or allowing them to use special parking spaces close to the building.

9.5.3 Service Failures, Customer Complaints, and Service Recovery Strategies

Service failures occur at critical incidents, or "moments of truth," in the service encounter, when customers interact with a firm's employees. It is important to provide service personnel with the authority and the recovery tools necessary to correct service failures as they occur. This section will discuss the types of service failures, common consumer complaints, and service recovery strategies that can be used to repair the service failures.

9.5.3.1 SERVICE FAILURES The timeliness and form of response by service providers to service failures will have a direct impact on customer satisfaction and quality perceptions. Service failures can be assigned to one of three major categories: (1) responses to service delivery system failures, (2) responses to customer needs and requests, and (3) unprompted and unsolicited employee actions.

The first category, system failures, refers to failures in the core service offering of the firm. These failures are the result of normally available services being unavailable, unreasonably slow service, or some other core service failure that will differ by industry. For example, a hotel's pool may have a leak and be closed, a customer may have to wait a long time for the shuttle to an airport car rental agency, or an airline might mishandle a passenger's luggage.

The second category, customer needs failures, are based on employee responses to customer needs or special requests. These failures come in the form of special needs, customer preferences, customer errors, and disruptive others (i.e., disputes between customers). For example, a hotel guest may want to have a pet in the room, a customer may want to be switched to an aisle seat on an airplane, a customer at an event may lose his ticket, or a customer in a restaurant may be smoking in a nonsmoking section.

The third category, unsolicited employee actions, refers to the unexpected actions, both good and bad, of employees that are observed or experienced by customers. These actions can be related to the level of attention an employee gives to customers, to unusual actions that can

Discretionary effort
Represents employee effort beyond the minimum requirements for his or her job.

Critical incidents
"Moments of truth" when customers interact with a firm's employees and have a positive or negative experience.

Service failures
Occur when a firm does not succeed in meeting customers' expectations.

System failures
When a failure or service breakdown occurs in a core service provided by the firm.

Customer needs failures
Based on employee responses to customer needs or special requests.

Unsolicited employee actions
Unexpected actions, both good and bad, of employees that are observed or experienced by customers.

be performed by employees, to an action's reinforcement of a customer's cultural norms, or to an employee's actions under adverse conditions. For example, a hostess in a restaurant could anticipate the needs of a family with a small child, a hotel front-desk clerk could give a free upgrade to a guest who waited in line too long, a flight attendant could ignore passengers with children, or a cruise ship employee could help evacuate passengers during a crisis.

9.5.3.2 CUSTOMER COMPLAINT BEHAVIOR.

As mentioned earlier in this chapter, certain undesired outcomes are associated with dissatisfied customers. Two of the most common are to engage in negative word of mouth and to change service providers. A third, less common, reaction is to engage in some form of retaliation. This retaliation can range from a negative word-of-mouth campaign to causing physical damage or launching a major protest. The way a firm approaches and handles complaints will determine its long-term performance. Some firms show a dislike for customers who complain, whereas other firms create an atmosphere that encourages customers to voice their concerns. Most customers complain in an attempt to reverse an undesirable state. Other more complicated reasons for complaining are to release pressure, to regain some form of control over a situation, or to get the sympathy of others. Whatever the reason, the outcome is that customers are not completely satisfied, and it is in the firm's best interest to know when this occurs. There are many other dissatisfied customers who do not complain because they don't know what to do or they don't think it will do any good.

9.5.3.3 SERVICE RECOVERY STRATEGIES.

When customers complain, firms are presented with the opportunity to recover from service failures. Service recovery strategies and actions occur when a firm's reaction to a service failure results in customer satisfaction and goodwill. In fact, customers who are involved in successful service recoveries often demonstrate higher levels of satisfaction than customers who do not report service failures or complain. The following list describes popular service recovery strategies:

Service recovery strategies
Strategies used to recover from service failures and satisfy customers.

- **Cost/benefit analysis.** Service firms should conduct a cost/benefit analysis to compare the costs of losing customers and obtaining new customers with the benefits of keeping existing customers. Most firms place a high value on retaining customers. However, some guests take advantage of satisfaction guarantees and complain on every occasion. Many hotel chains, such as Doubletree, maintain a database on complaints and will flag chronic complainers.

- **Actively encourage complaints.** It is better to know when customers are not satisfied so that action can be taken to rectify the situation. It is important to note that unhappy customers may not complain to service firms, but they will often complain to their family and friends. Hospitality and tourism firms use comment cards and toll-free numbers to encourage customers to provide feedback. Also, service personnel are trained to ask customers whether everything was satisfactory.

- **Anticipate the need for recovery.** Service firms should "blueprint" the service delivery process and determine the moments of truth, or critical incidents, where customers interact with employees (see Figure 9.5). The process can be designed to avoid failures, but recovery plans should be established for use in the event that a failure occurs.

- **Respond quickly.** The more timely the response in the event of a service failure, the more likely that recovery efforts will be successful. After a customer leaves a service establishment, the likelihood of a successful recovery falls dramatically. Based on this principle, firms such as Marriott International provide service hotlines at each hotel to help resolve problems quickly. Managers and associates know that the speed with which they respond is often as critical as what the final resolution becomes.

- **Train employees.** Employees should be informed of the critical incidents and provided with potential strategies for recovery. For example, some hotel training programs use videotaped scenarios of service failures to show employees potential problems and the appropriate solutions.

- **Empower the front line.** In many cases, a successful recovery will hinge on a front-line employee's ability to take timely action and make a decision. Firms should empower employees to handle service failures at the time they occur, within certain limits. For example, Ritz-Carlton allows its employees to spend up to $1,000 to take care of dissatisfied customers.

One of the classic examples of a service failure involved Northwest Airlines during a major winter storm at the Detroit airport. Unfortunately, due to the heavy snow, many outbound flights were canceled, and no gates were available for unloading passengers from the inbound flights. This traffic jam left many passengers stranded as the airplanes sat on the tarmacs and taxiways for several hours. Northwest's inability to provide the passengers with information or a solution resulted in hundreds of unhappy passengers and a class-action lawsuit. Having delayed flights and a shortage of gates is not a new phenomenon at airports in climates such as Detroit's, and Northwest Airlines should have had a viable service recovery program in place that could have lessened the severity of the problem.

9.6 TECHNIQUES TO ASSESS CUSTOMER SATISFACTION

One of the critical components of a firm's commitment to customer satisfaction is feedback that provides an assessment of the firm's performance. Benchmarks can then be established and future progress can be evaluated. Also, these measures can be used to reward service personnel in a way that stays consistent with a firm's customer satisfaction goals. The following section describes the most common techniques used by firms to assess customer satisfaction.

9.6.1 Spoken Comments and Complaints

Listening to consumer comments and complaints remains the most straightforward way to evaluate customer satisfaction. Service firms should set up formal systems that encourage customer and employee feedback regarding service experiences. Management should not overlook the value of the information obtained by boundary-spanning personnel through their normal contact with customers. One of the most recent approaches is providing toll-free numbers so that customers can call to voice complaints.

9.6.2 Surveys and Comment Cards

Many hospitality and tourism firms leave comment cards in guest rooms, on tables in restaurants, and at other points of contact so that the firms can obtain feedback. One of the problems associated with this method is the lack of representation. The response rate is small, and it tends to be biased toward those who are most upset and chronic complainers. Larger operations will conduct surveys through the corporate offices by either telephone or mail. Surveys will normally be more representative than comment cards and provide more detailed information. These types of surveys also provide for a more representative sample of customers.

9.6.3 Number of Repeat Customers

Service firms can gauge customer satisfaction by keeping track of repeat business. Higher levels of satisfaction would be associated with higher percentages of repeat customers. This models an unobtrusive method of assessing customer satisfaction, but it does not provide much detail.

9.6.4 Trends in Sales and Market Share

Another way to evaluate customer satisfaction without direct contact with customers is to examine the firm's internal sales records. Comparisons can be made on a month-to-month basis and within the same period of the previous year. Higher levels of satisfaction would be associated with increases in sales. However, firms should be careful with this method because there are many possible explanations for increases in sales. For example, the firm may have launched a new advertising campaign, a competitor may be renovating or going out of business, or the firm may have decreased its prices. In addition to examining sales records, firms should also look at market share. This measure considers sales in relation to the competition, which is a more accurate assessment of improved market performance. However, there could also be other explanations for changes in market share besides customer satisfaction.

9.6.5 Shopping Reports

Another approach used by hospitality and tourism firms involves having someone consume a service just like any other customer. The "secret shopper" can be an employee of the firm, an outside person chosen by the firm, or an employee of an outside company that specializes in this service assessment activity. These shoppers are normally equipped with detailed evaluation forms based on company guidelines that can be used to record the desired information. It is often recommended that someone outside the firm be used in an attempt to maintain some level of objectivity. It is important to have a particular operation evaluated by more than one shopper on several occasions throughout the desired period. Doing so will result in a more representative sample of service experiences.

SUMMARY OF CHAPTER OBJECTIVES

The product–service mix is an important component of a firm's marketing program. The other strategies (price, promotion, and distribution) are used to provide further assistance in positioning the brand in conjunction with the product–service mix. All of the strategies are based on the customers' wants and needs and the trade-offs that are necessary to offer a competitive product. When managing a product or service, it is necessary to consider all the product levels: the core product, the facilitating products, the supporting products, and the augmented product.

The product life cycle can be used to develop marketing strategies that are appropriate for the product or service throughout its useful life. Products evolve from introduction through growth into maturity and eventually decline. History shows us that certain marketing strategies or actions are more appropriate in certain stages in the life cycle. The pros and cons of the product life cycle were presented, as well as ways to extend the product life cycle and the use of the life cycle concept for tourist areas. Resource allocation models were introduced, and the Boston Consulting Group (BCG) matrix was presented in some detail. These types of models are useful to firms in establishing marketing budgets and developing marketing strategies in an attempt to achieve the firms' overall goals. Each strategic business unit has a unique set of conditions and competitors that must be monitored so that the firm can analyze cash flow. It was also shown how resource allocation models could be used by restaurants in menu sales mix analysis and menu engineering, and how resource allocation models are related to the product life cycle.

Finally, some issues unique to the managing of services were discussed in this chapter. Most of the problems stem from the fact that services are intangible and cannot be inventoried. Therefore, it is crucial that firms concentrate on managing supply and demand so they can maximize potential revenue. Customers are an integral part of the service delivery process and should be included in the product–service mix strategy. This makes service quality more difficult to assess than product quality, and the service quality process is presented to illustrate those differences. Customer satisfaction and customer service are important concepts for all types of products and services.

KEY TERMS AND CONCEPTS

Asset revenue generating efficiency
(ARGE)
Augmented product
Boston Consulting Group (BCG) matrix
Cash cows
Communications gap
Consolidation stage
Consumer expectations
Core product
Critical incidents
Customer needs failures
Customer satisfaction
Decline stage
Delivery gap
Development stage
Discretionary effort
Dogs
Economies of scale
Exploration stage
Facilitating products
Growth stage
Internal marketing

Introduction stage
Involvement stage
Knowledge gap
Market growth rate
Maturity stage
Menu engineering
Menu sales mix analysis
Peripheral services
Point-of-sale (POS) systems
Product levels
Product life cycle
Question marks
Relationship marketing
Relative market share
Resource allocation models
Revenue per available room (REVPAR)
Service blueprint
Service failures
Service gap
Service quality
Service recovery strategies
Stagnation stage

Standards gap
Stars
Strategic business units (SBUs)
Supporting products

System failures
Tourist area life cycle (TALC)
Unsolicited employee actions

QUESTIONS FOR REVIEW AND DISCUSSION

1 What are the four levels of a product? How can peripheral services be used to gain a competitive advantage?

2 What are the stages of the product life cycle? What are the characteristics of each stage?

3 What do you see as the advantages and disadvantages of using the product life cycle as a marketing tool?

4 How should a business go about developing a strategy for various stages in the product life cycle? What techniques are most appropriate for the various stages?

5 What are some ways to extend the product life cycle? Of these techniques, which one do you think is most useful? Why?

6 How is the tourist area life cycle similar to the product life cycle? How is it different?

7 What are resource allocation models? How are they related to the product life cycle?

8 What are the methods for managing supply and demand? Which methods are capable of increasing capacity for hospitality firms?

9 Define service quality. Discuss the service quality process.

10 What are the types of service failures? What recovery strategies can be used in the event of a service failure?

11 How would you define customer satisfaction? How can you improve customer satisfaction? What are the techniques that can be used to assess customer satisfaction?

NOTES

[1] R. W. Butler, "The Concept of a Tourist Area Cycle of Evolution," *Canadian Geographer* 24 (1980), pp. 5–12.

[2] A. Parasuraman, Valerie Zeithaml, and Leonard Berry, "A Conceptual Model of Service Quality and Its Implications for Service Quality Research," *Journal of Marketing* 49 (Fall 1985), pp. 41–50.

[3] Mission statement card, The Greenbrier, White Sulphur Springs, WV, 1994.

[4] Karl Albrecht and Ron Zemke, *Service America! Doing Business in the New Economy* (Homewood, IL: Business One Irwin, 1985), p. 6.

chapter review

CASE STUDY

Starbucks Coffee

Starbucks Coffee purchases and roasts high-quality coffee beans and sells them along with espresso beverages, pastries and confections, sandwiches, and recently, wine and beer. In addition to its retail sales through its own stores, Starbucks also sells coffee beans and bottled Frappuccino drinks through specialty stores and supermarkets. The company has had tremendous success since its inception in its quest to be the most recognized brand in the world. The following table contains data on the number of stores and total revenue by year, depicting the life cycle of the brand over time. The information regarding the number of units in operation over Starbucks Coffee's life cycle was taken from the "Timeline" and annual reports provided on the company's website (www.starbucks.com).

YEAR	TOTAL UNITS	U.S. UNITS	REVENUE ($BILLIONS)
1999	2498	1996	1.7
2000	3501	2729	2.2
2001	4709	3501	2.6
2002	5886	4272	3.3
2003	7225	5239	4.1
2004	8569	6177	5.3
2005	10241	7353	6.4
2006	12440	8896	7.8
2007	15011	10684	9.4
2008	16680	11567	10.4
2009	16635	11128	9.8
2010	16858	11131	10.7
2011	17003	10787	11.7
2012	18066	12903	13.3
2013	19767	11457	14.9
2014	21366	11962	16.5
2015	23043	12521	19.2

Case Study Questions and Issues

1. Use the data from 1999 through 2015 and construct a chart. What stage of the product life cycle was Starbucks in at the end of 2015? Explain your answer.

2. Would your answer be different if you consider global vs. United States units? Number of total units vs. revenue?

3. What product category would describe the Starbucks brand? What other companies would you consider direct and indirect competitors for Starbucks, and why?

4. In 2008, Starbucks announced plans to close more than 600 of its stores, most of which were opened in 2006. What led to this decision? Was the strategy successful? Explain.

5. What future strategies would you suggest for the Starbucks brand?

CASE STUDY

Service Quality at the Excelsior Hotel

Kristen Adams recently transferred to the Excelsior Hotel to improve the level of customer service. She had been with the company for 5 years and had been quite successful in improving the level of customer satisfaction at the two previous hotels to which she had been assigned. Kristen knew that the Excelsior was going to be a real challenge. The mix of business was 60 percent individual transient guests and 40 percent group business. Of this group business, about one-third was motor coach tour groups.

On her first day on the job, Kristen witnessed quite a sight. There was a line of about 20 guests waiting to check in when two motor coaches arrived and more than 80 additional guests and guides walked into the lobby to check in. Needless to say, the two front-desk agents had a look of terror in their eyes as they worked diligently to process the registrations for those waiting to check in. Some 40 minutes later, everyone had been checked in, but the general manager said to Kristen, "I'm glad that you are here; we need to work out a better system. Let's meet for lunch tomorrow to discuss your initial ideas." Kristen had just picked up a pen to start brainstorming ideas to present to the general manager when a guest approached her desk.

"Hello, my name is Bill Foster, and I stayed at your hotel last night with my family. We really did not have a good experience, and I want to tell you about it. I want to make sure that this does not happen again, to me or anyone else." Mr. Foster then proceeded to tell Kristen his account of the events. "I was traveling with my wife and our son, who is 4 years old. Our connecting flight was delayed, so we did not arrive at our final destination until 10 P.M. The Excelsior had an advertised check-in facility at the airport, and I assumed that I would be able to secure my room while waiting for the luggage. When I approached the employee at the hotel's airport facility, I was told that check-in service was not available at that time of the day. I found this to be surprising, because this was the very type of situation in which an airport facility would be beneficial.

"Next, my family took a shuttle van from the airport to the hotel, where we were given directions to the front desk. Two front-desk clerks were on duty when the passengers from the airport shuttle arrived a little before 11 P.M. However, one of the front-desk clerks was apparently going off duty at 11, and she proceeded to close her drawer at that exact moment. This left a line of approximately 10 or 12 guests to be checked in by one clerk. Needless to say, it took some time to process all of the guests, and we had to wait 20 or 30 minutes for our turn.

"We were assigned to a room, but at this point we had a few bags and my son was fast asleep and had to be carried. When I asked for assistance with our luggage, I was told that no one was available at that time of night. The hotel was large, having more than 1,000 rooms, and the rooms were spread out among several adjacent buildings. Our room was two buildings away from the lobby area. My wife and I struggled to carry the luggage and our son to the room. We arrived there about 11:30 and attempted to enter the room. The key unlocked the door, but the door would not open. After a couple of attempts, we heard a woman's voice in the room. Obviously, the room had been double-booked and the woman woke up from her sleep. I used the house phone to call the front desk and explain the predicament.

"The front-desk manager offered a quick apology and said that she would send someone with a key to a nearby room. About 10 minutes later, a housekeeper happened to be going through the hallway, and she let my family into the room that I had been given over the phone. However, the housekeeper had no idea what was going on and took my word. After we had been in the room for 10 minutes, the phone rang and I spoke with the front-desk manager. She acted as though she had sent the housekeeper to open the room, but she still needed to send someone with the room keys. She apologized one last time and told me to call the front desk if I had any other problems."

Case Study Questions and Issues

1. What steps should Kristen recommend to the general manager?

2. What action steps and timetable should she recommend? How should decisions be made about which steps should be done initially?

3. Develop a service blueprint of the check-in process. How might this be used to improve the situation?

4. Discuss the gaps in the service quality process that Bill Foster experienced.

5. What kind of service failures occurred and what recovery strategies were employed?

6. How did the Excelsior Hotel fail to meet Mr. Foster's expectations?

7. What other actions could have been taken?

case study

Distribution and Supply Chain Management

Courtesy Mobile Bay Convention and Visitors Bureau.

Chapter Objectives

After studying this chapter, you should be able to:

1. Outline the importance of distribution systems in hospitality and travel marketing, including the concept of supply chain management.

2. Provide an overview of distribution strategies used in hospitality and tourism.

3. Define franchising and list the advantages and disadvantages of franchisee/franchisor arrangements.

10.1 INTRODUCTION

Distribution is an important element of the marketing mix, but it is often difficult to understand its role in services marketing. A distribution channel is the path that products (goods and services) follow from manufacturers or vendors to final consumers, including intermediaries such as wholesalers and retailers. Service distribution channels are usually not traditional in the sense that there is a manufacturer, a wholesaler, and a retailer. Often, one firm performs all of the channel functions because there is no physical transportation of a product, and the production and consumption of the service occur simultaneously. However, service firms in industries such as hospitality and tourism must still make decisions regarding distribution and the supply chain.

The **supply chain** for hospitality and tourism services consists of all suppliers and vendors, intermediaries, procurement and delivery systems, and retail outlets that assist firms in obtaining products and services and using them to add value in producing and delivering the final service to customers. Supply chain management involves the integration of all these organizations, people, and activities so that services are produced and distributed in an efficient manner to customers at the right time and place. In addition, supply chain management focuses on the economic, environmental, and social sustainability goals of hospitality and tourism organizations. Finally, it is important to include supply chain management as part of the new product development process, and gather information to reduce the uncertainty and risk associated with business decisions.

Some of the typical activities included in the supply chain are transportation, procurement, distribution, financial transactions, order fulfillment, and gathering information on markets, suppliers, competitors, customers, and consumer demand. The information should be shared with other supply chain partners so that improvements can be made in efficiency and service quality. The supply chain for tourism destinations consists of suppliers such as lodging facilities, transportation firms (e.g., airlines, buses, rental car companies, shuttle services, taxis, etc.), food service operations, travel agents, tour operators, and tourist attractions. Figure 10.1 represents the basic supply chain for a hotel. Multiple suppliers and vendors provide products and services for the hospitality firm. The hospitality firm obtains the supply and uses it to produce its products and services, and then delivers the products and services to its customers.

Lodging and food service facilities have many of the same types of supplies. For example, both types of operations need food and beverages, linens, uniforms, furniture and fixtures, computer systems and software, signage, landscaping services, and artwork for their facilities. These items all become part of the "hospitality service" that is then delivered to customers. There is also a decision involving whether to produce these supplies in-house, or to outsource. For example, many hotels outsource their audiovisual needs to avoid purchasing and maintaining inventory. Others decide to take care of their own audiovisual needs. In fact, Marriott even went so far as to create a separate company to handle the audiovisual needs for the entire corporation.

Table 10.1 provides a summary of the advantages for each method. Performing the activities in-house enables the organization to have better control over costs of producing supplies and prices charged to acquire the resources, the quality of the resources and supplies, and the delivery time and available supply. The other advantages associated with in-house sourcing are the ability to protect propriety information related to the design of products and services and the processes involved in production and delivery of the services. Outsourcing the activities allows organizations to avoid large capital investments in facilities and resources (including labor), and the costs of maintaining inventory. It also enables the firm to free capacity, maintain multiple supplier sources to ensure availability of resources, and take advantage of supplier expertise and the specialization of labor. Finally, firms might not have the necessary knowledge and expertise among its employees and managers.

Supply chain

All suppliers and vendors, intermediaries, procurement and delivery systems, and retail outlets that assist firms in obtaining products and services and using them to add value in producing and delivering the final service to customers.

FIGURE 10.1 • Basic hotel supply chain.

PERFORMING ACTIVITIES IN-HOUSE	OUTSOURCING ACTIVITIES
Maintain quality standards	Avoid capital investment
Lower cost and control price	Take advantage of supplier expertise
Control delivery time and supply quantity	Reduce inventory costs and free capacity
Protect proprietary design or process	Maintain multiple sources of supply
Utilize employee strengths	Lack of necessary competencies

TABLE 10.1 • **In-House versus Outsourcing Supply Chain Activities**

10.2 DISTRIBUTION STRATEGY

A firm's distribution strategy must be consistent with the other elements of its marketing mix in order to be successful. The overall position of the firm in the marketplace is established by many factors, including price levels, product–service mix characteristics, and distribution. The promotion strategy is used to convey this positioning strategy to potential users of the firm's product or service. The delivery of products or services is intertwined with these other decisions. For example, consumers would not associate gourmet-quality food with an establishment that is part of a food court in a shopping mall. Similarly, consumers would not expect to pay high prices for food purchased through this type of outlet.

The main objective of the distribution function is to get products and services to consumers where, when, and how they prefer them. A good distribution system will result in a smooth flow of products and services to consumers while achieving the firm's goals concerning market coverage, sales, and profitability. Firms have limited resources and must determine the most efficient and effective way to distribute their products and services. Some of the necessary activities associated with distribution include:

- Communicating and negotiating
- Facilitating transactions
- Storing and moving physical goods
- Installing products and providing service

10.2.1 Channel Organization

Channel design decisions must be made with regard to channel width (i.e., desired market coverage) and channel length (i.e., number of intermediaries). It is also possible to use a single channel to distribute a firm's products and services or multiple channels of various widths and lengths. Channel decisions are affected by product–service mix characteristics, market characteristics, and environmental characteristics. Obviously, the intangible nature of services tends to minimize the length of the channel of distribution. As discussed earlier, the service delivery process often requires consumers to be present during the production process. This eliminates the need for the storage and movement of a physical product. However, distribution is still an important consideration in the delivery of services. Some firms use a variety of channels depending on the desired market coverage, the positioning of different services or brands, and the existence of different markets.

Channel width
Represents the number of distribution channel partners required to provide the desired market coverage.

10.2.1.1 CHANNEL WIDTH. The channel width decision is based on the desired amount of market coverage. In other words, larger widths would be associated with more market coverage. Basically, three channel width strategies are employed by firms: (1) exclusive distribution, (2) selective distribution, and (3) intensive distribution. The width of the channel ranges from exclusive distribution (one outlet) to intensive distribution (as many outlets as possible). As mentioned earlier, this decision must be consistent with the firm's other marketing mix strategies.

The narrowest channel width is exclusive distribution, where a firm limits the availability of its products or services to a particular outlet. This is common among independent operators in the hospitality industry. Le Cirque restaurant in New York City, for example, is a single-unit operation, and it is the only place consumers can purchase and experience this firm's product. This is also true of independent hotels such as the Palace Hotel in New York City and resorts such as The Greenbrier in West Virginia or The Homestead in Virginia. Many single-unit restaurants and lodging facilities offer a personal touch and a one-of-a-kind experience. However, this individual attention comes at the expense of market coverage and the cost economies associated with high-volume business.

The middle channel width is referred to as selective distribution, where a firm uses more than one outlet but restricts availability of the product or service to a limited number of outlets. In the hospitality industry, many firms limit market coverage based on geographic segmentation. Some multiunit operations are strictly local, but some are regional or national with a limited number of outlets. For example, The Cheesecake Factory tends to locate primarily in high-volume shopping centers in larger metropolitan areas. In contrast, Bertucci's Brick Oven Pizzeria, based in Somerville, Massachusetts, limits itself to the Northeast and recently expanded to the mid-Atlantic region. Many other multiunit restaurant operations are family-owned and stay within a very confined area. Some hotel chains, such as Omni Hotels and Four Seasons, have a limited number of hotels that are found mainly in large cities.

Finally, the widest channel strategy is intensive distribution, where firms attempt to make products and services available through as many outlets as possible. This is a common approach among franchise operations that use mass advertising and realize economies of scale. These firms, such as McDonald's and Marriott International, try to standardize their services so that consumers can expect a consistent experience at any of the firm's outlets. Corporate-owned chains—for instance, Applebee's—also use an intensive distribution strategy by adding units in as many suitable locations as possible. Consumers are more concerned with familiarity and consistency than with a one-of-a-kind experience. However, these firms do their best to provide consumers with a personal touch. Most airlines and car rental agencies use this distribution strategy as well.

10.2.1.2 CHANNEL LENGTH.

The channel length decision is based on the number of intermediaries between the manufacturer and the final consumer. In the case of services, the channel is usually very short because of simultaneous production and consumption. In other words, consumers must be present to consume a service such as airline transportation, a meal, or an overnight stay in a hotel. A channel can be either direct, from the manufacturer to the consumer, or indirect, with intermediaries performing some of the necessary channel functions (see Figure 10.2).

A direct channel is the most popular for hospitality and tourism firms, as well as for most other service industries. The manufacturer sells directly to the consumer, and the manufacturer performs all the channel functions. In product firms, this choice is made either because there are no qualified intermediaries or because the manufacturer feels it can do a better job. In service firms, there is often no choice because the service must be performed while the consumer is present. The direct channel enables the firm to have close contact with the final consumer and the ability to react quickly to changes in the market. For example, hotels use central reservation systems (CRS) and call centers to make the direct channel more accessible and to operate more efficiently.

Exclusive distribution
The narrowest channel width where a firm limits the availability of its products or services to a particular outlet.

Selective distribution
Refers to the middle channel width, where a firm uses more than one outlet but restricts availability of the product or service to a limited number of outlets.

Intensive distribution
The widest channel strategy, where firms attempt to make products and services available through as many outlets as possible.

Channel length
The number of intermediaries between the manufacturer and the final consumer.

Direct channel
The manufacturer sells directly to the consumer and performs all of the channel functions.

Central reservation systems (CRS)
Systems that are designed to improve the efficiency and effectiveness of the reservations function by providing a central point of contact for handling customers' requests in a timely fashion.

Courtesy of Foxwoods Resort Casino.

Foxwoods Resort Casino uses an exclusive distribution strategy by having only one location.

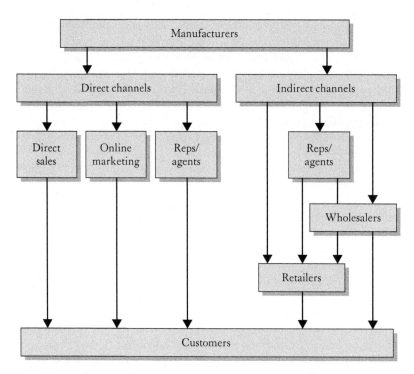

FIGURE 10.2 • Alternative channel systems.

Indirect channel

Involves at least one intermediary that is responsible for one or more channel functions.

Hotels allow direct access to booking rooms through the property, call centers, hotel website, or property-to-property. An **indirect channel** involves at least one intermediary that is responsible for one or more channel functions. This type of channel can exist in many forms, but it is not very common in service industries. Service firms are normally both producers and retailers.

There are a few indirect channels in the hospitality and tourism industries, but they seem to be more prevalent in the travel industry or in business markets that involve large-volume purchases. For example, tour operators (i.e., wholesalers) work directly with travel service firms such as hotels and airlines to combine services to market as a package to travel agents, who, in turn, market to the final consumers. Another example of an indirect channel is the meetings market. Hotel salespeople market their properties to meeting planners who purchase the hotel product on behalf of a group of final consumers. The various intermediaries will be discussed in more detail in the next section.

Global distribution systems (GDS)

Systems used by hospitality and travel firms to facilitate transactions within the distribution channel.

Most hospitality and travel firms use a combination of direct and indirect channels to reach as many consumers as possible. **Global distribution systems (GDS)** are used by airlines and hotels to coordinate their distribution activities and provide linkages to intermediaries. A GDS provides distribution channels that give customers the ability to easily search for hospitality and travel services and to conduct the transaction immediately. The system serves many roles, ranging from those that are transaction-based to those that are strategic in nature. In other words, a GDS is used for inventory control and rate management, storing data and disseminating information, revenue generation, and strategic positioning. Authors Nyheim, McFadden, and Connolly provide a thorough discussion of global distribution systems and other hospitality technologies in their book.[1]

Intermediaries

Specialists in certain functions in the distribution process that can add value to the product or service with their knowledge and expertise.

10.2.2 Intermediaries

One of the decisions that must be made by hotel and tourism firms concerns the use of **intermediaries**. Intermediaries such as wholesalers and retailers can be valuable to service firms because of their expertise and ability to specialize in certain channel functions. Also, government organizations such as travel bureaus exist to help promote and distribute travel services to individuals and groups for their constituents.

The fastest-growing procurement and distribution alternatives involve electronic commerce (e-commerce) over the Internet. Hospitality and tourism firms use this outlet to procure resources, promote their services, and offer a direct channel to consumers. This form of commerce is efficient and provides other advantages that will be discussed in this chapter.

Many of the distribution channels in service industries tend to be direct in nature, eliminating the need for intermediaries. However, the hospitality and tourism industries do have their share of valuable intermediaries that are responsible for volume business for hotels, airlines, and cruise ships. Intermediaries specialize in certain functions in the service delivery process, and they can add value to the service with their knowledge and expertise. This specialization results in more efficient production and distribution of services, as well as lower prices for consumers. Table 10.2 contains a list of the most common intermediaries in hospitality and tourism distribution channels.

10.2.2.1 TRAVEL AGENTS. Travel agents are responsible for a large volume of bookings for airlines, hotels, car rentals, and cruises. In addition, travel agents sell admissions to tourist attractions and special events. Although most of this volume comes from leisure travelers, corporate travelers can also account for a sizable amount of a travel agent's business. Rather than operate their own corporate travel departments, some firms choose to use travel agents who specialize in corporate business. The benefit of using a travel agent is that agents specialize in finding and securing good rates for their customers. Another reason that travelers use travel agents is because of their extensive knowledge regarding travel products. Most agents have traveled to many popular cities and destinations, and they have access to informative promotional materials. It is important for travel agents to provide some additional value or they will cease to exist. Consumers will make their own travel arrangements via the Internet or through direct contact with the service providers.

The travel agent's expertise and access to valuable markets can be useful to hotels, car rental agencies, airlines, and cruise operators. It is virtually impossible for any of these firms to operate their normal business while keeping abreast of the many market segments and having access to all their potential customers' preferred methods for purchasing travel products. Travel agents and hospitality and tourism firms seek to form relationships that will be mutually beneficial. Hospitality and tourism firms are looking for more volume, but they want consumers who will fit their overall customer mix. The current trend is for consumers to use Internet travel agencies such as Expedia, Travelocity, and Orbitz. This process is more cost-effective for the agency and the consumers because much of the process is automated and consumers take part in the search process. Some of the online travel agencies—for example, Priceline—offer an "opaque" service where consumers bid on travel products, like in an auction, without knowing the brand in order to get a lower price.

10.2.2.2 TOUR WHOLESALERS AND OPERATORS. Tour wholesalers and operators contract with hospitality and tourism firms to obtain services that can be combined in a package and offered to the leisure market. These packages can contain any combination of lodging, transportation, event or attraction tickets, and meals. These packages are marketed to travel agents and sometimes to consumers via the Internet or some other direct source. Tour wholesalers exist because they have access to the various suppliers and they specialize in packaging travel products, but they rely on travel agents to get the product to the mass market. This packaging concept appeals to consumers because of the convenience and the idea that the package can be purchased for a lower price than the components purchased individually. Once again, there is some value added to the services.

Electronic commerce (e-commerce)

A term used to describe the buying and selling process using electronic means such as the Internet.

CHANNEL RESOURCES	
Travel Agents	Hotel representatives
Tour wholesalers and operators	Travel bureaus
Meeting planners	Concierge

TABLE 10.2 • Most Common Intermediaries in Hospitality and Tourism

The package concept is particularly appealing to people engaged in international travel, senior citizens, groups, and novice travelers. There is some degree of risk associated with traveling to a new or foreign destination, but it is reduced by intermediaries such as tour wholesalers and travel agents. Tour wholesalers are able to sort services from suppliers into roughly the same grade and quality, package those services, and offer them to retailers. This is a more efficient way to sell travel products to large volumes of leisure customers. Each of the channel members has a specialty that improves the service delivery process as well as the overall value of the final product.

10.2.2.3 MEETING PLANNERS.   Large organizations such as corporations and trade associations have individuals or departments that are responsible for the travel plans of its members. These meeting planners negotiate with hotels, airlines, and other travel firms on behalf of their members for guest rooms and meeting space. There are also independent meeting planners and event planners who will work for organizations on a contract basis. As organizations seek to reduce overhead, outsourcing services such as meeting planning has become more common. Meeting planners are similar to travel agents in that they are familiar with many popular destinations. They have some expertise in areas such as negotiating, site selection, budgeting, and promotion, but it varies depending on whether they plan meetings for corporations, associations, or incentive groups. Each of these markets will be explained in more detail in Chapter 15, "Personal Selling."

10.2.2.4 HOTEL REPRESENTATIVES.   Large hotels have sales staffs that are responsible for selling guest rooms and meeting space to groups. These salespeople negotiate with meeting planners, tour operators, and travel agents in an effort to fill the hotel. Unfortunately, smaller hotels may not be able to justify the hiring of full-time salespeople, either because they don't have enough demand for the service or because they cannot afford to hire them. In this case, it may be in the hotel's best interest to hire an independent hotel representative to market the hotel to chosen market segments. Even large hotels may hire these independent representatives to take advantage of their access to certain markets. Much like travel agents, hotel representatives are able to deal with a wide array of consumers. Hotel representatives may not be as familiar with the hotel product as an in-house sales staff, but they may have more knowledge regarding the consumers that the hotel is targeting. Also, the hotel representatives may have better access to the targeted consumers.

Destination marketing organization (DMO)

An organization that promotes the long-term development and marketing of a destination.

Convention and visitors bureau (CVB)

Destination marketing organizations that represent cities and regions for the main purpose of promoting tourism and travel.

Destination management company (DMC)

A local firm that arranges activities and programs for meeting and event planners who are not familiar with the specific location or the local suppliers.

10.2.2.5 DESTINATION MARKETING ORGANIZATIONS.   Each tourism city, state, or region has some form of destination marketing organization (DMO) that is responsible for promoting the long-term development and marketing of a destination, focusing on convention sales, tourism marketing, and service. In the United States, each state has its own office for travel and tourism. These agencies, or bureaus, are responsible for promoting the state as a travel destination and securing major events. They are funded by the government and work in cooperation with the state's hospitality and tourism firms. In addition, each major city or region within a state will have a convention and visitors bureau (CVB) that is responsible for promoting that city or region. Convention and visitors bureaus work with local hospitality and travel firms to secure conventions, meetings, and special events for the region. Convention and visitors bureaus can receive funding from various sources such as the government, membership fees, hotel taxes, and fees for services. These bureaus also promote leisure travel to tour operators and travel agents, as well as the mass market of potential travelers. A CVB serves as a cooperative, representing hotels, motels, restaurants, convention facilities, tour operators, tourist attractions, transportation carriers, and other retail establishments that support tourists (see Figure 10.3). Most countries have a similar system focusing on regional, state, province, and city tourism destinations. (Destination marketing organizations and conventions and visitors bureaus were also discussed in Chapter 1.)

10.2.2.6 DESTINATION MANAGEMENT COMPANIES.   These companies specialize in the organization of meetings, incentives, and events. In addition, destination management companies (DMCs) arrange social activities and programs for meeting attendees and their companions. Other special services include catering, dinners, and entertainment. A DMC can also make hotel reservations, arrange transportation, and provide travel management, guides, and hostesses. Destination management companies remain behind the scenes while ensuring that everything runs according to plan. They are able to tailor their services to meet an organization's particular needs by using their many contacts and partners in the destination area. A list of destination

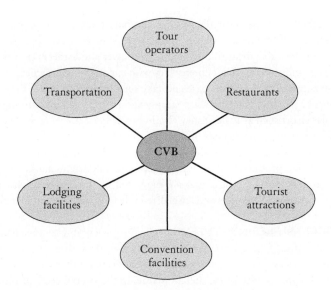

FIGURE 10.3 • **Convention and visitors bureau constituencies.**

management companies and suppliers/vendors is often available through destination marketing organizations' websites.

10.2.2.7 CONCIERGE.   Many full-service hotels employ an individual to help guests with local arrangements for restaurants and visitor attractions. In this sense, the concierge is an intermediary for the restaurants and local attractions. This individual will send business to retail operators with whom she or he has a good working relationship. As a result, it is in the best interest of the local restaurants and visitor attractions to introduce themselves to the hotel concierge and give him or her a tour of the facility. The quality of the guest's experience with the recommended restaurant or visitor attraction will reflect directly on the concierge and the hotel. Therefore, the retail establishments must assure the concierge that the consumer will be satisfied.

10.2.3   Channel Management

After a distribution channel is developed, it becomes an ongoing task to manage it over time. Many conflicts and problems can occur that will require the cooperation of the members of the channel. It is also important to note that the same company can be a part of more than one channel and occupy a different position in each channel. For example, a restaurant would be a consumer in the channel for bulk food items and napkins (i.e., its supply chain), but a producer or manufacturer in the market for meals and dining. Similarly, hotels purchase many products and services through supply chains, ranging from pens and soap to linens and pool chemicals. Therefore, a problem in one channel will affect the performance of the other channels in which the firm is a member. The Ritz-Carlton chain, a past recipient of the Malcolm Baldrige National Quality Award, recognizes the critical nature of these relationships and makes a special effort to recruit suppliers who understand and agree with its philosophy of customer service and quality.

There will always be conflicts between parties engaged in some form of negotiation over issues such as price, quantity, quality, and availability. Rather than attempt to eliminate these conflicts, it is better to find ways to manage them. In competitive markets, it is necessary to create fair exchanges so that both parties are satisfied. This mutual satisfaction can be the cornerstone of a loyal relationship that will benefit both parties in the future. Otherwise, it is in a firm's best interest to find a more equitable arrangement with other suppliers or retailers. Approaches to managing channel conflict can be behavioral (channel power and channel leadership) or contractual (vertical marketing systems).

10.2.3.1 CHANNEL LEADERSHIP.   At some point, one of the channel members should take a leadership role. The leader can then organize the other channel members and strive toward common goals and objectives. The channel leader can be a manufacturer, an intermediary, or a retailer. However, the leader will normally be large and have a sustainable, competitive advantage in its industry because of financial resources, marketing skills, or some other factor. These competitive advantages will enable firms to obtain channel power and leadership. It is often beneficial for other channel members to associate themselves with successful companies.

Manufacturers can obtain a power base and take on a leadership role if they maintain ample resources or control a product that is in short supply and in great demand among consumers. For example, a popular resort such as Walt Disney World can exercise power and leadership over travel agents, car rental companies, and airlines. Intermediaries such as wholesalers and retailers can gain control over a channel if they have the ability to group components from various manufacturers and create an attractive product or if they have access to important markets. Tour wholesalers combine travel products into packages that are marketed to travel agents who are retailers and who have access to important markets and specialize in dealing with the various market segments.

10.2.3.2 VERTICAL MARKETING SYSTEMS.

Vertical marketing system

In a vertical marketing system, channel members work together as if they were one organization, coordinating their efforts for the purpose of achieving a higher degree of efficiency, thereby reducing the overall costs of providing products and services.

One approach to reducing channel conflict and uncertainty is the vertical marketing system. In a vertical marketing system, channel members work together as if they were one organization. They coordinate their efforts for the purpose of achieving a higher degree of efficiency, thereby reducing the overall costs of providing products and services. Vertical marketing systems offer a unified approach to channel management and can be corporate, administered, or contractual.

Corporate vertical marketing system

All participants are members of the same organization. The original firm either develops or purchases other firms at the various levels in the channel.

In a corporate vertical marketing system, all participants are members of the same organization. In this case, the original firm either develops or purchases other firms at the various levels in the channel. For example, a restaurant chain might decide to operate its own food distributors in an effort to control price fluctuations and availability of its food supplies. A corporate system can be developed through *backward integration* (toward the manufacturer or supplier) or *forward integration* (toward the retailer or distributor). An example of forward integration would be a food distributor that decides to start a catering operation.

Administered vertical marketing system

A manufacturer or supplier attempts to control the flow of goods or services through the channel.

An administered vertical marketing system is one in which a manufacturer or supplier attempts to control the flow of goods or services through the channel. This is usually associated with expert power because distributors and retailers are willing to relinquish some of their control in order to benefit from the producer's knowledge and background. Event management companies may have this type of arrangement with ticket agents who market and sell their events. This arrangement is similar to a conventional channel, but a greater degree of cooperation and sharing of information is necessary for a successful operation.

Contractual vertical marketing system

A contractual vertical marketing system unifies the channel members by means of a legal and binding contract.

A contractual vertical marketing system unifies the channel members by means of a legal and binding contract. The firms agree to abide by the terms of the contract, the goal of which is to realize cost economies that would not be possible if the firms operated independently. This approach is similar to a corporate system, but it may be preferable when firms do not have the resources or expertise to develop operations at all channel levels. The firms benefit from pooling resources for functions such as advertising and research. Franchising is one example of a contractual distribution system.

10.2.3.3 CHANNEL MEMBER SELECTION AND RETENTION.

It is important that firms exercise good judgment when choosing channel members. Intermediaries must demonstrate the ability and willingness to perform the desired tasks. In addition, prospective channel members must buy in to the philosophy of the service provider. The service provider should determine the characteristics that it feels are critical in a channel member and then evaluate potential members on the basis of these characteristics. After a firm is selected, it is necessary to retain the firm through the use of financial and nonfinancial motivators.

Financial motivators are aimed at improving a channel member's profit. A service provider can improve a channel member's profit by offering more discounts or promotions related to desired outcomes, reducing prices, or increasing promotional support. Although financial motivators are effective, nonfinancial motivators should also be considered. Some nonfinancial motivators that could be used are training or improving products and services. For example, tour operators and tourism bureaus often invite travel agents on trips to the destination in order to familiarize the agents with the product. These trips are free of charge and allow travel agents to get a firsthand look at the destination so that they can relay the information to their customers. Hotels use a similar practice with meeting planners considering properties for their groups.

10.2.4 Building Customer Value through Distribution Systems

When choosing a distribution system to reach target customers, it is important for a firm to enhance customer value by increasing customer benefits (i.e., improve quality) and/or decreasing the customer's cost of purchase (i.e., lower the price).[2]

10.2.4.1 INCREASING CUSTOMER BENEFITS. Customer benefits can be increased by choosing a distribution system that delivers more product benefits, delivers more service benefits, builds brand image, and/or builds company benefits:

- **Delivering product benefits.** Product benefits can come in the form of product quality, product assortment, and product form. In hospitality and tourism, it is critical to meet customer quality expectations and provide consistent service. Direct channels provide the firm with the best opportunity to control quality, whereas indirect channels require a firm to place its trust in an intermediary. For example, tour operators rely on travel agents to sell their products to the final consumer. The channel system must also provide the range of products necessary to achieve a desired level of customer appeal. Travel bureaus need the full support of all businesses in the region to promote their tourism products to travelers.

- **Delivering service benefits.** Service benefits can come in the form of after-sale service, availability and delivery, and transaction services. After-sale service can be crucial in achieving customer satisfaction in the event of a service failure. For example, there are many stories of students going through tour operators or travel agents to purchase Spring Break package vacations, only to arrive in foreign cities and not have a room. Then when they try to contact the company that sold them the trip, it is often impossible to get through to someone. This reflects on all of the brands involved in the package, as well as the destination. Intermediaries are also used in indirect channels to make products more readily available. Internet travel companies such as Priceline and Expedia exist for this purpose. Customers get the best prices in a short period of time without having to search the alternatives. These intermediaries also facilitate the transaction and delivery of the hospitality or travel product. For example, tour wholesalers or operators can package the hospitality products and obtain one payment from the customer.

- **Building brand image.** One of the major issues facing hotels is the image that using Internet travel firms may convey. These companies tend to be viewed as discounters offering great values (i.e., low prices). It is relatively easy for hotels in the economy and budget categories to choose this channel, but higher-priced hotels have a much more difficult decision. Upscale and luxury hotels may diminish their brands by using Internet travel companies. Another problem is that some Internet travel companies sell hotel rooms at higher prices than the customer could get by going directly through the hotel. When customers become aware of this, it will reflect poorly on the hotel. Another common intermediary for hotels is the hotel sales representative who sells to groups and represents the hotel. The hotel loses some control over the message and the way the property is conveyed. Finally, building brand image is also an issue when franchising—the franchisor loses some control over brand image and must rely on the franchisees to adhere to the business system.

- **Building company benefits.** This form of benefit is related to brand image. The use of intermediaries such as hotel representatives and travel agents can actually benefit the firm because of the personal attention that customers get from qualified professionals. These types of intermediaries have good product knowledge and experience. They are experts in dealing with their respective target markets and provide a valuable asset in their use of relationship marketing with customers. Franchising is also a way to benefit from the relationships local owners already have with customers in the area, rather than opening a new restaurant without having any previous ties in the community.

10.2.4.2 IMPROVING COST EFFICIENCY. One of the other ways to increase customer value is to lower the cost of purchase, both actual and perceived. For instance, the cost of planning and purchasing a vacation may be higher when the customer has to contact hotels, car rental agencies, airlines, and tourist attractions to purchase each component separately. Meanwhile, tour operators package these same vacation components and offer them directly, or through travel agents for one price that is lower, or at least perceived to be lower, than if purchased separately. Convention and visitors bureaus serve as clearinghouses for travelers and reduce the number of transactions. Figures 10.4a and 10.4b illustrate the importance of this function in regard to meetings and conventions.

Assume there are five different meeting planners looking for a conference hotel in which to hold a meeting. If there are five conference hotels in a city, each of the meeting planners would have to contact all five hotels and send requests for proposal (RFP). With five hotels and five meeting planners, this would result in a total of 25 contacts or communications (see Figure 10.4a).

Consider this same situation with a convention bureau to act as an intermediary, or clearinghouse, for the two groups. Each of the meeting planners would send an RFP to the CVB, which would then forward the RFP to the conference hotels. This would result in a total of 10 contacts or communications between the meeting planners and the conference hotels (see Figure 10.4b). This example is simplistic; however, it does demonstrate the value of using an indirect channel system with an intermediary. The number of contacts was reduced from 25 to 10 with just five

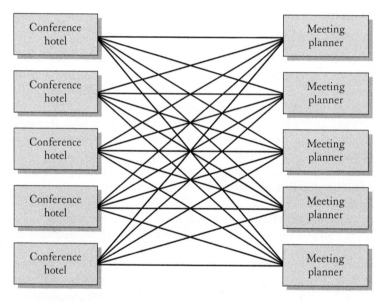

FIGURE 10.4a • Distribution system without an intermediary.

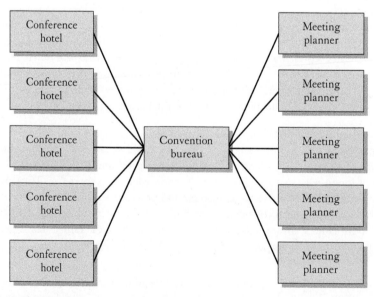

FIGURE 10.4b • Distribution system with an intermediary.

customers (i.e., meeting planners) and five service providers (i.e., hotels). As the number of customers and service providers increases, the number of contacts or transactions will increase exponentially. Therefore, it is necessary to weigh the benefits and costs of adding channel members and make a decision that is best for a particular service provider.

10.3 FRANCHISING

Franchising is a contractual arrangement whereby one firm (the franchisor) licenses a number of other firms (each firm is a franchisee) to use the franchisor's name and business practices. In other words, franchising is a network of interdependent business relationships that allows a number of operators to share a brand identification and a successful method of doing business (i.e., a proven marketing and distribution system). As a franchisee, you own the assets of your company, but you are licensed to operate someone else's business system. In 2003, there were over 2,500 franchise systems in the United States with more than 534,000 franchise units. This represents 3.2 percent of all businesses, controlling over 35 percent of all retail and service revenue in the U.S. economy.[3] Those numbers increased to over 3,000 different franchisers with over 900,000 franchise units, accounting for approximately 50 percent of all retail sales in 2014.[4]

Franchising opportunities can be found for a variety of industries, including hospitality and travel, through Internet sites such as Franchising.com, FranchiseOpportunities.com, and Entrepreneur.com. The restaurant industry, including quick service restaurants (QSR) and sit-down restaurants, is one of the top five industries in the United States for franchising.

As a method of distribution, franchising provides many opportunities for growth and profitability. However, when considering a franchising relationship, both parties should carefully evaluate the alternative forms of ownership and operation. The individual goals and objectives of each party have to be weighed against the trade-offs of a franchisor–franchisee relationship. In essence,

Franchising
A contractual arrangement whereby one firm licenses a number of other firms to use the franchisor's name and business practices.

Franchisor
The firm that licenses other firms to use its name and business practices.

Franchisee
A firm that obtains a license from another firm to use its name and business practices.

Julius Kielaitis/Shutterstock

The Subway chain is one of the largest franchise systems in hospitality.

	ADVANTAGES	DISADVANTAGES
FRANCHISEE	Established product/service	Additional fees/expenses
	Technical/managerial assistance	Loss of control
	Quality standards	Difficult to terminate
	Less operating capital	Pooled performance
	Opportunities for growth	
	Cooperative advertising	
FRANCHISOR	Rapid expansion	Loss of control
	Diversified risk	Reduced profits
	Cost economics	Legal issues
	Cooperative advertising	Recruitment
	Employee issues	

TABLE 10.3 • Franchising advantages and disadvantages.

franchising is a strategic alliance between groups of people who have contractual responsibilities and a common goal. By choosing to invest in a franchise operation, an owner is expressing the belief that he or she will be more successful using someone else's business system rather than investing his or her money in an independent operation and developing his or her own business system. Table 10.3 summarizes the advantages and disadvantages associated with franchising.

10.3.1 Franchisee

10.3.1.1 ADVANTAGES. There are many advantages to joining an existing operation rather than starting from the beginning.

1. There is an established product or service with a brand name and an identity in the marketplace. It is normally very costly and time-consuming to build a brand image. Trying to start a new pizza business would be much more cumbersome than opening a Domino's Pizza.

2. Second, franchisees receive technical and managerial assistance from the franchisor. This assistance could be in the form of recruitment and training of employees, or in the design of the facility. Franchisors transfer the knowledge they have accumulated as they progressed through the learning curve, thereby accelerating the process for franchisees.

3. Third, the franchisee benefits from the quality standards that are already in place for the franchise. There is a system of controls that guide the operations and provide for a certain level of quality and consistency.

4. Often, there is a smaller capital requirement for opening a franchise unit relative to the start-up costs for an independent operation. Franchises have a track record that can be used to estimate demand, design the facility, schedule employees, and order inventory.

5. There are opportunities to expand the business within the operating region. Franchisees are usually given some form of territorial rights to add units based on demand.

6. The franchisee benefits from the pooled resources of the many participants in advertising and promoting the product. The use of cooperative advertising results in a more efficient and effective means of communicating with customers. An independent restaurant would not be able to afford to place advertisements in major magazines or during prime-time television shows.

10.3.1.2 DISADVANTAGES. There are also some disadvantages to becoming a franchisee.

1. Franchise fees and royalties must be borne by the franchisee in return for the benefits just described. These expenses are normally a percentage of sales and result in a decrease in the profit margin.

2. The franchisee must adhere to the standards and procedures as set forth in the agreement. This restricts the franchisee's ability to control the entire operation in that certain requirements regarding products, price ranges, and expansion are imposed by the franchisor.

3. It may be difficult to terminate the agreement if the franchisee would like to change brands or sell the business.

4. The brand image is the result of the pooled performance of all corporate-owned and franchised units. The franchise's reputation and image can be negatively affected by the performance of individual units.

10.3.2 Franchisor

10.3.2.1 ADVANTAGES. Many companies are choosing to expand their operations using the franchise approach because of its advantages.

1. Companies can experience more rapid expansion, because franchisees provide additional investment capital and have access to untapped markets.

2. By limiting the investment and adding "partners," the franchisor is able to diversify the risk of doing business.

3. A byproduct of this rapid expansion is the realization of cost economies from operating at a higher level of volume. The organization will get better prices on supplies and be able to allocate fixed costs over a larger number of units, bringing down the cost per unit.

4. A related issue is the use of cooperative advertising. As mentioned before, this is an advantage for both the franchisor and the franchisees.

5. Certain human resources and management tasks are simplified by franchising. The franchisees play an important role in the selection and retention of employees. Plus, owners are very careful to monitor the performance of the franchise because they benefit directly from the profitability of the unit.

10.3.2.2 DISADVANTAGES. A few disadvantages are associated with being a franchisor.

1. There is a reduction in control of the operation. Having many owners or managers will have an effect on the overall performance of the franchise. Even though operating standards and procedures are written into the agreement, they are not always followed.

2. There is a trade-off between risk and return. The sharing of risk and ownership results in the sharing of profits as well.

3. The size and visibility of franchises exposes them to more potential litigation. They are easy targets for legal actions such as antitrust suits and class action suits. Also, injury claims are prevalent in many service industries. For example, McDonald's was once sued by a customer who spilled coffee in her lap while driving her car, and has been sued by obese people who accused the fast-food restaurant of causing their weight problems.

4. It is difficult to find qualified prospects to be franchisees. Although many investors have the necessary capital, they may lack the necessary knowledge and experience to run a successful franchise unit in the product or service category.

SUMMARY OF CHAPTER OBJECTIVES

This chapter discussed the role of distribution and supply chain management in planning the marketing strategy for hospitality and tourism services. Decisions must be made regarding whether to perform activities and take care of supply needs in-house or to outsource. In addition, decisions need to be made regarding channel width (how many outlets) and channel length (number and type of intermediaries). If the decision is made to use an indirect channel (at least one intermediary), then the firm must examine channel management issues such as channel leadership and channel power. Finally, the extent of the relationships with other channel members will need to be considered.

Intermediaries exist in channels because they perform certain channel functions more effectively than the other channel members. One advantage of using intermediaries is the fact that they often have access to markets that are desired by a manufacturer or producer. Travel agents and tour operators specialize in packaging trips and selling them to groups and individuals for pleasure travel, and meeting planners and travel bureaus work more with business groups for conferences and conventions.

Some type of vertical marketing system can be used to provide more certainty in the relationships. Franchising is probably the most common form of vertical marketing system. There are advantages and disadvantages associated with franchising versus remaining corporate owned and operated. In general, the franchisor gives up control and some of the profit margin in an attempt to reduce risk and grow at a faster rate. The franchisee gives up control and some of the profit margin as well, but gets the advantage of an established brand, a proven operation, and increased advertising.

KEY TERMS AND CONCEPTS

Administered vertical marketing system	Exclusive distribution
Central reservation systems (CRS)	Franchisee
Channel length	Franchising
Channel width	Franchisor
Contractual vertical marketing system	Global distribution systems (GDS)
Convention and visitors bureau (CVB)	Indirect channel
Corporate vertical marketing system	Intensive distribution
Destination management companies (DMCs)	Intermediaries
Destination marketing organization (DMO)	Selective distribution
Direct channel	Supply chain
Electronic commerce (e-commerce)	Vertical marketing system

QUESTIONS FOR REVIEW AND DISCUSSION

1. What is a supply chain? What are the reasons for performing the supply chain activities in-house versus outsourcing?

2. What factors are considered in determining a firm's channel width and channel length?

3. List and give examples of the intermediaries that exist in the hospitality and tourism industry.

4. Explain the three types of vertical marketing systems.

5. What are the ways a firm can enhance customer value through channel systems?

6. What is franchising? Why would firms or individuals choose to enter this type of arrangement?

chapter review

7 If you have 10 tour operators and 100 customers, what is the difference in the number of transactions with, and without, a travel agent acting as an intermediary?

8 Internet exercise: Use the Internet resources for identifying franchise opportunities and put together a proposal for a group of investors who want to start a restaurant operation in the Midwest. The investors are looking to become franchisees with an existing casual dining restaurant chain that will have a good potential for success. The investors are starting a management company and pooling their resources, so there shouldn't be any capital or net worth restrictions. Choose a franchise operation and justify your decision based on the Midwest market and the restaurant concept's potential appeal.

NOTES

[1] Peter D. Nyheim, Francis M. McFadden, and Daniel J. Connolly, *Technology Strategies for the Hospitality Industry* (Upper Saddle River, NJ: Prentice-Hall, 2005), pp. 153–186.

[2] Roger J. Best, *Market-Based Management: Strategies for Growing Customer Value and Profitability*, 2nd ed. (Upper Saddle River, NJ: Prentice-Hall, 2000), pp. 204–207.

[3] Robert Gappa, "What Is Franchising?" (2003). Available at www.franchising.com.

[4] Quick Franchise Facts, Franchising Industry Statistics (2014). www.azfranchises.com/franchisefacts.htm.

chapter review

CASE STUDY

Ice Cream Heaven

Ice Cream Heaven is an independent, family-owned restaurant that offers an extensive selection of ice cream and desserts, along with basic sandwiches and comfort food. There is also a playground for children. The target market consists of families with young children and sports teams. The restaurant is a popular place for teams to come after Little League and soccer games. Most of the items on the menu are between $5 and $10, and that price point is not flexible—customers are not willing to pay more than that. Also, many of the customers buy only ice cream or milk shakes. Therefore, the business is very seasonal because the restaurant is located in the northeastern United States.

The majority of revenue is obtained during the summer months, and the annual revenue is approximately $500,000. Most of the workers are local high school students, so labor is relatively inexpensive. However, the food costs run about 35 percent, even though it is a simple menu. The owner tries to use local companies and quality ingredients. One of the problems is that there is only one Ice Cream Heaven and the amount of volume doesn't result in significant discounts from large suppliers (e.g., Sysco). The owner is trying to decide what to do at this point to increase profits.

Case Study Questions and Issues

1. Can anything be done to minimize costs in the supply chain? What are the possible sources of supplies?

2. What are some of the advantages and disadvantages of opening one or more additional restaurants? Should they be the same concept?

3. How would franchising affect the supply chain?

case study

CASE STUDY

The Wing Shack

A couple of college students decided to start a business together after graduating. The two friends traveled the region in search of the ultimate buffalo chicken wings. After researching these other operations, the two returned to their town and started to put the wheels in motion to find a location and develop a business system. The idea was to open a small restaurant and focus on delivery within the local area, including the college campus. As luck would have it, a restaurant recently had gone out of business in a high-traffic area. The two young men found themselves meeting with realtors, bankers, accountants, lawyers, and town officials in an attempt to achieve their dream of opening a restaurant. After many negotiations, the two began planning for the opening of their restaurant. They decided to call it The Wing Shack and cater to the college crowd.

The restaurant had a small bar area, a pool table, a few televisions, a jukebox, and 12 tables for dining. The menu consisted of chicken wings (including boneless), chicken sandwiches, a few appetizers, and a few sides (e.g., french fries). The chicken wings were meatier than those of most restaurants, and 20 flavors were offered. For beverages, the owners decided to put 20 beers on tap, showcasing the regional microbrews. Business was slow at first, but word of mouth quickly spread and the restaurant started to get more and more customers. One of the early strategies employed by the owners was to have all-you-can-eat wings on the slower nights of the week (Sunday to Wednesday). Eventually, the restaurant had people waiting in line to get a table, and the sit-down business was as good as the delivery business.

After 3 years of successfully running the business and seeing increased profits, the owners considered expanding. The business system was solid and the restaurant benefited from a good marketing strategy, including being a sponsor of the college's athletic programs. Initially, the owners decided to open another restaurant in a city about one hour away. This required the owners to commute on a regular basis, which soon put a strain on their partnership and relationships. They felt they were spread too thin, and in hindsight they weren't sure if this was the best idea. This led the young entrepreneurs to investigate the possibility of franchising. The profit after taxes for the original restaurant was approximately 28 percent of revenue. Franchise fees for restaurants in this category usually run around 3 to 4 percent.

Case Study Questions and Issues

1. What issues must the owners consider before deciding whether to open more restaurants on their own or to franchise?

2. Assuming the original restaurant is in the Northeast, what cities or towns would you suggest for the next five restaurants?

3. How many franchised units would the owners have to contract to make the same profit as they do in the original unit (assuming the revenue will be similar for all units)?

Electronic Commerce

Courtesy of Mila Supinskaya/Shutterstock

Chapter Objectives

After studying this chapter, you should be able to:

1. Describe the impact of the Internet on the hospitality and tourism industry.

2. Discuss the attributes and scope of electronic commerce, including traits of a networked economy and security issues.

3. Explain the various strategies and business models used in electronic commerce.

4. Describe Internet marketing strategies for websites and e-mail campaigns.

11.1 INTRODUCTION

Electronic commerce, or *e-commerce,* refers to the practice of carrying out business transactions over computer networks in an effort to generate sales and improve organizational performance. Previous forms of electronic business included electronic data interchange (EDI) by businesses and the use of automated teller machines (ATMs) by consumers. These applications were limited to one-to-one or one-to-many, whereas the newer form of electronic business application (the Internet) allows many-to-many communications. The number of companies engaging in online commerce has been growing at a rapid rate since its global consumer introduction in the early 1990s. Organizations can communicate with all their stakeholders through this form of electronic commerce. For instance, investors can obtain information about the company, consumers can obtain information about products or complain about customer service, and suppliers can communicate with their business partners. In addition, firms can gather information about their customers with online surveys and sales promotions.

One of the major reasons for the popularity of electronic commerce is the ability of manufacturers, retailers, and service providers to sell directly to consumers at retail or near-retail profit margins without sharing the revenue with other channel members. Firms are able to increase profitability, gain market share, improve customer service, and deliver products more quickly as a result of this direct channel to the consumer. Before discussing the details of electronic commerce, it is necessary to provide some background on the Internet and the Web.

> **Electronic commerce (e-commerce)**
> A term used to describe the buying and selling of goods and services through electronic means such as the Internet.

11.1.1 The Internet

The precursor of the Internet was first introduced by the Rand Corporation in 1964 as a method for secure contact between the Pentagon and units of the U.S. armed forces.[1] It was a decentralized computer communications network with no central computer or governing authority. In the event that one or more computers on the network were destroyed, it would still be possible to send information between the remaining computers. In other words, the Internet began simply as a network of networks. Its use was expanded to university faculty and other researchers in the early 1970s, and it was improved with the National Science Foundation's creation of a high-speed long-distance telecommunications network in the mid-1980s. The government restricted the use of the Internet to nonprofit, educational, and government organizations until 1991, at which time commercial sites were allowed to participate.

The Internet is a complex collection of wires, protocols, and hardware that allows for the transmission of data using *transmission control protocol and Internet protocol (TCP/IP).* These protocols ensure that information sent from one computer to another arrives in the format in which it was sent, despite being broken up during the transmission. Internet protocol software sets the rules for data transfer over a network, and transmission control protocol software ensures the safe and reliable transfer of the data.

Another important element developed in the 1980s is the **domain name system (DNS).** Each computer connected to the Internet has a unique name and number. For each website, the DNS gives each computer on the Internet a unique and easily recognizable name that is used instead of the IP address. In addition to the name associated with each computer, the last portion of the domain address refers to the type of organization. For example, *.com* and *.biz* represent businesses, *.edu* represents colleges and universities, *.gov* represents the federal government, and *.mil* represents the U.S. military.

> **Domain name system (DNS)**
> The unique name given to a computer connected to the Internet.

Web content normally consists of five types of items: text, links, forms, images, and multimedia. The *text* is the copy that has been developed for the website. The *links* are the hypertext links that connect one webpage to other webpages. *Forms* are the pages that contain fields, which when completed are then submitted to a firm through its website. Using forms, customers can complete inquiries and purchases. *Images* are photos that bring webpages to life. Two photo formats commonly used in Web design are *graphics image format (GIF)* and *joint picture encoding group (JPEG).* Finally, *multimedia* content in the form of audio or video clips is often placed on websites.

Since the early 1990s, the Internet has become an avenue for sharing information, obtaining software, selling products and services, retrieving data, exchanging messages via e-mail, allowing interactive discussion groups, and displaying video and audio files. The Web was first developed in 1989 at the European Organization for Nuclear Research (CERN) in Geneva, Switzerland, as a means of communication that could be used while simultaneously working on another project. This was made possible by the use of hypertext, which is a method of linking related information without a hierarchy or menu system. An example of this concept is the use of help screens in software applications. The software that is used to access the documents stored on servers located throughout the world is called a browser. Several browsers are available for both the Windows and Apple operating systems, including Internet Explorer, Firefox, and Safari. The actual link to the Internet is made through a commercial service or Internet service provider (ISP) that sells services that connect individuals and organizations to the Internet.

11.1.1.1 THE CYBERSPACE COMMUNITY.   *Cyberspace* is a term coined by William Gibson in his novel *Neuromancer* to describe the electronic communities that formed on the Internet. These communities are similar to normal communities in that members do not like being bothered by salespeople, and they have formed their own rules of "netiquette" concerning such actions.

Therefore, most marketing of products and services has been restricted to the Web. The Web offers the greatest flexibility regarding the use of graphics and interactive communication, and it is the easiest area of the Internet to navigate. Also, as mentioned before, the ability to use many-to-many communication allows firms to mass-market their products and services within these electronic communities. In addition to mass marketing, the use of personalized content management allows companies to tailor Web content based on a user's Web behavior and preferences. Amazon.com was among the first to offer personalized Web content based on past purchase behavior and online browsing behavior.

11.2 THE SCOPE OF ELECTRONIC COMMERCE

Although we may think that electronic commerce is a phenomenon of the 1990s, its roots date back to the 1970s. At that time, the primary commercial application was electronic funds transfer (EFT) between financial institutions. This evolved into electronic data interchange (EDI), which is the routine transfer of documents. Among the first types of EDI transfer were orders from one company to another, typically from a retailer to a manufacturer.

Today, electronic commerce is classified in a number of ways:

- **Business-to-business (B2B).**   E-commerce that involves one business selling to or creating an exchange with another business is called business-to-business (B2B). For example, if a restaurant electronically buys food or other supplies from a supplier, this would be classified as B2B.

- **Business-to-consumer (B2C).**   The electronic form of retailing when a business sells a product or service to a consumer is called business-to-consumer (B2C). Amazon.com is among the most well known B2C companies, but nearly all of the national brands in the hospitality and tourism industry have a presence in the B2C environment.

- **Consumer-to-business (C2B).**   The situation in which an individual seeks to sell products or services to a business (e.g., advertising links on consumer websites), or when consumers bid for products and services offered for sale by a firm (i.e., reverse auction), is classified as consumer-to-business (C2B). One such example is Priceline.com, where consumers bid for airline tickets.

- **Consumer-to-consumer (C2C).**   Although not common in the hospitality and tourism industry, consumers selling directly to other consumers make up the consumer-to-consumer (C2C) segment of e-commerce. Individuals selling or exchanging timeshare units is an example of this type of exchange.

Hypertext
A method of linking related information without a hierarchy or menu system.

Browser
An application program that allows users to display HTML files obtained from the Web.

Business-to-business (B2B)
E-commerce that involves one business selling to or creating an exchange with another business.

Business-to-consumer (B2C)
The electronic form of retailing when a business sells a product or service to a consumer.

Consumer-to-business (C2B)
The situation in which an individual seeks to sell products or services to a business, or when consumers bid for products and services offered for sale by a firm.

Consumer-to-consumer (C2C)
The situation in which consumers sell directly to other consumers.

11.2.1 Traits of a Networked Economy

Some people view electronic commerce as a boom-and-bust cycle, but that is actually not true. In the mid-1990s, there was a dramatic increase in activity in the broad field of e-commerce. Companies such as eBay, Amazon, and Expedia provide tangible evidence of the impact that e-commerce has had on the business world. These companies, and hundreds like them, created an economic boom unlike anything seen before. Most traditional companies, including those in the hospitality and tourism industry, were forced to change their business practices and business models. Online reservations for hotels, airlines, and restaurants, as well as online check-in for airlines and hotels, and other forms of electronic exchanges, are now quite common. In the airline industry, these transactions are ubiquitous.

Those who follow the evolution of electronic commerce agree that a networked economy, based on firms that have an Internet presence and conduct business on line (at least in part), has several important traits:[2]

- **It creates value largely or exclusively through the gathering, synthesizing, and distribution of information.**   Firms that engage in e-commerce activities can collect significant data about their customers. They can more easily determine consumers' likes, dislikes, and responses to various marketing stimuli. The wealth of data, which is readily analyzed, allows marketing managers to make better-informed decisions.

- **It formulates strategy in ways that result in a convergence of management of the business and management of various technologies.**   The management of technology is viewed not as a separate function but as a core business competency. The development of e-commerce applications is viewed not as a parallel activity but as part of the core set of activities within the firm.

- **It allows firms to compete in real time, not in cycle time or in asynchronous time.**   Historically, businesses made changes on an intermittent basis, as a result of data about, for instance, financial performance or guest response. With the increasing use of technology, this lag time can be nearly eliminated. For example, an airline can post price changes to an e-commerce website and then monitor site transactions to determine within a very short time whether the price change has resulted in the desired change in buyer behavior.

- **It operates in business environments in which there are low barriers to entry and extremely low variable costs.**   This trait is applicable to pure e-commerce companies that operate solely on the Internet, but less so to companies in the hospitality and tourism industry that have physical facilities. Hospitality and tourism firms have higher capital costs for buildings, fixtures, and equipment than do firms that are pure electronic commerce companies.

  > **Pure e-commerce companies** Refers to firms that operate solely on the Internet. They do not operate any physical facilities.

- **It organizes resources around the demand side of the business (i.e., the level of demand from potential buyers of the products and services).**   Demand from potential customers is constantly monitored to determine changes. These firms then attempt to influence demand by changing marketing variables such as price and availability.

- **It examines relationships with customers in "screen-to-face" interfaces in which technology is used to manage and customize customers' experiences.**   In order to increase relationship-building interactions and reduce labor costs at the same time, technology is used to "push" customized information to the consumer. This can take many forms, including e-mail and website information that is customized to match the interests and past behavior of individual consumers.

- **It uses technology-mediated methods to measure and track customer behavior and interaction patterns.**   These data are then used to customize future interaction with individual customers and customer groups with similar buyer behavior.

The use of digital technology has dramatically shifted the business paradigm, both domestically and internationally. Digital technology has created entire new industries, shifted others, and forced managers and leaders of firms to look at their customers, markets, and competitors in entirely new ways. The size and scope of e-commerce has changed dramatically in the past 10 years. Numerous industry publications and research organizations report on these trends. Among the most notable are www.emarketer.com, www.cnet.com, and www.forester.com. Electronic commerce is characterized by the following attributes.[3]

- **Exchange of digitized information.** The foundation of e-commerce includes exchange of digitized information. These exchanges can involve information or communications, or they can be related to the purchase of goods or services in a digital format. The exchanges occur between organizations or individuals.

- **Technology-enabled transactions.** E-commerce is about technology-enabled transactions. Use of Web browsers is the most common form of e-commerce, but there are others. When banks use ATM machines or companies use phone or personal digital assistant (PDA) interfaces to create exchanges, these are part of e-commerce as well. Years ago, companies managed these exchanges through human interaction, but technology is used more frequently today. The result is generally better response to customer needs and a reduction in the cost of the exchange. Perhaps the best example of an effective technology-enabled exchange is the use of online reservations for airlines and hotels. Consumers are able to access vastly more information than would be possible through a voice-only interaction with the airline or hotel company. The company is able to provide the information and make a less expensive sale when using an e-commerce exchange.

- **Technology-mediated transactions.** With each passing year, e-commerce is moving beyond technology-enabled transactions to technology-mediated transactions. For example, when a customer makes a transaction at a large discount retail chain and the individual items are scanned, they are subtracted from the store inventory. When a predetermined inventory level is reached, this will automatically trigger a reorder from the manufacturer. Orders from hundreds of stores are automatically combined and placed as a single daily order with the manufacturer. Similar mediation is occurring within the hospitality and tourism industry. For example, when a guest checks out of a room via the interactive video services in the room, the now vacant room is added to the inventory of those that need to be serviced by housekeeping. Once the room is cleaned, it is automatically added back into the available room inventory. Similarly, when items are sold in a fast-food restaurant, this inventory can be tracked and reorder points established so that managers can spend more time interacting with customers and employees instead of tracking and ordering inventory.

- **Intra- and interorganizational activities.** Within hospitality and tourism organizations, there are many electronically based activities both within the organizations and between organizations and individuals. All of these activities are considered part of electronic commerce. Any electronic activity that directly or indirectly supports exchanges is part of the world of e-commerce.

11.2.1.1 ELECTRONIC COMMERCE SECURITY ISSUES. One of the appealing features of the Internet is the fact that there is open access without a governing body. This lack of governance or authority has left many to question the security and safety of the Internet. Some potential applications have been slow to develop because of the hysteria surrounding Internet security. Online banking, investing, and travel reservations were initially slow to gain volume due to consumers' concerns about security. Initially, firms promoted products and services online but provided a toll-free number that consumers could call to place orders. More recently, more consumers are placing their orders online, but companies still provide toll-free numbers for those who are hesitant to provide confidential information, such as credit card numbers, online. Airlines were among the first providers to provide a financial incentive to purchase electronically. Later, they shifted to an additional financial cost if toll-free numbers of support personnel were accessed to make a purchase.

Concerns about Internet security have been blown out of proportion. Although online business transactions are not perfectly secure, they are no riskier than ordering via telephone or fax. Computer hackers are similar to everyday criminals who try to find ways to circumvent security systems and procedures, although there are some additional security issues associated with electronic commerce. First, the Internet is an open network without any physical barriers to prevent theft (e.g., hidden cameras, safes, security guards). Second, the same technologies that are being used for commerce can be used to breach security (e.g., computer software used to search for passwords).

Several methods can be used to restrict access and improve security in electronic commerce. First, a form of **authentication** can be required through the use of some combination of account numbers, passwords, and IP (Internet protocol) addresses. Second, a **firewall** can be used to monitor traffic between an organization's network and the Internet. This barrier can restrict access to certain IP addresses or applications. A third method is to use coding or **encryption** techniques to transform data to protect their meaning. These security methods can be used individually or together, depending on the level of security desired. For instance, firms that are transmitting payment information will be more inclined to use all three levels of defense.

11.2.2.   Benefits of Electronic Commerce

The advent of electronic commerce has brought many benefits to businesses, which far outweigh the limitations.

- **International reach.**   Even small firms are able to create a worldwide marketing presence, allowing them to expand their customer base. In addition, firms are able to seek out higher-quality and lower-cost suppliers on a worldwide basis.

- **Cost reduction and supply chain improvements.**   Electronic commerce allows firms to reduce the cost of paper-based marketing and business process systems. Inventories can be reduced and the firm's assets used more efficiently.

- **Improved customer communication and relations.**   The use of electronic means of communication allows firms to be in more frequent and more personal communication with customers. The use of customer relationship management (CRM) software allows firms to know more about all their customers, but especially the best customers.

- **Availability of updated materials.**   When hospitality and tourism firms relied on printed brochures and collateral materials, it was a constant battle to have up-to-date material. Now, information, rates, and other data can be changed in real time on corporate websites.

- **Ubiquity.**   Consumers can use e-commerce 24 hours a day, 7 days a week.

- **Instant delivery and confirmation.**   When consumers purchase airline tickets, they receive nearly instant confirmation and have access to tickets and other travel documents immediately.

Authentication

Verifying the appropriate access by a user through the use of some combination of account numbers, passwords, and IP (Internet protocol) addresses.

Firewall

A filter used to monitor traffic between an organization's network and the Internet. This barrier can restrict access to certain IP addresses, applications, or content.

Encryption

Transmitted data are scrambled to prevent unauthorized access by users or hackers.

11.3   ELECTRONIC COMMERCE STRATEGY

The use of electronic commerce is a multifaceted industry. There are pure e-commerce companies such as Expedia.com, Hotels.com, and Kayak.com, as well as established firms such as Marriott International and Hilton Hotels and Resorts that use e-commerce as a supplement to their other forms of marketing. All are correct approaches and are designed to be an important part of a firm's overall marketing strategy. Any hospitality or tourism firm should carefully consider how the use of the World Wide Web and electronic commerce fits with the balance of the marketing strategy before investing significant time, effort, and resources in an e-commerce strategy. A decision about entering the e-commerce space is a critical one and should not be taken lightly. Managers should fully consider broad perspectives before making decisions and moving forward. The following are some of the specific questions that should be addressed before action is taken:[4]

- What is the firm's purpose for engaging in online communications?
- What are the firm's goals and specific objectives? What outcome is the firm seeking to achieve?

- Why should the firm want to go online? Is it to introduce new products and services? Is cost reduction one of the goals? Are enhanced relations with current customers an objective?

- What expectations does the firm have for its online activities? Are there different objectives for different divisions of the firm, such as marketing, human resources, or finance?

- How will electronic commerce efforts be integrated with other forms of communication? How will consistency of branding and identity be maintained?

- Who will be in charge of website creation, maintenance, and evaluation?

- Who will establish the budget for electronic commerce? How will costs be allocated among units?

- Does the firm have the talent and patience to allow the website and electronic commerce efforts to mature into a productive communications and distribution channel?

The size of the firm is not the driving factor when deciding what role electronic commerce might play in a firm's marketing program. Large firms such as Marriott International (www .marriott.com) and Hilton (www.hilton.com) receive major benefits from using the Internet in a variety of ways to meet marketing objectives, but small startups and single-unit lodging companies can use the Internet successfully, as well. For example, a bed-and-breakfast might choose to belong to the Select Registry (www.selectregistry.com) and derive many of the same benefits of a much larger organization. Decisions about use of the Internet and other e-commerce strategies are driven by how managers want to integrate the use of the Web into their overall marketing strategies. In the case of Marriott International and Hilton Worldwide, it seems that their objectives related to the Internet are to do the following:

- Create brand awareness
- Sell products and services, room reservations, group meeting space, and so on
- Create interest in and sales related to promotions
- Provide information about the many products and services that the firm offers
- Build loyalty through frequent-guest programs and provide automated 24/7 access to these accounts
- Promote employment with the firm
- Provide positive information about the community service work that the firm and related foundations accomplish

Many types of businesses find it necessary to offer their services through websites.

11.3.1 Electronic Commerce Business Model Components

A variety of business models are used within electronic commerce. These will vary greatly depending on the industry and the company. This section provides an overview of the broad framework of e-commerce business models and then focuses on the models and examples most common in the hospitality and tourism industry. There are two critical components for all e-commerce business models: the revenue model and the value proposition.

11.3.1.1 REVENUE MODEL. A revenue model simply shows how the firm will generate revenue or income. Without some income stream that exceeds the level of expenses, the business model is not going to be successful and the company will not be able to sustain its operations. There are five primary revenue models.[5]

> **Revenue model**
> A type of electronic commerce business model that focuses on how the firm will generate revenue or income.

1. **Sales.** Firms generate revenue from the sales of products or services on their websites. For example, hotel chains allow consumers to book rooms through their websites, and airlines allow consumers to book flights.

2. **Transaction fees.** Firms generate revenue based on commissions or fees on each transaction. Expedia.com is an example of a hospitality and tourism firm that uses this model. Expedia generates revenue each time a reservation is made, and it also collects commissions on some transactions on its website.

3. **Subscription fees.** For a fixed fee, monthly or yearly, hospitality firms may choose subscription-based cloud platforms for point-of-sale (POS) and restaurant ordering, and for client relationship management through vendors such as Salesforce.com[6]. Hotels subscribe to convention and visitor bureau (CVB) sites to increase request-for-proposal (RFP) opportunities.

4. **Advertising fees.** Firms charge for placing banner advertisements and other forms of advertising on their websites. Kayak.com is an example of such a website.

5. **Affiliate fees and other sources of revenue.** Firms receive commissions and other forms of compensation for referring customers to other websites. They may receive a small fee for those who click through to the second website and a larger commission based on the purchases made on the second site. Amazon.com was among the first companies to offer this type of financial arrangement. One of its goals was to increase the number of visitors to its website.

11.3.1.2 VALUE PROPOSITION. Any business plan for a firm engaged in electronic commerce should include a value proposition for the business model. How will the firm create value for the buyer? The value proposition defines how the firm will fulfill the needs of the consumer. Amit and Zott identified four primary ways that firms create successful value propositions:[7]

> **Value proposition**
> A component of electronic commerce business models that focuses on how the firm creates value for the buyer.

1. **Search and transaction cost efficiency.** This value proposition allows for faster and more informed decision making by providing a wider selection of products and services, as well as economies of scale. Marriott International and Hilton have been leaders in developing websites that set the standard for the hospitality and tourism industry in this regard.

2. **Complementarities.** This involves bundling products and services together to provide more value than if purchased separately. Expedia.com and Travelocity.com were among the early leaders in bundling the services of a travel agent together in an e-commerce business model. Many websites now provide bundled services such as airfare, lodging, rental car, and tourist attraction admission fees for a bundled price that is significantly less than purchasing the same services separately.

3. **Lock-in.** The high cost of switching will keep customers from changing suppliers. Many hospitality and tourism firms, including the airlines and major hotel chains, use frequent flyer and guest programs to lock in customers.

4. **Novelty.** This approach creates value by using innovative ways to structure transactions, connect business partners, and open new markets.

11.3.2 Types of Electronic Commerce Business Models

Numerous researchers have developed and identified many different forms of business models. Turban, King, Lee, and Viehland summarized these in several models, which encompass the vast majority of models used by electronic commerce firms:[8]

- *Online direct marketing.*
- *Electronic tendering systems.*
- *Name your own price.* Consumers are able to set a price at which they will buy the product or service. When that price becomes available, the transaction is made.
- *Find the best price.* Online services such as Hotels.com™ and Expedia.com allow consumers to compare prices and find the lowest-cost providers.
- *Viral marketing.* This emulates word-of-mouth advertising by spreading the word electronically. With the use of message boards, instant messaging, and e-mail, news of an excellent "deal" spreads rapidly.
- *Online auctions.* These provide a venue for buyers and sellers to come together to exchange products and services. The best-known online auction is ebay.com™.

11.3.3 Server-Based Gaming

One of the newest technologies being used by casinos is server-based gaming (SBG). Basically, SBG is a technology that allows casinos to operate electronic gaming machines (e.g., slot machines) from a remote location through a central system over a network. The network can either be a local area network (LAN) or a wide area network (WAN), and electronic gaming machines (EGM) are merely terminals through which game logic and random number generation can be controlled from the central location. For example, multiple game programs can be accessed from a single slot machine, and slot managers can change the machine's themes, the amount that can be wagered, the hold (amount kept by the casino) or payouts, and promotions from the central server. Server-based gaming is a newer variation of server-supported gaming (SSG). With SSG, each terminal (i.e., slot machine) has to have its own random number generator and the games have to be stored on the machine itself. Server-based gaming is more flexible than server-supported gaming and is considered the future of the gaming industry. The SBG variation is similar to Internet gaming,

The Cosmopolitan Hotel in Las Vegas uses server-based gaming technology in its slot machines.

Kobby Dagan/Shutterstock

but the machines (terminals) are within the confines of the casino. Some of the benefits that are expected from SBG include multi-channeling of games (e.g., mobile phone access), ability to continually update games, more game variety, larger cash prizes through multiplayer and progressive jackpots, ability to obtain player profiles and offer loyalty rewards, and improve security.

11.4 INTERNET STRATEGIES

Not all firms use the Internet for the same purpose. Some companies take orders through their websites; others simply use the sites to provide information to consumers and other stakeholders. Some of the more popular uses of websites are listed here:

- Providing customer service
- Selling products or services
- Educating and informing potential customers
- Offering discounts
- Promoting products and improving brand image
- Obtaining customer information and building a database

It is incumbent on the firm to determine how its we site will fit into the overall marketing plan. Strategies can then be formulated to attain the firm's goals and objectives. Customer service has played an important role in the quest for product or service quality. As the number of Internet users continues to grow, websites become more attractive as outlets for customer service. This approach has proven to be more efficient than the telephone call centers. Firms can list answers to commonly asked questions and guide inquiries or complaints through the proper channels. Customers can go directly to the needed information rather than wait for service via a call center. Customers' concerns can be expressed via e-mail or "live-chat."

Another reason for having a website would be to sell products and services. Most hotel and resort sites have a link to reservations so that consumers can easily purchase the product after browsing the site. Airlines and rental car agencies provide similar services as well. The easier it is for consumers to find your product and complete a transaction, the more successful you will be in selling your product. Many Internet users value the convenience associated with electronic commerce. For example, consumers have 24-hour, 7-day-a-week (24/7) access to the website. They are not bound by the normal hours of operation that a firm chooses, and can shop whenever they wish.

Websites can also be used to educate and inform consumers about a firm's products or services. Information search is the step after problem recognition in the consumer decision-making process. In the past, this information was obtained through word of mouth, past experience, an on-site visit, speaking with salespeople over the telephone, or reviewing printed brochures. Now it is possible to provide basic information regarding a hotel or restaurant over the Internet. Consumers can get prices, availability, hours of operation, directions, and menus. Hotels can provide materials for meeting planners at a fraction of the cost of producing and mailing brochures, planning guides, and videos. Travel agents also find websites to be valuable resources that can be accessed easily and are more convenient than maintaining large inventories of brochures and pamphlets that become outdated.

The Internet has become a useful outlet for reaching price-sensitive consumers. Firms offer reduced prices to attract bargain hunters who are familiar with normal price ranges for products and services. These consumers are aware that many firms offer discount prices through their Internet sites, and they take the time and effort to search for deals. For example, airlines use the Internet to sell unused capacity to consumers who are willing to make their arrangements on short notice. The participating airports and routes are announced midweek for travel originating Friday or Saturday and returning on Monday or Tuesday. International flights are even included in this service, as well as hotel rooms and rental cars from the airline's partners. The discounts are normally for periods of slow demand or packages of services and are often accompanied by certain restrictions involving time or quantity.

Companies can use websites to provide product information and promote events.

Some firms categorize their use of the Internet as a component of the promotional mix. In some ways, it is a form of advertising, but it can also be used for sales promotions. Therefore, the firm's website should be integrated with the other components of the promotion mix in an effort to position the firm in the marketplace and improve its brand image. It is imperative that a hospitality or tourism organization develops a Web strategy that is consistent with and integrated with all other elements of the promotional strategy. Marriott International has developed its Web strategy to drive traffic to the website. Marriott customers can make reservations at the guaranteed lowest rate, check frequent-guest program points, redeem points, and fully manage their relationship with Marriott branded hotels. When customers visit the website, Marriott is able to draw from vast quantities of personal purchase behavior to personalize the purchase experience for guests. Their approach integrates web-browsing behavior with prior-purchase behavior to target the specific needs of the individual.

As a part of the strategy development, sales promotions such as contests and sweepstakes can be used to attract customers and create an awareness of and interest in the brand. These promotions should be creative and entertaining so that consumers become involved with the brand while trying to win free services and merchandise. Finally, most of the aforementioned Internet uses have the added advantage of gaining access to customer information. Firms can build databases filled with customers' names, addresses (including e-mail addresses), telephone numbers, and purchase histories. These databases can be used for future mailings and promotions. One popular use of these databases is to survey customers and prospects about their behaviors, perceptions, and backgrounds. This information can be used to design products and services, promotions, and competitive strategies. In fact, surveys can be placed on websites, resulting in an efficient data collection process.

11.4.1 Website Design and Layout

A firm's website needs to be creative and to catch the attention of visitors to the site. However, it is important to avoid overly complex layouts with hard-to-find links that slow movement between areas of the site. There should be a balance regarding the use of graphics and the speed of movement. The following are some useful tips regarding page layout:

- Include the corporate logo at the top of every page as if it were a letterhead.
- Use graphic links for effect, but make sure there are also text links.
- Code pages so that the text is displayed before graphics are downloaded.

- Use a common style on every page and provide a link to the home page (and other pages if possible) through the use of frames or tables, which can keep important links constantly available throughout the website.

The rest of the content included on the site depends on the type of product or service that is being marketed. There are not many graphics that would need to accompany an airline's product information. However, hotels can give visitors a "tour" of the facility using photos or a video file. To conserve space, the hotel could use a thumbnail gallery with small pictures visitors can click on if they want to see a larger version. It is important to remember that consumers will access websites using a wide array of Internet connections that vary in speed. Therefore, it is important to design the content of the website in such a way that an individual with a slower connection will not become discouraged and disconnect due to long download times.

Tourism bureaus and convention and visitors bureaus provide users with many useful links to related sites. Travelers can go to a state's website and find general information regarding that state. From there, they can narrow their search to a city or region, where they can find more detailed information. Finally, they can follow links to hospitality and tourism firms such as hotels, restaurants, and tourist attractions and obtain very detailed information on a specific firm. Similarly, most of the search engines have links to travel reservations systems and tourism destinations. Therefore, it is crucial that hospitality and tourism firms register their sites with these important directories so that their sites are easily accessed through a basic search. Also, firms should provide links to related pages that may benefit consumers. For example, restaurants and hotels can provide a link to a city map or the tourism bureau's list of events. The Appendix at the end of this chapter shows a Website Evaluation Sheet with a list of attributes or characteristics normally found on hospitality and tourism websites.

11.4.2 Taking Orders and Accepting Payment

After a website is developed, it is necessary to determine the methods and procedures that will be used for completing transactions. One of the most important considerations is to make sure the process is fast, simple, and secure. The more complicated the process or the longer it takes to complete a purchase, the less likely it is that consumers will use the service. Firms should make it easy for customers to tell them what they want, and make it secure and convenient to pay. A button found on most pages of commercial websites is the "purchase" button. Other common labels for this button are "place order," "submit," or "shopping cart."

Placing this button on every page makes it convenient for consumers to make a purchase when they are ready. If consumers have to search for the purchase button within the website, they

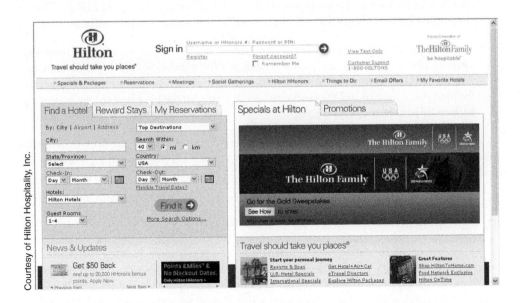

Courtesy of Hilton Hospitality, Inc.

The Hilton website is an example of how effective site layout and design promote the corporate brand.

may give up and move on. The order section of the website will depend on the complexity of the shopping task. A checklist approach can be used for less complicated purchase situations involving fewer decisions. However, a "shopping cart" approach may be necessary when consumers are likely to purchase multiple items. This allows consumers to browse through the various product offerings and add items to their shopping carts as they decide to purchase them. When they have finished shopping, they can place one order for all the items in the cart. Regardless of the approach, all commercial websites should do the following:

- Itemize costs, provide totals for each line item (quantities purchased multiplied by price), and give the overall total for the order.

- Explain the delivery process, including alternative methods and prices, and let customers know when to expect delivery.

- Offer a special discount for Internet purchases and use reference prices so that consumers are aware of the savings.

Sometimes consumers become confused while shopping. They may not know how to proceed, or they may have questions about a product or service. This can be addressed either by providing a link to an online customer service representative via e-mail or real-time online customer service, or by providing a toll-free number to call. As mentioned earlier, a toll-free number or "live-chat" may also be necessary for consumers who are not comfortable with the security of the Internet for placing orders and giving confidential information.

The next step is to determine the method of payment. A firm's first line of defense in ensuring a secure transaction is to avoid having its internal records connected to the web server while the server is connected to the Internet. The firm can store the electronic transactions in temporary files and transfer the data to the internal records later. Once again, there really is not any more risk of fraud with Internet transactions than there would be with telephone or fax transactions. The basic options for accepting payment include:

- **Having customers apply for credit accounts before they make any purchases.** Personal information such as name, address, phone number, and credit card number is provided online, by telephone, by mail, or by fax. Customers are assigned an account name or number and a password or personal identification number (PIN). Orders can be billed to the credit card and delivered to the address in the preexisting account. The major drawback of this option is that consumers must take the time to establish accounts before they can make a purchase.

- **Using encryption techniques with electronic transactions.** The confidential information provided by customers is encrypted before it is sent, and then decrypted by the firm. All of the major Internet browsers provide this service. It would take a great deal of effort on the part of a hacker to break the code, and consumers can make purchases without any delay.

- **Using a digital cash intermediary.** Individuals open accounts with a third party that operates like a bank and are provided with a PIN (similar to a debit card account). The intermediary completes the transactions with the merchant off line, but it is necessary for both the individual and the vendor to be affiliated with the intermediary. An example of such an intermediary is PayPal.com.

None of the methods discussed is without its drawbacks. However, the popularity of the Internet has attracted many firms that specialize in computer security, and the environment for electronic commerce is constantly improving.

11.4.3 E-mail

E-mail marketing is a very effective and inexpensive means of communicating with customers or prospective customers. The number of e-mail users in the United States is expected to reach 236.8 million by 2017.[9] As of 2014, 95 percent of online consumers use e-mail, and 91 percent of consumers check their e-mail at least once a day. E-mail ad revenue reached $156 million in 2012, and for every $1 spent on e-mail marketing, the average return on investment is $44.25. E-mail is an effective tool for retaining customers, especially when customers opt-in to receive e-mails and other information that is pushed to them electronically. (Customers are also free to opt-out, which will remove their names from the distribution list.) Using e-mail to acquire new customers is less effective. With the growth of e-mail, end-users, corporate IT departments, and Internet service providers are becoming more sophisticated in their use of spam filters and other methodologies to reduce the amount of unwanted e-mail that appears in user's inboxes.

However, e-mail marketing does present challenges. Marketers express several reservations about the use of e-mail, including:[10]

RESERVATIONS ABOUT E-MAIL	PERCENTAGE OF RESPONDENTS
Recipient e-mail boxes are swamped and all e-mail suffers	36%
Spam is eroding trust in e-mail	21%
E-mail doesn't get the budget or attention it deserves	11%
Willingness of people to opt-in to new e-mail lists	11%
Lack of accountability or measurement	6%
Difficulty with effective e-mail creative due to image blocking	5%
Deliverability	2%

E-mail can be considered both a mass-market methodology as well as a target market methodology. When many companies began using e-mail as a marketing tool, they sent messages to large lists, either purchased from outside sources or developed internally from customer lists. Over time, this approach has become less effective. More recently, successful firms use e-mail messages in much more targeted fashion. Using market segmentation strategies discussed earlier, successful companies use e-mail messaging to deliver a specific message to a narrowly defined target market. The results are much greater impact, acceptance, and success.

Consumers have varying reactions to e-mail marketing. If consumers have an established relationship with a firm and the firm does e-mail marketing in a professional manner, fully 74 percent of the customers view the e-mail messages as valuable. Conversely, if there is no relationship with a firm, only 17 percent of consumers view the e-mail messages as valuable. There are a number of best practices that will increase the acceptance of e-mail and increase customer satisfaction with received e-mail:[11]

- Requiring a name to sign up for opt-in e-mails, in addition to an e-mail address
- Offering a link to the company privacy policy on the registration page
- Offering a one-click sign-up from the home page
- Offering content tailored to the specific interest, products, or services desired by the e-mail recipient
- Requesting that the company domain or e-mail address be added to the recipient's address book to reduce the impact of spam filters
- Offering a text-only delivery option
- Requiring subscribers to confirm their opt-in registration by responding positively to the first e-mail
- Featuring the company name in the e-mail subject line or the "from" line
- Featuring the privacy policy or opt-out mechanism within each message
- Placing key points of content in the first two paragraphs of the e-mail message
- Having a mixture of graphics and text content

Opt-in and opt-out
The approach to building e-mail distribution lists that empowers consumers to choose whether to participate (opt-in) or withdraw (opt-out).

Spam
Any e-mail received that is unwanted or unsolicited by the recipient.

One of the issues that e-mail marketers must address is how frequently to send messages. The frequency with which consumers wish to receive e-mail messages from companies is shown here.[12]

FREQUENCY OF E-MAIL	PERCENTAGE OF RESPONDENTS
Daily	1%
Few times per week	2%
Weekly	17%
Every other week	21%
Monthly	36%
Quarterly	10%
Seasonally	13%

11.4.4 Search Engine Optimization

A company's success online may depend on how high its website is listed when a prospect looks for guidance from Google, Bing, and Yahoo!, the dominant search engines. There are a variety of techniques and best practices that will lead to success in search marketing.[13] These approaches are divided into three areas: (1) natural or organic search optimization, or search engine optimization (SEO); (2) paid keyword search; and (3) search feeds.

1. **Natural or organic search optimization.** This approach is sometimes called free or unpaid search because it is based on developing webpages so that the search engines will successfully find your content and position it prominently on search results. This approach normally requires considerable up-front work, but does not incur ongoing per-click-through fees.

2. **Paid keyword search.** As the name implies, this approach involves paying the search engine companies to show advertisements for your site when users initiate relevant searches. Most search engines charge on a pay-per-click basis; that is, every time a user clicks on the advertising link, a fee is incurred.

3. **Search feeds.** This approach is used when data describing your website are sent to the search engines and a fee is charged to ensure that your pages are part of the site engine's index.

One of the issues that electronic marketers must address is whether to do the work in-house or outsource the work to a third party. There are advantages to both approaches. If the firm is developing and hosting its own website, it makes sense to develop the search engine optimization in-house. This is especially true if the number of keywords that are part of a paid search is small. Conversely, if the size and scope of the project are beyond the skills, talents, and capacity of the firm, outsourcing is a good decision. As a general rule, if any of the following are true, outsourcing is a desired approach.[14]

- The monthly paid key word search advertising expense exceeds $10,000.
- The terms list exceeds 2,000 terms.
- Your firm competes in a highly competitive market in which the cost-per-click is above 60 cents.
- The in-house staff spends more than 20 hours per week managing your program.
- The firm changes more than 20 percent of the ad copy monthly.
- The term list changes more than 20 percent per quarter.
- You are frustrated or dissatisfied with the services provided by the in-house operation.

If the firm decides to outsource, the decision about which firm to select is similar to any outsourcing decision. Among the questions and issues that all potential bidders should address is how many years the company has been providing search engine optimization. The field of search marketing evolved very quickly and is changing very rapidly. You want to have a firm that is both experienced and at the same time nimble enough to be current with technology and technique:

- What is the range of services that the firm provides?
- What percentage of the firm's revenue is provided by search marketing services? A firm that specializes in search marketing may be more desirable than one that is more general, with only a limited scope of business in the search engine optimization specialty.
- What firms similar to your firm have they provided services for? Check these references.

Whether the firm decides to do the work in-house or outsource, there are two primary approaches to increasing the probability of a potential customer finding your website based on a search—natural or organic search optimization and paid search advertising, or pay-per-click.

Search optimization is based on processes that increases the chances that your website will rank well with the dominant search engines, Google and Yahoo!. These processes are based on putting the keywords in the right place on the website and having Web content that is sufficient. Search engines use *spiders* to find and review websites. These spiders, often called robots, crawl from webpage to webpage, reviewing and indexing content, following links to other websites and webpages.

One of the most important beginning steps to increase search engine effectiveness is to be sure that your website is linked to other sites. Without such links, a spider might not even find your website. Consider links to your site as votes. Each time another site links to your website, it increases the probability of your site being listed higher on search engine results. Links to highly regarded sites are even more valuable. You can easily check which sites are linked to your site by typing "Link:yourdomainname.com" into any of the major search engines.

Keywords are used by search engines to identify content and then rank the content in order of relevancy for users. For example, instead of using the keyword *coffee* it would be more desirable to use *Nicaraguan coffee*. Individuals within your own firm could be used to brainstorm keywords. In addition, Google, the leading search engine, provides free online assistance. The following URL provides a free tool that is used to identify keywords and provides a ranking of how well each word would work in a Google search: adwords.google.com/select/KeywordToolExternal.

It is easy to study the keywords of other sites, including those of competitors. Simply open the site, select "view" and "source," and the listing of keywords will appear. For example, the website of two international hotel chains included the following:

meta name="description" content="Hotel and resort information, make reservations and book events, or find special offers at XYZ.com."

meta name="Description" content="ABC Hotels online reservations for leisure and business travel at leading airport, resort, and business hotels worldwide. ABC Hotels is a member of the ABC Family."

After the keywords are identified, it is important to place them in the titles, headings, and subheadings on each page. The title of each page should be directly tied to the content of the page. Search engines will use these titles to index the content of the particular page.

Meta description tags are used to determine how the author wants the page to be described when a search engine views the page. *Meta tags* are normally between 50 and 200 characters. It is best that a single word not be repeated more than four times, nor any keyword phrase more than once.

Meta keywords are not visible when the page is viewed, but are viewable when the source code is revealed. Words should be inserted that are relevant to the content of the particular page. Limit the number of characters to 75 to 120. An example from two major hotel chains follows:

meta name="keywords" content="hotel, hotel reservations, hotel rates, XYZ, XYZ hotels"

meta name="Keywords" content="ABC hotels, airport hotels, ABC hotels worldwide, ABC international, resort hotels, business travel, vacation travel, holiday travel, hotel reservations, on-line hotel booking, ABC, family vacation"

Pay-per-click
When an advertiser pays the host each time a user clicks on an advertisement and opens the advertiser's web page.

Each page should contain 200 to 600 words of actual content. Among this content, keywords should be used four to six times, to increase search engine effectiveness.

When the site is up and running, it is important to track results. How many visitors does the site attract? How many click-throughs from other sites or pay-per-click advertising click-throughs does the site receive? What are the visitors doing? How many seek more information? How many make purchases? Google offers a free analytics tool for websites that can provide very useful information to the marketer.

11.4.5 Budgeting for Online Marketing

There is no simple answer concerning how much to budget for online advertising, search, and e-mail. The correct proportion will vary by company, market, and a host of other variables. A consistent trend is that online marketing contributes more to total marketing spending each year, with the most growth coming in the areas of mobile marketing and social media. An article on the Entrepreneur website suggests five ways a firm can optimize its digital marketing budget.[15] First, focus on what works best. Use tools like Google Analytics to determine the return on investment (ROI) from various outlets. Second, stay in control of the budget and targeting. It is best to focus on the platforms where you are in full control of costs and placements. Third, don't scale until it is profitable. Start campaigns on a small scale with narrow targeting, after which the campaign can be scaled with larger investments when it is determined what platforms contribute the most in terms of ROI. Fourth, align marketing efforts across channels. All of the firm's efforts should be focused on communicating the same message on all platforms. Fifth, engage in cross-channel remarketing. Instead of just remarketing through the same platform that first attracted a visitor, retarget the same visitor on other platforms. For example, if the visitor first engaged on an ad in Google, you could try to target the same visitor through ads on social media.

SUMMARY OF CHAPTER OBJECTIVES

This chapter discussed the dynamic marketing specialty of electronic commerce. A relatively recent phenomenon, e-commerce, has had a dramatic and fundamental impact on the methods used by hospitality and tourism firms to market products and services. Electronic commerce is the logical extension of bringing commercial transactions and business processes to the Internet. The historical roots of electronic commerce were discussed and the four classifications of electronic commerce were presented, including business-to-business (B2B), business-to-consumer (B2C), consumer-to-business (C2B), and consumer-to-consumer (C2C).

The chapter explored key traits of a networked economy and the scope of electronic commerce. Numerous trends were presented that illustrated the worldwide impact of electronic commerce and the growth of the entire subdiscipline of marketing. Electronic commerce is characterized by four primary attributes: exchange of digital information, technology-enabled transactions, technology-mediated transactions, and intra- and interorganizational activities.

Several management issues related to electronic commerce were presented, including the structure of business models. The foundation for these models includes the revenue model and the value proposition. Finally, design and implementation issues related to electronic commerce were discussed and the benefits of electronic commerce were explored.

E-mail marketing is becoming increasingly important. Spending on e-mail is increasing, and is especially effective for retaining current customers. Unwanted e-mail (i.e., Spam) continues to be a challenge for marketers. It is estimated that as much as 50 percent of the e-mail received is considered spam. There are numerous best practices for e-mail marketers that will significantly increase the effectiveness of e-mail.

Search engine optimization is also an important component of a firm's Internet strategy. This optimization, whether done in-house or outsourced, relies on effective use of key word search in the form of meta descriptions and meta words.

KEY TERMS AND CONCEPTS

Authentication	Firewall
Browser	Hypertext
Business-to-business (B2B)	Opt-in
Business-to-consumer (B2C)	Opt-out
Consumer-to-business (C2B)	Pay-per-click
Consumer-to-consumer (C2C)	Pure e-commerce companies
Domain name system (DNS)	Revenue model
Electronic commerce	Spam
Encryption	Value proposition

QUESTIONS FOR REVIEW AND DISCUSSION

1 What are the pros and cons of the openness and interconnectedness of the Internet?

2 Why are security issues of such importance in developing an Internet strategy and business plan?

3 What are the traits of a networked economy? Which trait do you believe is the most significant? Why?

4 What is server-based gaming? How will it impact the casino industry?

chapter review

5 Review two or three well-known hospitality and tourism company websites. Based on your review, prepare the responses to the following questions for class discussion:

  a What is the firm's purpose for engaging in online communications?

  b What is the firm's website strategy? What are the goals and specific objectives? What outcomes do you believe the firm is seeking to achieve?

  c How are the electronic commerce efforts being integrated with other forms of communication? How will consistency of branding and identity be maintained?

6 What are the four primary classifications of electronic commerce? Which is the most common in the hospitality and tourism industry?

7 What revenue models are most common in electronic commerce? Which one(s) are most applicable to the hospitality and tourism industry? Why?

NOTES

[1] Herschell Gordon Lewis and Robert D. Lewis, *Selling on the Net: The Complete Guide* (Lincolnwood, IL: NTC Business Books, 1997).

[2] Jeffrey F. Rayport and Bernard J. Jaworski, *Introduction to E-Commerce*, 2nd ed. (Boston: McGraw-Hill Irwin marketspaceU, 2004), p. 3.

[3] Ibid., p. 3.

[4] Joel Reedy and Shauna Schullo, *Electronic Marketing*, 2nd ed. (Mason, OH: Thompson Southwestern, 2004), p. 30.

[5] Efrain Turban, David King, Jae Lee, and Dennis Viehland, *Electronic Commerce 2004* (Upper Saddle River, NJ: Pearson Prentice Hall, 2004), p. 12.

[6] Lev-Ram, Michal. 2014. "It's a subscription economy, and you're just living in it." *Fortune*, June 6. www.fortune.com/2014/06/06/welcome-to-the-subscription-economy/.

[7] Amit, R., Zott, C. 2001. "Value creation in e-business." *Strategic Management Journal*, 22: 493–520.

[8] Efrain Turban, David King, Jae Lee, and Dennis Viehland, *Electronic Commerce 2004* (Upper Saddle River, NJ: Pearson Prentice Hall, 2004), pp. 14–16.

[9] Jaegel, Wolfgang. 2014. "[Infographic] 10 Must Know Email Marketing Stats 2014." Available at wolfgangjaegel.com/infographic-10-must-know-email-marketing-stats-2014/.

[10] Clarke, Tad, ed. 2007. *MarketingSherpa Email Marketing Benchmark Guide 2008*, p. 5. Available at www.marketingsherpa.com.

[11] David Hallerman, "E-mail Marketing: Getting Through to Customers," eMarketer.com, 2007, pp. 17–18.

[12] Ibid., pp. 19–11.

[13] Alan Rimm-Kaufman, *Search Marketing Firms: A MarketingProfs Shopper's Handbook*, 2005, pp. 5–7.

[14] Ibid., pp. 9–11.

[15] Baldassarre, Rocco. 2015. "5 Ways to Optimize Your Digital Marketing Budget." *Entrepreneur*, March 6. www.entrepreneur.com/article/243586.

chapter review

INTERNET CASE STUDY

Hospitality and Tourism Website Analysis

Hospitality firms (e.g., hotels and restaurants) and tourism organizations often have the same customers in their target markets, especially people who are engaged in travel. However, the core service of the business is somewhat different. Go on the Internet and review the websites for some of your favorite local restaurants, popular hotels in your area, and destination marketing organizations (e.g., convention and visitors bureau, tourist attractions, the state tourism bureau, etc.).

Questions for Review and Discussion

1. Using the Website Evaluation Sheet in the Appendix of this chapter, rate the websites.

2. What are the similarities and differences between the various websites?

3. Do you think you can use a standard evaluation instrument, or does each type of business need a separate form adapted for that industry?

case study

CASE STUDY

Electronic Commerce Strategy at Malone Golf Club

Derek Sprague, general manager of the Malone Golf Club, pondered changes in the marketing and distribution strategy for his club for the upcoming season. The Malone Golf Club had made significant progress in the past 3 years. The club completed the construction of a new clubhouse, made minor design changes to several of the 36 holes that make up the two golf courses, and upgraded the food and beverage offerings of the club.

The Malone Golf Club operates as a semi-private club, offering both annual memberships and daily greens fee access. Many of the daily fee players come to the club, located in Malone, New York, from Canada—Montreal is only a 90-minute drive from the club. The club has used a website for several years to promote its golf, golf packages, food and beverage service, and other amenities. The club's approach to the website (www.malonegolfclub.com) has been primarily "brochure-ware"—that is, it is used as an addition to the printed brochures. Derek is thinking of taking a more aggressive approach to electronic commerce. He is considering a number of options, including accepting reservations online; developing a chat-room where members and players could discuss the course, trade stories, and stay in touch with each other; and developing an online push e-mail and promotional strategy for frequent daily fee players and members of the club.

You have been retained as a consultant to the club. Derek has asked you to research the following questions and then meet with him next week. He wants to review your early research before proceeding further or retaining additional consulting assistance.

Questions for Review and Discussion

1. What are the pros and cons of accepting tee time reservations online?

2. Will online reservations impact the staffing of the pro shop?

3. What electronic commerce business model should Malone Golf Club adopt? Should it auction off tee times at low-demand periods or keep the traditional pricing model in place? What are the financial implications of these options?

4. Should the club consider developing its own online reservation system or outsource this endeavor to another company that provides the service for other golf clubs?

5. What increase in greens fee and membership revenue will be required to offset the costs of an online reservation system?

6. How will potential online systems integrate with the current tee time system?

7. How might the members and frequent players react to online reservations? Will it be viewed positively or negatively?

case study

APPENDIX

Website Evaluation Sheet

ATTRIBUTE	POOR	FAIR	GOOD	EXCELLENT
Company Information				
Company Information				
Contact Information				
Logo/Brand Name/Tagline				
Product Offering				
Product/Service Information				
Program/Activities				
Prices/Rates				
Special Offers/Discounts				
Transactions				
Describe Payment Methods				
OnLine Reservations/Ordering				
Transaction Security Info				
Support Services				
Maps and Directions				
Calendar of Events				
Links to Related Websites				
OnLine Customer Service				
FAQs				
Interactive Functions				
Newsletters/Club Membership				
Career Services/Employment				
Internal Search Engine				
Multimedia (videos/clips)				

Poor = 1, Fair = 2, Good = 3, Excellent = 4

appendix

Integrated Marketing Communications

Courtesy of testing/Shutterstock.

Chapter Objectives

After studying this chapter, you should be able to:

1. Define integrated marketing communications and list the elements of the promotion mix.

2. Explain how to handle promotion over the four stages of the product life cycle and the methods for establishing promotional budgets.

3. Discuss the various forms of advertising and how to manage the advertising function.

4. Describe how to plan and evaluate an advertising campaign.

5. Identify the social, ethical, and economic criticisms of advertising.

12.1   INTRODUCTION

Hospitality and tourism firms engage in a good deal of advertising and promotion. In fact, these firms are often at the forefront in terms of creativity and spending. As the marketing environment in which hospitality and tourism organizations operate becomes more competitive, the importance of advertising and other forms of promotion increases. This chapter focuses on the concept of integrating the marketing communications stemming from the use of the promotion mix. The components of the promotion mix include advertising, personal selling, sales promotion, and public relations. This chapter provides a general overview of the promotion mix and the business side of advertising. The next three chapters will address the creative side of advertising and social media, sales promotions and public relations, and personal selling.

Integrated marketing communications (IMC) is a strategic approach designed to achieve the objectives of a marketing campaign using the elements of the promotion mix to convey a unified message to the firm's various audiences. These audiences include the customers and other stakeholders of the firm such as the community, employees, shareholders, and suppliers. Researchers have identified four levels of IMC that represent the evolution of organizations in terms of marketing communications:[1]

- Level 1: Tactical coordination and marketing communications
- Level 2: Redefining the scope of marketing communications
- Level 3: Application of information technology
- Level 4: Financial and strategic integration

The basic progression is from the focus on unifying the message from the organization through its traditional media and special events. Next, the focus is on the communications from the customer's perspective, including all messages received regarding all the products and services offered by the organization. Also, as indicated in the definition, this includes other stakeholders as well as customers. At this stage, organizations find themselves collecting empirical data through information technology systems that can aid in monitoring and implementing integrated marketing communications programs. Finally, this information is used to determine strategies and evaluate activities based on financial performance.

The popularity of IMC is due in large part to advances in information technology. Organizations are now able to collect large amounts of data, store it, and analyze it using sophisticated software with real-time applications. In addition, the advent of the Internet increased the number of communications options to include corporate websites and social media. The traditional advertising mediums saw changes as well. Digital marketing offered alternatives for billboard advertising and introduced new media vehicles such as smartphones, tablets, and game consoles. The following is a detailed discussion of the promotion mix and the functions of promotion and advertising as part of the integrated marketing communications program.

12.1.1   The Promotion mix

The more visible forms of advertising are often used to help increase sales and profits. However, all of the elements of the promotion mix are equally important. The following is a brief description of each of the four original components of the promotion mix:

1. **Advertising** is any paid form of nonpersonal presentation of ideas and promotion of ideas, goods, or services by an identified sponsor.

2. **Personal selling** involves interpersonal communication between an organization's representatives and prospective consumers for the purpose of making a sale.

3. **Sales promotion** includes marketing activities other than advertising, personal selling, and public relations that attempt to stimulate short-term consumer demand and increase sales. Commonly, sales promotion is a direct inducement offering an extra incentive to try a product (e.g., coupon, free sample, or premium).

Promotion mix
The basic elements (advertising, public relations, sales promotions, and personal selling) used by organizations to communicate with consumers.

Integrated marketing communicatons (IMC)
A strategic approach designed to achieve the objectives of a marketing campaign using the elements of the promotion mix to convey a unified message to the firm's various audiences.

Advertising
Consists of any paid form of nonpersonal presentation of ideas and promotion of ideas, goods, or services by an identified sponsor.

Personal selling
An interpersonal process whereby a salesperson attempts to create a mutually satisfactory exchange with a buyer using various sales techniques.

Sales promotion
Includes marketing activities other than advertising, personal selling, and public relations that attempt to stimulate short-term consumer demand and increase sales.

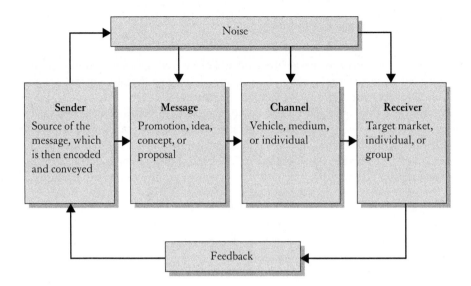

FIGURE 12.1 • Communications model.

4. **Public relations** is a nonpersonal stimulation of demand for a product or service by providing commercially significant news about the product or service in a published medium or obtaining favorable presentation in a medium that is not paid for by the sponsor.

In all forms of the promotion mix, it remains critical that the intended message be delivered to the potential target markets. A model of communication is shown in Figure 12.1 to illustrate how this process takes place.

Remember that both the sender and the receiver are humans and are subject to the failings common to everyone. With this in mind, all communication attempts with target markets should be as clear and concise as possible. In addition to the human failings, potential difficulties arise with the message, the channels that are used, and the noise level in the environment, so efforts must be made to overcome these difficulties. When management designs a new form of promotion, it is sometimes expected that the entire target market can be reached with a limited number of contacts. This is simply not possible, because the target market is being bombarded with other messages; as a result, sometimes the intended message is not received and retained above the noise in the environment. It is important to keep this communications model in mind when designing any type of communications with target markets. It is also critical to review the feedback received, study it carefully, and look for ways to improve the identified weakness.

12.1.2 The Functions of Promotion and Advertising

Advertising and promotion are marketing functions that need to be managed along with other functions. First, advertising and promotion present information to the consumer about new products, new services, new decor, and other items of interest in an attempt to create awareness of the products and services. Second, they reinforce consumer behavior by communicating with individuals who have patronized a particular hotel or restaurant in the past. Exposing these consumers to a continuous flow of advertising is likely to induce repeat patronage by reinforcing their positive experiences. Third, advertising induces first-time patronage. When consumers are exposed to a continual flow of advertising, their curiosity is aroused, and this often results in patronage. If a first-time guest is rewarded with a pleasant experience, the foundation for repeat patronage has been successfully established. And last, advertising enhances the image of hospitality and tourism operations. In addition, advertising can be used to enhance perceived quality and perceived value for hospitality and tourism organizations.

12.2 MANAGING THE PROMOTION MIX

It is important for firms to create promotion mixes that will lead to a strong position in the marketplace. Each firm must choose its own mix of advertising, publicity, personal selling, and sales promotions, depending on the firm's positioning and image. However, one marketing tool that is helpful in determining baseline strategies for promotion is the product life cycle.

12.2.1 Promoting over the Product Life Cycle

As discussed in Chapter 9, all hospitality and tourism organizations progress through a distinct life cycle (see Figure 12.2). As an organization moves through the stages of the life cycle, different marketing strategies are recommended. Promotion is one component of the marketing mix that changes over the life cycle of a product.

12.2.1.1 INTRODUCTION STAGE.   Rarely does a new hotel or restaurant open without creating some interest in the local community. The goal of all hospitality managers should be to capitalize on this natural curiosity and make it work to the advantage of the business. The main focus of the promotional campaign in the introduction stage is to inform consumers in an effort to create awareness. The principal objective during this phase is to build volume within the operation by reaching individuals who are innovators and are most likely to patronize a new operation. This approach is very critical to an independently owned operation. Every effort must be made to reach potential consumers and encourage first-time patronage. All targeted segments should be identified and strategies developed to reach each of these markets.

All elements of the promotion mix are applied at this point. Advertising and publicity are used to create awareness and interest in the new operation. Depending on the size of the operation, local, regional, and/or national media are contacted to cover the story surrounding the opening. Personal selling is used to generate awareness and interest among intermediaries. Restaurants will contact hotels, retail businesses, and tourist information sources that are likely to make referrals. In addition, hotels will contact tour operators and travel agents. Finally, sales promotions are used to induce trial. For example, hotels will offer familiarization trips to intermediaries such as travel agents or tour operators, and many hospitality and tourism firms will offer discounted rates to reduce the perceived risk of consuming the service.

12.2.1.2 GROWTH STAGE.   During the growth stage, promotion and advertising focus on building name recognition and persuading consumers to purchase the brand. If the introductory stage has been successful, a solid core of consumers has been established. With this core, the promotional objective must be twofold: (1) to reinforce and remind those consumers who have patronized the hospitality establishment to continue their patronage, and (2) to reach those consumers who have not patronized the operation, thereby expanding volume with a significant number of first-time buyers.

During the growth stage, the mention of the name of the hospitality establishment brings a distinct image to the consumer's mind. Therefore, promotion and advertising should seek to reinforce the most positive aspects of this image. The strategies used during this stage include comparative advertising and stressing the special advantages offered by the product–service mix of the operation. In addition, personal selling is still used to build awareness, interest, and desire among intermediaries. However, less emphasis is placed on publicity and sales promotions to build image and persuade consumers to purchase.

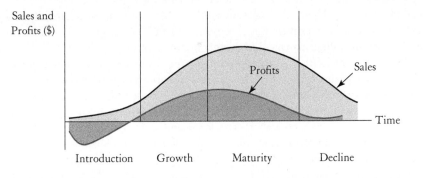

FIGURE 12.2 • The product life cycle.

12.2.1.3 MATURITY STAGE. Only the largest and most successful hospitality and tourism organizations progress to this stage of the life cycle. The firms that achieve this level are very well established and have the tremendous advantage of nearly universal name recognition and reinforcement. Food service firms that have achieved this level include McDonald's, Wendy's, Chili's, and Red Lobster. Well-known hotel firms include Hilton and Marriott. For example, a McDonald's advertisement need not even mention the product or service to be successful. Simply by using the word *McDonald's,* showing the restaurant and the people who patronize it, or simply the golden arches logo, the advertisement reinforces the image in the minds of consumers.

The primary goal of a firm at this stage is to use the organization's size and brand recognition to remind consumers of the product's benefits and continue to differentiate it from the competition. When a company is in the maturity stage, sales growth is usually obtained by taking market share away from competitors, rather than through growth in the overall market. An example of this is the fast-food segment, as each of the largest competitors (McDonald's, Burger King, and Wendy's) attempts to differentiate its product–service mix from the others.

In addition to reminder advertising, sales promotions in the form of coupons and discounts are popular. Coupons are normally distributed through a variety of print media or by direct mail. They are generally most effective in increasing consumer counts. Coupons are merely short-term inducements to purchase a brand and are not a means to build long-term loyalty among customers. Rather, the consumer uses coupons as the method to shop for the best deal at any given moment. If a large number of hospitality and tourism operations in a given geographic area offer coupon discounts, consumers can become conditioned to coupons as a way of life, with the result that they will patronize only those operations that offer such discounts. Finally, limited attention is given to personal selling and publicity during this stage.

12.2.1.4 DECLINE STAGE. The goal of any firm that reaches this stage of its life cycle is to use its competitive advantage to launch new products and services that will further strengthen the organization. By adding to its product–service mix, the firm can attract new consumers and extend its product life cycle. For example, McDonald's has repeatedly used its number-one position in the fast-food segment to launch new products and services, most notably a variety of breakfast items, specialty sandwiches, and salads. These products contribute to the sales mix of the organization and serve to broaden the market appeal. All have, of course, been test-marketed prior to being introduced into the system. They are examples of ways an organization can market new products and services from a position of strength and, as a result, become stronger still.

If a firm cannot find ways to extend its product life cycle, then the appropriate strategy is to maximize short-term profit and eventually divest. This strategy calls for the firm to reduce marketing expenditures to the minimum effective level, including a reduction in the promotional budget. At this stage, there is virtually no effort in the areas of personal selling and publicity. In addition, advertising is kept to a minimum and sales promotions are used sparingly. It is assumed that these expenditures will have little effect on consumer purchasing, serving only to decrease the firm's profitability. An example of a firm that went through this phase is Boston Market. Later, it emerged from reorganization and continued in operation.

12.2.2 Establishing the Promotional Budget

Promotional expenses should be carefully planned, monitored, and controlled. Promotional budgets should be set to maximize the use of the sales force and other promotional elements such as advertising, publicity, and sales promotions. Management must carefully establish the promotional budget to maximize the effectiveness of the dollars spent (i.e., return on investment). For example, some managers promote more when business volume is slow, thereby hoping to increase volume. Others attempt to reduce expenses by cutting back on promotion when a decline in sales volume occurs. Both approaches are subject to error because they are based on intuition rather than on a rational decision-making and budgeting process. Promotional budgets serve several useful and important functions: (1) to provide a detailed projection of future expenditures, (2) to provide both short- and long-range planning guides for management, and (3) to provide a method for monitoring and controlling promotional expenses by comparing actual expenses against projections.

Developing budgets forces management to look into the future. Although both past and current conditions certainly need to be considered, the future is key. All management personnel must develop the ability to project future trends, revenues, and expenses. Failure to do so can easily lead to "management by crisis." Budgets also serve as reference points. Budget projections need not be financial projections cast in stone. Budgeted figures and media plans are, of course, subject to modification if the marketing situation changes dramatically. The budget, however, is important as a point of reference, a goal, and a standard against which actual performance can be compared. When promotional budgets are established, all management personnel with marketing responsibilities should be involved in their preparation. This involvement fosters improved communication among individuals. In addition, when all managers have input into the development of the plan, support for the plan increases, as each manager "owns a piece" of the plan. When individuals identify with the budget as it is developed, it will increase their personal motivation to see that it is implemented successfully.

12.2.2.1 THE BUDGETING PROCESS.   Those exposed to the budget preparation process for the first time can be overwhelmed. The process is often associated with internal corporate processes that can seem bureaucratic. Figure 12.3 illustrates the budget process in a manner that encapsulates the process in an easily understood format. Initially, senior management must determine future objectives. At the same time, the desired future performance for advertising is projected by taking into consideration trends, future influential factors, past performance, and input

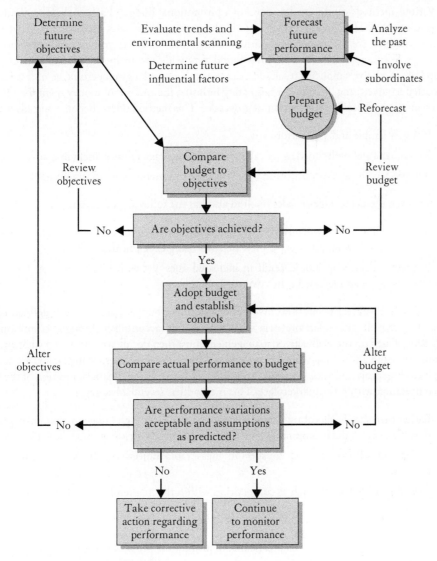

FIGURE 12.3 • **The budgeting process.**

from subordinates. A preliminary budget is prepared and then compared with the short- and long-range objectives of senior management. If the budget appears to have a high probability of satisfying the objectives, it is adopted, and controls are established. If the budget fails to meet the objectives, then the objectives and/or the budget must be revised to bring the two into harmony.

Following the implementation of the budget, management uses a simple control process. If the promotion mix performs as planned, the monitoring process continues. If, however, evaluation shows that the promotion mix is not successful, several avenues exist:

- The promotion mix can be changed to increase the probability of satisfying evaluation standards.
- The budget can be modified based on changing market conditions.
- The short- and long-range objectives can be changed based on new available information.

12.2.2.2 BUDGETING METHODS.

Promotional budgets are normally either fixed or contingent. *Fixed budgets* are based on predictions of sales volume and expected levels of advertising. Projected expenditures are normally held firm, even if the assumptions on which the budget was based prove to be incorrect. Conversely, *contingent budgets* are developed based on several sets of assumptions. This development means that if situation A happens, then implement plan A; if situation B occurs, then implement plan B; and so on. This type of budget draws its name from being based on a number of contingencies, or plans developed to be appropriate for several possible outcomes.

Various methods can be used to develop a promotional budget. Each of these methods falls into one of the four following categories: (1) the percentage-of-sales method, (2) the desired-objective method, (3) the competitive-parity method, and (4) the all-you-can-afford method.

The percentage-of-sales method has found very wide use in the hospitality industry. The method offers relative simplicity: a sales forecast is obtained, and a given percentage of this forecast is allocated to advertising. Within the hospitality industry, the amount of money spent for advertising is typically between 2 and 8 percent of gross sales. This method offers the following advantages:

Percentage-of-sales method
A given percentage of a sales forecast is allocated to promotion and advertising.

- It is very simple and straightforward.
- Some managers prefer to view all expenses as a percentage of sales, including advertising.
- It works well if sales can be forecasted accurately and market conditions are stable.

However, the percentage-of-sales method also has the following disadvantages:

- If sales decline, so too will advertising expenditures. This is not a valid argument; instead, in this situation it would be wise to increase advertising expenditures.
- Increased advertising should result in increased sales, yet with this method an increase in sales results in an increase in the advertising budget.

Desired-objective method
The promotional budget based on achieving well-defined objectives.

The desired-objective method involves developing a budget based on well-defined objectives. Management must plan precisely what it wishes to accomplish through promotion and advertising. Based on these objectives, management must then decide what type and what amount of promotion and advertising will be necessary to achieve the objectives. Many factors are considered, including projected sales, previous promotion and advertising, financial position of the firm, and competition within the marketplace. This method has several advantages:

- Rather than simply allocating a fixed percentage of sales for each budget period, management must critically evaluate promotion and advertising expenditures in accordance with objectives.
- Advertising efforts are tied to specific measurable objectives, thereby making evaluation easier.
- Several variable factors, such as competition within the marketplace, are considered.

However, two major disadvantages must also be considered:

- It is difficult to determine the precise mix of promotion and advertising that will accomplish the objectives satisfactorily.

- Engaging in this type of budget preparation is very time-consuming, especially when one considers that advertising and promotion represent only one area on an income statement and only one aspect of the marketing mix.

The competitive-parity method for establishing a budget involves direct comparison with the promotion and advertising efforts of major competitors. Based on the type and amount of promotion done by the competition, management then establishes a budget that will roughly match the activities of the major competition. The following advantages are associated with the competitive-parity method:

- A relative level of equilibrium is established with regard to the competition.
- The method is simple and straightforward, especially if an industry average is used.

The disadvantages of the competitive-parity method include the following:

- Relative promotion and advertising budgets and media decisions made by one firm usually are not applicable to other firms. For example, how can management be assured that the competition's advertising is appropriate for its hotel or restaurant?
- Basing future plans on the past performance of others is reactive rather than proactive.

The all-you-can-afford method is usually a last resort practiced by small firms that do not have the luxury of setting resources aside for promotion and advertising. For example, independent restaurants and lodging companies that operate on very tight cash flows must meet their expenses such as payroll and inventory before they can consider the allocation of resources to promotion and advertising. If a small restaurant has only $2,000 to allocate, then the manager or owner must determine the most effective use of the funds.

The all-you-can-afford method is often a reality for small firms, but it is not a sound method to use in determining the promotional budget. Once again, as sales decrease and profits are down, the firm will allocate less money for promotion and advertising at a time when it would be most beneficial. Conversely, when business is good, the firm will have more money to spend on promotion. This is counter to what would make sense from a logical perspective. The main advantage associated with this method is its simplicity; it does not require managers to perform any formal budgeting for promotion, and spending is not related to goals and objectives.

Competitive-parity method
The promotional budget based on direct comparison with the promotion and advertising efforts of major competitors.

All-you-can-afford method
The promotional budget based on the amount of limited resources a firm can reasonably afford to allocate to promotion and advertising.

12.3   MANAGING THE ADVERTISING FUNCTION

The American Marketing Association defines advertising as "the placement of announcements and persuasive messages in time or space purchased in any of the mass media by business firms, nonprofit organizations, government agencies, and individuals who seek to inform and/or persuade members of a particular target market or audience about their products, services, organizations, or ideas."[2] This definition is widely accepted throughout the business community. The key components of the definition are:

1. Advertising is paid for and controlled by the individual or group that is the sponsor. Because someone is paying for the space (newspaper, outdoor) or time (radio, television), this individual or group has complete control over what is said, printed, or shown. Any media attention that is not paid for is called publicity. Because the individual or group is not paying for the time or space, those involved do not have complete control and are at the mercy of the writer or producer.

2. Advertising is done through the mass media without personal contact or interaction between the seller and the potential buyer.

3. Advertising need not be restricted to the promotion of a tangible physical product or good. It may try to influence individuals to change their way of thinking or their behavior about a product, service, organization, or idea.

Publicity
A form of public relations used solely to attract media attention.

National advertising

Advertising aimed at a national audience by using network television and radio, or national print media such as magazines or newspapers.

Local advertising

Advertising placed in local media to reach a local target market.

Cooperative advertising

When two or more firms are involved in a common advertising campaign that benefits all of the parties involved.

Advertising can be divided into two broad categories, national and local. National advertising is aimed at a national audience by using network television and radio or national print media such as magazines or newspapers. This form of advertising normally promotes the general name of the chain, not individual locations or stores.

Local advertising is used not only by the major hospitality and tourism chains but also by second-tier chains, regional chains, and independent operations. Local advertising, including television, radio, print, and other media, is used extensively in the hospitality and tourism industry. This is where the action is, and to coin a phrase, the battle of market share is won or lost in the trenches of local advertising.

A simple fact of business life for many managers is that specific advertising media are too expensive for the organization to use. For many managers, cooperative advertising is an excellent alternative. Cooperative advertising, as the name implies, involves two or more firms working together to sponsor an advertisement that provides benefit to all parties involved. For example, a group of restaurants located in a given geographic area may join together and promote dining in the area without promoting any one operation specifically. By joining together and sharing the expenses, managers are able to advertise in more expensive media and reach new audiences. Cooperative advertising is an area of tremendous promise because it allows a manager to expand the advertising media selection.

12.3.1 Advertising Positioning and Strategy

Advertising terms and jargon often sound like the language of war—campaigns are launched and advertisements are aimed at target markets. Advertising need not be anything like war, but successful advertising is the result of a carefully planned strategy. A manager must first decide how to position the product–service mix. Positioning is the manner in which the consumer views the product–service mix, and each hospitality and tourism operation is positioned differently. Before owners or managers make any advertising decisions or plot strategy, they must determine the proper market position.

A successful advertising campaign does not result from haphazard planning and execution. A single advertisement may be very good, but prosperous companies produce consistently superior advertising. Advertising succeeds when good strategy is developed. According to advertising experts Kenneth Roman and Jane Maas, strategy development revolves around five key points:[3]

1. **Objectives.** What should the advertising do? What goals does management want to achieve? For example, a new hospitality operation may set recognition among local residents as an objective, whereas another hospitality operation might seek to increase sales on slow nights. For the latter operation, most of the money would concentrate on promotions designed to increase volume on these nights.

2. **Targeted audience.** Who is the customer or potential customer? Advertising is not a success when used in a hit-or-miss manner. Successful advertising addresses a specifically targeted market and talks directly to that market. Many advertising programs fail because they attempt to appeal to too broad a targeted market.

3. **Key consumer benefit.** Consumers can be skeptical and often need a benefit or a reason to buy before they are persuaded. This is a pitch to the consumer to come to this operation instead of another. True differences between hospitality and tourism operations are rare, but a list of products and services the operation offers should stress those different from or superior to those offered by other hospitality and tourism facilities.

4. **Support.** To have a successful advertising campaign, the key benefit must be supported. Consumers are skeptical of advertising claims, and who can blame them? Included in any advertisement should be a reason for the consumer to believe in the benefit. Consumer testimonials or test results showing superiority are often used for this purpose.

5. **Tone and manner.** The advertising strategy must have a personality. This personality should blend with the image and positioning of the hospitality and tourism operation. For many years,

McDonald's has successfully used the Ronald McDonald character when advertising to children. This character makes McDonald's seem like a fun place to be, and children respond to the advertising. The tone and manner selected should blend with the overall theme that management is trying to create and should show the potential customer the nature of the operation.

Companies can benefit by working together to promote and advertise their products and services.

12.3.1.1 DEVELOPING A CENTRAL APPEAL.

Developing a central advertising appeal is not an easy process. Considerable time and thought must be devoted to the creative process before a viable appeal is developed. Several rules of thumb exist for the development of this appeal:

- **A central appeal must offer some value to the consumer.** If the central appeal does not speak directly to the needs of the primary target market, the chances for success are greatly reduced. A well-developed marketing information system should provide specific data about the marketplace, enabling management to be in tune with the preferences of consumers.

- **The appeal must be distinctive.** All advertising must compete not only with all other hospitality and tourism organizations but also with advertising for everything from automobiles to washing machines. For the advertising to be effective, the appeal must offer something that separates it from everything else. Distinctive and unusual appeals are needed.

- **The appeal must be believable.** Claims made for the product–service mix must be backed up if the appeal is to have credibility. Because some consumers are more skeptical than others, the appeal should be believable to those who might at first have doubts.

- **The appeal should be simple.** Consumers are confronted each day with hundreds of advertising stimuli, and if one is to be recalled, it must be simple and straightforward. Effective and simple appeals that have been used successfully include "We do it all for you," "You, you're the one," "It's a good time for the great taste" (McDonald's), as well as "America's business address" and "Travel should take you places" (Hilton).

12.3.1.2 KEYS TO SUCCESSFUL ADVERTISING.

To be successful, advertising needs to be approached in a systematic manner. The following are several suggestions on how to improve advertising efficiency:[4]

- **Time.** Advertising should not be considered a necessary evil. Sales and operations are equally important and require time for an advertising program to generate satisfactory results. In order to be effective, advertising must normally be repeated. Frequent exposure to targeted markets will increase the impact of advertising.

- **Budgets.** Budgets should be developed for the needs of each operation. It makes little sense to base an advertising budget on figures and percentages that represent the national average. Generally, a manager must have the courage to spend enough to produce successful results.

- **Study.** A manager needs to analyze the operation and determine the operation's advantages as compared with those of the competition. Disadvantages also need to be identified so that they can be minimized or eliminated completely. The evaluation must be done constantly so that any changes in the competitive situation are noted and adjustments are made quickly.

- **Analysis of market segments.** Each year, many people change jobs and move, and as they do, their lifestyles change, too. No market segment is constant; people are always changing. For this reason, management must know the patrons of the hospitality operation. By doing this, management can modify the operation to meet changing consumer demands.

- **Media.** Media must be selected very carefully to be effective. Media used must match the intended targeted markets. Each type of medium offers advantages and drawbacks, which are discussed in Chapter 13.

- **Formation of a plan.** Advertising cannot be successful if it is approached in a haphazard manner. It is important that continuity be established among all forms of advertising so that it gains momentum. Continuity can be established through the consistent use of logos, distinctive type styles, music, or creative touches to make the advertising stand out from other advertisements. Managers should not be afraid of advertising and should develop plans designed to produce results. Nothing is worse than spending too little money on advertising; thus, advertising expenditures should not be cut. To be successful, advertising must be used regularly, not intermittently. Successful advertising is based on repetition.

Courtesy of The Breakers, Palm Beach, Florida.

Good advertising should have a central appeal that offers something of value to the customer.

Single advertisements may be creative or humorous and may convey a message, but by themselves they are not able to achieve the necessary degree of advertising effectiveness. Many independent hospitality advertisers purchase print advertising or a few radio spots during certain times of the year, particularly when business is slow. This type of advertising is not likely to be as effective as it could be, because continuity between the advertisements is lost. Such advertisements are

IF IT DID ANY MORE OF THE

OPERATOR'S JOB,

YOU'D HAVE TO GIVE IT FULL EMPLOYEE BENEFITS.

Microban

A more resourceful, productive and tireless worker would be hard to find. Like an operator, the Hobart 2000 Series Slicer cuts portions by weight or slice count. Unlike ordinary operators, it makes every cut precisely and automatically. The 2000 Series is easy to work with, too, with a smooth aluminum base for faster wiping. Loath to lose a second of uptime, the 2000 Series saves you up to 15 minutes per cleaning. Now with Microban antimicrobial product protection permanently built-in—a Hobart exclusive—it's cleaner between cleanings, too. There are a lot of benefits to the 2000 Series, not the least being that you won't have to offer it any employee benefits

WAREWASHING	COOKING	BAKERY
REFRIGERATION	WEIGHING AND WRAPPING	SERVICE
FOOD PREPARATION		

2912PS SLICER

HOBART
Solid equipment. Sound advice.

www.hobartcorp.com

Courtesy of Hobart Corporation.

This advertisement explains the appeal of the product and provides the customer with specific information.

not packaged as a campaign but are instead a hit-or-miss approach. An **advertising campaign** includes all forms of advertising held together by a single message or comprehensive theme. A campaign is the overall plan or strategy that guides the development of all forms of advertising. When developing the theme for an advertising campaign, Roman and Maas suggest that the advertiser consider four checkpoints:[5]

1. **Maintain visual similarity.** This applies to the use of a well-defined logo or applying the same format and typeface to all of your marketing communications.

2. **Maintain verbal similarity.** This applies to using the same phrases and statements in all marketing communications to reinforce the image and message.

3. **Maintain similarity of sound.** This applies to maintaining similarity of sound by using the same narrator or spokesperson and/or the same music.

4. **Maintain similarity of attitude.** This applies to projecting a consistent attitude or perspective that reinforces the product's image.

12.4 PLANNING AND EVALUATING ADVERTISING CAMPAIGNS

Campaign planning is initiated by considering the competitive situation, currently targeted markets, potentially targeted markets, and market positioning. An astute manager should always be aware of the advertising activities of major competitors. This, of course, is not to say that the competition should dictate advertising activities, but awareness of competitors' activities may indicate trends. For example, what product–service attributes is the competition stressing? Is it food quality, service quality, physical facilities, extra amenities, room atmosphere, or something else? Awareness of the efforts of direct competition may allow a manager to counter the competition's benefits and gain a competitive advantage.

Both the current target markets and the potential new markets must be evaluated. How can management best reinforce current markets to promote repeat patronage? What type of message will reach these markets most effectively? In addition, what new markets should be explored? What is the best type of message to use to overcome uncertainty and resistance and to promote first-time patronage? Can these two messages be combined, or are they best kept separate? Market positioning must also be considered. How is the operation perceived by repeat consumers and by potential consumers? Is this the same perception that management wishes to project?

Advertising campaigns come in all patterns and sizes, depending on the resources and needs of the individual hospitality and tourism organization. Generally, campaigns are organized geographically on a national, regional, or local level. Each level will differ in sophistication and media selection. Local campaign planners often feel that they are at a distinct disadvantage because they have smaller advertising budgets and less marketing expertise. This need not be a disadvantage; instead, it is often just the opposite. The use of local radio spots and local print and/or television advertising allows the advertiser to speak directly with the local clientele. Often the local advertiser has a much clearer understanding of the target market and is able to achieve a competitive advantage over regional and national advertisers.

12.4.1 An Advertising Planning Model

For many managers, one of the most difficult aspects of managing the advertising and promotional function is the detail of planning, implementing, and evaluating an advertising campaign. Figure 12.4 illustrates an advertising planning model. This visual format makes it easier to

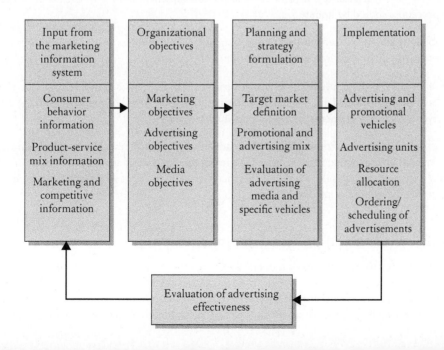

FIGURE 12.4 • An advertising planning model.

conceptualize all aspects of the process and should provide a novice planner with a structured framework from which to work. The model contains five components: (1) input from the marketing information system, (2) organizational objectives, (3) planning and strategy formulation, (4) implementation, and (5) evaluation of advertising effectiveness.

The first component, *input from the marketing information system,* includes information from three separate areas. First, relevant information concerning consumer behavior should be reviewed and analyzed. What are the trends in consumer behavior? How are dining habits changing? How are the travel patterns of the key market segments changing? What hospitality concepts are hot, and which ones are not so hot? Input concerning the product–service mix is also important. What are the sales trends for the various products and services offered? Information concerning the activities of direct and indirect competition is also of value in planning the advertising campaign. The process of gathering information for marketing decisions was covered in detail in Chapter 6.

The second component, *organizational objectives,* should be established in three separate areas: marketing, advertising, and media. *Marketing objectives* focus on such things as market share and producing a specified percentage of increase in sales volume or a specified percentage of increase in repeat patronage. *Advertising objectives* focus on such topics as increasing consumer awareness and drawing consumers away from the competition with advertisements demonstrating the superiority of the organization's product–service mix. *Media objectives* focus on the selection of individual media to achieve the marketing and advertising objectives. For example, an objective might be "To plan media selections so that 90 percent of the target market segments are exposed to at least two of the advertisements."

The third component, *planning and strategy formulation,* involves the formal definition of the specific target markets. Given the limited resources available, it is virtually impossible to reach the saturation point with all target market segments. Therefore, what specific target market segments are most important? Weights should be established for all of the desired advertising and promotional activities. For example, what proportion of the total resources available should be allocated for radio, print, direct mail, and all other activities? Finally, each advertising medium and its individual vehicles are evaluated based on effectiveness and cost efficiency in reaching the target market segments.

Next is the *implementation* of the advertising plan. This component includes working with each of the selected advertising vehicles, determining the advertising units (e.g., half-page print advertisements or 30-second radio spots), allocating resources to pay for the advertising time and space, and ordering and scheduling the time and space with each individual vehicle.

The fifth and final component is *evaluation of advertising effectiveness.* Without engaging in some form of evaluation process, how will management know to what degree the advertising efforts have met with success? There are three important explanations of why some form of evaluation procedure should be undertaken:

- **To gain an understanding of the consumer.** This involves learning what consumers want, why they want it, and how best to serve their needs.

- **To avoid costly mistakes.** When advertising effectiveness is tested, errors that might have gone undetected are noted, and adjustments can be made. In this way, both the effectiveness and cost efficiency of advertising are increased.

- **To add structure.** Rather than viewing advertising as a business expense whose impact is impossible to measure, management can measure the impact of advertising. If sales increase by 10 percent, what is the reason for this increase? What types of advertising and promotion have had the greatest impact on sales?[6]

12.4.2 Evaluating an Advertising Campaign

Advertising effectiveness should be measured for both short- and long-term impact. However, large hospitality organizations engaged in national and regional campaigns usually have the resources to evaluate advertising effectively; smaller firms often do not. Short-term measurements are normally given most attention because they directly reflect the income statement and the financial position of the organization. In addition, managers' tenure and bonuses are typically based on short-term performance. This is not to say that the long-term effects of advertising should be disregarded. Repeat patronage, brand loyalty, and an asset called *goodwill* reflect long-term effects. Nevertheless, it is difficult to measure the long-term residual effects of advertising within a reasonable margin for error, though in the last several years, econometric techniques have advanced to the point where measuring advertising effectiveness is more precise.

The management of a hospitality operation can evaluate advertising subjectively, either alone or in conjunction with an advertising agency. Experienced management plays a key role in this type of evaluation. If management has successfully directed advertising campaigns, subjective evaluation may indeed be adequate. This is especially true of agency executives, as they often have a wealth of experience that allows them to gauge the overall effectiveness of advertising efforts. It is also wise to maintain a file of all advertisements that can be available for easy reference and reviewed periodically.

It is almost impossible to measure advertising effectiveness empirically unless well-defined objectives were formulated prior to initiating the advertising campaign. How would management know whether advertising has been successful if they are not able to compare actual performance with specific objectives? As stressed in Chapter 5, clearly defined, quantifiable objectives are very important. Variances between actual performance and objectives are noted and corrective action taken. The following is a brief review of commonly used techniques, although they are not all suitable for all types of operations:

- **Copy testing.**   The process of copy testing involves pretesting the copy of an advertisement prior to running it in the media. Several advertisements are normally shown to a group of consumers, and questions are asked of the group—typically, "Which advertisement would interest you most?" "Which advertisement is most convincing?" and "Which advertisement is most likely to cause you to patronize the hospitality establishment?" These questions can be asked of an entire group assembled for review of a series of advertisements, or personal interviews can be conducted.

- **Inquiry and sales.**   Direct-mail advertising lends itself to the inquiry and sales method. This involves keeping a tally of each inquiry and sale. For example, if a series of advertisements was run to promote banquet business, how many people phoned or contacted the operation? How many of these inquiries were converted into sales? From these tallies, it is easy to compute a cost per inquiry and a cost per sale for this type of advertising.

- **Coupons and split runs.**   Coupons can be tallied to evaluate the effectiveness of one promotion against others. For example, did the sundae special sell more than the french fries promotion? Coupons are used extensively by the hospitality and tourism industry because they allow for easy evaluation. Coupons can be carried one step further and used to compare one medium against another. For example, suppose that management had a choice among three print media in which to place advertisements. Which one will reach the target market most effectively? The same advertisements and coupons could be run in the three media, with each coupon coded so that a tally could be made of the number of coupons from media A, B, and C. In this way, a relative ranking of effectiveness is possible.

- **Sales tests.**   The level of gross sales or sales of specific items can be monitored following a specific period of advertising aimed at increasing one or the other. It is often difficult to take into account all the variables that affect sales both positively and negatively and thereby establish a cause-and-effect relationship.

- **Consumer testing of awareness, recall, and attitude.**   Through assembled groups, telephone surveys, direct-mail surveys, and personal interviews, consumers can be tested to determine their relative awareness concerning a specific hospitality operation. Have they heard of the operation? Do they patronize it? If so, how frequently do they visit? Do they recall seeing any advertisements? Which ones do they recall? When shown certain advertisements, do they recall seeing these? This is known as *aided recall*.

Copy testing
Involves pretesting the copy of an advertisement prior to running it in the media.

12.4.3 The Role of an Advertising Agency

An **advertising agency** (also referred to as an *ad agency*) is an independent business that works for the client who is purchasing the advertising. Agencies come in all shapes and sizes, from one-person operations to large agencies employing hundreds of individuals. Basically, an agency develops and implements an advertising plan tailored to the needs of the individual client. Then, the creative staff develops the advertisements, and the business staff secures the advertising time and space in the various media. An agency can actually save the client money because the fees earned by the agency are paid as commissions by the medium in which the advertisements are placed. The decision regarding the use of an ad agency is influenced by factors such as the amount of resources (i.e., time and money) the firm is willing to commit to advertising, the size of the firm and the market(s), the types of media being considered, and the knowledge and expertise of the hospitality firm's managers and employees.

The decision to use an ad agency depends on the unique circumstances faced by each hospitality or tourism organization, but agencies offer several advantages and disadvantages. Table 12.1 lists the potential advantages and disadvantages associated with using an advertising agency.

12.4.3.1 TYPES OF ADVERTISING AGENCIES. There are several types of advertising agencies. They are classified based on two criteria: the type of business they handle and the range of services they offer. Agencies may serve a broad range of consumer products, or they may specialize in one field such as consumer goods, industrial products, financial services, retail sales, or real estate. It is wise to select an agency with a proven track record in working with service or hospitality industry clients. An advertising agency may offer specific functions, such as media-buying services or creative services, or it may be a full-service agency. Full-service agencies will handle not only the advertising that the client elects to purchase, but also nonadvertising activities such as sales promotional materials, trade show exhibits, publicity, and public relations.

Advertising agencies provide a wide variety of professional services, including campaign planning, market research, media selection and production, public relations, and campaign evaluations. When selecting an agency, it is important to determine your service needs and find an agency that fits those needs. It can also be helpful if the agency has experienced your product category and customer markets. The following list represents the most common services that ad agencies provide:

- Studying the client's product–service mix to determine strengths and weaknesses and the client's relation to the competition
- Conducting an analysis of the current and potential market segments to determine future potential

ADVANTAGES	DISADVANTAGES
An agency can increase the effectiveness of advertising; its work is more professional, and its use of media is better.	Using an agency can be expensive; you are paying for the expertise and talent.
An agency can be especially helpful in dealing with the special production requirements of radio and television advertising.	Some agencies might resort to using a production-line (or "cookie cutter") approach that lacks creativity.
Using an agency is like maintaining a staff of part-time specialists—copywriters, artists, and layout professionals.	Firms lose some control over the advertising function.
Agencies are able to maintain closer contacts with media representatives than most independent advertisers.	The agency might not be familiar with the target market.
Agencies can offer consultative services related to advertising research and evaluation.	

TABLE 12.1 • Summary of Advertising Agency Advantages and Disadvantages

- Providing direction and leadership with regard to selecting available media and the best method to advertise and promote the product–service mix
- Formulating a detailed plan to reach the stated advertising and promotional objectives
- Executing the plan by coordinating the creative process (writing and designing the advertisements) and the business process (securing the desired advertising time and space)
- Verifying that the desired advertisements have been run in the media selected
- Evaluating the effectiveness of the advertising campaign and submitting a report to the client

12.4.3.2 AGENCY COMPENSATION.   How are advertising agencies compensated? Typically, agencies receive payment in several ways: (1) commissions from media, (2) fees or retainers paid by the client, (3) service charges for creative and production work, (4) markups on outside purchases, and (5) trade-outs.

Commissions of 15 percent are normally paid to the agency by the media. For example, if an advertisement costs $5,000, the agency would collect $5,000 from the client but would pay the medium $5,000 minus $750 (15 percent), or a total of $4,250. Agencies often do not generate sufficient revenue from small advertisers to cover production and creative costs, and therefore they charge other fees, such as monthly retainers or hourly charges for creative work.

Charges are also levied for such production work as photography and graphics. These are usually billed at cost plus a certain percentage. If services are performed for the agency by a third party, the agency may add a markup to the amount billed by the third party. This markup would cover the costs of securing the services and coordinating the services of several third-party providers. Charges are made for advertising on which commissions are not paid, such as direct mail and local newspaper advertising.

Agencies may also accept trade-outs as a form of compensation. Trade-outs consist of trading services for services. The agency performs services for the hotel or restaurant in exchange for services in the form of food and beverages or guest rooms that are provided on a complimentary basis up to the retail value of the services provided by the advertising agency. This method is widely used by hotels and restaurants, for it increases the purchasing power of each dollar spent.

> **Trade-outs**
> When firms trade products or services in lieu of cash.

Establishing a positive agency-client relationship is of critical importance. Management should be willing to work closely with the agency and be honest and open in communication. A manager should be critical of the agency's work without being overly critical of every advertisement, focusing instead on the broader overall strategy. Taking an active interest in the relationship is a very positive step in making the relationship an effective one.

12.5   CRITICISMS OF ADVERTISING

Advertising is a common practice by firms selling products and services in our society. Consumers are often amused and entertained by advertisements during special events such as the Super Bowl. Every year, the nation is astonished at the cost of advertising for 30 seconds during such major events. In addition, advertisers are given awards for their creativity and special effects, and celebrities receive large sums of money to participate in advertisements. Therefore, it is no wonder that economists and consumer advocates debate the overall impact of advertising on our society.

12.5.1   Social and Ethical Criticisms of Advertising

Many critics of advertising raise questions about the social and ethical issues surrounding the use of advertising and other forms of promotion. The following is a list of the most common criticisms regarding advertising.[7]

12.5.1.1 ADVERTISING IS MISLEADING OR DECEPTIVE. Originally, advertising was a practice used to inform consumers about products and product uses. It was a way for firms to convey their messages to consumers so that consumers could make informed purchase decisions. Over the years, as the country prospered and firms sold more products to more consumers with more discretionary income, advertising has become a major strategic tool used to differentiate products and services. Unfortunately, in the heat of competition, some firms choose to stretch the truth or deceive the consumer in an attempt to gain a competitive advantage.

12.5.1.2 ADVERTISING IS OFFENSIVE OR IN POOR TASTE. As mentioned before, the increase in competition has resulted in some firms engaging in questionable advertising practices in an attempt to gain market share. In addition to being misleading or deceptive, a number of critics have also argued, some advertising is offensive or in poor taste. For example, insurance firms may use "fear appeal" to sell their products, automobile manufacturers may use sex to sell cars, and marketers of children's products target children directly. Firms may argue their First Amendment rights to free speech, but many critics feel that advertisers have crossed the line. Advertising has also been accused of creating and perpetuating stereotypes based on its depiction of certain groups of people.

12.5.1.3 ADVERTISING ENCOURAGES MATERIALISM. Rather than merely informing and educating consumers about product benefits, much advertising focuses on creating needs and promoting materialism. Products and services are being promoted as symbols of status and accomplishment, to the detriment of basic values. Celebrities are used in ads in an attempt to influence consumers and act as a point of reference. Another common practice in advertising is to seek product placement in popular movies, many of which target impressionable youths.

12.5.1.4 ADVERTISING ENCOURAGES PEOPLE TO BUY THINGS THEY DO NOT NEED. Advertising seeks to persuade consumers to purchase specific products and services from the advertiser. It is the term *persuade* that bothers critics. As previously mentioned, advertising could be limited to informing and educating consumers so they can make informed decisions. However, many firms launch campaigns targeting vulnerable consumers (e.g., lonely seniors, less-educated people, etc.) to achieve profit goals. This criticism can overlap with all of the other criticisms.

12.5.2 Economic Criticisms of Advertising

Advertising has become a very important strategic tool used by companies to position and gain some form of competitive advantage. There is no doubt that there are advantages to advertising at the brand level. However, some critics question the effects of advertising at the industry level or on the economy as a whole. The following is a brief discussion of the economic effects of advertising.

12.5.2.1 EFFECTS ON CONSUMER CHOICE. Most firms use advertising to differentiate their products and services from those of their competitors. Although consumers still have the option of purchasing from several different brands, in most product categories, there are advantages realized by larger firms that can afford to spend more on advertising. Therefore, some critics would argue that large firms have the ability to dominate the market and charge lower prices than their smaller counterparts. As a result, larger firms may have the potential to reduce the competition based on price or product and services attributes and make it difficult for smaller firms to create brand loyalty among consumers.

12.5.2.2 EFFECTS ON COMPETITION. One of the major criticisms of advertising is its ability to create barriers of entry to firms wishing to enter a market. When large firms spend large amounts of money on advertising, it makes it increasingly difficult for new brands to enter the market with any reasonable level of success. Instead, new brands are relegated to pursuing niche strategies in an attempt to profit and survive. Large firms also enjoy economies of scale in advertising, much the way they do in other areas such as ordering supplies, recruiting and training, and financing. This is especially true in the area of media buying, where firms that purchase more volume get more favorable rates. This results in large firms controlling the major media that have the most impact on consumers. Based on these assertions, some critics would argue that advertising could have an anticompetitive effect on the market.

12.5.2.3 EFFECTS ON PRODUCT COSTS AND PRICES. Probably the most common criticism of advertising is that it results in higher costs that lead to higher prices charged to consumers for products and services. There is no question that advertising is a cost of doing business, similar to a firm's payroll, supply, building leases, insurance, and financing. It appears as a line item on the statement of income and expense as an expense, and it must be covered if a firm expects to be profitable. Basically, any increase in expenses must be offset by an increase in price or a decrease in other expenses if a firm is to maintain its current level of profitability at the same level of volume.

SUMMARY OF CHAPTER OBJECTIVES

This chapter reviewed promotion as applied to hospitality marketing, providing a broad-based overview of the four elements of the promotion mix: advertising, personal selling, public relations, and sales promotion. The management of the promotion mix over the product life cycle was discussed, and methods for setting the promotional budget were examined. They included the percentage of sales, desired objective, competitive parity, and all-you-can-afford methods. A budgeting system provided an easily understood presentation of budget development.

Advertising can be national, local, or cooperative, depending on the size and scope of the firm. To reach the highest level of success, management must engage in various advertising efforts. Generally, advertising seeks to satisfy three goals: (1) to establish awareness in the minds of consumers, (2) to establish a positive perceived value in the minds of consumers, and (3) to promote repeat patronage and brand loyalty among consumers. Advertising positioning and strategy include forming an objective, identifying a target audience, highlighting key consumer benefits, establishing support for the benefits, and employing an appropriate tone or manner. The development of an advertising appeal includes six keys to successful advertising.

In some cases, firms choose to enter a relationship with an advertising agency. The chapter provided an overview of the advantages and disadvantages of working with an agency, the role of the agency, the types of agencies, the methods that can be used to select an agency, and the methods for compensation.

Planning and evaluating advertising involve noting campaign checkpoints. A five-component advertising planning model includes input from the marketing information system, organizational objectives, planning and strategy formulation, implementation, and evaluating advertising effectiveness.

Finally, the chapter discussed the effects of advertising on society. There are critics who feel advertising has many negative social consequences and economic effects on competition. In general, critics argue that advertising limits consumer choices and leads to unfair competition as larger firms create barriers to entry and enjoy economies of scale that are not available to smaller firms.

KEY TERMS AND CONCEPTS

Advertising
Advertising agency
Advertising campaign
All-you-can-afford method
Competitive-parity method
Cooperative advertising
Copy testing
Desired-objective method
Integrated marketing communications (IMC)

Local advertising
National advertising
Percentage-of-sales method
Personal selling
Promotion mix
Publicity
Public relations
Sales promotion
Trade-outs

QUESTIONS FOR REVIEW AND DISCUSSION

1　What are the four elements of the promotion mix?

2　How is the promotion mix used throughout the stages of the product life cycle?

3　Select restaurants in your local area, placing each in one of the stages of the product life cycle. Explain why you placed each restaurant in that particular stage.

4　List and discuss the various methods used to establish promotional budgets. Which is the most common? Which one is the best from a theoretical standpoint? If you were a manager of an independent restaurant with $800,000 in annual sales, which method would you use? Why?

chapter review

5   **What are the three forms of advertising? Give examples of each form.**

6   **How would you describe the process of positioning? Cite two examples of hospitality or tourism firms that you believe have done an excellent job of positioning the product–service mix. Why do you believe they have done an excellent job?**

7   **Select four advertisements featuring hotel chains from print media. Which one do you think does the best job of positioning and conveying the message to the target markets? Why? How could the others be improved?**

8   **What are the three major goals of advertising?**

9   **What are the advantages and disadvantages associated with using an advertising agency?**

10   **How are ad agencies compensated for their work?**

11   **What are the keys to successful advertising?**

12   **What is an advertising campaign? What factors should be considered when planning a campaign?**

13   **What techniques are used to evaluate advertising effectiveness?**

14   **What are some of the criticisms associated with advertising?**

NOTES

[1] D. E. Schultz and H. F. Schultz, "Transitioning Marketing Communication into the Twenty-First Century," *Journal of Marketing Communications*, 4(1) (1998), pp. 9–26.

[2] *American Marketing Association Resources Library Dictionary*, www.marketingpower.com/_layouts/dictionary.aspx.

[3] Kenneth Roman and Jane Maas, *How to Advertise* (New York: St. Martin's Press, 1976), pp. 1–3.

[4] H. Victor Grohmann, "Ten Keys to Successful Advertising," *Cornell Hotel and Restaurant Administration Quarterly* 17, No. 2.

[5] Roman and Maas, pp. 1–3.

[6] C. H. Sandge, V. Fryburger, and K. Rotzoll, *Advertising Theory and Practice* (Homewood, IL: Richard D. Irwin, 1979), pp. 533–536.

[7] George E. Belch and Michael A. Belch, *Introduction to Advertising and Promotion: An Integrated Marketing Communications Perspective*, 2nd ed. (Boston: Richard D. Irwin, 1993), pp. 811–834.

chapter review

CASE STUDY

The Glen Pub

Melissa Clark recently became the manager of a full-service restaurant. The restaurant is in a midwestern resort town of 10,000 people. The town is located along the coastline of one of the Great Lakes and is approximately 10 miles from an industrial town of 150,000 people and 35 miles from a progressive city of almost 200,000 residents. The summers are mild and seldom hot, and the winters are often bitter and snowy. The restaurant is part of a small, well-known upper Midwest chain. The resort town, although only about 2 miles from a substantial four-lane, limited-access road that connects coastal communities, is 10 miles from the nearest inter-state highway.

The restaurant is upscale and attractive to summer vacationers. The restaurant has an English pub look and feel to it, with yards of ale and artifacts from England and Scotland. The food prices are considered to be moderately expensive for this midwestern resort town. There is no restaurant of comparable quality within a 20-mile radius. The restaurant dining area can accommodate 250 guests at one sitting and can comfortably seat another 40 to 50 people in the bar area for cocktails. The bar sales consist primarily of guests waiting to be seated or who drink after dinner. On Friday and Saturday nights the bar has a folk singer or musician for entertainment. The restaurant is open seven days a week during the summer months, and Monday through Saturday after Labor Day. Lunch is served from 11 A.M. to 5 P.M. Monday through Saturday, with dinner from 5 to 11 P.M.

A typical lunch count in the summer is 100 to 120 meals, while a weekend dinner in the summer serves as many as 550 guests. During the off-season, Labor Day to Memorial Day, lunches shrink to 50 to 70 covers and dinner during the week ranges from 10 to 50 guests. Friday and Saturday nights a range from 80 to 150 guests are served, depending on weather, holidays, and other local events. To accommodate the wide fluctuation in guests, the restaurant relies on college students in the summer. There are approximately 10 long-term employees and three managers who work year-round: a restaurant manager, a back-of-the-house manager, and a front-of-the-house manager.

The Problem

Every year during the resort season the restaurant is extremely busy. After Labor Day, business drops substantially and meeting operating costs becomes difficult. How would the manager get more local residents to frequent the restaurant in the off-season? With almost 150,000 residents living approximately 10 miles away, and another populated area of 200,000 people approximately 35 miles away, how would the manager get them to be part of your off-season market? There are no comparable restaurants within a 20-mile radius. The city 35 miles away has a couple of full-service restaurants with quality food and atmosphere, but they do not have the regional reputation that the resort restaurant has.

The restaurant is active in the local community. The Rotary and Lions Clubs hold their weekly luncheon meetings at the restaurant. The restaurant occasionally does outside catering, but demand is minimal. Special functions at the restaurant can be accommodated in the off-season, but the dining rooms are contiguous and relatively intimate, making it difficult to rearrange and close one off from the rest of the restaurant.

The restaurant benefits from billboard advertising and the positive reputation of the chain's five other restaurants. The closest of the other five chain restaurants are 80 miles and 120 miles away. The restaurant has just hired a part-time person as public relations director to help pump up community involvement and increase the restaurant's profile.

Case Study Questions and Issues

1. How can Melissa and her new public relations employee generate more local customer business in the off-season?

2. What can they do to entice residents of neighboring communities to drive 10 to 35 miles for an upscale dinner?

3. What type of advertising and promotions might increase local community traffic?

4. What other information is necessary to make advertising and promotion decisions?

CASE STUDY

Mr. C's Sandwich Shoppes

You've been working for Mr. C's Sandwich Shoppes for nearly a year as a manager of one of the five stores operated within a medium-sized city. Edward Callahan, "Mr. C," opened his first store nearly 20 years ago and has steadily expanded since that time. The restaurants feature both eat-in and take-out dining, and are open from 6 A.M. until 10 P.M. every day. In addition to freshly prepared sandwiches and salads, the restaurants feature a variety of baked goods, prepared in a central commissary on a daily basis. The specialty bakery items include bagels, muffins, and other breakfast items, along with exceptional breads in a wide variety of forms.

In recent years, same-store sales have flattened somewhat, with the increased completion from larger companies such as Panera Bread, Chipotle, and Atlanta Bread Company. These chains have each opened a store in the city and have gained customers and market share in the past 3 years. Each of these competitors advertises and promotes frequently in the local area, using a variety of methods.

For the past two months, you've been encouraging Mr. C to begin advertising and promoting the restaurants. He has responded consistently that word-of-mouth referrals have built the restaurants for many years. He sees no reason to change now. You believe that more aggressive use of advertising and promotions would result in increased sales and market share. In a conversation yesterday with Mr. C, he asked you to develop an analysis of the advantages and disadvantages of increasing advertising and promotion within the local trading area. He also asked you to prepare a summary for his review in seven days. Now that he's agreed to let you proceed, how can you best prepare the requested summary?

case study

Advertising and Social Media

Courtesy of Luciano Mortula/Shutterstock

Chapter Objectives

After studying this chapter, you should be able to:

1. Outline the media planning process.

2. Discuss the advantages and disadvantages of using various types of print media.

3. Discuss the advantages and disadvantages of using various types of broadcast media.

4. Discuss the advantages and disadvantages associated with direct-mail campaigns.

5. Discuss the advantages and disadvantages of using other support media such as outdoor advertising.

6. Discuss the various types of social media, their relevance to the hospitality and travel industry, and social media strategies.

13.1 INTRODUCTION

No one questions that advertising remains an extremely powerful force in the hospitality and tourism industry. Advertising programs must be managed with care and used to the maximum advantage of the organization. Advertising and promotion constitute a major area of marketing effort for most hospitality and tourism organizations, as numerous media are employed in an effort to communicate with selected target markets. The success of these advertising efforts rests to a large degree on the media and the manner in which they are used. Many times, advertisers spend large amounts of money without achieving the desired results. In other cases, advertisers spend only a relatively small amount, yet the results are dramatic. It is useful to remember that it is not how much is invested but *how* it is invested. Dollars allocated to advertising are expected to increase sales.

One of the fastest-growing areas of promotion and advertising is the use of social media and digital marketing. Larger percentages of hospitality and tourism firm budgets are shifting to digital marketing efforts concerning the firm's website, e-mail campaigns, and social media. (The importance of the Internet and electronic commerce was discussed in Chapter 11.) Digital marketing provides a highly cost effective means to reach many important consumer segments in the population. In particular, younger generations are heavily invested in social media such as Facebook and Twitter because of its easy access with smartphones and computer tablets. This chapter begins with a discussion of the traditional print and broadcast advertising vehicles, and then introduces the use of direct mail and other support media, as well as social media.

13.2 DEVELOPING MEDIA PLANS

The stages in the **media planning process** are similar to those in the marketing planning process. First, the firm must perform a market analysis to determine the current situation. Second, the firm needs to establish its media objectives. That is, what does the firm want to accomplish with its media program? For example, is the firm focusing on creating awareness or increasing sales? Third, the firm must develop media strategies to use in attaining the objectives. Media strategies would entail developing a media mix, determining the desired coverage in regard to target markets and geographic area(s), and scheduling the specific media.

> **Media planning process**
> The process firms use to determine and implement media strategies that help achieve the desired goals and objectives for its products and services.

13.2.1 Performing a Market Analysis

The first stage of the process involves a thorough analysis of the market to identify the target markets that become the focus of the media program. This decision is based on the history of the firm, its competitors, and trends in the general population. Advertising is a key element in the positioning of firms and their products or services. Therefore, it is important to select target markets that offer potential for long-term growth and survival. These market segments then become the focus of the media program in an attempt to communicate the firm's products in a favorable light that is consistent with the overall image of the firm. For example, all advertising might be aimed at men and women between the ages of 25 and 35 with annual incomes above $45,000. Or advertising might be slanted toward women such that a 60-to-40 ratio of female-to-male exposure is achieved.

13.2.2 Establishing Media Objectives

Media objectives should be tied to the overall marketing objectives of the firm, as well as the promotion or communications objectives. The media objectives should be focused on the goals associated with the media program and be attainable using media strategies. After determining the target market(s) in the market analysis stage, a firm should establish media objectives for these markets considering the distribution of exposures, the media environment, and budget limitations.[1] Some of the more common objectives for media programs are as follows:

- To increase awareness among consumers in the target markets
- To increase coverage in target markets
- To maintain a positive impact on consumer attitudes and perceptions in regard to the firm's image and brand recognition

Good objectives will (1) be stated in clear and concise language, (2) include a specific time frame in which to accomplish the objective, and (3) include quantifiable terms that can be used as a standard by which to evaluate performance. For example, a local restaurant chain may want to improve the awareness of its restaurant to 75 percent of its target audience with a television ad campaign over the next 60 days.

13.2.3 Developing Media Strategies

Once media objectives are established, it is necessary to develop media strategies that will lead to the attainment of the firm's goals. Selecting the proper media mix, determining the target market and geographic coverage, and scheduling the media achieve this.

13.2.3.1 SELECTING THE MEDIA MIX. When selecting the media mix, it is important to examine the general nature of the target market segments. A medium should be selected based on its ability to reach the maximum number of potential consumers at the lowest cost. However, it is also necessary to minimize wasted coverage while trying to maximize reach. *Wasted coverage* refers to advertising exposures that do not involve members of the target market. For example, if low-income households are exposed to ads for an expensive restaurant, the restaurant is wasting money because it is paying to reach consumers who are not in its target market and would be unlikely to dine at the restaurant. If one million people subscribe to a newspaper, advertisers are charged based on a readership of one million, whether the readers are in the target market or not.

Also, the objectives of the overall campaign must be considered in choosing media vehicles. Howard Heinsius, president of Needham and Grohmann, Inc. suggests several essentials in media selection:[2]

- **Market focus.** Carefully examine your market by product–service mix category or brand and by target market segment. Determine if your hotel or restaurant appeals to the target market and the important attributes that need to be focused on.

- **Media focus.** Follow trends in the national and local media, and evaluate the effectiveness of each. Media time and space are perishable, so you should look for special purchase opportunities.

- **Periodic media update.** Make sure that information about rates and circulation is current.

- **Establish media effectiveness guidelines.** Make sure the media is appropriate for the type of message and that it reaches the preferred target audience.

- **Advertising by objective.** Establish specific advertising objectives such as sales targets or consumer awareness levels to help you determine the best media combination.

- **Coordinate advertising with marketing campaigns.** Advertising is only one part of the promotion mix, and promotion is only one part of the marketing mix. Be sure that it is coordinated with the other efforts in the areas of personal selling, promotion, and public relations, as well as pricing and branding strategies.

- **Develop a sound advertising budget.** Choose the appropriate method for developing an advertising budget so that your campaign is efficient and effective.

- **Plan around media pollution.** Evaluate your media schedule in order to avoid potential noise in the communication process and extensive competition.

- **Coordinate local efforts to match the national advertising efforts.** Local advertising should supplement and complement your national and regional advertising.

- **Use a variety of media.** Extend the number of customers you reach and the frequency of exposure by using multiple advertising channels.

- **Keep accurate files.** Maintain accurate records of budgets, media schedules, and sales results to use in evaluating your performance.

The media selection process involves matching available media with the firm's objectives. There may be multiple objectives and many media alternatives from which to choose. Therefore, the process is one of making choices at various levels. For example, once a decision is made to use some form of print media, the decision between newspaper and magazine follows. Then a decision must be made regarding the particular magazines or newspapers that will be used.

13.2.3.2 DETERMINING TARGET MARKET AND GEOGRAPHIC COVERAGE.

Consideration must be given to the amount of coverage desired. Also, when making decisions, determine the relative costs of the various media. Additionally, be sure to carefully analyze the sizes and frequency of advertisements. Hospitality and tourism firms have the option to advertise on an international, national, regional, or local level. Then, at each level, a firm must decide how long or how often to run an ad in a given geographic market.

13.2.3.3 SCHEDULING THE MEDIA.

Each hospitality or tourism organization must tailor the scheduling of media to fit its individual needs. Figure 13.1 illustrates the three most common approaches to media scheduling. **Continuous advertising** refers to the practice of keeping

Continuous advertising
The practice of keeping the amount of advertising relatively constant over time.

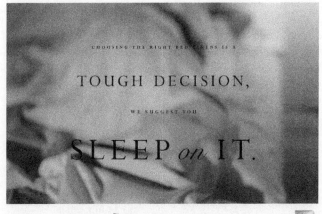

Courtesy of Artex International.

It's important that ads meet the objective determined by the media strategy.

Continuous

Flighting

Pulsing

FIGURE 13.1 • Approaches to media scheduling.

the amount of advertising relatively constant over time. This type is appropriate for hospitality operations with very stable volumes. **Flighting media scheduling** involves a schedule that is set up in spurts and stops. Periods of blitz advertising are used, with no advertising between blitzes. **Pulsing advertising** balances the previous two approaches in that it provides a constant low-level flow of advertising with intermittent periods of blitz advertising. Normally, high levels of continuous advertising are thought to be superior, but economic considerations may necessitate the adoption of either flighting or pulsing media scheduling.

13.3 PRINT MEDIA

The two most common forms of print media are newspapers and magazines. Another form of print media is the yellow pages offered by local telephone companies or similar products offered by competing companies. Advertising in the yellow pages can result in immediate action, but it is difficult to differentiate a firm's product and there is little flexibility because the advertisement runs for a 12-month period. However, all print media vehicles are popular among hospitality and tourism firms because of their ability to provide detailed information and target specific markets. In general, newspapers are a valuable form of media for local hospitality and tourism firms. Advertisements will reach a broad audience at a relatively low cost. Newspapers offer the following advantages and disadvantages:

Flighting media scheduling
The practice of scheduling advertising blitzes followed by periods of no advertising over a given time period.

Pulsing advertising
Constant low-level flow of advertising with intermittent periods of blitz advertising.

ADVANTAGES	DISADVANTAGES
Short lead time for placing ads. It normally takes only 1 to 2 days advance notice to run an ad.	*Short life span of the advertisement.* Newspapers generally have a one-day life span because they are published on a daily basis.
Low cost. An advertisement in a local newspaper is usually lower in both absolute cost and cost per thousand in comparison to other types of media.	*Wasted coverage.* Advertisers pay to reach the total number of newspaper subscribers, many of whom are not in the target market based on demographics or lifestyles.
Can be used for coupons. Newspapers allow for the use of coupons, which can increase volume and provide the information necessary for evaluating advertising effectiveness.	*Clutter.* There is a lot of competition for the reader's attention within the newspaper. It is easy to have an advertisement buried amid other advertisements, decreasing readership and effectiveness.
Good coverage. Newspapers reach all demographic segments in a geographic area.	

In general, magazines offer better reproduction (e.g., color) than newspapers and allow market-ers to segment on a regional basis. Magazines offer the following advantages and disadvantages:

ADVANTAGES	DISADVANTAGES
Quality reproduction. Color photographs reproduce particularly well.	*Long lead time for ad placement.* Magazine publishers require advertisers to adhere to closing dates far in advance of the distribution date (e.g., 30 days).
Long life span. Through pass-along readership, magazine advertisements are seen by more people and have a longer life span than that of newspapers and other media.	*High production costs.* Costs associated with magazine advertising are generally substantially higher than those for newspapers, including both absolute costs and the cost per thousand.
Audience selectivity. Some magazines are aimed at the general population, but through the use of regional and metropolitan editions as well as selective market magazines, advertisers can pinpoint specific target markets.	*Lack of flexibility.* Magazines are not as well suited for local markets as newspapers, direct mail, or radio. Magazines are generally either regional or national in scope, but local city "what to do" magazines are an exception.
High information content. Magazines provide ample space to cover detailed topics and supply a good deal of information.	

13.3.1 Techniques for Successful Print Advertising

First, every effort should be made to attract the consumer's attention with the ad's headline. Many print advertisements are ineffective because a large percentage of consumers skim through the pages and never read the entire advertisement. The headline must therefore get the attention of the reader and deliver the message.

Second, print advertising is more effective if visual components, such as artwork and photographs, are used. Both of these formats are effective in magazines and newspapers.

Third, every effort should be made to keep the layout and copy simple and straightforward. Print readers are less likely to read an advertisement that looks crowded and contains many ideas. Instead, the advertisement should have one or perhaps two points and no more. Print advertising is an example of where less is more, and this means more effectiveness.

Fourth, print advertising lends itself to the use of coupons. Coupons serve to increase volume and can add value in assessing the effectiveness of print advertising media. Coupons should be designed as mini-advertisements with all necessary information so that the consumer does not need to save the rest of the ad. Placement of coupons is important both within the advertisement and on the page on which the advertisement appears. They should be placed at the edge of the advertisement, and the advertisement itself should be at the edge of the page to make it easier to clip the coupon. Simple things such as coupon placement can dramatically increase advertising effectiveness.

Finally, when a given print advertisement has been effective, management should not hesitate to repeat it. The advertisement may seem old hat to the management of the hospitality or tourism

Courtesy of Allied Domecq.

It is important for print advertising to attract the attention of the consumer and have a clear message.

firm, but many potential consumers have not seen the advertisement or do not recall it. Therefore, what has proven successful in the past should be repeated.

13.3.2 Print Advertising Terms

The following terms are commonly used in print media, although some apply to other media as well:

- *Agate line* is a measurement by which newspaper and some magazine advertising space is sold, regardless of the actual type size used. There are 14 agate lines to the inch. Therefore, if a manager wanted advertising space two columns wide and three inches deep, the firm would be charged for 84 agate lines (i.e., 3 inches deep × 14 agate lines = 42 for first column + 42 for second column).

- The *base rate* is the lowest rate for advertising in print media. This rate is for run of paper (ROP) and means that the medium, at its discretion, puts advertisements wherever there is space.

- A *bleed advertisement* is an advertisement that extends into all or part of the margin of a page. Rates for bleeds vary with the medium used. Most media charge extra for bleeds.

- The number of copies distributed is the *circulation*. *Primary circulation* includes those who subscribe, whereas *secondary circulation* includes those who read pass-along copies; secondary circulation is very difficult to measure. Some business publications are provided, often at little or no cost, to those individuals who qualify by engaging in a specific line of business (*qualified circulation*). For example, meeting planners typically receive publications targeted toward individuals who plan meetings. These publications are not available to the general public.

- The *cost per thousand (CPM)* formula is the oldest means for comparing media rates. For print, the cost per 1,000 units of circulation is calculated on the basis of the one-time rate for one black-and-white page.

- The number of times the same audience—listeners, readers, or viewers—is reached is the *frequency*. It is expressed as an average, because some people may see or hear an advertisement only once, while others see it a dozen times. Placing more advertising in the media currently being used, adding more vehicles in a medium currently being used, and/or expanding into other media, such as radio as well as newspapers, can increase frequency.

- The *milline formula* is used to determine the cost per line per million circulation and is used to compare the costs of advertising in different newspapers. The formula is (line rate = 1,000,000)/circulation = milline rate. The reason for multiplying by 1,000,000 is that larger figures are easier to compare. If the rates compared are quoted in column inches, this rate can be used in the formula instead of the line rate. The same rate—baseline or column inch—must be used for all newspapers compared.

- The number or percentage of people exposed to a specific publication is the *reach* and is usually measured throughout publication of a number of issues. It is the net unduplicated audience.

- The *volume rate,* or *bulk rate,* may be for total space, time used, or total dollars expended during a contract period, usually 12 months. As more advertising is done, unit costs decrease. Newspapers generally quote their rates in agate lines or column inches. Rates get progressively lower as the number of lines increases.

13.4 BROADCAST MEDIA

Broadcast media—radio and television—are distributed over the airwaves. The level of involvement is lower than with print media and other advertising mediums, as listeners or viewers can be very passive if they choose.

13.4.1 Radio Advertising

Radio advertising finds extensive use in the food service segment of the industry, and in most cases, it is extremely effective. Radio is able to develop a distinct personality for a hospitality or tourism operation, and it can reach consumers 24 hours a day. Radio advertising offers the following advantages and disadvantages:

ADVANTAGES	DISADVANTAGES
Personal. Radio spots can be written so that they speak directly to the consumer.	*Lack of visual appeal.* Extra effort must be made when developing the copy and sound effects for a radio commercial to stretch the listener's imagination.
Low relative cost. The cost of radio is usually quite low for local advertising, especially when a package involving several spots is purchased. The production costs for the ad are also relatively low.	*Clutter.* The airwaves are filled with advertisements for other hospitality or tourism operations and for every consumer product and service imaginable. Given this noise, it is often necessary to maintain higher levels of advertising to achieve the desired effectiveness.
Flexibility. Radio copy can be changed quickly in response to rapid changes in market conditions.	*Fleeting message.* Once the commercial has aired, it is gone. The listener cannot refer to the advertisement to check the price, phone number, or hours of operation.
Audience selectivity. Radio stations have specific formats that appeal to certain target markets. The characteristics of these markets can be matched with the firm's consumer profile.	

13.4.1.1 TECHNIQUES FOR SUCCESSFUL RADIO ADVERTISING. It is important to recognize that people who are listening to the radio are also engaged in other activities. They may be cleaning house, driving cars, working in the office, or playing at the beach, but they are doing something besides listening to the radio. Because listeners are not devoting 100 percent of their attention to the radio, commercials should be kept simple, focusing on one or two major ideas. It is not effective to bombard listeners with several ideas in each commercial; they simply will not remember everything. It is also important to mention the name of the hospitality or tourism operation and the benefit early in the commercial. Many consumers have a tendency to tune out commercials, but advertisers must work hard to make sure they hear at least part of the commercial. The following is a list of techniques that can improve the success of radio advertising:

- Short and simple music helps in developing ad recognition, especially if it is repeated as a musical logo in all radio commercials. The use of jingles and sound effects helps give consumers a mental image.
- Consumers will quickly forget the radio commercial, and unless the advertiser can encourage almost immediate action, the effectiveness of the advertising will be decreased.
- The advertisement should talk directly to consumers in a language and a tone that they will understand. The approach should be personal, much as if it were a conversation, albeit a one-way conversation.

13.4.1.2 SELECTING RADIO SPOTS. Radio spots can be purchased in a wide variety of lengths, ranging from 10 seconds to 1 minute. Special attention should be paid to (1) the number of spots, (2) the days the spots are broadcast, and (3) the times of day the spots are broadcast.

The number of spots purchased is important in achieving effectiveness in radio advertising. Consumers often require several exposures to the message before they begin to retain it. Repetition is critical to success in radio, as it is in all advertising. The days of the week selected are also important, for they suggest when the hospitality advertiser is seeking to promote business. For example, for an upscale restaurant, is early-week advertising more important, or should the focus be on traditional weekend dining?

CLASSIFICATIONS	TIME	RELATIVE COST
Class AA—morning drive time	6 A.M. to 10 A.M.	High
Class BB—daytime	10 A.M. to 3 P.M.	Moderate
Class A—afternoon drive time	3 P.M. to 7 P.M.	Moderate to high
Class C—evening	7 P.M. to 12 A.M.	Low to moderate
Class D—night time	12 A.M. to 6 A.M.	Low

TABLE 13.1 • Radio Time Classifications

The time of day must also be considered. Radio should reach the consumer at a time when a decision is being made or when the advertiser is seeking to stimulate demand. Table 13.1 shows the time classifications used by radio stations. The most expensive times are morning and afternoon commuting times. A hospitality advertiser should seriously consider these times, despite the increased cost, because they are likely to prove the most effective, especially for restaurants.

13.4.1.3 PRODUCING RADIO COMMERCIALS. Figure 13.2 illustrates a time guide for producing a radio commercial. This guide can, of course, be modified, but generally a commercial should consist of introduction, commercial copy, recap of pertinent points, and musical logo. The introduction usually consists of music and copy written to get the listener's attention. It serves the same function as the headline in a print advertisement.

The copy of the commercial is the real heart of the selling proposition. The copy should explain the benefits of purchasing the product to the consumer. The recap of pertinent points should repeat points that the consumer should remember, such as a special price or new hours of operation. Finally, a musical logo is often used to fade out the commercial. Many advertisements allow 5 to 10 seconds at the end for the announcer to read a live segment of the commercial. This segment often calls for immediate action by the listener. Both of these approaches can be very effective.

13.4.1.4 RADIO ADVERTISING TERMS. As with other forms of media, radio has its own unique terms that are used within the industry. The following are terms commonly used in radio advertising:

- An *advertising spot* is a short advertising message on a participating program or between other radio programs that an advertiser does not sponsor. This is what most people call a *commercial*. Advertising spots may be (1) fixed, broadcast at a time guaranteed by contract; (2) preemptible, broadcast at a certain time unless bumped by an advertiser willing to pay a higher rate; or (3) floating, broadcast when the station decides (run of station, or ROS).

- *Drive time* is the early morning and late afternoon/early evening hours when radio has its largest audiences and highest rates.

- Another way of comparing media vehicles and programs is by referring to *gross rating points*. This rating can be calculated by multiplying the rating points (percentage of households, according to surveys, listening to a program or station at a particular time) by the number of times that program or station is heard or viewed during a given period (usually 4 weeks). Twenty percent of a potential audience equals 20 rating points.

- *Preemptible rates* are charges for broadcast advertising spots that may be bumped to different time periods by advertisers paying higher rates. They vary in cost by the amount of notice the station must give the advertiser before moving an advertisement: The longer the notice, the higher the rate.

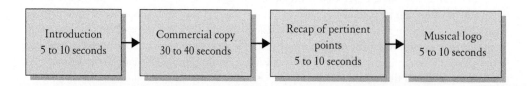

FIGURE 13.2 • Production guide for a 60-second radio commercial.

13.4.2 Television Advertising

Each year, more and more hospitality and tourism organizations use television as an advertising medium. For some, the move into television brings increased sales; for others, it is not such a bright picture. Television is a very demanding medium, one that delivers large audiences but requires great skill in advertising. Before a hospitality or tourism organization decides to commit resources for television, very careful thought must be given to its impact on the remainder of the organization's advertising efforts. The advantages and disadvantages of television advertising include the following:

ADVANTAGES	DISADVANTAGES
Large audiences. Television, even at the local level, is able to deliver large numbers of viewers.	*Low selectivity.* It may be difficult to segment the target audience as narrowly as preferred, leading to some amount of wasted coverage.
High impact of message. The combination of quality sight, sound, and motion holds the potential for tremendous impact on viewers.	*Fleeting message.* Much like radio, once a television advertisement is broadcast, it is gone, and a potential consumer cannot refer back to it.
Low cost per exposure. The absolute cost is high, but the cost per person reached is low due to the large volume of viewers.	*High absolute cost.* For many hospitality and tourism organizations, the absolute cost of purchasing television time and producing commercials is simply too high.
Credibility. Consumers perceive claims made in television commercials as credible (e.g., celebrity endorsers).	*Clutter.* Television commercials tend to be grouped together at certain times each hour. This creates a certain amount of competition for the viewer's attention and interest.

13.4.2.1 TECHNIQUES FOR SUCCESSFUL TELEVISION ADVERTISING. First, the visual aspect of the commercial must convey the message to the consumer. The sound should enhance the message, but the message should be able to stand on its visual impact alone. Television is a visual medium; the visual aspect is the key to successful television advertising. Messages that hospitality advertisers try to convey include the luxury and high living of upscale hotels or the fun people have at a restaurant. Showing people in the actual setting, not just showing the facilities or the food and beverages, does this.

Second, television advertising must capture the viewer's attention immediately, or it is doomed to failure. Facing facts, a manager must remember that consumers use commercial time to do other things, such as get snacks in the kitchen. If a commercial does not spark interest, people will not even watch.

Third, the advertisement should stay with one idea and repeat it within the time allocated. Television viewers see many advertisements throughout the day, and they cannot possibly remember all that they see and hear. Therefore, advertisements should focus on one key point. For example, Wendy's, Burger King, and Taco Bell achieved success with campaigns centered on themes that were simple, direct, and memorable. Every effort should be made to trim commercials that talk too much. The adage "A picture is worth a thousand words" should be a guide when evaluating television storyboards.

Fourth, television advertisements should accurately project the image of the hotel or restaurant to consumers. Much time, effort, and money have been invested in staffing and in the physical facilities in order to create an image; advertising should not muddy that image with poor television commercials. For example, one upscale restaurant operating in a major metropolitan area enjoyed a fine reputation and steady clientele. In an effort to increase sales during slow periods, management ventured into television advertising. After work with the creative staff, a storyboard and script were created, and production began. The result was a commercial that featured several still photographs of the restaurant depicting dining situations. These were well done, but the announcer was talking in a hard-sell tone and at a very fast pace. This commercial cheapened the image of the restaurant and, in fact, hurt sales figures.

13.4.2.2 TYPES OF TELEVISION COMMERCIALS. Advertisements can be creative and may use several different approaches. Television commercials can be categorized into six types:

1. **Demonstration.** Showing an actual part of the operation can be very effective. For example, preparing a certain menu item or banquet service in action within a hotel can help create an image.

2. **Straight announcer.** This involves the use of only one announcer offering the benefit and support.

3. **Testimonial.** This is a form of word-of-mouth promotion in which satisfied consumers talk about elements of the product–service mix.

4. **Problem solving.** This type of commercial offers a problem or series of problems and shows how a given hospitality or tourism operation can be the proper solution. For example, "How can you best celebrate your fortieth birthday? Why of course, come to the famous XYZ restaurant!"

5. **Story line.** Some commercials tell a story in 30 to 60 seconds. For example, imagine a young boy sitting in a classroom at school daydreaming about a hamburger and french fries. The visual pieces and the sound discuss the benefits of the products, and when the commercial concludes, school is out, and the young boy is eating his favorite fast-food meal.

6. **Musical.** Several successful television commercials have used the appealing visual effect of food products backed with appropriate music. If done well, this can be a very effective soft sell.

13.4.2.3 TELEVISION ADVERTISING TERMS. Many industry-specific terms are used by television stations and advertisers in business negotiations. The following are terms commonly used in television advertising:

- In a *dissolve,* one scene fades into the next, with the two showing simultaneously for a moment.
- *Dubbing* refers to recording the sound portion of the commercial separately and then synchronizing it with the visual components.
- With a *fade in/fade out,* the screen goes from black to the visual material, or the final visual shot is faded into black.
- The term *fringe time* refers to the periods immediately before and after TV prime time, 4 P.M. to 8 P.M. and after 11 P.M. in all time zones except the Central time zone, where periods run an hour earlier.
- A *network* is a link of many stations by cable or microwave for simultaneous broadcast from a single originating point. The stations may be owned by or affiliated with the network. Major networks are ABC, CBS, NBC, and Fox. However, with the increase in specialized stations because of the growth of cable and satellite television, the importance of the three major networks has declined. Other networks such as CNN, ESPN, Food Network, and more targeted networks have increased their impact on the television market.
- *Prime time* is the time period when television has the largest audiences and highest advertising rates. In the Eastern, Mountain, and Pacific time zones, it is from 8 P.M. to 11 P.M. In the Central time zone, it is from 7 P.M. to 10 P.M.

13.5 DIRECT MAIL

There are those who refer to direct-mail advertising as "junk mail." These individuals believe that direct-mail advertising is of little value and is not appropriate for the hospitality and tourism industry. These beliefs simply are not true. Direct mail can and does work for many hospitality and tourism advertisers. It is used to solicit group and banquet business. Most hotels routinely send direct-mail pieces describing guest room and meeting facilities to potential meeting planners and then follow up with inquiries and personal calls to generate leads from the mailing. Direct mail is also used to promote special events, such as holidays or special packages, and often to offer promotional discounts. Following are the advantages and disadvantages associated with the use of direct-mail campaigns:

ADVANTAGES	DISADVANTAGES
Highly selective, low wasted coverage. With direct mail, an advertiser can be very selective with the target market using lists collected from customers and/or bought from list companies or other firms.	*Poor image.* Direct mail suffers from a poor image in the minds of many consumers. Unless the piece is able to attract immediate attention, most consumers will not read it.
Easily evaluated. It is easy to monitor the effectiveness of direct-mail pieces by looking at inquiries and sales related to "dropped" pieces.	*High relative cost per contact.* Costs include mailing lists, printing, production of letters, envelope stuffing, and postage.
High information content. There are no time or space limits, as is the case with other media. Therefore, managers can be very creative and they have a great deal of control over the design, production, and distribution of the direct-mail efforts.	*Clutter.* The number of direct-mail pieces that the typical consumer receives each day is increasing, and it is becoming more difficult to get the desired message to the consumer.
Short lead time. It is relatively easy to produce, copy, and send direct-mail pieces.	

13.5.1   Techniques for Successful Direct Mail Advertising

First, any direct-mail piece that achieves success must capture the potential consumer's attention. Many consumers throw out direct-mail advertising without opening it; others open it but do not read it. If the advertisement fails to motivate the consumer to act immediately, chances are that it will be set aside and eventually forgotten. Second, special attention needs to be given to the layout and copywriting of direct-mail pieces. Generally, long paragraphs of copy should be avoided because most people simply will not read them. Research has shown that the more personal the appearance of the direct mail piece, the greater the likelihood that the recipient will read it. Many firms doing small, selective mailings will personalize them with a regular stamp and/or envelopes that are addressed by hand. Both techniques usually prove to be more effective than using bulk rate postage and peel-off address labels. Finally, direct-mail efforts are often successful because of the creativity on the part of the advertiser. It helps to do something different or unique to set yourself apart from other firms. For example, one restaurant used brown lunch bags instead of standard envelopes. The phrase "Are you still brown-bagging it?" was printed on the outside of the bag.

The DMA (formerly *Direct Marketing Association*) offers a wealth of information that will be useful to any hospitality and tourism organization. Additional educational and training resources in data and direct mail techniques can be found at www.thedma.org.

13.5.2   Mailing Lists

Mailing lists fall into two categories: in-house lists and external lists. The management generates *in-house lists* internally. These lists should include those who have patronized the hotel, restaurant, or tourist attraction or who have the potential to generate a significant amount of business. Many restaurants use the guest book concept very successfully. They place a guest book at the entrance and ask each individual to sign it. Another approach is to keep a large bowl at the host's stand into which guests may place business cards. The names and addresses provided by the guests become an excellent foundation on which to build a mailing list. Within hotels, it is relatively easy to build a mailing list based on registration information, as well as the contacts that are made by the sales

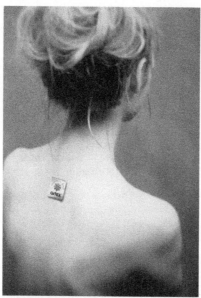

INTRODUCING ARTEX SHIRTS AND COATS.

For years, we've dressed tables in the world's finest linens. It was only a matter of time before we got around to people. For information on the Artex Apparel Collection including coats, pants, shirts, aprons and hats, please call 1.800.851.8671 or visit us at www.artexapparel.com.

ARTEX APPAREL • A DIVISION *of* ARTEX INTERNATIONAL, INC.
MANUFACTURERS *of* FINE LINENS SINCE 1933 • *www.artex-int.com*

Courtesy of Artex International.

Artex International direct-mail pieces are successful at capturing the attention of potential customers.

and marketing staff. *External lists* are obtained from companies that sell mailing lists based on demographics, socioeconomic levels, geographic areas, and numerous other variables. Costs of these lists vary depending on selectivity and size. Lists purchased externally should be guaranteed to be current. Reputable companies will guarantee lists to be 90 to 95 percent accurate and current. Mailing lists can also be purchased from magazines, clubs, associations, and other businesses.

Maintaining mailing lists is critical to the cost-effectiveness and success of any direct-mail advertising program. Only names of potential consumers should be included, and names that are duplicated because several lists are used should be avoided.

The results of direct mail advertising campaigns may seem discouraging based on the total number of pieces mailed. Typically, the response rate on mail promotions is less than 1 percent. Anything more than 1 percent is very good, and more than 5 percent is outstanding. Consider a restaurant that sent a mailing to 20,000 potential consumers advertising a promotional item.

A response rate of 1 percent would be 200, 2 percent would be 400, and 5 percent would be 1,000. As few as 200 extra covers can have a substantial impact on sales.

13.6 SUPPORT MEDIA

In addition to the major types of media discussed earlier, there are other forms of media that are used by firms to support, or supplement, the media effort. This section covers four forms of support media: outdoor advertising, Internet and Web advertising, brochures and collateral materials, and specialty advertising.

13.6.1 Outdoor Advertising

Outdoor advertising has widespread use among those hospitality operations located near interstate highways, but it can be effective in other locations as well. According to the Outdoor Advertising Association of America, restaurants and hotels are among the top 10 categories for the use of out-of-home advertising, led by companies such as McDonald's, Walt Disney, and Cracker Barrel Old Country Restaurant.[3] The advantages and disadvantages associated with outdoor advertising include:

ADVANTAGES	DISADVANTAGES
Low cost per exposure. The number of people exposed to outdoor advertising is large compared to the cost of producing and placing it.	*Poor audience selectivity/high wasted coverage.* Although the cost per thousand is low, outdoor advertising does not lend itself to reaching small target market segments. It is a mass-market method.
High repetition. Consumers who frequent a given route will experience many exposures to an outdoor ad. This repetition aids in recall and retention.	*Long lead time.* It requires considerable planning and it takes a relatively long time to create and display an outdoor ad.
Ability to target location. Outdoor advertising is particularly useful for hospitality and tourism firms in targeting customers looking for lodging, restaurants, or attractions in the immediate area.	*Legislation/local restrictions.* Beginning with the Highway Beautification Act in 1965, all levels of government have discussed and often have enacted legislation to limit and tightly control the construction of outdoor billboards and signs.
Availability of digital media. The development of digital billboards has improved the quality and flexibility of outdoor advertising.	*Lack of flexibility.* Once outdoor advertising is in place, it is not subject to change without considerable effort and cost.

13.6.1.1 TECHNIQUES FOR SUCCESSFUL OUTDOOR ADVERTISING. Two simple rules should govern all outdoor advertising. First, the copy should be kept short and the print large. Those viewing outdoor advertising will be riding in buses, cabs, and cars or walking down the street. They focus their attention on the advertisement for only a few seconds, so the message must be brief. The message should be a maximum of five to seven words—the fewer, the better. Information such as the telephone number or hours of operation is not likely to be remembered and should not be included. Second, a picture or illustration is often helpful in gaining attention. The picture or illustration should convey the message and be used to provide clear name recognition. The best example is the McDonald's golden arches. The arches are used on most outdoor advertising for McDonald's. The visual image is easily recognized.

13.6.1.2 TYPES OF OUTDOOR ADVERTISING. Standard outdoor advertising consists of posters and painted bulletins. Posters are blank boards on which the printed advertising is mounted. Painted bulletins are more permanent signs on which the message is painted. Digital billboards placed in high traffic interior and exterior locations provide moving, eye-catching images presented in high-definition resolution. Posters and painted bulletins and digital billboards are available in a wide variety of sizes. Painted bulletins are sold individually, and posters are sold by showings. A *showing* refers to the coverage of a market within a 30-day period, not the number of posters. A 100 showing is complete coverage of a market, a 50 showing is half of it, and so on. In some communities, 10 posters might be a 100 showing, but in much smaller places, 2 posters could be a 100 showing. An *outdoor advertising plant* is a company that buys or leases real estate (where it erects standard-size boards) or rents walls of buildings. It then sells use of space at these locations to advertisers.

When renting posters, one should consider the circulation, or the number of people who will see the board. The length of time a passerby can see the poster clearly should be considered. Not all locations are good ones. The physical condition of the posters and painted bulletins should also be considered. Nothing will reflect more negatively on an advertiser than a poorly maintained board or one with its lights burned out.

Another type of outdoor advertising is referred to as *transit advertising*. This refers to advertising placed on vehicles used in transporting people or in public places that people encounter in their daily travel routines. For example, most cities sell advertising space on buses, taxis, and subways, as well as on walls in the stations where people wait for these forms of transportation. In addition, transit advertising can be found in airports and on the side of trucks. Street furniture such as bus shelters, phone kiosks, and news racks are also used. Finally, there are other alternative outdoor display mediums such as cinemas, digital place-based screens, arenas and stadiums, shopping malls, and marinas. Some interior place-based displays can be found in convenience stores, health clubs, and restaurants or bars.

13.6.2 Internet and Web Advertising

The use of Internet advertising has increased substantially in the past few years. By using websites that attract tourists or others that are part of the target market for a hotel, restaurant, or tourist destination, the advertiser is able to reach new potential customers via Internet advertising. The advantages and disadvantages of Internet advertising include the following:

ADVANTAGES	DISADVANTAGES
High selectivity. By selecting websites that have traffic from users that match the target market closely, the advertising can be highly targeted.	*Low target market selectivity of some websites.* Websites that attract a broad array of users may provide little selectivity for hospitality companies.
Easy to monitor. Internet advertising allows advertisers to monitor the number of "hits" that an advertisement receives and then the number of individuals that "click through" to the advertiser's website to gather additional information.	*Clutter of banner advertising.* Often websites have a number of banner advertisements that creates clutter and reduces that effectiveness of any single advertisement. In addition, software that blocks advertising is readily available.
Low cost per exposure. The cost per thousand to place an Internet ad (e.g., banner ad) is extremely low.	
Short lead time. Once designed, Internet banner advertisements can be placed very quickly and can be changed equally quickly.	

Brochures
A small pamphlet containing information and images related to products, services, and events.

13.6.3 Brochures and Collateral Materials

Brochures are developed and used to supplement other forms of advertising, as well as personal selling efforts. Normally, **brochures** are used in direct-mail campaigns in addition to being placed in hotels, restaurants, tourist attractions, and tourist information centers. Other forms of collateral materials include meeting planner guides and video brochures. Hotels, cruises, and resorts use video brochures that provide a quick 4- to 6-minute tour of the property. However, written brochures are still the most common item for creating awareness and interest among potential consumers.

Brochures play a vital role in the advertising and promotional efforts of hotels, and they can be beneficial to restaurants and travel firms as well. They can be used in a wide variety of situations. It will not be possible to tell the entire story within a brochure, as there are space restrictions. The most important point to remember is to communicate your facility's positioning. It is imperative that you create and maintain an image in the consumer's mind. After you have determined the type of positioning statement you want to communicate, you can move on to the key benefits and support that the brochure will communicate. The following guidelines will lead to more successful brochures:

- **Brochure cover.** First, the cover design is very critical. It should communicate where your property is located and your positioning statement. The cover is valuable space, and it should be used to convey your primary selling message and the key consumer benefit. The photograph used on the front cover should capture the attention and interest of potential guests.

- **Photographs.** All photographs should help stretch potential guests' imaginations. They should be able to see themselves in the setting. Photographs of activities are more useful than photographs of just the facilities. If you plan to use food in the photographs, use close-up photos of finished products, not just the ingredients. Avoid the use of standard types of photographs that are all too common in hotel brochures. These include the smiling chef standing beside the buffet table and service personnel serving food in a restaurant. Strive for a fresh approach.

- **Information.** Potential guests need information that will help them to better understand things about your product–service mix. The use of maps and/or graphics on the brochure helps the reader gain a better understanding of where you are located, as well as some specifics about the types of products and services offered. Basic information such as street address, website address, telephone number(s), and chain affiliation should also be included.

- **Copy.** Just as with any type of advertising, the copy used in a brochure must talk to the consumer in his or her own language and must speak directly in terms of important benefits. A professional copywriter might be useful in this venture. It is important to avoid cliches, as these will actually turn off potential guests.

> **Collateral materials**
> Printed and electronic materials such as brochures and websites that support the sales of products and services.

13.6.4 Specialty Advertising

In addition to the basic media used by hospitality and tourism firms, specialty advertising materials bearing the firm's name and logo can be given or sold to a targeted consumer group. There are literally thousands of specialty items, including pens, pencils, calendars, rulers, paperweights, jewelry, matches, programs, candy jars, travel bags, T-shirts, and much more. Here are some of the advantages and disadvantages commonly associated with specialty advertising:

> **Specialty advertising**
> Materials bearing the firm's name and logo that are given or sold to a targeted consumer group.

ADVANTAGES	DISADVANTAGES
Retention. If the item is of value or usefulness to the recipient, it is likely to be retained, and the advertising message is seen repeatedly.	*Clutter.* Many firms distribute similar items such as pens and key chains. Firms must develop unique items that will be of some value to consumers.
Selectivity. Most specialty items are distributed directly to consumers in the firm's target market. For example, free items such as hotel pens and cups from children's meals can be taken home.	*Image.* It is important to use items that are consistent in quality with the overall quality perceptions that consumers have of the firm. If the items are cheap, they will have a negative impact on the image of the firm.
Low cost. When purchased in large quantities, many specialty advertising items can be fairly inexpensive per unit.	

13.7 SOCIAL MEDIA

Social media
Internet-based applications that allow organizations and individuals to exchange information in virtual communities and networks.

Social network
Individuals and organizations build personal webpages to share content and communicate with friends, colleagues, fans, and customers.

Social media can be defined as "a group of Internet-based applications that build on the ideological and technological foundations of Web 2.0, and that allow the creation and exchange of user-generated content."[4] Web 2.0 is simply the next generation of technology that allowed webpages to be interactive and accessed from the desktop (or smartphones and tablets). Social media is interactive in that it allows individuals and organizations to share and modify the content created on the Web. Participants are encouraged to contribute and provide feedback, engage in conversations, and form virtual communities and networks. The most common type of social media is a **social network** such as Facebook or LinkedIn that allows individuals and organizations to share content and communicate with people that have common interests. Other types of social media include:

- **Microblogs.** Short messages (updates) are distributed to subscribers (e.g., Twitter)

- **Blogs.** Online forums that allow members to hold conversations by posting messages (e.g., WordPress)

- **Media sharing.** Online services that enable individuals and organizations to upload and share media such as audio and video files and photos (e.g., YouTube, iTunes podcasts, and Flickr)

- **Wikis and collaborative projects.** Open sources allow anyone to make changes and edit content, whereas closed sources allow only members to make changes and edit content (e.g., Wikipedia)

13.7.1 Types of Social Media Users

Social media usage is growing every year. In 2015, more than 2.3 billion people worldwide actively communicated through social media, and an estimated 65 percent of the U.S. population used one or more social networking platforms. However, the growth in social media has started to plateau, with the largest growth rate in the age group 65 and older.[5]

Many classification schemes exist for categorizing social media users, ranging from 5 user types to as many as 12 or more. They use different variables to classify users such as demographics,

There are many well-known social media brands.

Bloomua/Shutterstock

participation, exposure, and usage frequency. One classification scheme was provided in an online marketing blog that is simple (5 types) and provides their characteristics and recommendations for strategies that marketers can use to connect with each type.[6] Table 13.2 summarizes the types, their characteristics, and strategies for connecting with them.

13.7.2 Tips for Using Social Media in Business

It is obvious that social media and social networking have become ingrained in the U.S. culture and around the globe. In fact, although the United States has the largest number of Facebook users, the active reach is actually better in several other countries, including Brazil, most of the developed countries in Europe, Japan, and Taiwan.[7] In terms of commercial use, 27 percent of small businesses and 34 percent of medium-sized businesses are using social media, and 87 percent of the Fortune 100 companies use social media. The following is a list of 10 social media tips from Kodak's chief blogger:[8]

1. **Know what you are talking about.** Provide content that is accurate.

2. **Always be transparent.** Be genuine and be real.

3. **Be yourself.** Present content in a conversational format.

4. **Post frequently.** Post on a regular basis to keep the content current.

TYPE	CHARACTERISTICS	STRATEGIES
The Lurker	• Always listening and observing, but not participating	• Don't expect regular interaction • Reach out directly using a direct message • More likely to respond to thought-provoking message
The Newbie	• New to social media and social networks; they follow for a while before they participate	• Provide information to help them with social media • Check new followers to identify them
The Predictable User	• They share regularly and interact when prompted • Looking for things to share • Easy to spot	• Provide useful and easy-to-share information • Research their feed to determine content they like to publish • Ping them regularly with content similar to what they normally share
The Chronic Oversharer	• Share on a regular basis and divulge a lot of personal information • They send multiple messages at a time; might cause others to tune out unless they are credible	• They will be quick to share, so send interesting content • If credible, they are a good opinion leader you can use to reach others
The Power User	• Found proper balance between sharing, interacting, and providing value • Large quantity of followers, possible expert, and powerful social message content	• Looking for quality over quantity, so you have to provide useful content to attract them • Social networking asset if you can connect with them

TABLE 13.2 • Social Media User Types and Strategies to Connect with Them

5. **Add value.** Provide something that can be used by the reader.

6. **Respond.** Follow-up to questions and posts.

7. **Listen to what others have to say.** Make it easy for readers to provide feedback that will help you improve.

8. **Learn from your mistakes.** Be willing to admit you are wrong and make the appropriate changes.

9. **Be external.** Link to other blogs, videos, news articles, websites, and so on.

10. **Have fun.** Make it enjoyable and you will be more successful.

13.7.3   Social Media Usage in Hospitality and Travel

There are many different types of social media, as discussed in the beginning of this section. The trick is to be able to choose those that are most relevant to your operation and leverage them to your advantage. Not all hotels and restaurant have the same level of knowledge and expertise in regard to the use of social media. For instance, independent restaurants are often owned and operated by men and women who didn't attend college, and are over the age of 50. Many of these people do not engage with computers and social media on a regular basis, if at all. Conversely, large chains usually have one or more experienced employees dedicated to the social media function. However, all types of hospitality and travel organizations can benefit from the use of social media. The following is a brief discussion of the various social media tools that are used most in hospitality and travel, and some of their common uses.

13.7.3.1 USER-GENERATED COMMENTS AND REVIEWS.   In the past, hospitality and travel firms relied on reviews from their own websites and monitored how they would be conveyed to others. Now, consumers obtain most of this type of information from third-party providers who offer complete transparency. The objectivity of firms such as TripAdvisor and WikiTravel allow consumers to differentiate between hotels, restaurants, and other travel firms based on the quality of their operations. This has become one of the most influential forms of social media for hospitality and travel firms. Therefore, it is imperative that firms monitor these sites and take actions to address negative feedback from customers. In a way, this is a type of publicity, given that firms do not sponsor or pay for the communications, nor can they control the message.

13.7.3.2 BLOGS AND MICROBLOGS.   *Blogs* and *microblogs* allow hospitality and travel firms to interact with their customers by posting content related to the firm and the local destination. Firms can link other websites that provide information on local restaurants, attractions, travel firms, and events. Microblogs such as Twitter can be used to keep customers apprised of special promotions, announcements and awards, new products and services, and local events. Twitter can also be used to get real-time customer feedback. Similarly, blogs can be used to post basic thoughts (by the firm and its customers) and chronicle the history of the firm through a "diary" of sorts. If the content on blogs and microblogs is interesting, it will add value and be shared by the customer with friends, relatives, and colleagues. Finally, posting content on blogs can also benefit firms by increasing their visibility and ranking on search engines. Blogs and microblogs can be particularly useful in the restaurant industry because of the frequency of dining out and the reliance on word of mouth.

13.7.3.3 SOCIAL NETWORKS.   It should be clear by now that social media and social networks are becoming increasingly popular among the young and old, alike. More and more "older" people (e.g., baby boomers) have joined social networks and participate on a regular basis. In addition, younger generations are growing up with the Internet and social media, making it a part of culture and their everyday lives. As previously mentioned, Facebook has become the most used online application, including smartphones. Social networks can be used to share information regarding the firm, its products and services, and local destination-specific information. This information can be shared, "liked," and tagged by social network users. They can also create "fan" pages to help promote your business. LinkedIn is a professional social network that can be used by firms to recruit employees, find suppliers, and network with other hospitality and travel industry professionals.

13.7.3.4 MEDIA SHARING. The last category involves the sharing of videos and photos and, to a lesser extent, audio files such as podcasts. Video brochures have taken the place of the traditional brochures on hospitality websites and the Internet. Links to video platforms (e.g., YouTube) allow hotels to provide a visual representation of their properties for transient customers and meeting planners. This supplements the written description of the property (e.g., guest rooms, restaurants, recreational facilities, etc.) and the specifications provided for meeting planners regarding the meeting facilities and catering services. The visual aspect of the video brochures allows hospitality firms such as resorts and cruise lines to simulate the service experience for potential customers. In addition to online videos, hospitality and travel firms can also share photos through platforms such as flickr and create audio files for podcasts using platforms such as iTunes. All of these types of media can be "tagged" to drive traffic to the firm's website and increase rankings in search engines if optimized.

13.7.4   Measuring the Impact of Social Media

One of the benefits of social media over other forms of advertising and communications is that the impact can be measured using objective techniques. Also, the metrics used to evaluate social media campaigns can be integrated, and compared, with those used for other components of the marketing mix. Table 13.3 contains a summary of the most common types of social media and

MEDIA TYPE	EXPOSURE	ENGAGEMENT
Twitter	• Number of followers (reach) • Number of followers for those who re-tweeted your message • Use "TweetReach"	• Number of times link clicked • Number of times message re-tweeted • Number of times hashtag used
Facebook	• Number of fans for brand page • Number of friends from those who became fans during given period of time or promotion • Number of friends from those posting comments or "likes" • Use "Facebook Insights"	• Number of times link clicked • Number of comments and "likes" • Number of wall posts and private messages
YouTube	• Number of views tied to promotion or specific period of time • Number of total subscribers	• Number of comments on your video • Number of times the video was rated • Number of times the video is shared • Number of new subscribers
Blogs	• Number of visitors who viewed the posts tied to the promotion or specific period of time	• Number of comments • Number of generated subscribers • Number of times posts were shared and where they were shared • Number of third-party blog referrals
E-mail	• Number of people on the distribution list • Number of people who actually received the e-mail	• Number of people who opened the e-mail • Number of people who clicked on links • Number of people who shared the e-mail • Number of new subscriptions generated by the e-mail

TABLE 13.3 • Social Media Metrics for Exposure and Engagement

the metrics that can be used to measure exposure and engagement.[9] It should be noted that there is some disagreement as to whether e-mail should be classified as a type of social media, but it is included here.

The final metric that really matters is the return on investment (ROI). This starts with the number of leads for potential business that are generated through exposure to your social media and e-mail campaigns. Then, it is important to determine the conversion rate of leads to sales. Finally, it is necessary to calculate the ROI based on the costs of creating and maintaining the social media vehicles, and the amount of revenue that can be directly linked to the social media campaign. Social media is one of the most cost effective forms of advertising and promotion, but it is often difficult to accurately measure its financial impact.

SUMMARY OF CHAPTER OBJECTIVES

This chapter covered the vast area of external advertising and promotional media. These media constitute an invaluable resource that, if managed properly, can generate increased sales and substantial profits. Managed poorly, these media will drain away advertising resources and leave little or nothing to show in return. As with all investments, management must evaluate advertising for its return on investment. The relationships between a hospitality client and an advertising agency involve both positive and negative aspects. Management should consider several factors when selecting an agency and should consider compensation practices within the industry.

Media selection involves several factors. These include the nature of the target market, the campaign objectives, the desired amount of coverage, and the activities of direct competition. Media plans must be developed to achieve maximum effectiveness. These plans must closely consider the target markets to blend the media to achieve the desired results. Media scheduling includes the following approaches: continuous, flighting, and pulsing advertising.

External advertising media include newspapers, magazines, radio, television, direct mail, outdoor, Internet, and supplemental advertising. Each of these media has its appropriate uses, advantages, drawbacks, and techniques that are generally successful. An understanding of advertising terms allows a manager to communicate more intelligently with media and advertising agency personnel.

Finally, social media is fast becoming a necessary component for all hospitality and travel firms. The various types of social media include blogs and microblogs, social networks, media sharing, and wikis or collaborative projects. There are various types of social media users based on their levels of viewing and participation. It is important for hospitality and travel firms to understand the users and develop strategies using various social media to reach these users. After implementing these strategies, their impact should be monitored and measured using common metrics to determine the level of success.

KEY TERMS AND CONCEPTS

Brochures

Collateral materials

Continuous advertising

Flighting media scheduling

Media planning process

Pulsing advertising

Social media

Social network

Specialty advertising

QUESTIONS FOR REVIEW AND DISCUSSION

1 **What factors affect the selection of advertising media?**

2 **Discuss the media planning process. What are the steps involved?**

3 **What are the advantages and disadvantages of each of the major media types?**

4 **Cite and discuss techniques for successful print advertising and for developing copy for print advertising.**

5 **What are the methods of media scheduling? Which one do you consider the best? Why?**

6 **Compare and contrast the various types of media based on their respective characteristics.**

7 **What are the most common types of social media?**

⑧ Discuss the types of social media users and how you would target them if you were organizing a special event such as the Boston Marathon.

⑨ What specific types of social media platforms would you use if you wanted to promote your new bed and breakfast?

⑩ How would you measure the impact of a Twitter campaign to increase the awareness of your new restaurant?

NOTES

[1] David W. Nylen, *Marketing Decision-Making Handbook* (Englewood Cliffs, NJ: Prentice-Hall, 1990), p. G-150.

[2] Howard A. Heinsius, "How to Select Advertising Media More Effectively," in *Strategic Marketing Planning in the Hospitality Industry*, ed. Robert L. Blomstrom (East Lansing, MI: Educational Institute of the American Hotel and Motel Association, 1983), pp. 256–258.

[3] Outdoor Advertising Association of America, Resource Center, 2014. www.oaaa.org/ResourceCenter/MarketingSales/Factsamp;Figures/Revenue/TopOOHSpenders.aspx.

[4] Andreas M. Kaplan and Michael Haenlein, "Users of the World, Unite! The Challenges and Opportunities of Social Media," *Business Horizons*, 53(1), p. 61.

[5] Dave Chaffey. "Global social media research summary 2016," *Smart Insights*, February 16, 2016, www.smartinsights.com/social-media-marketing/social-media-strategy/new-global-social-media-research/.

[6] Ashley Zeckman, "5 Social Media User Types and Tips for Marketers to Connect with Each One," *TopRank Online Marketing Blog*, 2012, www.toprankblog.com/2012/11/5-social-media-user-types/.

[7] Pring, Cara. 2012. "216 Social Media and Internet Statistics." September 15. www.thesocialskinny.com/216-social-media-and-internet-statistics-september-2012/.

[8] Kodak's Chief Blogger, "10 Social Media Tips," *Social Media Tips*, Kodak, 2009, p. 6.

[9] Nichole Kelly, "4 Ways to Measure Social Media and Its Impact on Your Brand," *Social Media Examiner*, June 15, 2010, www.socialmediaexaminer.com/4-ways-measure-social-media-and-its-impact-on-your-brand/.

chapter review

INTERNET CASE STUDY

Social Media Use by Restaurants

Identify several of your favorite restaurants (both chains and independent operations) in your college/university town and/or where you permanently reside with your family (if different). Next, search for information about that restaurant using a basic search engine and the common types of social media (e.g., Facebook, Twitter, YouTube, and Flickr). Finally, determine the level of social media use by the various restaurants you have chosen and create a spreadsheet detailing the types being used. Also, record some details regarding the level of social media use. Does the level of social media use differ between large chains and independent restaurants? If so, explain how.

1. Does the level of use differ by location (e.g., large city, small city, college town, etc.), especially for restaurants that are independently owned and operated? Why or why not?

2. Do you think the use of social media would be more prevalent in the hotel industry or the restaurant industry? Explain your answer.

3. What other hospitality and travel organizations would benefit the most from using social media? Can you think of any type of hospitality organizations that would not see much of a benefit to using social media?

CASE STUDY

Advertising Decisions for the Alexandria Inn

Bill Walker is a co-owner of the Alexandria Inn, an independently owned casual restaurant located in an urban area in the southeastern United States. The city in which the Alexandria Inn is located has a year-round population of 200,000 that increases to nearly 350,000 during the tourist season, which lasts for 6 months each year, with the peak being in the summer months. The restaurant has seating for 200, divided between three separate dining areas. An additional 45 seats are in the lounge area. There is currently no outside seating, although Bill has considered adding an outside dining area. During the most recent fiscal year, the restaurant had annual sales totaling $2.1 million, of which 70 percent was food, with the remaining 30 percent representing alcoholic beverages. There is a modest amount of offsite catering, which accounts for $125,000 annually.

The Alexandria Inn, which Bill and his co-owners developed as a mid-priced restaurant, competes with several national chains located within a 2-mile radius. These chains include Macaroni Grill, Chili's, and TGI Friday's, all of which are quite successful. During the last year, Bill has noticed that each of these national chains has been much more aggressive in advertising and promotions. These and other regional and national chains are running advertisements on a continuous basis, both on radio and in print, as well as pulsating advertising on television. Most of this television advertising is during the period of high tourist demand. In addition to their use of advertising, these chains offer nearly constant promotions of one or more items on their menus, and are again more aggressive during the height of the tourist season.

Bill asserts that the target market for the Alexandria Inn consists of more than 125,000 people who live within an 8-mile radius of the restaurant. About 40 percent of the restaurant's business comes during the lunch period, and the largest demand during lunch is from individuals who work within 2 miles of the restaurant. Bill has cultivated a strong demand from several corporate office parks located near the restaurant. His strategy asserts that this demand is more consistent than catering to tourists. His goal is to keep a more even demand throughout the entire year, something that focusing on tourists as his primary target market would not allow.

Bill's dilemma is quite clear. Should he start to more aggressively advertise and promote the restaurant? If yes, where and how? The restaurant has an ongoing relationship with a marketing and public relations firm that Bill has worked with for the past 3 years. This firm creates and produces all the posters, banners, and similar work used inside the restaurant. In addition, this same firm does all the menu design and production. Bill has been very pleased with their work, and the prices have been quite reasonable.

In recent weeks, Bill has been approached by both another marketing firm and a radio station soliciting his business. The marketing firm has promised a 10 percent discount on all design and production costs. The radio station is offering a commercial package that offers 20 percent more advertising time than regular advertising rates. In order to secure his business, the radio station is willing to tie future advertising rates to documented increases in business at the Alexandria Inn.

Last evening, Bill told his general manager, Chris Williams, that he felt overwhelmed and confused. At times like this he wished that his restaurant were part of a chain so that he could get some help with advertising and promotion. The two of them talked for a while about what to do. They developed the following questions, agreed to think about them, and will meet again in a week to consider options. What should Bill do?

Case Study Questions and Issues

1. As an independent restaurateur, should Bill start advertising?

2. How should Bill achieve his goal of increasing dinner volume by 10 to 15 percent?

3. How should Bill achieve his goal of increasing lunchtime off-site catering by 10 percent?

4. Bill is being given the hard sell by the radio station sales representative. Should he consider advertising in other media, such as print or television? Is direct mail an option he should consider?

5. The Alexandria Inn has a loyal clientele, with approximately 60 percent of the customers being repeat customers. How can Bill best attract more business from this group while bringing in first-time guests?

6. Only about 10 percent of Bill's business comes from tourists visiting the area. Should he advertise to attract this market? If so, how?

case study

14

Sales Promotions and Public Relations

Courtesy LEGOLAND California. LEGO, LEGOLAND, the LEGO and LEGOLAND logos and the brick configuration are trademarks of the LEGO Group and are used here with special permission. 2004 The LEGO Group.

Chapter Objectives

After studying this chapter, you should be able to:

1. Compare and contrast the various types of sales promotions and the advantages and disadvantages associated with their use.

2. Identify merchandising techniques and how they can be used in hospitality and tourism.

3. Discuss the concept of public relations and its role in marketing strategy.

14.1 INTRODUCTION

The hospitality and tourism industry is a people-oriented business. Hospitality operations promote hospitality, yet hospitality cannot be purchased, cannot be traded, and does not appear on the menu. Hospitality is intangible, yet it is absolutely necessary for success. When service personnel project the spirit of hospitality, the results can be dramatic: increased sales, increased profits, increased consumer satisfaction, and, yes, increased employee satisfaction and motivation. Hospitality and tourism companies also sell atmosphere, convenience, entertainment, escape, and social contact. All of these are related to the spirit of hospitality and are equally intangible. All deserve consideration as promotable items. In addition, hospitality and tourism firms are concerned about their images and work hard to maintain good images through advertising and public relations. Unlike advertising, public relations is an objective form of promotion because it isn't sponsored by an organization. The following sections discuss the sales promotions, merchandising, and public relations.

14.2 SALES PROMOTIONS

Sales promotions include marketing activities other than advertising, personal selling, and public relations that attempt to stimulate consumer demand and increase sales. In recent years, most companies have devoted an ever-increasing percentage of their budgets to sales promotions and have reduced the percentage devoted solely to advertising. Sales promotions seek to accomplish several broad objectives and can be used for several reasons:

Sales promotions
Marketing activities other than advertising, personal selling, and public relations that attempt to stimulate consumer demand and increase sales.

- **To increase consumer awareness.** This is the first step in attracting new guests or customers. To attract a guest, one must first stimulate interest and a desire to act. Advertising seeks to increase awareness as well, but sometimes it takes a targeted promotion to turn that awareness into consumer purchasing action.

- **To introduce new products and services.** Every hotel and restaurant launches new products and services. The best way to ensure that the target markets are aware of these products and services is to initiate a special promotion to draw attention to them. When McDonald's or Taco Bell launches a new product, it supports the introduction with extra advertising and special promotions designed to promote trial of the new product. Merely introducing the new product or service to the target markets is not enough; you need to create interest, encourage trial purchases, and stimulate future demand for the new products and services.

- **To increase guest occupancy and customer counts.** With increasing competition in many markets, one of the few avenues for market share growth is to take business away from the direct competition. To accomplish this, it is necessary to feature promotions that offer consumers a better deal or greater value than they can receive elsewhere. Promotions are used to spread the word to potential guests.

- **To combat competitors' actions.** If the direct competition is gaining market share at the expense of your hotel or restaurant, you may be forced to match their promotion or to add one of your own with a new twist. For example, Marriott International was among the first hotel companies to offer a frequent-guest program. This program proved to be so successful that competing hotel chains were forced to offer frequent-traveler programs to compete with Marriott. Each company offered a slightly different program, seeking to gain a competitive advantage and therefore promote brand loyalty.

- **To encourage present guests to purchase more.** Total sales can be increased by packaging (bundling) different products and services at a total price that is less than the cost of purchasing the components separately. Promotions can also be used to encourage guests to trade up to more expensive products and services by offering a discounted price on the more expensive product or service. The primary purpose is to increase sales by encouraging present guests to purchase more.

- **To stimulate demand in nonpeak periods.** All hospitality and tourism operations have periods when demand is weak. Promotions can be used to increase weekend business for a business-oriented hotel or stimulate offseason and shoulder-season business at a resort. Within the food service segment, promotions can be used to increase sales during periods of the day or days of the week when demand is slow. For example, some restaurants stimulate early evening business by offering a discount to senior citizens who dine between 5:00 and 7:00 P.M., when business is often slow. They take advantage of the fact that seniors usually try to dine earlier and are often more conscious of the price–value relationship. Early dining promotions directed at this target market are often quite successful.

14.2.1 Types of Sales Promotions

Push promotional strategy

A sales promotion strategy used to push the product–service mix through the service delivery system or channels of distribution.

Pull promotional strategy

A sales promotion strategy aimed at stimulating the interest of consumers and having them pull the product through the channels of distribution.

Point-of-sale (POS) displays

Advertisements or promotions placed in retail outlets where customers select products in an attempt to stimulate demand through impulse purchases.

Firms use two common strategies within the broad sphere of sales promotion: push promotion and pull promotion. A marketing manager uses the **push promotional strategy** when he or she wants to push the product–service mix through the service delivery system or channels of distribution. This approach encourages increased purchases and increased consumption by consumers. A **pull promotional strategy**, by contrast, is aimed at stimulating consumers' interest and having them pull the product through the channels of distribution. This, in turn, puts additional pressure on the retail outlets or hospitality facilities to supply the products and services most in demand by consumers. Descriptions of some of the more commonly used push and pull techniques follow.

14.2.1.1 TECHNIQUES FOR PUSH PROMOTIONS. There are several common techniques used by firms to create demand through promotion, either to channel members or directly to customers. The following is a list of the most common techniques used for push promotional strategies:

- **Point-of-sale (POS) displays.** The displays usually seen at the counter of fast-food restaurants or as table tents in other types of restaurants, called **point-of-sale (POS) displays**, are designed to stimulate increased sales. Similarly, signs, banners, and table tents are often displayed by hotels in their lobbies, restaurants, and guest rooms.

- **Cooperative advertising.** A national chain normally provides advertising at the national, regional, and local levels to support its outlets. Also, franchisees will often receive financial assistance with local advertising, in addition to the chain's national advertising, as part of the franchise agreement. This practice is called cooperative advertising.

- **Advertising materials.** To encourage the local property to run advertising, the national chain will supply camera-ready advertising materials as well as prepared radio commercials.

- **Traditional and electronic collateral material.** Many firms supplement their other promotional efforts with materials such as brochures, flyers, or directories of other outlets within the chain. Beyond the traditional print collateral materials, firms use Web-based promotions to communicate with current and prospective customers.

- **Convention and owners'/managers' meetings.** National chains use these meetings as a method to introduce new products and services to those who will be working in the individual units. These meetings are used for sales and service training.

14.2.1.2 TECHNIQUES FOR PULL PROMOTIONS. In addition to push promotional strategies, there are several pull promotional strategies that are aimed at building demand for a product by targeting customers directly. The following is a list of the most common pull promotional strategies:

- **Sampling.** This technique can be used effectively by food service managers. For example, samples of menu items can be distributed in the lobby area of a fast-food restaurant or food court, thereby encouraging customers to try the product. The goal is to convert this trial into regular use and repeat purchase. Within the lodging field, this technique is common as well. Meeting planners usually visit the potential hotel meeting site to "sample" the product and service before they make a final decision about the host hotel for an upcoming meeting.

- **Price reduction promotions.**   Price reductions for a limited time can encourage trial business and increase sales. Many business-oriented hotels that are normally busiest Monday through Thursday have used weekend price reductions to increase volume during otherwise slow periods. By promoting getaway weekends at discounted prices, these hotels built weekend business. Chains such as Marriott International, Hyatt Hotels and Resorts, and Hilton Worldwide have used this approach very successfully. As with all promotions of this type, restrictions should apply and a definite time period should be stated. By contrast, recreation-oriented hotels, such as Great Wolf Lodges, charge higher prices on the weekend and offer discounts during the week.

- **Coupons.**   These are certificates that entitle the consumer to receive a discount when presented at the retail outlet. Coupons can be distributed in newspapers or magazines, face-to-face, or via direct mail.

- **Combination offers or bundling.**   This involves combining two or more products or services and offering them for less than what they would cost if purchased separately.

- **Premiums.**   Extra merchandise or gifts that the hotel or restaurant gives away or sells at a very favorable price to guests are premiums. Examples include items such as hats, tote bags, glassware, and T-shirts with the logo printed on them. If the hotel or restaurant is able to cover the direct costs of the item, the premium is called *self-liquidating*. Some operations, such as Cheers in Boston or Emeril Lagasse's restaurants, have historically sold a considerable volume of logo merchandise. Frequent-flyer, frequent-guest, and frequent-diner programs are another type of premium that adds value by rewarding consumers in relation to the amount of products or services that they purchase. Recently, some airlines have changed the reward criteria from the number of miles flown to the amount of money spent. Frequent-customer programs have become very popular as a means for firms to build repeat business

Coupons
Certificates that entitle the consumer to receive a discount when presented at the retail outlet.

Premiums
Something that is given away or sold at a reduced cost to bring in new guests, to encourage more frequent visits by current guests, and to build positive word of mouth about the operation.

Nadalina/Shutterstock

Frequent-customer programs are effective for building repeat business.

and brand loyalty. However, these programs do have some drawbacks. For instance, frequent-diner programs can be inexpensive to maintain, but the start-up costs can be high.[1] Also, a great deal of time and effort is required to plan the program's structure and benefits. Customers find ways to "cheat" the program, and restaurants risk alienating customers when changes are made to the programs. Finally, customers may get bored with the program, and it could become difficult to track customer visits and points over time. And, in the case of airlines or hotels, customers redeeming points could displace paying customers during periods of high demand.

Contests
Require some skill on the part of the participant to win prizes.

Sweepstakes
Prizes are awarded solely based on chance.

- **Contests and sweepstakes.**   The attraction of contests and sweepstakes is the highly desirable prizes that consumers can win. There is one minor difference between a contest and a sweepstakes. Contests require some skill on the part of the participant, but sweepstakes are based solely on chance. In all states, non–state-run lotteries are illegal. Lotteries consist of three elements: (1) the element of chance; (2) consideration, or giving something in return—for example, having to make a purchase in order to enter the sweepstakes; and (3) a valuable prize. To avoid illegal activities in most localities, it is necessary to eliminate one of these elements. If a purchase is not required to enter the sweepstakes, it is not classified as a lottery and is therefore legal in most localities. Contests, because they require some skill on the part of the participant, are not considered to be lotteries because there is no element of chance involved.

14.2.2 Commonly Used Techniques

The most common sales promotion techniques in the hospitality and tourism industry are coupons, sampling, premiums, and contests and sweepstakes. The following sections provide a complete discussion of these techniques.

14.2.2.1 COUPONS.   The primary objectives for coupons are to stimulate trial of your products and services by reducing the price, encouraging multiple purchases, and generating temporary sales increases.

Coupons offer several advantages:

- The coupon represents a tangible inducement, offering a savings or benefit.
- The price reduction is for a limited time and will not affect profit margins in the long term.
- Coupons can be used to accomplish specific objectives, such as boosting business during nonpeak periods.
- The maximum cost of the promotion can be calculated in advance. For example, past experience will allow you to estimate the percentage of the coupons likely to be redeemed.

Coupons have disadvantages as well:

- Some employees will be tempted to defraud the business. It is possible for them to take cash and substitute coupons. The higher the value of the coupon, the more supervision is necessary.
- Redemption rates are not easily predicted. Among the environmental factors that can affect the redemption rate are the value of the coupon, timing, and the activities of direct competitors. This is most common with new promotions because there is no prior history on which to predict future coupon redemption rates.

Sampling
Offering products and services for free to create awareness and generate interest.

14.2.2.2 SAMPLING.   Encouraging trial of new products is the primary objective of sampling. If consumers will at least try the product, they are more likely to purchase it in the future. Sampling is also an excellent way to persuade consumers to trade up to more expensive products and services. Sampling can be tied in with other types of promotions. For example, quick service restaurants in food courts often provide free samples of menu items to lure customers to choose them over the competition. Airlines may offer free WiFi the first few minutes after takeoff to entice consumers to purchase the service for the remainder of the flight. Offering free samples is one of the most effective ways to get consumers to try a product.

Sampling offers these advantages:

- Getting consumers to try the product is superior to getting them to look at an advertisement. It provides the consumer with instant feedback.
- Sampling represents value to the consumer. Many consumers like to think that they can get something free. For example, including small portions of entree and appetizer items in the free offerings during "happy hours" is an excellent way to stimulate dining-room business.

Some disadvantages of sampling include:

- Giving away products can become a major expense if it is done for an extended period of time.
- Samples of food products must be served when they are freshly prepared. If the products are to be held for any period of time, care must be taken to ensure that the quality can be maintained.

14.2.2.3 PREMIUMS. Premiums—items that are given away—are used to bring in new guests, to encourage more frequent visits by current guests, and to build positive word of mouth about the operation.

Advantages include the following:

- Most consumers like to get something for nothing or for a good price. It helps to build goodwill for your business, especially if the premium is highly valued by the consumer.
- If the premium is clever or unique, it will build positive word of mouth as consumers tell others where they found it. When your logo is included on the premium, the message is always in front of the consumer.

Disadvantages of premiums include:

- Storing and handling the premium items can be a challenge if they are large or bulky.
- Employees and others may take the premiums for their own use or for their families and friends.
- The quality of the premium must be equal or superior to the image of the hospitality facility. If the premium does not work properly or breaks, it will diminish the image the consumer has of the facility organization.
- Anticipating demand for premiums is difficult. If they are to be advertised as being available, it is imperative that a sufficient inventory be maintained so that consumers are not disappointed. Raising expectations and then not delivering will result in negative consumer perceptions.

14.2.2.4 CONTESTS AND SWEEPSTAKES. Contests and sweepstakes are being used with increasing frequency, especially within the more competitive segments of the industry such as fast food. They are designed to increase the number of customers and build market share, often at the expense of the competition.

Advantages of contests include the following:

- Consumers are more involved in the process because there is some element of skill and thinking required, thereby presenting an opportunity to create and support a more lasting positive image in the consumer's mind.
- Those who enter have already shown an interest in your products and services and are more likely to purchase them. This eliminates the potential for chance winners who do not usually purchase the product.

Disadvantages of contests include these:

- There can be some difficulty in judging entries because the criteria are often subjective. Those selected to judge must take the responsibility seriously, because the contestants will be serious about the outcome.

- Often the rules and guidelines for the contest are lengthy and may turn off potential participants.

The advantages of sweepstakes include the following:

- Entry is very easy; no purchase is necessary. The names and addresses of those who enter can be stored in a database and used in future direct-mail advertising efforts.
- Because the rules are usually quite simple, attention can be focused on the prizes in advertising.
- Sweepstakes will attract more participants than contests because it is easier to enter. No skill is involved, and it takes little time or effort to complete the entry.
- Selection of the winner is easy and judging is not required.

Disadvantages of sweepstakes include these:

- The entry box may be stuffed. It is possible for a consumer to reproduce the entry blank and enter thousands of times. For this reason, the rules should prohibit mechanical reproduction of the entry forms.
- An individual's chances of winning the large prizes are very small, so people may get discouraged and not enter.

14.2.3 Managing Successful Promotions

When developing a sales promotion campaign, the marketer must consider several major aspects. First, it is necessary to determine the size of the incentive that has to be offered to get consumers to participate. The larger the incentive, the more likely it is to attract attention. Second, the firm must establish the conditions for participation. Hospitality and tourism firms often limit offers to certain times of day or days of the week. In addition, offers may require reservations in advance and depend on availability. Third, the marketer must determine the timing of the promotion, including its duration. Will it be combined with other promotions, such as advertising? Will it be offered during peak or nonpeak periods? How long will the sales promotion be available?

Finally, it is necessary to determine how consumers will be informed of the promotion, and to estimate the total budget for the promotion. Coupons are normally distributed by mail, and other promotions are advertised at the point of purchase or via some other media vehicle. Coupons can also be distributed via the Internet.

The hospitality industry trade journals are filled with terrific ideas for promotions. There is never a need to reinvent the wheel. Rather, simply modify the ideas that others have used successfully before. Like anything else managers do, developing a promotion calls for careful planning, execution of the plan, and evaluation:

1. **Select the target market for the promotion.** Analyze sales records to determine the most likely target markets for a special promotion, as these segments offer the greatest potential for increased sales.

2. **Establish specific objectives for the promotion.** Objectives should be very specific, detailing exactly what the promotion should accomplish. Desired results should be quantified.

3. **Select the promotional technique.** Based on the situation and the advantages and disadvantages of each of the techniques, select the one best suited to the situation.

4. **Brainstorm about the potential offer.** There are hundreds of excellent ideas. Make a list of those being considered and seek input from others. All potential offers should be examined carefully from two perspectives: the potential appeal to the target market and the potential sales increase in light of the projected costs and expenses.

5. **Create the promotional theme.** This is the area where you can be very creative. What will be included in the promotional copy or tag line? Does it capture the interest of potential guests? Can it be used both internally and externally in the promotion? For a promotion to

achieve the maximum potential, it needs to be carried forward both outside and inside the operation. Externally, it should build business. Internally, it should create excitement among the staff and build morale.

6. **Develop the promotional budget.**   A projection of the total anticipated costs should be prepared to include all internal and external costs. To be able to evaluate the promotion, all costs, both direct and indirect, must be measured. It is wise to project the impact on costs and revenues at several different levels of consumer participation.

7. **Select the advertising media and vehicles to support the promotion.**   Based on your knowledge of the media, those that will best support the total promotional campaign should be contacted. Advertising space and time should be secured.

8. **Develop an implementation timetable.**   Promotions require attention to detail so that all phases are integrated and implemented properly. To accomplish this, a timetable is required. Specific dates should be established for each task. Assigning responsibility to a specific individual or team for the completion of these tasks will increase accountability.

9. **Conduct internal training for the entire staff.**   Just prior to the implementation of the program, the entire staff should be briefed so that they are familiar with the details of the promotion. Items of interest are how long the promotion will last and how the details will be handled by the different members of the staff.

10. **Work the plan.**   Put the promotional plan into action and follow the timetable.

11. **Monitor results.**   Feedback should be followed very carefully and should be compared with the timetable. Are things progressing as planned? Is the level of consumer participation within the projected range? Are the staff members working as planned? Attention to detail is very important. All information collected should be retained for future use in other promotions.

14.2.4   Evaluating the Impact of Sales Promotions

Several elements of a sales promotion must be evaluated in order to determine the actual impact of the final promotion. The following is a brief description of the major elements.

14.2.4.1 ADMINISTRATIVE COSTS ASSOCIATED WITH CONDUCTING A SALES PROMOTION.   Some costs are directly related to conducting a sales promotion, such as printing, mailing, and advertising. The firm should estimate these fixed costs prior to launching a sales promotion.

14.2.4.2 COST OF DISPLACED SALES.   A certain number of customers would have consumed the service at the regular price. When these customers participate in a promotion, such as a coupon or some other form of price discount, the firm loses revenue equal to the difference in price multiplied by the number of consumers. For example, some consumers order pizza delivery from the same provider time after time. If the firm offers a $1-off coupon that is redeemed by 200 regular customers, the firm loses $200 in revenue.

14.2.4.3 ADDITIONAL REVENUE FROM NEW CUSTOMERS.   One of the main objectives of sales promotions is to induce new customers to accept a trial offer, with the eventual goal of having them become repeat customers. Any revenue received from new customers is positive and will offset the administrative costs and losses from displaced sales. For example, the pizza delivery restaurant may have had 200 new customers pay an average of $10 per order, resulting in additional revenue in the amount of $2,000. In that example, after accounting for displaced sales, this would leave $1,800 to cover the administrative costs of offering the promotion.

It is important for firms to consider all these costs to determine the necessary budget, as well as the viability of a particular sales promotion. The elements listed earlier are short term in nature and should be evaluated in conjunction with the potential long-term effects of having additional customers. The increase in revenues may be accompanied by a decrease in unit costs as the overall volume increases. In some cases, a hospitality or tourism firm may be content to break even or actually lose some money on a sales promotion in the short run in order to achieve its long-term objectives.

14.3 MERCHANDISING

Hospitality is a form of retail business. A sincere effort should be made to merchandise hospitality services to consumers when they enter the establishment or visit the website. Therefore, merchandising involves any practice or activity that leads to the sale of products and services to retail customers. This includes product design, pricing, packaging, point-of-sale displays, promotions, and advertising. In addition to the regular promotional practices, it is becoming more common to see hotels and restaurants selling branded merchandise as well. For example, even independent restaurants and bars are selling T-shirts, hats, golf accessories, and other items with the company's name and logo like the popular chains have been doing for years (e.g., Bubba Gump Shrimp, Hard Rock Café, Hooters). These items are usually in a display case at the entrance, in a separate store area, or over the bar in plain sight. Similarly, hotels have realized there is a market for branded products such as bathrobes, hats, shirts, and so on.). In fact, Starwood Hotels & Resorts Worldwide even started a "Hotels at Home" online concept store to sell the popular beds, pillows, linens, and blankets used at its Westin and Sheraton hotels to retail customers.

14.3.1 Entertainment

Entertainment can generate increased sales and more satisfied guests. In recent years, entertainment has taken on new forms, including in-room movies and video games, large-screen television and multiscreen sports bars, various forms of disk jockey and music video entertainment, comedy clubs, Podcasts and YouTube, and other types of media entertainment. Many forms of entertainment are suitable, but live entertainment has long been regarded as the most powerful form. When entertainment of any type is selected, the marketing concept should be the paramount concern. Management should focus on the needs and wants of the guests, not their own likes and dislikes. Live entertainment is not the right choice for all hospitality and tourism operations, but it can be considered for some, based on the following factors:

- What impact will the entertainment have on volume, both in sales and in the number of guests?
- Is the physical layout of the facility suitable for live entertainment?
- How will the costs associated with live entertainment, such as payment to performers and increased advertising, be covered?

First, the impact that entertainment will have on sales volume should be analyzed closely. The break-even point should be calculated. Different methods to cover the costs of entertainment are feasible; these include charging higher prices for food and beverage to offset the increased cost, instituting a cover charge or a cover charge and minimum purchase, and covering costs through increased sales. Second, the physical layout of the facility must be examined closely. Is the configuration of the facility suitable for live entertainment and perhaps for dancing? Many operators have learned that their facilities were simply too small for live entertainment—but not until after they had made the commitment.

14.3.2 Other Merchandising Techniques

Many other techniques should be considered. These include brochures and meeting planner guides, directories, flyers, in-house signs, and tent cards. All of these techniques offer a great deal of potential when they are used properly and directed toward the appropriate target audience. For example, brochures are not as easy to design as one might think. When brochures are placed in a rack with others, it becomes clear how difficult it is to design a brochure that will stand out from the others, capture the potential consumer's interest, and spark further inquiry or action. If a brochure is able to accomplish this, it truly is successful. The following is a list of tips that can be used to create an effective brochure:

- **Understand your customer.** It is important to know your customers' wants and needs, and the salient attributes used in making a decision.

- **Use visuals and colors to enhance the brochure.** You should include your logo and company colors to support your branding efforts. The visuals should be high quality images and provide a good representation of your product.

- **Focus on readability.** Make sure your brochure is easy to read and keep the number of different fonts to a minimum (three at most). Use short paragraphs that focus on a specific objective, and bullet points to focus on key features.

- **Include important information.** There is limited space on a brochure that can be used to provide basic facts and sell your product. Make sure you have the information that will help customers evaluate your product and differentiate it from your competitors. Also, include all of your contact information, including your website address.

- **Remember to sell.** The main purpose of the brochure is to get customers to buy your product. Use the brochure to persuade customers to act by focusing on the benefits of your product.

14.4 PUBLIC RELATIONS

The term *public relations* is widely misunderstood and is often misused within business, and the hospitality and tourism business is no exception. Every business interacts with a variety of publics: consumers, the general public, the financial community, the organization's employees, government, the media, suppliers, and many others. **Public relations** is the process by which the relationships with each of these publics is managed. All businesses must realize that the general public is affected by everything that companies say and do. Public relations are most obvious in the event of a disaster, such as a hotel fire, but public relations encompass many other facets, and can and should take a positive tone. The following section will discuss aspects of public relations, effective techniques for managing public relations, important guidelines for effective public relations, and a specific application of public relations: the opening of a hotel.

It requires great skill to effectively manage public relations, which is why many firms use external consultants and agencies to assist them with this effort. Public relations should be an integrated part of the overall marketing plan. Just as objectives, strategies, tactics, action plans,

Public relations
A nonpersonal stimulation of demand for a product or service by providing commercially significant news about the product or service in a published medium or obtaining favorable presentation in a medium that is not paid for by the sponsor.

Courtesy of Brennan's Restaurant. The Brennan's logo is a registered trademark.

It is important for brochures to include valuable information, as well as pictures and a logo.

target audiences, implementation schedules, and methods for evaluation are a part of the development of a marketing plan, the same approach should be applied to public relations. Positive and beneficial public relations do not just happen by chance; they must be the result of individuals making it happen according to a plan. One of the basic needs of public relations is for the organization to provide accurate information. The development of a press kit can help accomplish this goal. Here are the essential components of a typical hotel press kit:[2]

- **Fact sheet.** This should contain basic information such as property name, address, telephone number, names of contact personnel, a list of hotel facilities and amenities, and detailed specifications for meeting facilities.

- **Description of the local trading area.** This should include the geographic location of the facility and its proximity to the city or town where it is located.

- **Special features of the product–service mix.** This should include the main features of the facility and how they would add value for, or benefit, consumers.

- **Specific details about the product–service mix.** This should provide information about each of the components of the hotel, including guest rooms, meeting facilities, restaurants, and recreation facilities.

- **Photographs.** Stock photographs should be maintained of both the exterior and interior of the facility, showing the facilities being used by guests.

- **Biographical sketch of the general manager.** Provide a brief biography of the general manager, including items of particular interest in his background and experience.

The press kit is useful when interacting with members of the media, as well as the other publics. Table 14.1 provides a list of members of the media with whom public relations personnel should be familiar.

14.4.1 Public Relations Techniques

Public relations can be applied in several ways. Some of the more common techniques include the following:

- **News releases.** These should be routinely sent to the media, providing information about people and events of potential interest. Certainly, not all the releases will result in positive coverage, but some will.

PRINT MEDIA	BROADCAST MEDIA
City editor	Station manager
Food editor	News director
Travel editor	Assignment editor
Finance editor	Reporters
Style section editor	
Travel editor	
Business editor	
Feature columnists	

TABLE 14.1 • Public Relations Media Contacts

- **Photographs.** These will be particularly effective if they feature a famous personality or create a human-interest angle.

- **Letters, inserts, and enclosures.** Letters might be sent to government officials urging them to take some type of action. Inserts can be used as envelope stuffers in employee paychecks, or they can be sent as follow-up correspondence to guests or clients.

- **House newsletters.** These can be both internal and external but should be focused on a specific target audience. The purpose is to communicate positive images, increase sales, and influence public opinion.

- **Speeches and public appearances.** Members of the management staff should speak before groups with either professional or civic applications. Special care should be taken to ensure that the speech is well prepared and delivered.

- **Posters, bulletin boards, and exhibits.** These help draw attention to your organization.

- **Audiovisual materials.** CDs, DVDs, or flash drives with presentations can be distributed to the media and travel professionals.

- **Open houses and tours.** Inviting the media and travel professionals to your property can increase awareness and create interest.

14.4.2 Guidelines for Public Relations

It is difficult to provide a complete list of possible public relations techniques. However, the following guidelines offer several good ideas for increasing the effectiveness of public relations activities:

- Always identify individuals in photographs when submitted so that the recipient does not play "editor's bingo" in guessing who's who. Send photos only of people involved, not the person making the announcement. In group shots, identify individuals from left to right, standing, and so on.

- Do not fold, staple, crease, or otherwise mutilate photos, or write on the front or back with a heavy hand, thereby damaging the photo.

- Know the publications that you send material to so that you do not waste your company's money or the editor's time. Do not develop a reputation for sending out worthless material, or your important releases may one day be overlooked or discarded.

- Always provide pertinent information such as the company's name and address (not just the public relations or ad agency's name and address), retail price, or cost of the product so that the reader can evaluate its appeal and marketability, and so on. Stick to the facts—no puffery.

- Do not send too many releases at one time and then complain that the publication did not select "the most important one." If one is more important from a marketing standpoint, send it separately or properly identify it. It is really best to space out releases. Few publications maintain files of releases, because they receive hundreds each week.

- Be brief and provide a summary of the release so that it can be judged quickly (and properly) by someone who is not an expert in your field. Complete information can be briefly stated without reams of company history!

- Do not threaten editors with loss of advertising if they do not run your items or bait them with promises of advertising if they do.

Public relations requires careful planning and attention to detail. Unlike advertising, in which the sponsor controls the content and the timing of the message, public relations requires coordination with many other parties. These parties do not have the interests of the hotel or restaurant as their primary objective. Therefore, hospitality and travel firms cannot control the actual content of the message, but they do their best to maintain good relationships with the travel media to avoid negative publicity.

14.4.3 Evaluating Public Relations

As with the other promotional program elements previously discussed, it is important to evaluate the effectiveness of the public relations effort. In general, public relations programs are effective because they cost little (in both relative and absolute terms), are not subject to the same clutter as advertising and sales promotions, and have the ability to generate interest in a firm's product or service. Also, when the source is credible, well-managed public relations programs can improve the image of the firm. However, the firm does not determine the message that is sent to consumers because there is no exchange of money, and the publicity can be negative.

The public relations efforts of firms need to be evaluated to ensure an effective long-term program. The following is a list of possible methods that can be used to evaluate these programs:

- **Personal observation.** All members of a firm should take an active interest in the image that is being portrayed by the media. Both positive and negative publicity should be conveyed to proper authorities within the organization. Some companies hire public relations firms or designate employees to be responsible for this task.

- **Public opinion surveys.** Firms can conduct their own studies of public opinion, or purchase the results of syndicated research performed by independent agencies. These studies enable firms to track their progress over time.

- **Objective measures.** Firms or their representatives can simply count the number of impressions over a certain time period. More specifically, these impressions can be separated into positive and negative categories. Percentages can be calculated for each category as a percent of the total, and the ratio of positive to negative impressions can be examined as well.

Firms should use a combination of all these types of evaluation techniques. As more companies hire public relations firms and organize public relations departments, more emphasis will be placed on this activity. Public relations is no longer considered a passive practice that cannot be controlled by firms.

14.4.4 Types of Media Relations Plans

Communications plan
An overall plan composed of several individual plans designed for each of the target markets or "publics".

A comprehensive communications plan is composed of several individual plans designed for each of the target markets or "publics." It is important that the organization is proactive in its communications rather than merely responding to inquiries as they come in. The sales staff needs to actively seek out and continually explore leads. In addition, the organization should actively listen to its publics in order to determine their wants and needs. There should be an open dialogue between the organization and these publics, including the local community. Finally, it is beneficial to create a theme for the organization that can be consistent throughout all its communications. The theme should fit the organization's unique selling proposition and take advantage of its favorable attributes, thereby supporting its brand and image.

The primary target publics or markets include customers, residents of the local community, investors, the government, and the news media. The major objectives are to increase awareness and interest among the primary target publics, and develop and maintain good relationships with the media so they can help communicate the organization's goals and objectives to the target publics. The communication goals and objectives are achieved through the use of carefully planned strategies. The strategies should utilize a multimedia and multilevel communication approach that consists of a variety of integrated marketing communications activities. These communication tools should involve the target publics or markets in the process and gain their commitment for the desired outcomes. Finally, both qualitative and quantitative research techniques should be used to monitor the communications program and measure the effectiveness and the performance of the campaign.

Organizations are responsible for developing media relations strategies for each of the target publics. The most obvious plan is aimed at the customer markets. The organization should create a separate marketing program, including communications, for each target market. The goal of the customer relations plan is to create awareness and interest in the organization and its products. The customer relations plan details the use of the organization's integrated marketing communications in targeting potential customers. A separate plan is created for each of the organization's various target markets, and various marketing techniques are used for the different types of customers (e.g., individual and organizational buyers).

The community relations plan is developed to create a favorable environment in the local community within which the organization operates.

The stakeholders relations plan is aimed at producing business partnerships and alliances that result in additional revenue and marketing resources for the organization.

The crisis management plan should be launched in the event of natural or manmade disasters, and any other factors that might raise public concerns and/or negatively affect the image of the business and the safety of people. It is important to provide the pertinent facts in a timely manner.

The internal relations plan is aimed at improving employee morale and ensuring a positive and productive work environment. This component of the media relations strategies is normally handled by human resources rather than the sales and marketing department.

Customer relations plan
The component of the communications plan used to market the organization to various consumer segments.

Community relations plan
The component of the communications plan developed to create a favorable environment in the local community.

Stakeholders relations plan
The component of the communications plan developed to foster business partnerships and alliances.

Crisis management plan
The component of the communications plan prepared in the event of a natural or manmade disaster.

Internal relations plan
The component of the communications plan developed to improve employee morale and the work environment.

SUMMARY OF CHAPTER OBJECTIVES

This chapter focused on the important aspect of promotions and public relations. The role of sales promotion was discussed, including increasing consumer awareness, introducing new products and services, increasing guest occupancy and customer counts, combating competition, encouraging present guests to purchase more, and stimulating demand in nonpeak periods.

The two basic types of sales promotion strategies are push and pull. Push strategies attempt to push the product–service mix through the service delivery system, whereas the pull strategy encourages increased purchases and consumption by consumers. Several common techniques were discussed, including coupons, sampling, premiums, and contests and sweepstakes. Recommendations for managing successful promotions were also discussed, and merchandising techniques were reviewed.

The broad field of public relations was introduced. Public relations involve the management of relationships with the publics with which the firm comes in contact. Specific material presented included the development of a public relations press kit as well as the most commonly used public relations techniques. In addition, the types media relations plans were presented.

KEY TERMS AND CONCEPTS

Communications plan
Community relations plan
Contests
Coupons
Crisis management plan
Customer relations plan
Internal relations plan
Point-of-sale (POS) displays
Premiums

Public relations
Pull promotional strategy
Push promotional strategy
Sales promotions
Sampling
Stakeholders relations plan
Sweepstakes

QUESTIONS FOR REVIEW AND DISCUSSION

1 What is the role of sales promotion?

2 What are several of the objectives of sales promotion? Which of these elements do you believe is the most important for an independent restaurateur? For a mid-priced hotel? Why?

3 What is the difference between push and pull promotional strategies? Use an example to illustrate the difference.

4 When and under what conditions would you recommend push and pull techniques? Why?

5 Cite and discuss the pros and cons of each of the major sales promotional techniques discussed in the chapter.

6 If you were given the job of designing and managing a sales promotion, how might you use the guidelines presented in the chapter? What would you do differently? Why?

7 What is public relations? What do public relations personnel do?

8 What are the different types of media relations plans and what is their purpose?

NOTES

[1] Melanie A. Crosby, "Rewarding Regulars: Frequent-Diner Programs Keep Customers Coming Back for More," *Restaurants USA* (September 1998), pp. 12–17.

[2] Jacques C. Cosse, "Ink and Air Time: A Public Relations Primer," *The Cornell Hotel and Restaurant Administration Quarterly* 21, 1 (1980), pp. 37–40.

chapter review

CASE STUDY

Restaurant Sales Promotions

You have just been hired to handle marketing for a small chain of local Mexican restaurants in San Antonio. The chain has five locations scattered throughout San Antonio and sales have slumped over the past 2 years. The owner has asked you to come up with some strategies for improving sales in the short run that will lead to long-term profits as well. One of the strategies you are considering is to offer "deals" to customers in the form of sales promotions, such as coupons. You have come up with three alternatives: (1) put a coupon in the Sunday supplement of the local newspaper, (2) use ValPak, or (3) use Groupon.

Advertising supplements in the Sunday edition of the local newspaper have traditionally been a popular vehicle for restaurant advertising and discount coupons. Normally, restaurants provide cut out coupons for a percentage off a meal, a discounted meal price, or a buy one get one free. ValPak provides a packet of coupons, sometimes including those from competitors, to a zone of houses. For example, a business might pay $500 to reach a zone of 10,000 residents. Then, the retailer provides the discount listed on the coupon at the point-of-sale. There is an expiration date on the coupon, usually a month's duration because the ValPak is issued once a month. The offers on ValPak coupons are similar to the offers in newspaper coupons.

Groupon is a combination of the words *group* and *coupon*. The company offers a "deal-of-the-day" through its website for each of the markets it serves. Basically, customers have the option to sign up for the "deal-of-the-day" offer, and if the required minimum number of customers is met, then they all receive the coupon. The coupon is offered at a discount of the normal price and Groupon keeps half of the money the customer pays for the coupon and the retailer keeps the other half. For example, on Groupon, a restaurant might offer a $20 certificate for $10. Groupon and the restaurant would each get $5 and the restaurant would have to honor the $20 certificate when the customer purchases food at the restaurant.

Case Study Questions and Issues

1. What are the advantages and disadvantages of each alternative?

2. Which alternative has the most downside risk?

3. Which alternative has the best potential for creating repeat business (i.e., long-term profits)?

4. What information would you want before you make the decision?

5. What information would be useful to you after you run the sales promotion?

case study

CASE STUDY

Promotion at Princess Suites

Katherine Jones, Director of Sales and Marketing of the 128-room Indianapolis Princess Suites, strongly subscribes to the 80/20 rule when it comes to marketing. She feels that 80 percent of her business comes from 20 percent of her customers. Katherine has built solid relations with the firms and customers that represent 80 percent of her business. She has established numerous programs and incentives that result in repeat business from these key customers.

The first Princess Suites was built in 1994 outside of Cleveland, Ohio, and the chain has expanded to its current size of 64 hotels. These limited-service hotels offer a queen-size bed or two double beds, two televisions with remote control and 50-channel cable, and a fully equipped kitchen with a two-burner cooking surface, full-size refrigerator, microwave, coffeemaker, and cooking utensils, dishes, and flatware. Also standard for each room are a sofa sleeper, dining table and chairs, and a free local newspaper. Princess Suites offers free local phone calls, broadband Internet connection, voice mail, access to a fax machine, a 24-hour coin-operated guest laundry, an outdoor swimming pool, and a fitness room.

The Indianapolis Princess Suites, located on the south side of Indianapolis, recorded 63.5 percent occupancy last year with a rack rate of $87 single/$92 double. The average daily rate for the past year was $74.21. The hotel is usually sold out on Tuesday and Wednesday nights and occasionally on Mondays and Thursdays. There is little all-suite competition except for a Mickey Suites located across the interstate. Princess Suites provides the same amenities as Mickey Suites in order to directly compete with it. Princess Suites also offers its guests a complimentary breakfast, as well as a happy hour with complimentary beer and wine. Two full-service hotels, the Pacer Inn and the Macron Hotel, are close, but Katherine does not view them as direct competition. The Pacer and Macron both have bell service, restaurants serving three meals a day, room service, and meeting facilities that are not available at the Princess Suites. The rates of both hotels are significantly higher than those at the Princess Suites, according to the latest shopping survey.

Katherine takes advantage of co-op advertising dollars offered by Princess Suites by advertising in *USA Today* and *BusinessWeek*. There is a listing in the AAA book, and she takes out a half-page ad in the Indianapolis yellow pages. A local cable channel has been courting her lately, but she feels that television and the local paper are not effective uses of her money. Katherine has been exploring billboard advertising, but she's not familiar with whether this medium is effective. The Princess Suites website is basic; it is not on par with the competition's websites.

Princess Suites has created a Secretary's Club to reward secretaries when they book the hotel. Every 15 room nights booked at a net rate results in a $15 gift certificate to a local restaurant of their choice. Katherine allows local restaurants to put fliers in the guest rooms in exchange for $45 worth of gift certificates per month. She also purchases additional certificates from the restaurants as needed. Last year alone, she distributed more than $1,200 worth of certificates to the Secretary's Club, which she sees as 1,200 room nights she would not have sold without the club.

Chris Wood, the GM of Princess Suites, believes that Princess Suites must develop a promotion that will result in increased sales on Friday through Monday nights, which the hotel rarely sells out and in general has low demand. The business traveler, representing the 80 percent group, provides excellent volume during the week. Chris has challenged Katherine to develop a promotion that will increase weekend volume and increase occupancy and sales at the Princess Suites.

Case Study Questions and Issues

1. What steps might Katherine take to respond to Chris Wood's request for a promotion to increase weekend business?

2. How might Katherine develop a promotional strategy using the steps outlined in the chapter?

3. What would be reasonable financial results for the promotion? How did you determine these results?

4. What costs will Katherine incur in launching such a promotion?

5. How can Katherine ensure that the promotion will not adversely impact business from her current key customers?

Personal Selling

Courtesy of Pacific Edge Hotel, A Joie de Vivre Hotel, Laguna Beach, California.

Chapter Objectives

After studying this chapter, you should be able to:

1. List the types of sales roles in the hospitality industry.

2. Identify the basic markets for hospitality group sales and discuss their decision factors.

3. Describe the four stages of the personal selling process.

4. Explain how to use common personal selling tools.

5. Discuss ethical issues related to personal selling.

15.1 INTRODUCTION

In the competitive world of hospitality sales and marketing, the ability to effectively identify potential business, qualify the prospects, engage in personal selling activities, and eventually book the business is critical to the success of the property. The term *selling* is often used synonymously with the term *marketing*. Marketing encompasses all of the activities that are necessary in creating an exchange between a buyer and a seller. These activities include promotion, pricing, product design, and distribution. Personal selling is merely one component of the promotion mix, which refers to the personal communication of information to persuade a prospective customer to buy something (e.g., a product or service) that satisfies that individual's needs.[1] The range of activities that are under the umbrella of personal selling is quite broad. Sales managers communicate with clients and prospects by means of the telephone, personal sales calls resulting from appointments, cold sales calls without appointments, and contacts with clients at trade shows, professional meetings, and conventions.

15.1.1 Sales Roles

Sales jobs can vary widely in their nature and requirements, even within the same company or industry. This chapter focuses mainly on hotel sales, but the fundamentals and techniques can apply to any type of hospitality or tourism sales. One of the main factors that can be used to classify sales positions is the extent to which the salesperson is responsible for creating sales and developing new accounts. Order takers are salespeople who ask customers what they want or respond to purchasing requests. This type of salesperson is most common in organizations that have high demand for their products and services, or organizations that engage in a great deal of mass advertising and use the pull strategy for promotion. In other words, customers seek them out. Order getters are salespeople who are responsible for creating sales and developing new accounts. They still service their existing accounts, but they are also expected to use sales strategies to obtain new accounts.

> **Order takers**
> Salespeople who attend to customer inquiries and repeat purchases.

> **Order getters**
> Salespeople who are responsible for creating sales and developing new accounts.

Many resort hotels and luxury properties enjoy good demand and have many repeat customers. The salespeople in these establishments are able to spend more time in the office responding to inquiries and following up with repeat customers. The goal is to create a good mix of customers who will maximize the firm's potential revenue over the long run. Conversely, hotels that do not have high demand because of various components of their product–service mixes find it more challenging to obtain group business. When there is excess room capacity, lodging facilities require salespeople to be good order getters and create sales. However, some hotels do not target group markets, and even with excess capacity, they choose to have only one or two people responsible for taking orders and not actively soliciting business.

Some firms employ both order takers and order getters to obtain a customer mix. For example, telemarketing systems use the hotel's telecommunication technology, and trained personnel conduct marketing campaigns aimed at certain target markets. Hotels advertise a toll-free number that can be used by customers to contact the hotel. When calls are received, they are sent through the proper channels. Transient customers can be handled by reservations, and group business can be directed to the sales department. Once the call is in the sales department, it can be determined whether to use an order taker or an order getter. Hotels that focus on group business tend to have separate toll-free numbers for the sales department.

> **Telemarketing**
> The use of telecommunication technology to conduct marketing campaigns aimed at certain target markets.

A sales blitz is another type of personal selling activity that targets specific groups within a condensed time frame. A sales blitz can be done in person or over the telephone, and hotels will often use staff members from different departments within the hotel. The goal of most sales blitzes is to make a large number of sales calls in a short period of time, with the objective of generating as large a number of qualified potential buyers as possible. Blitzes are often used to requalify prior clients who have not booked any business for a year or more.

> **Sales blitz**
> A selling activity that targets specific groups within a condensed time frame.

The importance of sales has increased as the competitiveness of the group meetings business has intensified. Today, through the efforts of the major hotel corporations and professional associations such as the Hospitality Sales and Marketing Association International (HSMAI), sales and marketing professionals employed within the hospitality and tourism industry are better trained than ever before. They have to be to remain successful.

15.1.2 Profile of a Successful Salesperson

What makes a salesperson successful? A profile of a successful salesperson would reveal several factors that contribute to the individual's success. Courtesy pays a big part in making an individual successful. It is imperative that the sales manager always strives to make certain that the client is satisfied. This means having to expend some extra effort or occasionally doing something that is not routine. It might even mean bending the rules or standard operating procedures to ensure client satisfaction. Courtesy also means being able to smile and handle a difficult situation even when those around you are angry or in a panic.

A second aspect in the profile of a successful salesperson is complete knowledge of the product–service mix that is being sold. The salesperson should understand every aspect of the operation and should be able to answer any questions that the prospect might raise. For example, hotel salespeople should be knowledgeable about all facets of the hotel, including items such as meeting-room setup, booking policies and procedures, weight capacity of freight elevators, audiovisual capabilities of the hotel, and food and beverage skills and talents of the hotel's staff. However, if the salesperson is not able to provide the information requested by a customer or prospect, the salesperson should know where to get the information, or refer the customer to the right person.

A third part of the profile is professional appearance and behavior. This does not mean that the individual needs to be a "pretty face." Rather, this requires professional clothing, such as business suits, and good personal grooming. First impressions are critical in selling, and professional appearance can be a real asset in establishing rapport with a prospective client.

The desire and willingness to work is a fourth characteristic in the profile of a successful salesperson. Only a small percentage of sales calls and contacts will result in sales or signed contracts. A successful salesperson must have the perseverance to keep going and to keep asking for the business, even when many others have said no. Keep in mind that if one call out of ten results in a signed contract, a sales manager has been told no nine times before making a sale. For this reason, when a prospect says no, the sales manager should give a reply of "Thank you," knowing that the next prospect might say yes. A conversation with one of the leading salespeople for a major manufacturing company revealed an interesting philosophy when he stated, "I'm not in sales, I'm in rejections. I get rejected a lot more than I make sales."

Another quality that is a real asset in sales is organizational ability. Keeping in constant communication with dozens of clients and keeping all the many separate details straight requires superior organization. Also, there are several contact management software programs such as Act, Maximizer, or Microsoft Outlook that make it relatively easy for sales managers to maintain profiles for each of their clients. In addition, contact management capability is often part of the sales and catering software used in hotels and other meeting facilities. The ability to recall names and faces is also important. When a salesperson meets clients, it is imperative to remember their names, the company they work for, and other pertinent details. Following up with trace dates and the details of each client's contract calls for superior organizational skills.

A final quality that is an asset to the successful salesperson is a strong personality. This does not mean that to be successful in sales, you must be extroverted and the life of the party. Rather, it means that you need to have some warmth, some empathy, and the ability to make others believe in and trust you. If prospects do not feel comfortable with the salesperson, it is very unlikely they will make a purchase. Numerous articles detail the traits shared by successful salespeople: They tend to be persistent, resourceful, effective at multitasking and managing time, they ask good questions, and they are good listeners. Hotel sales and marketing is a dynamic environment in which to work. It is demanding and full of challenges, but the rewards are commensurate with the efforts required. In the hotel industry, salespeople are normally referred to as *sales managers,* and the person responsible for the sales function is referred to as the *director of sales.* In larger hotels, the director of sales reports to the *director of marketing,* and in some smaller hotels the two positions are combined into a *director of sales and marketing.* The remainder of the chapter will explore aspects of hotel sales and personal selling.

15.2 SELLING TO GROUP MARKETS

Before a single telephone call or personal sales call is made, the sales manager must begin to develop a clear understanding of the nature of the buyer: the meeting planner. **Meeting planners** plan meetings that will be attended by all sorts of individuals who are part of a vast array of groups, from large national associations to small local civic groups. Many meeting planners, especially those representing large associations and companies, are very knowledgeable professionals. They usually know as much or more about the operation of a hotel than an entry-level sales manager. At the other extreme are those individuals who only occasionally plan meetings and whom the sales manager must educate, as well as sell. Such is the challenge faced by the sales and marketing team—selling to many different individuals, each holding the title of meeting planner. Chapter 3 covers some of the complexities of organizational buying behavior when dealing with large-volume sales and buying units composed of more than one individual.

If sales managers are to effectively sell to the meeting planner, several things are necessary. First, sales managers must thoroughly understand the product–service mix that they are representing. They must know everything or be able to find the answers quickly to questions raised by the meeting planner. Second, they must know how to sell. Selling is a skill that is first learned and then refined. Few individuals are born to be in sales; for nearly everyone, selling is a learned skill. Selling in the hospitality industry is just like selling in other industries, especially service industries. One must learn to sell effectively.

Meeting planners
A person who organizes and plans meetings that will be attended by groups of individuals.

15.2.1 FAB Selling Technique

One of the most common approaches to selling is to focus on the benefits that a product or service offers consumers. In selling benefits, the salesperson relates a product's benefits to the consumer's needs by stressing its features and advantages. This technique can be referred to as the **FAB selling technique.** The *F* refers to product *features,* or the physical characteristics of the product. The *A* refers to the *advantages,* or performance characteristics, that will be of benefit to the buyer. And finally, the *B* refers to the *benefit,* or favorable outcome, that the buyer experiences. In other words, salespeople take the product's features and demonstrate how they can be advantageous to the buyer, resulting in the end benefit that is being sought. Table 15.1 summarizes the components of the FAB selling technique. This technique will be described using a hotel as an example.

FAB selling technique
FAB is a common selling approach that focuses on the features, benefits, and advantages that a product or service offers consumers.

15.2.1.1 FEATURES. All products have physical characteristics such as price, shape, color, and size. Hotel services are no exception. In the past, many firms attempted to sell products and services based on features, until they realized that it was more effective to focus on the benefits provided by the product or service. Many hotels have front desks, guest rooms, restaurants, pools, meeting facilities, and parking lots. Consumers can fill their basic needs at any of these establishments, but those that are superior in terms of performance have a competitive advantage when it comes to benefiting consumers. Figure 15.1 is an example of a **property analysis checklist** that can be used to evaluate a hotel's basic features.

Property analysis checklist
A form used to evaluate a hotel's basic features such as location, guest-room accommodations, meeting facilities, general facilities and services, and transportation.

TYPE OF CHARACTERISTIC	DEFINITION	IMPACT ON LARGE SALES
Features	Describe facts, data, and product characteristics	Neutral or slightly negative
Advantages	Show product strengths in relation to competitors' products	Slightly positive
Benefits	Show how product meets the customer's needs	Very positive

TABLE 15.1 • Summary of FAB Selling

Location

 Rural or urban; location within city or town

 Type of area: industrial, agricultural, political

 Accessibility by highway and major carrier; by membership

 Facilities for sharing and overflow; attractions for free time

Guest-Room Accommodations

 Total number and amount that can be committed; when they can be committed

 Types of rooms: singles, doubles, suites, and so on; special rooms: nonsmoking, handicapped-accessible

 Rate schemes: rack rates, discounted rates (volume, time of purchase, etc.), upgrades

General Facilities and Services

 Public dining and lounge facilities

 Entertainment, recreation, and fitness facilities

 Business or corporate services: faxing, copying, shipping, and so on.

 Other services: room service, valet parking, laundry, and so on.

Meeting Facilities

 Total number and dimensions of meeting rooms; possible setups

 Location and dimensions of exhibit areas

 Equipment: tables, podiums, audiovisual, and so on.

 Banquet rooms and reception areas

Outside Facilities and Services

 Restaurants and tourist attractions

 Sports and recreation facilities (e.g., golf and tennis.)

 Additional business services

Transportation

 Mass transit and taxis

 Rental cars, charters, and sightseeing vehicles

FIGURE 15.1 • **Property analysis checklist.**

15.2.1.2 ADVANTAGES. After the basic features are determined, it is necessary to compare these features with those of the competitors' offerings to assess a firm's strengths and weaknesses. This analysis provides salespeople with the information that they need to persuade buyers. The salespeople should focus on the firm's strengths or the advantages associated with the product, and should stress its benefits to the consumer. However, it is important to determine consumers' needs and the benefits that they are seeking. Hotel chains train salespeople to know the property's physical characteristics, but it is also necessary to train them to know the property's performance characteristics. For example, the following product advantages could exist:

- The hotel has the best location in town.
- The hotel's restaurant has been rated the best in town.
- The hotel has free or less expensive parking.
- The hotel's banquet facilities are the largest.

- The hotel's guest rooms have been recently renovated.
- The hotel has been given an award for service quality.

As you can see, there are many ways to gain a competitive advantage over the competition. However, it is critical to match a hotel's advantages and benefits with markets that highly value those particular attributes.

15.2.1.3 BENEFITS.   To sell products and services to consumers, salespeople must be able to tell consumers how their needs will be fulfilled. Benefit selling can address a consumer's personal motives by answering the question, "What's in it for me?" In discussing benefits, salespeople should stress the favorable outcomes that will result if the consumer purchases the product or service. To sell effectively, the sales manager must possess a thorough understanding of the needs of the prospective client. He or she should be a professional in identifying client needs and then showing how the hotel's product–service mix will help meet those needs. It is much easier to sell when you are demonstrating how your product–service mix will solve the client's problems than when you are merely trying to push your product–service mix.

Knowledge of the meeting planners' needs begins with background information about the group that the meeting planner represents, as well as the more specific needs directly related to the meeting. For example, the needs of most meeting planners will fall into the following categories: costs, location, image and status, professional service, adaptability and flexibility, and professional operations and management.

If a sales manager is to be successful, he or she must help the meeting planner solve the problems faced in planning the meeting. This includes finding answers to all the critical decisions that confront the meeting planner. The role of the salesperson begins with preplanning, which can be very important if the meeting planner is not experienced. The sales manager can assist the meeting planner with the following:

- Defining the purpose of the meeting and identifying who will attend and the total number of attendees.
- Identifying and managing the expectations of those who will attend the meeting.
- Developing a central theme for the meeting, or themes for specific events within the larger meeting.
- Developing a schedule for the events that are planned.
- Developing a budget for all meeting expenses such as rooms, food and beverage, and other items.
- Developing criteria by which to select a geographic location and hotel site.
- Deciding on first, second, and third most preferred meeting dates.

In most cases, the meeting planner will have already done much of this preplanning before visiting with the hotel sales manager, but even so, the discussion related to some of these issues will serve to qualify the prospective client and establish the meeting planner's expectations.

After the preplanning is completed, the role of the sales manager becomes more critical. The meeting planner needs to make decisions about the type of guest-room accommodations needed. This will include several particulars:

- Determining the total number of rooms that should be blocked, as well as the arrival and departure patterns of the attendees.
- Assessing the need for hospitality suites and suites for VIPs and speakers.
- Making decisions about the billing procedures, such as each guest being responsible for individual charges, all of the charges being billed to a master account, or some combination of the two methods.
- Finalizing a meeting schedule to include the necessary meeting-room configurations, meeting lengths, food and beverage functions, coffee breaks, and the proper audiovisual requirements.

After these issues have been addressed, further discussion with the meeting planner is necessary to work out the details of the meeting-room setups and meeting logistics.

15.2.2   Meetings Market Segments

Selling to any group begins with understanding the needs of the prospective client and then showing the client how your firm's product–service mix can satisfy those needs. To do this well, the sales manager must have a great deal of background information about the client's group, the group's needs, past meeting behavior and patterns, and objectives and plans for future meetings. The second step is to link the features offered by the firm's product–service mix with benefits that the client will find attractive and that will satisfy the client's stated needs and objectives.

Association market segment
A group market consisting of organizations that have members who share a common cause or purpose.

15.2.2.1 ASSOCIATION MARKET SEGMENT.   The association market segment is very broad, ranging from large national and international conventions attended by thousands of individuals to very small but expensive board of directors meetings. When one thinks of the association market, one tends to think of the large conventions, but this is only a small segment of the total associations meeting market. Associations hold several different types of meetings each year, including the following:

- **Annual convention for the entire membership.**   This meeting is usually the largest that the association will hold. It will often include exhibits, especially within the trade association market.

- **Board of directors meetings.**   These are typically held three or four times a year and are often quite elaborate. The expenditures per attendee are higher than for other association meetings.

- **Seminars and workshops.**   Associations provide continuing education for the members, and these meetings are held throughout the year.

- **Committee meetings.**   Associations operate by means of a volunteer committee approach, and each of the committees may need to meet several times a year.

The decision-making process and long lead time for the association market can be quite frustrating for the hotel sales manager. This market segment is often assigned to the most experienced sales manager or the director of sales because that individual's additional experience will prove beneficial in working with this business segment. The meeting planners working with the larger associations are normally quite experienced and professional, so the hotel's representative must be equally knowledgeable and experienced. The decision making is scattered among several people within an association. For example, the meeting planner may decide where to hold small meetings and workshops, but decisions about larger meetings such as annual conventions normally involve the executive committee and/or the board of directors. For this reason, the sales manager must be prepared for a lengthy decision-making process. The initial contact may be with the association's meeting planner, but it may take several weeks or months before the board of directors makes a final decision concerning the location for a large meeting.

The lead time for planning meetings can also be quite long. For the largest of the national associations, it is common for the site of the annual convention to be selected 5 to 10 years in advance. Even smaller associations typically plan their annual conventions 1 to 3 years in advance. This lead time creates some real challenges for the sales and marketing staff. Even if a large annual meeting is booked now, the revenue will not be realized for quite some time in the future.

An association often uses its annual convention as a revenue-producing event; the revenue is then used to fund some of the association's annual operating expenses. For this reason, associations are sensitive about such negotiable items as meeting-room rental, complimentary room policies, food and beverage prices, and, in some cases, room rates. Keep in mind that association attendees will be paying their own expenses to attend meetings and may be very sensitive about prices for guest rooms, suites, and food and beverages.

Another popular component of the association market is the **SMERF group**. This acronym represents a combination of several market segments: social, military, educational, religious, and fraternal. Basically, SMERF groups tend to be nonprofit groups that have limited budgets and volunteer meeting planners (i.e., not professionals). Therefore, these groups tend to be very price-sensitive and do not spend as much on rooms or food and beverages as other associations and corporate groups. Some of the SMERF meetings are small, but the total number of meetings that the SMERF market segment generates makes the overall contribution significant. Also, the SMERF segment is important to hotels because these groups are willing to book rooms during nonpeak periods in order to get a lower price. This allows hotels to maintain a decent occupancy rate and keep more full-time employees.

SMERF group
An acronym for a combination of several market segments: social, military, educational, religious, and fraternal.

15.2.2.2 CORPORATE MARKET SEGMENT.

The **corporate market segment** is very broad and is widely solicited by hotels. This market is quite different from the association market segment. The differences include needs and objectives, the type and number of individuals in attendance, and the lead time required. Corporations hold many more meetings than associations. The meetings tend to be smaller, have a much shorter lead time, are less price-sensitive, are subject to quicker site decisions, and involve fewer individuals in the decision-making process.

Corporate meetings are attractive to hotels for several reasons: They are held throughout the year rather than being concentrated in certain periods or months, and they do not require as extensive a use of meeting rooms as the association market segment. The typical corporation meeting involves fewer than 50 attendees. Types of corporate meetings vary widely, including the following:

Corporate market segment
A group market consisting of employees and stakeholders of corporations that meet to address specific issues related to business operations.

- **Training meetings.** With the advent of new technology, corporations frequently hold meetings to train new staff and provide up-to-date training for current staff. This type of meeting is perhaps the most common. Many hotels located near the offices of major corporations will solicit this type of meeting on a continual basis.

- **Sales meetings.** Most corporations maintain a sales staff that meets on a frequent basis. These meetings serve both to provide information to the sales staff and to motivate them. This is an excellent type of meeting to solicit because the group is normally less concerned about price than other types of organizations. The corporation is concerned about providing attendees with convenience and comfort.

- **New product introduction meetings.** When a corporation introduces a new product, it is often done with great fanfare. The meeting is likely to be attended by dealers, corporate sales staff, and the media. This type of meeting can be very extensive and very price-insensitive.

- **Management meetings.** Management staff often need to get away from the place of business to meet and discuss issues in a quiet environment, where they will not be interrupted by telephones and other office distractions.

- **Technical meetings.** Technical specialists need to meet to discuss items of mutual concern. This type of meeting is less elaborate than the other types of corporate meetings.

- **Annual stockholders meetings.** All publicly held corporations are required to have annual stockholders meetings that may be attended by a large number of individuals. Some food and beverage events associated with this type of meeting can be very extensive.

- **Board of directors meetings.** These meetings are perhaps the most elaborate and expensive, and they often feature extensive food and beverage presentations. They also require more expensive and specialized meeting rooms within the hotel.

Meeting planning within corporations is typically spread among several departments. Larger corporations tend to have many meetings and may have established meeting planning departments. However, in many corporations, meetings are planned by people with other areas of responsibility, such as marketing or human resources. The other alternative is to use an independent

Courtesy Pacific Edge Hotel, A Joie de Vivre Hotel, Laguna Beach, CA.

Corporate meetings often use small breakout rooms.

Incentive trip
An all-expenses-paid vacation offered by corporations to reward employees for outstanding performance.

meeting planner. The decision making is usually rapid and does not involve as many individuals as the association market does. If the meeting planner is not the final decision maker, he or she is usually highly influential.

In addition to business meetings, incentive trips are often planned for corporations' employees as a reward for outstanding performance. Incentive meetings tend to be held at resort properties in exotic locations and aboard cruise liners. In many ways, incentive meetings are similar to association meetings. For instance, location and climate are very important, and there is an emphasis on recreation and relaxation. Also, attendance is voluntary, spouses often attend, and the trips must be heavily promoted to encourage employees to perform well in hopes of "winning" a place on the trip. The lead time for planning incentive trips is a year or more, they last four to five days on average, and they can be attended by anywhere from 10 to 1,000 people (the average is around 100). Business-related meetings are normally scheduled during these incentive trips for tax purposes (participants do not have to report business trips as taxable income), but those meetings are often canceled or ignored by the meeting attendees. However, incentive trips do resemble corporate meetings in that the decision making is centralized, a master account is used for billing, service is important, planners are not price-sensitive, and there are established guarantees for rooms and meals.

15.2.2.3 DECISION FACTORS. The association and corporate markets are natural segments for the group business market in hotels because of their clear distinctions in meeting characteristics. In addition, sales managers need to understand the factors that are important to each meeting planner in selecting a facility.

Convene magazine held a forum with a small group of highly respected meeting planners to discuss important meeting topics.[2] They identified the top 10 most important factors that meeting and event planners consider when selecting a meeting location. The following is a list of the factors in order of importance:

1. Location and accessibility

2. Meeting room capacity

3. Flow and layout of space

4. Quality and capability of AV equipment

5. Room flexibility

6. Décor

7. Intelligent staff, from sales to service

8. Price flexibility

9. Quality of food

10. Participant experience

Once again, it is necessary for salespeople to perform an objective assessment of their properties and facilities based on these factors so that they can devise ways to accentuate their strengths and mitigate the effect of their weaknesses. In other words, they should anticipate the complaints or negative appraisals of their properties from meeting planners and determine ways to deflect their concerns.

15.2.2.4 OTHER MEETINGS MARKET SEGMENTS.
In addition to association and corporate meetings, lodging and food service facilities have other leisure groups that can generate revenue. Banquet and catering facilities (e.g., hotels, restaurants, and country clubs) focus on weddings, reunions, anniversary parties, and other events that are mainly centered on the food component. However, these events can also generate room revenue when held at a lodging facility. The sports market is another leisure segment with the potential for generating revenue. Professional, college, and other amateur teams travel to competitor sites and might have a need for overnight accommodations. Sports events occur throughout the year, but this market segment has some special needs such as late arrival and early checkout.

Another market segment that can be very profitable for lodging and food service facilities is the tour group market. Tour groups can be from the local region or other states, provinces, or other countries. One of the preferred modes of travel for many tour groups is the chartered bus, or motorcoach.

These tours can travel to more than one destination and provide lodging and food service revenues for multiple properties. This market segment is similar to the SMERF segment in that the members tend to be price-sensitive. The tour groups will often stay at limited-service hotels or motels and travel throughout the year.

Courtesy Pacific Edge Hotel, A Joie de Vivre Hotel, Laguna Beach, CA.

Hotels normally book groups of 10 or more through their sales departments.

15.3 THE PERSONAL SELLING PROCESS

As mentioned previously, **personal selling** is an interpersonal process where the seller ascertains, activates, and satisfies the needs and wants of the buyer so that both the seller and the buyer benefit. Selling need not be one-sided; it can satisfy both parties. Prospective clients can derive benefits in that the burden of planning, organizing, and directing the various aspects of a group meeting function is shared by the hospitality firm. For most clients, this is a tremendous relief, as they no longer are directly responsible for the event. Of course, the hospitality firm also benefits through increased sales and profits.

Why should a hospitality firm engage in personal selling? First, it allows the firm to be presented in an interpersonal manner to a prospective client. The sales presentation need not be supported by expensive visual aids. Sales calls and presentations can be as simple as having a sales manager engage in telephone and personal solicitation. These sales calls give the hospitality firm exposure and provide prospective clients with another choice when arranging group meetings and banquet functions. Second, sales calls allow for two-way communication between the hotel sales manager and prospective clients. Prospects are able to ask questions, and the representative has the opportunity to present the hospitality firm more thoroughly than is possible through advertising. The representative can personally demonstrate how the operation will be able to satisfy the specific needs of the prospect.

Sales calls should be made on prospective clients as well as previous clients. Previous clients should receive follow-up calls to cultivate an ongoing business relationship. If the previous experiences did not satisfy the client, there is all the more reason to follow up with a sales call. Perhaps the situation can be corrected and negative word of mouth prevented. Often, mere attention to the client's needs and a sincere effort to improve will be enough to convince the client that the hospitality firm should be given some additional business. The goal is to continually meet or exceed customers' expectations, thereby ensuring their satisfaction.

Three basic types of sales calls are follow-up calls, initiating calls, and blitz calls. *Follow-up calls* are arranged with representatives of groups and organizations that have previously been clients of the hospitality firm. Their main purpose is to remind the client of the firm's willingness to be of service in the future. *Initiating calls* are made to people who have not been clients in the past but represent solid prospects for future business. The purpose of these calls is to create awareness of the products and services and to encourage a site visit so that the prospective client may see firsthand what the facility has to offer. Few bookings are made at the time of initiating calls, but it is the first step in cultivating a better relationship. And, as mentioned earlier, a sales blitz saturates an area by making many times the normal number of *blitz calls* and distributing literature describing the product–service mix. A successful blitz reaches as many potential clients as possible. Sales blitzes often use a varied approach involving not only personal sales calls but also telephone selling, as well as other forms of advertising using the mass media.

Successful salespeople generally focus on four components of successful selling: (1) prospecting and qualifying, (2) planning and delivering sales presentations, (3) overcoming objections, and (4) closing the sale (see Figure 15.2).

15.3.1 Prospecting and Qualifying

Identifying prospective clients is a critical activity if the sales manager's efforts are to be successful. Generally, 20 to 30 percent of all telephone sales calls are scheduled with prospective clients—those who have not previously booked a banquet or a meeting function with the hospitality firm. No firm can rely entirely on repeat business, so the organization must commit itself to seeking and cultivating new business and expanding its market.

In the process of **prospecting and qualifying** sales managers should determine whether prospective clients represent good prospects before they invest a large amount of time. The following questions are helpful in determining whether a prospect is a good one:

- **Does the prospect have needs and wants that can be satisfied by the products and services of the hospitality firm?** If the needs and wants of the prospect differ substantially

FIGURE 15.2 • The personal selling process.

from the product–service mix of the firm and personal selling is undertaken anyway, sales managers are likely wasting their time as well as that of the meeting planner. In addition, it can create a poor image for the firm, because the sales manager has not done enough background checking and homework to determine if the facility fits the prospect's needs.

- **Does the prospect have the ability to pay?**   It is important to determine whether the prospect has income or credit reserves to pay for a meeting or banquet function. This is a particularly important question to consider when dealing with small associations, corporations, and SMERF groups, as well as the leisure groups.

- **Does the prospect have the willingness to pay?**   In some cases, the meeting planner may have the ability to pay for the nicest facilities but not the willingness. For example, some corporations have policies against using luxury hotels because they feel it is too extravagant, even though they have deep pockets. Or a corporation may have contracts set up with various hotel chains, limiting the list of potential sites.

- **Does the prospect have the authority to sign a contract and commit the organization for the meeting function?**   It is terribly frustrating for a sales manager to cultivate prospective sales only to find that the individuals with whom the manager has been dealing do not have the authority to sign a contract and commit the organization for a function. It is important to know what the decision-making process is, who is involved, and when a decision will be made. If this information is not available from the hospitality firm's records, the best way to find out is to ask the meeting planner.

- **Is the prospect readily accessible?**   It is important that the sales manager be able to contact the meeting planner by telephone and schedule an appointment with the prospect. Part of prospecting involves determining the best time and method to contact the prospect. It may be difficult to schedule a sales presentation with company presidents, so they may prove to be poor prospects.

Locating suitable prospects is a task confronting all sales representatives. What methods can be used to obtain leads that will result in good prospects? The following list represents a few potential sources.

- **Inquiries.** Often, individuals visit or call the hospitality firm directly and request information concerning banquets and/or meeting facilities. These individuals and the groups they represent are ready-made prospects.

- **Names given by existing clients.** This approach is sometimes called the *endless chain* or *networking*. Simply ask each of the existing clients to supply the names of additional individuals, groups, or companies that might be prospective clients. The resulting list is then qualified to determine the most attractive prospects, and personal selling begins. It is important to follow up with a thank-you letter to the individual who supplied the name of the prospect, especially when the lead results in booked business. The mutual contact also serves as a means of introduction with the new prospect.

- **Centers of influence.** Every community has its own leaders and influential people. These individuals make excellent prospects because they tend to be active in the community; they are "joiners." Additionally, it is an excellent idea for the sales manager and other members of the management staff to belong to community and civic organizations. In this way, they can establish personal relationships with these community leaders.

- **Developed lists.** Often, lists of prospects are simply developed from sources such as the telephone directory, Chamber of Commerce, and local clubs and organizations. These lists should then be qualified to identify the most likely prospects.

- **Direct-mail prospecting.** Lists can also be used to initiate direct-mail prospecting. Promotional material is mailed to a list of prospects, and the sales manager can either follow up with a telephone call seeking an appointment or wait for an inquiry.

- **Corporate sales offices.** All major hotel chains maintain national and regional sales offices. One of the responsibilities of these offices is to direct prospective leads to the chain's hotels that are in the best position to service the prospective clients. In addition, hotels within a chain may refer potential business to other hotels within the chain. For example, if a sales manager has made a contact with a meeting planner and learns that the group is planning to meet in another city, the sales manager should refer the client to the sales department of the chain's hotel in that city.

- **Cold calls.** Finally, personal sales calls can be made without prior arrangements or appointments. These are called cold calls. The sales manager simply contacts the prospect by telephone or may make a personal call to the prospect's office and ask to see the prospect. Rarely does this type of call result in a signed contract, but it does open some doors for future contact with the prospect. When made as personal sales calls, however, cold calls are quite time-consuming and, as a result, are very expensive.

Cold calls
Personal sales calls made without prior arrangements or appointments.

15.3.2 Planning and Delivering Sales Presentations

Soon after qualifying a prospect as a good candidate for the product–service mix of the hospitality firm, a sales manager should make contact. This is usually done by telephone. Subsequent contact may also be by telephone, or the sales manager may make a personal visit to the prospect's place of business, or the prospect may visit the property to inspect the facilities. Sales managers should be assertive and honest. They should introduce themselves to the prospect, identify the property they represent, and state the reason for the call. Mentioning a mutual acquaintance or a common interest may help break the ice, but sales managers should be candid and "up front." They should not attempt to schedule the appointment under false pretenses, as this will only hurt in the long run.

The overall goal of any personal selling activity is, of course, to promote purchase on the part of the prospect. Rarely, however, does this occur without a well-planned sales presentation. The AIDA model (attention, interest, desire, and action) is one that has long been used in training sales personnel. To sell the prospect successfully, the sales manager must help move the prospect through each of the four steps of the AIDA model. Supplemental materials such as magazine

AIDA model
A model sellers use to match presentations with the current level of consumer engagement, that starts with attention (or awareness) and proceeds through interest, desire, and action.

Young businesswoman shaking hands with customer.

advertising and direct mail can help get the consumer's attention or create awareness and, to some extent, interest, but it is the responsibility of sales managers to create desire and action.

Before making the sales call, a sales manager should develop an outline of the presentation. What are the prospect's needs and objectives for the meeting or function? How can the firm's products and services help the organization meet its needs and objectives? It is important to make the products and services offered by the firm as tangible as possible and to link them directly with the stated needs and objectives of the prospect. What points should be stressed? How should they be presented so that the firm is perceived positively? What should the sales call accomplish?

It is not advisable to prepare a canned sales pitch that is merely replayed for each new prospect. Instead, a sales manager should be natural and straightforward, not waste words, and get right to the point. The sales presentation should begin with a formal introduction, followed with questions probing the prospect about his or her needs and objectives. These needs and objectives can then be used as the basis for the remainder of the sales presentation, focusing on how the property's features and performance characteristics match the buyer's needs. It is important to let the prospect know that the firm values, wants, and deserves the prospect's business. It may be best to use a checklist of points to be covered, for it is better to refer to a list than to appear disorganized during the presentation.

It is also important to be aware of the nature of the prospect. Some individuals have time to sit and talk; others are too busy. A sales manager should be able to vary the presentation to suit the needs of the prospect. Every effort should be made to make the prospect comfortable by establishing rapport. The sales manager must emphasize the strong selling points of the hotel operation's product–service mix, while linking these strengths to the stated needs and objectives of the prospect.

Finally, one of the most important skills that can be acquired by sales managers is the art of listening. Often, sales managers feel they must do all the talking if a sale is to be made. Nothing could be further from the truth. Selling also requires concentrating on what the prospect is saying and on nonverbal behavior. A good sales manager allows the prospect to ask questions uninterrupted and does not try to anticipate questions and jump in with a canned response before the prospect has finished asking the question. Active listening is a learned skill, and one that is critical to successful selling. Selling means focusing attention on prospects and learning to hear what they are really saying.

Asking probing questions is an important part of the sales presentation. The use of probing questions helps avoid objections and gain commitment from the prospect. The commitment can be in the form of an advance in the sales process (e.g., a hotel site visit or a meeting with more members of the committee) or an actual sale (i.e., close). The following questions are used to progress through this alternative personal selling process. There are basically three types of probing questions: information gathering, problem identification, and problem resolution:

1. **Information gathering.**   Questions that focus on gathering information are aimed at learning background information and facts about the prospect, his or her needs, and the organization he or she represents. Much of this information can be gathered before the actual sales. The salesperson should not ask simple questions such as, "What does your company do?" or bore the prospect with a series of basic questions. Instead, the salesperson should do some research before the meeting to demonstrate his commitment to getting the prospect's account.

2. **Problem identification.**   Questions that focus on identifying problems are meant to uncover any issues or dissatisfaction the prospect has with the current supplier (e.g., hotel for meetings, food service contractor for college dining, or corporate travel agent). In some cases, these inquiries could uncover problems that the prospect does not even know exist. The questions could be as simple as, "Do you have any problems with your current supplier?" or "Are you satisfied with your current supplier?" in an attempt to get the prospect thinking.

3. **Problem resolution.**   Questions that focus on resolving problems are attempts at getting the prospect to realize how any problems or dissatisfaction with the current supplier could have a negative impact on her or his business, and the positive outcome of purchasing your product. This could be a financial issue or something more subjective, such as attendee satisfaction at a meeting or convention. The salesperson for a contract food service firm could ask a college administrator, "Do you think the students' dissatisfaction with the current supplier might lead to fewer dining contracts?" to bring up a possible consequence associated with a specific problem. This could then be followed with a question such as, "If I could demonstrate how our product would result in higher quality and student satisfaction, and an increase in the number of dining contracts, would you consider hiring my company as your food service provider?"

Active listening
When a salesperson listens carefully to the buyer to understand the buyer's point of view.

Active listening requires a salesperson to hear and understand what the buyer is trying to say, from the buyer's point of view. The key is that the salesperson actually needs to understand the buyer, not merely hear what the buyer is saying. It is important to let the buyer know that you are listening and that you know what he or she means. There are four techniques that can be used in active listening:[3]

1. **Encourage talking.**   Let prospects know that you are listening and that you want them to continue talking. Use responses such as "I see" and "Go on," and/or nod and use facial expressions.

2. **Take notes.**   Note taking sends prospects the message that you are interested in what they are saying and you are concerned about getting the details correct.

3. **Paraphrase the customer's meaning with a confirmation question.**   If in doubt, restate what you think the prospect meant. This will help clarify any misunderstandings and give the prospect a feeling of assurance.

4. **Express an understanding of the customer's feelings and perceptions.**   Show empathy. It is helpful to express similar opinions or feelings, especially when the prospect demonstrates feelings of doubt or frustration. Let the prospect know that you are concerned about his or her feelings and ask him or her to elaborate.

All of these techniques will go a long way toward building the prospect's level of confidence with you and your organization. In addition, listening and obtaining feedback will provide valuable information to use in the sales presentation.

15.3.3   Overcoming Objections

No matter how good a sales manager may be, sooner or later (and probably sooner) a prospect will object during the sales call. Before you proceed, you need to determine if the prospect's response is a request for more information, a condition of the sale, or an actual objection. In most cases, objections can be anticipated based on past experiences with other prospects and a thorough knowledge of the property and the competition. Most objections fall into one of the following categories:

- **Price.**   The perceived value of the products and services being offered may not be high enough. This calls for the sales manager to reassure the prospect and to continue to negotiate.

- **Products and services offered.**   The prospect may not feel comfortable with the assurances that the sales manager has made about the quality or consistency of the products and services provided by the hospitality firm's staff. It may be easy to show the prospect firsthand how the firm performs.

- **Facility or brand.**   The prospect may hold a negative image of the individual property or the entire brand. If this is the case, efforts must be made to change the perceptions and to ask the prospect for a second chance, especially if the prospect represents a sizable piece of business.

- **Pressure to decide.**   Sometimes the prospect simply does not like being put under pressure to make a decision immediately. This can occur when another group is thinking of booking the same space on the same days, or when sales managers are pressuring the prospect to decide in order to make a quota.

- **Individual sales manager.**   Once in a while, there can be a personality conflict between the sales manager and the prospect. Sales managers need to be flexible and able to work effectively with a wide variety of individuals.

For the sales call to be successful, of course, these objections must be overcome. A simple yet effective approach directs the sales manager to use four steps:

1. Listen; allow the prospect to explain the objections fully.

2. Reflect or rephrase the prospect's feelings to assure the prospect that you fully understand the objection.

3. Handle the objection.

4. Get a commitment from the prospect that the objective has been met.

Several methods are used to effectively handle the objections that prospects will raise:

- **Agree and counter.**   Acknowledge the prospect's objection but then offer support for why the objection really is not important or is not an objection. It is important to offer support or a reasoned argument for your response. If the prospect has incorrect facts, that is easily remedied. If the prospect has an incorrect perception, this is much more difficult to change. A perception represents an individual's view of reality, and this is not easily changed.

- **Turn the objection into a reason for buying.**   For example, if the prospect objects to the price, it might be useful to talk about a hotel's employee-to-guest ratio and how this allows the hotel to provide a higher level of service than the competition and therefore is justification for the higher price.

- **Seek more information.**   Often, the stated objection is not the full reason why the prospect is not ready to make a commitment. The sales manager must probe further to determine if the meeting planner's facts are incorrect or incomplete, or if the objection is based on a bad experience in the past. Sometimes, prospects appear to be objecting when they are actually trying to obtain more information.

- **Postpone the objection.**   If the prospect raises an objection early in the sales presentation and it would be best dealt with later, ask to defer it for a few minutes, indicating that it will be discussed at length shortly. For example, if the prospect objects to a hotel's price, it is unwise to discuss price until the hotel's product–service quality is well established in the prospect's mind. However, it is imperative that objections be dealt with openly and in a timely manner. Do not just ignore them in the hope that prospects will forget about them—they will not.

If the prospect indicates that the objection has been satisfactorily addressed, it is advisable to ask for the business and attempt a trial close (i.e., get a commitment). The following types of questions can be used to determine if the objections have been properly handled:

- "Is that the answer you are looking for?"
- "Do you agree that we have covered your question and given you a way to handle it?"
- "Does that solve your problem?"

After attempting the trial close, if you cannot overcome an objection or close the sale because of an objection, you will need to either return to your presentation or consider walking away if the objection seems insurmountable. If your trial close suggests that you have overcome the prospect's objection(s), then it is time to close the sale. The next section covers some common closing techniques.

15.3.4 Closing the Sale

Despite otherwise successful sales efforts, many sales managers fail to get a firm commitment from the prospect. They simply fail to close the sale. Closure can be as simple as saying, "Can we confirm your meeting for October 15th?" Closure involves summarizing the major selling points and striving for agreement on the part of the prospect. Simply stated, closure involves asking for business. A number of methods can be used to close a sale. These are among the most common:

- **Continued affirmation.**   If the sales manager can ask questions to which the prospect will answer yes, this can set up prospects for closing the sale. The prospect has already responded positively to a series of questions, and the sales manager has led the prospect to a point where he or she can then ask for the business.

- **Prestige or status close.**   This is often used by upscale or exclusive properties. The sales manager discusses the other groups that have met in the facility and, by affiliating the prospect's group with the other, more prestigious groups, encourages the prospect to decide to hold the meeting or function at the facility as well.

- **Assumptive close.**   This is a bold approach in which the sales manager simply assumes that the sale is closed and asks the prospect questions that relate to details of the contract or hands the prospect the pen and asks him or her to sign the contract.

- **Closing on a minor point.**   This is useful when the prospect has raised an objection that the sales manager has successfully dealt with. If there is agreement on a minor point, the sales manager can then ask for the business. This approach involves offering the prospect choices and asking "which" questions rather than "if" questions. In this way, the prospect will not respond with a simple no, but rather will agree and offer an explanation.

- **Standing room only.**   If another group is looking at the same dates and space in a hotel or restaurant, it may be useful to tell the prospect that he or she will need to make a decision quickly in order to reserve the meeting space and/or a block of guest rooms.

15.4   PERSONAL SELLING TOOLS

A number of tools can be developed and used by salespeople to improve their performance. These tools increase the efficiency and effectiveness of sales presentations. We have chosen to discuss two such tools: key account management and negotiation skills.

15.4.1   Key Account Management

A rule that has been applied to sales for some time is the *80/20 rule*. This proposition holds that 80 percent of the profitable business will be generated by 20 percent of the customers. Not all prospects, guests, or meeting planners should be treated equally. Rather, special attention should be given to those who are producing the largest share of the revenue and profits or who have the potential to do so. The groups that make up this 20 percent are termed *key accounts*. They deserve key account management—special attention and extra-personalized selling efforts.

Each sales and marketing department should keep a very close watch on the level of business provided by each account. Trends should be studied to determine which accounts are growing and which are declining. An analysis of each account should be conducted periodically to determine the total revenue and contribution margin for each account. Based on this analysis, accounts can be classified as shown in Figure 15.3.

Based on this analysis, key accounts can be identified and strategies and action plans developed to foster the development of exceptional accounts. Accounts with the most current business and greatest potential must be given extra attention, while those that are marginal should not consume too much of a sales manager's time and effort. Keep in mind that resources are limited, and they should be directed toward the accounts with the most profit potential.

Key account management
A management model in which the level of attention increases for customers who are producing the largest share of the revenue and profits, or who have the potential to do so.

15.4.2   Negotiation Skills

In today's competitive environment, salespeople need to be able to negotiate effectively in order to achieve mutually beneficial outcomes with buyers. There is a proliferation of information available to consumers, including tips and suggestions for getting the best deals from manufacturers and retailers. Advances in technology make this information easy to access, thereby allowing consumers to compare alternatives easily. The negotiation process is particularly critical in industrial markets because of the high volume. For example, if a hotel sales manager is negotiating the room rate for 500 rooms over 4 nights (2,000 room nights), a reduction of $5 in price results in a decrease in revenue of $10,000. This transaction could take place in a matter of seconds.

The goal of any negotiation is to achieve a win-win situation. It is important not to view the negotiation process as a competition, because someone will end up losing. Dissatisfied customers do not return, and they provide negative word of mouth to their colleagues. Rather, it is important to create an exchange that results in the mutual satisfaction of the involved parties. A good sales manager will plan for the sales presentation and the inevitable negotiation process. A complete knowledge of the competitive environment will provide useful parameters for steering the negotiations. In addition, the sales manager should develop acceptable ranges and options for negotiating to ensure profitability. Finally, the following tips will improve the sales manager's potential for success in negotiating.[4]

Negotiation
Communication between two or more individuals or parties seeking an outcome that is mutually beneficial.

- **When you give something up, try to gain something in return.** Once you show a tendency to negotiate, prospects will try to negotiate on every item. Therefore, make it clear that you expect something in return for making concessions. For example, a hotel sales manager could say, "I'll lower the room rate by $5 per night if you guarantee 100 rooms for four nights."

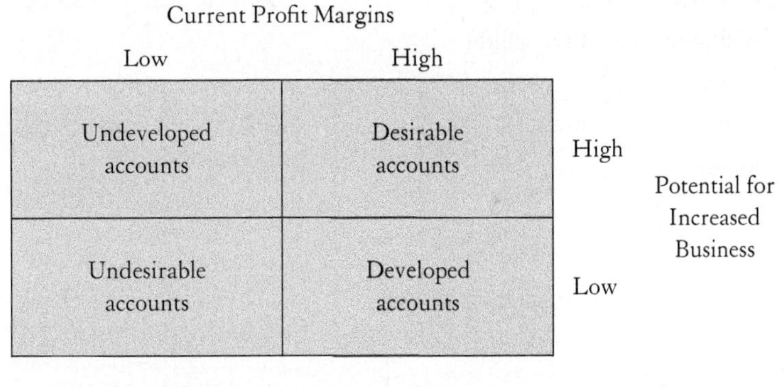

Current Profit Margins

	Low	High	
High	Undeveloped accounts	Desirable accounts	
Low	Undesirable accounts	Developed accounts	

Potential for Increased Business

FIGURE 15.3 • Account profile.

- **Look for items other than price to negotiate.** As mentioned earlier, a small reduction in price could result in a large decrease in revenue when dealing with volume business. Hotel sales managers can focus on items other than room rates. For example, planners could be given free meeting space, room upgrades, reduced meal prices, or free audiovisual equipment. All of these items would have a much smaller impact on the hotel's bottom line, and they provide meeting planners with a sense of accomplishment.

- **Do not attack your prospect's demand; look for the motive behind it.** Try not to tell a prospect that his or her demand is ridiculous or unreasonable. This will only anger the prospect and have a negative impact on the negotiations. Instead, remain calm and ask for an explanation. For example, if a meeting planner asks for a very low room rate, it may be because of a small or restricted budget.

- **Do not defend your position; ask for feedback and advice from the prospect.** If you meet resistance to your offer, do not get defensive. Simply ask the prospect why he or she thinks it is unreasonable. Asking "What would you do if you were in my position?" is often beneficial in this situation.

15.4.3 Suggestive Selling

Suggestive-selling
Attempting to enhance an initial sale by recommending compatible products and services.

Another common sales technique in the hospitality industry is suggestive selling. This is the process in which a salesperson (e.g., sales manager, reservation clerk, or waiter) provides suggestions for the consumer that result in more revenue or profit for the firm, better service to the consumer, and more money for the salesperson. For example, a waiter might recommend a certain appetizer or wine for his guests before taking their order. This might result in the sale of additional items that wouldn't have been ordered because the guests didn't think about it. Similarly, a catering salesperson might suggest some additional services for a couple planning their wedding. It could be a certain food item or something to do with the decorations.

The lack of active selling on the part of a service organization's employees results in lower sales and less-satisfied consumers. All of this is simply a matter of missed opportunities. For example, consider the following situation in which four friends were planning to have dinner at a restaurant. After they had waited about five minutes for a server to approach the table, she presented each guest with a closed menu, and asked, "Would anyone like anything from the bar?" Each responded no, and the server said that she would be back in a few minutes to take their dinner orders. She returned in a few minutes, asking, "Are you ready to order?" When a guest inquired about any special items or recommendations, the server responded, "There isn't a special today, but everything on the menu is good. Can I take your order?" The guests then placed their orders.

Clearly, the server failed to sell; she merely took the orders. She did not use suggestive-selling techniques to recommend a round of drinks, a bottle of wine, an appetizer, or a specialty of the house. Figure 15.4 summarizes the loss of potential revenue from the table in the example. The total potential lost revenue is $80 for the party of four. Although they might not have spent

Drink sales	4 @ $6.00	$24.00
Wine sale	1 bottle @ $28	$28.00
Trading up/suggestive selling a more expensive entrée or accompanying item	4 @ 2.00	$ 8.00
Dessert	4 @ 5.00	$20.00
Potential lost revenue		$80.00
Potential lost gratuity @ 15%		$12.00

FIGURE 15.4 • Potential impact of missed selling opportunities.

the entire $80, they might easily have spent an additional $10, $20, or $30. The point is that service people are salespeople. They must be taught to suggestive-sell—to increase the check averages, to deliver additional profits, and to ensure guests' satisfaction. If employees suggestive-sell, they have a 50/50 chance of being successful. However, if they do not suggestive-sell, the chances of success are nil. Suggestions for ways to effectively suggestive-sell are shown in Figure 15.5.

This example focused on a food service operation, but similar examples can be seen in other segments of the hospitality and tourism business. For instance, cruise lines could encourage passengers to book higher-priced cabins, purchase trip insurance, or buy excursion packages for ports of call. Similarly, car rental agencies could offer promotions that encourage customers to upgrade their vehicles, extend their rental periods, or purchase additional rental services such as GPS navigation systems. Suggestive selling can result in the sale of additional items or increase revenues and profits by up-selling, or encouraging consumers to buy items that are more expensive or provide a greater profit margin.

15.4.4 Information Technology

Salespeople have access to information technology that automates many aspects of their jobs, from creating a database for customers and prospects to evaluating the profitability of accounts. In the hospitality and tourism industry, there are products that focus primarily on catering (e.g., Caterease and Cater Pro) and products that are directed at hotel sales and catering departments (e.g., Delphi and Skyware). These software products are normally Microsoft Windows–based and able to be integrated with the operation's other software systems (point-of-sale systems, reservation systems, etc.). For example, Delphi is a sales and catering software product developed by Newmarket International for larger hotels, hotel chains, casinos, and convention centers. All editions of Delphi provide key features such as dashboard interfaces with critical metrics, complete account and contact management capabilities, catering and event management with banquet event orders, meeting and guest room control logs, and report analytics. In addition, Delphi

Up-selling
A technique that involves encouraging consumers to purchase relatively more expensive products and services, or those that provide a greater profit margin.

Information technology
The use of computer systems and applications to improve operating efficiency and effectiveness.

---

1. Develop a positive mental attitude. Not everyone will accept the suggestions, but all guests will appreciate the desire to serve and attend to their needs.

2. Do not try to manipulate the guest; simply make positive and upbeat suggestions.

3. Suggest favorite items or aspects of the product–service mix with which the employee is most familiar. This makes the suggestion more personal and sincere, increasing the chances of success.

4. Use props to support suggestive selling. For example, it is relatively easy to turn down an offer for dessert, but if a dessert tray is brought to the table and the server offers the right suggestion, sales of desserts will increase. Offering samples of wine will increase the sale of wine by the glass. Some restaurants offer "flights of wine" in which several small samples are provided at about the same cost as a glass of wine. Some guests will merely try the samples, but others will purchase additional wine after trying the samples.

5. Always make positive suggestions; always focus on the positive aspects of the product–service mix. If a guest makes a negative comment, acknowledge the comment, but try to turn the negative into a positive.

6. Always be attentive to guests' needs. Some will be very receptive to suggestive selling, but others will want speedy treatment with a minimum of extra conversation and suggestive selling. Do not use a "canned presentation" to suggestive-sell. Stay tuned to the guests' needs and vary the suggestive-selling presentations.

7. Never make excuses for why suggestive selling will not work or has not worked in the past.

FIGURE 15.5 · Suggestions for effective suggestive selling.

added a product (N2GO) that provides convenient access to Delphi software through mobile devices such as smartphones and tablets to take advantage of current trends in technology.

15.5 ETHICAL ISSUES IN PERSONAL SELLING

As with most other areas of business, there is the potential for unethical behavior by salespeople. A firm's policies and practices should provide salespeople with a good understanding of acceptable behavior or conduct. When these policies are written and used in training, salespeople are more likely to uphold the firm's ethical standards. The following is a brief description of the most common types of unethical behavior among salespeople:

- **Sharing confidential information.** Salespeople and customers build close relationships over time that lead to the disclosure of confidential information based on trust. There is a potential for salespeople to share this information with a customer's competitors, either deliberately or accidentally. Salespeople need to be cognizant of this possible breach. This behavior speaks to the character of the salesperson.

- **Reciprocity.** This refers to the mutual exchange of benefits between buyers and sellers. If a firm has a policy of reciprocity, it can be viewed as an exclusive *tying arrangement,* which is illegal. For example, a hotel might purchase supplies only from firms that agree to use its services for corporate travel.

- **Bribery.** Bribes in the form of monetary payoffs or kickbacks are unethical, if not illegal. Many U.S. firms find themselves at a disadvantage in international markets because their corporate policies and U.S. laws forbid them from offering bribes in countries where it is accepted as a normal business practice. Some meeting planners have coaxed hotels into giving them kickbacks from the room revenues for their meetings.

- **Gift giving and entertainment.** There is a fine line between gift giving, entertainment, and bribery. If the gift is being used to obtain the customer's business, then it amounts to a bribe. Gifts should be given only after contracts are signed, as a symbol of the firm's gratitude. Meeting planners are inundated with gifts in the form of hotel coupons and frequent guest points or even frequent flyer miles. Wining and dining clients is another popular sales technique. "Fam" (familiarization) trips provide meeting planners with free hotel rooms, airline travel, and entrance to tourist attractions or special events. In response, some firms have policies regarding the acceptance of gifts and entertainment by meeting planners and travel agents.

- **Making misleading sales claims.** In their pursuit of sales and quotas, salespeople may decide to provide customers or prospects with misleading information. It is not uncommon in hotel sales for a sales manager to promise meeting planners things that the food and beverage department cannot deliver. This results in some difficult negotiations at the time of the meeting. Another practice that is found in hotel sales departments is *blind cutting.* This refers to the practice of promising a certain quantity of rooms in a contract but then setting the actual room block at a lower amount to account for slippage or artificially high estimates from meeting planners.

- **Business defamation.** Salespeople sometimes make disparaging comments about their competitors when dealing with customers. Not only does this reflect poorly on the salesperson and the hotel, but in some instances it is actually illegal (e.g., slander or libel). It is very tempting to take a cheap shot at a competitor when making comparisons between properties or firms. However, salespeople should constrain themselves to answering specific questions with factual information.

The extent to which a firm is successful in deterring unethical behavior on the part of its employees will depend on how it treats employees who violate its policies and the level of support for the policies throughout the organization.

SUMMARY OF CHAPTER OBJECTIVES

This chapter has focused on a vital link in hotel sales and marketing: the sales and solicitation of group business. The initial section of the chapter examined the selling function and the attributes that make a salesperson successful. These attributes include courtesy, knowledge of the products and services, professional appearance, a strong desire for and willingness to work, and, finally, a strong personality.

The role of the meeting planner was reviewed. Each meeting planner is different, and the needs and objectives of each group will be different, presenting a real challenge for the sales manager. However, common needs of meeting planners include costs, location, image and status, professional service, adaptability and flexibility, and professional operations and management. In working with a meeting planner, the sales manager should strive to build a solid working relationship based on trust and the hotel's ability to meet the meeting planner's needs and objectives. The sales manager should become a problem solver.

Selling effectively to group markets was discussed at length, especially as it relates to the needs and objectives of the association and corporate market segments. Characteristics of each of these markets were discussed and generalizations made. The FAB selling technique was introduced as a means of tying product features to advantages and benefits that can be marketed to prospective customers.

The personal selling process was presented, including four important steps: prospecting and qualifying, planning and delivering the sales presentation, handling objections, and closing the sale. Each step was explained and techniques provided for achieving the efficiency and effectiveness necessary to succeed. The importance of listening was discussed, and several options were presented for handling objections and closing the sale. Some additional personal selling tools, such as key account management, help salespeople expend their effort where the potential payback is greatest, and some tips were provided for improving negotiating skills. The use of information technology in sales was discussed.

Finally, the chapter discussed the ethical issues surrounding the personal selling process. There are many areas for potential abuse, including the sharing of confidential information, reciprocity, bribery, gift giving and entertainment, and business defamation. It is important for hotels and travel firms to establish a written code of ethical behavior that is conveyed to their employees during orientation and job training. There must be penalties for violating the firm's ethical standards, and the entire firm should support them.

KEY TERMS AND CONCEPTS

Active listening
AIDA model
Association market segment
Cold calls
Corporate market segment
FAB selling technique
Incentive trips
Information technology
Key account management
Meeting planners
Negotiation

Order getters
Order takers
Personal selling
Property analysis checklist
Prospecting and qualifying
Sales blitz
SMERF group
Suggestive selling
Telemarketing
Up-selling

QUESTIONS FOR REVIEW AND DISCUSSION

1 **Cite and discuss the attributes of a successful sales manager. Which one do you consider to be the most important? Why?**

2 **What do you see as the pros and cons of a career in sales?**

3　What is the role of the meeting planner? How does this individual interact with the hotel sales and marketing staff?

4　Cite and discuss the nature of the association and corporate market segments, including decision making, lead time, types of meetings, and site selection criteria.

5　What are the steps in the personal selling process? Provide a brief description of the activities at each step.

6　Discuss some of the procedures that can be used to qualify a prospect.

7　When a sales manager encounters objections, how might these be handled?

8　What does it mean to close a sale? What methods can be used to accomplish this?

9　How does gaining a commitment differ from closing a sale?

10　What is the proposed benefit of asking probing questions during the personal selling approach?

11　What is account management? How can it be done?

12　What are some common negotiating skills?

13　List and discuss the ethical issues in personal selling.

NOTES

[1] Charles M. Futrell, *Fundamentals of Selling: Customers for Life* (Chicago: McGraw-Hill, 1996).

[2] Bromberg, Joyce. 2014., "Top 10 Factors to Consider When Selecting a Meeting Location." February 3." www.convene.com/top-10-factors-to-consider-when-selecting-a-meeting-location-meeting-planner-forum-session-one-recap/.

[3] Gerald L. Manning and Barry L. Reece, *Selling Today*, 6th ed. (Upper Saddle River, NJ: Prentice Hall, 1995), pp. 256–258.

[4] Futrell, *Fundamentals of Selling*, p. 243.

chapter review

ROLE-PLAY EXERCISE

College Sports Team

The goal of this exercise is to give students an opportunity to engage in a mock sales call. Put students into groups of two or more, depending on the size of the class. Have one or more students participate in the role of a travel planner for a college sports team and one or more students participate in the role of a hotel sales manager. You can change the type of sport (e.g., basketball, football, soccer, etc.) as well as the gender (i.e., male or female) to vary the room requirements, season, day of the week, and so on. Have the students participating as sales managers choose a local hotel that can accommodate the number of rooms required by the sports team. They will have to look online and/or visit the hotel to become familiar with the accommodations and amenities, including meeting facilities and food service operations. (Note: It helps if one of the students actually has working experience at the hotel). The students participating as travel planners can either be assigned a sport or choose one. The college or university isn't extremely important, but choose one that is in the same conference. There might be some differences based on the location of the institution and whether it is private or public.

The sales managers need to address the features, benefits, and advantages associated with the hotel relative to the needs of the travel planners. The travel planners should think carefully about the needs of a sports team and what the players would be looking for in terms of lodging facilities. Assume the sales managers are making a sales call at the office of the travel planners. They should try to make the exercise as realistic as possible, starting the sales call with introductions and moving on through the personal selling process. The students can be evaluated based on how well they utilize the tools and concepts provided in the chapter.

CASE STUDY

Atlantis Resort

Atlantis Resort is located in Paradise Island in the Bahamas. The resort has 2,280 guest rooms and suites located in three towers and the Cove Atlantis. In addition, there are 392 villas to provide a variety of accommodation types to satisfy any needs. The resort's meeting facilities include a 50,000 square-foot ballroom—the largest in the Bahamas and Caribbean, with more than 30,000 square feet of prefunction space. In addition to 30 break-out rooms, there are three board rooms, a large staging area, and a banquet kitchen with additional pantries and facilities to accommodate up to 5,000 guests. More detailed information on guest-room rates, meeting facilities, and packages can be obtained by examining the resort's website (www.atlantis.com).

Case Study Questions and Issues

1. Which of the meetings market segments discussed in the chapter would be good target markets for the Atlantis Resort? Explain your answer.

2. What other destinations or hotels/resorts do you think would be competitors for each of the meetings markets you listed?

3. What are some potential objections that the salespeople at the Atlantis Resort might expect? Be specific.

4. Provide examples of how you would use the techniques for handling objections for each of the specific objections you've anticipated.

Glossary

Accessibility The target markets must be reachable, or accessible, through a variety of marketing communication efforts.

Acquisitions A firm can acquire the rights to new products or services by entering into a legal arrangement with another firm, thereby combining the two firms' products and services.

Actionability Consumers in the same market segment should react similarly to the marketing program used to target them.

Active listening When a salesperson listens carefully to the buyer to understand the buyer's point of view.

Administered vertical marketing system A manufacturer or supplier attempts to control the flow of goods or services through the channel.

Advertising Consists of any paid form of nonpersonal presentation of ideas and promotion of ideas, goods, or services by an identified sponsor.

Advertising agency An independent firm that works for the client to produce creative work and media scheduling.

Advertising campaign Includes all forms of advertising held together by a single message or comprehensive theme. A campaign is the overall plan or strategy that guides the development of all forms of advertising.

Advertising spot A short advertising message on a participating program.

Agate line A measurement by which advertising space is sold in newspapers and magazines. There are 14 agate lines to an inch.

AIDA model A model sellers use to match presentations with the current level of consumer engagement, that starts with attention (or awareness) and proceeds through interest, desire, and action.

AIO statements Data collected regarding consumer activities (e.g., hobbies and sports), interests (e.g., family), and opinions (e.g., politics) that help firms understand market perceptions about their brand or product.

Alliances Firms pool resources for a specific goal or purpose instead of combining ownership.

All-you-can-afford method The promotional budget based on the amount of limited resources a firm can reasonably afford to allocate to promotion and advertising.

Asset revenue generating efficiency (ARGE) A measure of the relationship between actual revenue and maximum potential revenue.

Association market segment A group market consisting of organizations that have members who share a common cause or purpose.

Attitudes Learned predispositions to act in a consistently favorable or unfavorable manner.

Attribute data Data that involve asking consumers to rate brands on a predetermined list of attributes.

Augmented product The core product and peripheral services that combine to form the overall package of benefits offered by a product or service.

Average daily rate (ADR) Average rate paid for occupied hotel rooms on a daily basis.

Authentication Verifying the appropriate access by a user through the use of some combination of account numbers, passwords, and IP (Internet protocol) addresses.

Barter A process of exchanging goods and services rather than money.

Bartering Individuals or organizations exchange goods and services with one another without the use of money.

Base rate The lowest rate for advertising in print media. This rate is for run of paper (ROP) and means that the medium, at its discretion, puts advertisements wherever there is space.

Behavioral segmentation Segmentation technique that focuses on the purchasing behaviors exhibited by consumers in the marketplace.

Benchmarking A process whereby a firm establishes a level of performance by comparing current performance against past performance, or by comparing current performance against the performance of other companies or an entire industry.

Benefit segmentation Segmentation technique that focuses on benefits sought by consumers when purchasing a product.

Bleed advertisement An advertisement that extends into all or part of the margin of a page.

Boston Consulting Group (BCG) matrix   A 2 × 2 resource allocation matrix consisting of four quadrants based on two axes representing relative market share and the market growth rate.

Boundary-spanning roles   Roles that frontline employees (e.g., front-desk clerks, waiters, flight attendants, travel agents) perform.

Brand   The name, sign, symbol, design, or any combination of these items that is used to identify the product or service in an attempt to establish an identity that is separate and unique from competitors' offerings.

Brand mark   The symbol or logo design used to identify the product or service.

Brand name   A part of the brand consisting of the words or letters that can be used to identify the firm.

Break-even analysis   Uses the break-even point (BEP) to examine the relationships between costs, sales, and profits.

Brochures   A small pamphlet containing information and images related to products, services, and events.

Browser   An application program that allows users to display HTML files obtained from the Web.

Business analysis   Represents the qualitative and quantitative assessment of a firm's potential or a firm's strategies.

Business-to-business (B2B)   E-commerce that involves one business selling to or creating an exchange with another business.

Business-to-consumer (B2C)   The electronic form of retailing when a business sells a product or service to a consumer.

Buying center or buying unit   Groups of people that influence buying decisions for organizations.

Carbon footprint   The total amount of greenhouse gas emissions caused by people, organizations, products, and events through everyday activities.

Cash cows   Products and services with the best opportunity for positive cash flow: they have high relative market shares in industries with low market growth rates.

Causal analysis   Analysis techniques that look for cause-and-effect relationships between two or more variables.

Causal methods   These are often referred to as explanatory methods because they use historical data to establish the relationship between sales and other factors that are believed to influence sales. The other factors, or causal factors, can differ based on the level of the forecast.

Causal research   Research used to define cause-and-effect relationships between variables.

Census   A sample consisting of the entire population.

Central reservation systems (CRS)   Systems that are designed to improve the efficiency and effectiveness of the reservations function by providing a central point of contact for handling customers' requests in a timely fashion.

Channel length   The number of intermediaries between the manufacturer and the final consumer.

Channel power   The ability of one channel member to influence the behavior of other channel members in such a way as to get them to do things that they normally would not do. The most common forms of power are reward, coercive, expert, legitimate, and referent.

Channel width   Represents the number of distribution channel partners required to provide the desired market coverage.

Circulation   The number of copies of a publication that get distributed.

Click-through   Number of images that are requested when an Internet browser clicks on an image or link, in order to access additional information. Click-through rates are often less than 1 percent. Click-throughs are often expressed as unique page views.

Closed-ended question   Provides the respondent with options from which to select a response. It is much easier to collect and analyze information in this type of question. The respondents' answers are consistent and the data are in a form that is simple to record.

Co-branding   Using multiple brand names to promote and/or sell a single product, service, event, or cause.

Cognitive dissonance   Stress or discomfort experienced by a consumer because of conflicting beliefs or second thoughts after they have purchased a product or service.

Cold calls   Personal sales calls made without prior arrangements or appointments.

Collateral materials   Printed and electronic materials such as brochures and websites that support the sales of products and services.

Communications gap   Occurs when there is a difference between the service delivered and the service promised.

Communications plan   An overall plan composed of several individual plans designed for each of the target markets or "publics".

Community relations plan The component of the communications plan developed to create a favorable environment in the local community.

Compensatory strategies   Consumers use one or more of a product's strengths to compensate for deficiencies in other areas.

Competitive advantage   An advantage over competitors gained by offering greater relative value based on lower prices and/or higher quality.

Competitive-parity method The promotional budget based on direct comparison with the promotion and advertising efforts of major competitors.

Competitive pricing   Setting prices within the same range as prices for competitive products in the immediate geographic area.

Competitive structure   A combination of buyers and sellers in a market.

Concept testing   A written or oral description and/or a visual representation of a new product or service is tested on consumers in the target market.

Consolidated metropolitan statistical area (CMSAs)   The largest type of metropolitan statistical area, consisting of at least two primary metropolitan statistical areas (PMSA).

Consolidation stage   The fourth stage of the tourist area life cycle occurs when tourism has become a major component of the local economy, and a welldelineated business district has begun to take shape.

Consumer adoption process Consumers will adopt new products at different rates, depending on their level of aversion to risk and change.

Consumer decision-making model This model consists of five stages that a consumer experiences when making decisions about the purchase of a product or service. The five stages consist of recognizing a problem, seeking information, evaluating alternatives, making a purchase decision, and evaluating the product or service after the purchase.

Consumer expectations   Each consumer forms a set of expectations for the performance of a product or service based on past experiences and other internal and external sources.

Consumer feedback   Information received directly from consumers regarding their experiences with a product or service.

Consumer price index (CPI)   A measure of the relative level of prices for consumer goods in the economy.

Consumer price sensitivity   The degree to which a change in price will affect a consumer's purchase decision.

Consumer problem-solving techniques   Consumers typically use one of three types of problem-solving techniques when they encounter a problem: routine response behavior, limited problem solving, and extended problem-solving.

Consumer-to-business (C2B)   The situation in which an individual seeks to sell products or services to a business, or when consumers bid for products and services offered for sale by a firm.

Consumer-to-consumer (C2C)   The situation in which consumers sell directly to other consumers.

Contests   Require some skill on the part of the participant to win prizes.

Continuous advertising   The practice of keeping the amount of advertising relatively constant over time.

Contractual vertical marketing system   A contractual vertical marketing system unifies the channel members by means of a legal and binding contract.

Convenience sample   The most basic method of nonprobability sampling because the researcher chooses a sample of population members that, in his or her opinion, represent the target population (e.g., professors use a class of students, or research firms intercept people at shopping malls).

Convention and visitors bureau (CVB)   Destination marketing organizations that represent cities and regions for the main purpose promoting tourism and travel.

Conversion study   A process to measure the effectiveness of the destination marketing organization's advertising and promotion by determining the number of inquiries that are converted to visitors.

Convivial dimension   This refers to the human element (e.g., body language, saying the guest's name) in the service delivery.

Cooperative advertising   When two or more firms are involved in a common advertising campaign that benefits all of the parties involved.

Copy testing   Involves pretesting the copy of an advertisement prior to running it in the media.

Core product   The most basic form of the product represented by the main benefit sought by customers to fulfill their needs.

Corporate market segment   A group market consisting of employees and stakeholders of corporations that meet to address specific issues related to business operations.

Corporate vertical marketing system   All participants are members of the same organization. The original firm either develops or purchases other firms at the various levels in the channel.

Cost per thousand (CPM)   The CPM (from *mille*, the Latin word for thousand), the oldest means for comparing media rates, examines the cost to reach 1,000 consumers through an advertising medium.

Cost/benefit analysis   Firms compare the costs of losing customers and obtaining new customers with the benefits of keeping existing customers.

Cost control data   Data focused on the firm's costs and expenses for each market segment.

Cost-oriented pricing   Basing pricing decisions on the cost of providing a product or service.

Cost-plus pricing   Determining the price for a product or service by adding a desired markup to the cost of producing and marketing the item.

Coupons   Certificates that entitle the consumer to receive a discount when presented at the retail outlet. The primary objectives for coupons are to stimulate trial of a firm's products and/or services by reducing the price, encouraging multiple purchases, and generating temporary sales increases.

Credence qualities   Attributes that are difficult to evaluate even after the service is consumed.

Crisis management plan   The component of the communications plan prepared in the event of a natural or manmade disaster.

Critical incidents   "Moments of truth" when customers interact with a firm's employees and have a positive or negative experience.

Cross-sectional study   A study used to measure the population of interest at one point in time.

Culture   Patterns of behavior and social relations that characterize a society and separate it from others.

Customer needs failures   Based on employee responses to customer needs or special requests.

Customer-oriented strategy   A proactive strategy that focuses on the wants and needs of current and prospective customers.

Customer relations plan   The component of the communications plan used to market the organization to various consumer segments.

Customer satisfaction   Occurs when a firm's service, as perceived by customers, meets or exceeds their expectations.

Decline stage   The last stage in the product life cycle when industry sales and profits decline more rapidly, and the number of competitors gets reduced to only those with strong positions.

Defensive strategy   A reactive strategy that is used to counter the effects on an existing product from a competitor's new product.

Delivery gap   Occurs when there is a difference between the service delivery specifications and the actual service delivery.

Delphi technique   The Delphi technique involves collecting forecasts, developing composites, and sending the data to those participating several times until a consensus results.

Demand-oriented pricing   Approaches to pricing that use consumer perceptions of value as a basis for setting prices.

Demographic segmentation   Segmentation technique that focuses on consumer demographics such as age, income, gender, and ethnicity.

Demographics   Characteristics that describe the population such as age, income, education, occupation, family size, marital status, and gender.

Descriptive analysis   An analysis using aggregate data to describe the "average" or "typical" respondent, and to what degree respondents vary from this profile.

Descriptive research   Research that helps answer the questions who, what, where, when, why, and how.

Desired-objective method
The promotional budget based on achieving well-defined objectives.

Destination attributes   Combination of tangible and intangible elements that define the location.

Destination branding   Process of capturing the distinct elements of the destination and communicating them through components such as identity, personality, and image.

Destination image study   Diagnosis of the destination's strengths and weaknesses on salient attributes, relative to competitive destinations, is helpful in designing the tourism offerings and marketing programs.

Destination management company (DMC)   A local firm that arranges activities and programs for meeting and event planners who are not familiar with the specific location or the local suppliers.

Destination marketing organization (DMO)   An organization that promotes the long-term development and marketing of a destination.

Development stage   The third stage in the tourist area life cycle occurs when there is continued growth in the number of visitor arrivals.

Dichotomous question   The simplest form of a closed-ended question is a dichotomous question, which contains two possible options. Examples include questions with "yes" or "no" answers or a categorical question such as gender with two possible responses, "male" and "female."

Differentiation value   The value to the consumer (both positive and negative) of any differences between a firm's offering and the reference product.

Digital marketing   The marketing of products and services using the Internet and other forms of electronic media.

Direct channel   The manufacturer sells directly to the consumer and performs all of the channel functions.

Direct marketing   The firm contacts consumers at home or work with promotions.

Discretionary effort   Represents employee effort beyond the minimum requirements for his or her job.

Discretionary income   An individual's income that is available for spending after deducting taxes and necessary expenditures on housing, food, and basic clothing.

Disposable income   An individual's income that remains for spending after required deductions such as taxes.

Dissolve   When one scene in a television commercial fades into the next, with the two showing simultaneously for a moment.

Distribution   The manner in which the products and services are being delivered to consumers. It involves decisions related to the location of facilities and the use of intermediaries.

Diversification strategy   A strategy for growth that involves introducing new products and services into new markets.

Dogs   Products and services with low relative market shares in industries with low market growth rates that incur negative cash flows and show little promise for future growth.

Domain name system (DNS)   The unique name given to a computer connected to the Internet.

Drive time   The early morning and late afternoon/early evening hours when radio has its largest audiences and highest rates.

Dubbing   Recording the sound portion of the commercial separately and then synchronizing it with the visual components.

Dynamic pricing   Continually changing prices based on market conditions.

Econometric models   This model uses statistical techniques to solve a simultaneous set of multiple regression equations.

Economic impact study   An analysis that is used to estimate the revenues that come from the spending of tourists within the local area, change in regional incomes, and changes in employment.

Economic sustainability   The ability to support a given level of economic production indefinitely.

Economic value   The sum of a product's reference value and a product's differentiation value.

Economies of scale   Cost efficiencies derived from operating at high volumes.

Electronic commerce (e-commerce)
A term used to describe the buying and selling process using electronic means such as the Internet.

Encryption   Transmitted data are scrambled to prevent unauthorized access by users or hackers.

Entrepreneurial strategy A proactive strategy where firms generate new ideas internally through means other than research and development.

Environmental scanning Environmental scanning can be a formal mechanism within a firm, or merely the result of salespeople and managers consciously monitoring changes in the environment.

Environmental sustainability The ability to maintain reasonable levels of renewable and nonrenewable energy, waste, water, and pollution indefinitely.

Evoked set The qualified set of brands that will be considered in the final purchase decision.

Exclusive distribution The narrowest channel width where a firm limits the availability of its products or services to a particular outlet.

Experience qualities Attributes that can be evaluated only after the purchase and consumption of a service.

Experiments A data collection process used to compare a control group with one or more treatment groups to determine if there are any differences attributed to the variable(s) being tested.

Expert opinion Marketers look to a panel of experts with knowledge of the industry and the marketplace to provide a forecast.

Expert power Expert power is the result of the superior knowledge of one channel member relative to another. Some hotels agree to pay commissions and employ independent hotel representatives because of their expertise in dealing with certain market segments.

Exploration stage The first stage in the tourist area life cycle when a small number of adventurous tourists visit sites with limited public facilities.

Exploratory research Research used to determine the general nature of the problem.

Exponential smoothing This technique uses the trend line to predict future sales; however, it places more weight on the most recent periods.

External environment The outside influences on the marketing process that are not under the control of the organization.

External influences External influences include culture, socioeconomic status, reference groups, and household.

FAB selling technique FAB is a common selling approach that focuses on the features, advantages, and benefits that a product or service offers consumers.

Facilitating products Services that enable the customer to consume the core product by making it available where and when the customer wants it.

Fade in/fade out The screen goes from black to the visual material, or the final visual shot is faded into black.

Family life cycle A concept that attempts to describe the way purchasing behaviors change as consumers pass through various life stages.

Firewall A filter used to monitor traffic between an organization's network and the Internet. This barrier can restrict access to certain IP addresses, applications, or content.

Flighting media scheduling The practice of scheduling advertising blitzes followed by periods of no advertising over a given period of time.

Focus group A group of 8 to 12 people who represent the population being studied and are brought together in an informal setting to discuss the issues surrounding a research problem.

Follow-the-leader An approach that introduces competing products and services soon after the market leader introduces its products and services.

Franchisee A firm that obtains a license from another firm to use its name and business practices.

Franchising A contractual arrangement where one firm licenses a number of other firms to use the franchisor's name and business practices.

Franchisor The firm that licenses other firms to use its name and business practices.

Frequency The number of times the same audience—listeners, readers, or viewers—is reached. It is expressed as an average, because some people may see or hear an advertisement only once, whereas others see it a dozen times.

Frequent traveler programs Loyalty programs that reward customers commensurate with their level of purchase and use.

Fringe time The periods immediately before and after TV prime time, 4 P.M. to 8 P.M., and after 11 P.M. in all time zones except the Central time zone, where periods run an hour earlier.

General Electric (GE) matrix The GE Matrix is similar to the BCG Matrix in that it examines strategic business units based market attractiveness (i.e., market growth rate) and business strength (i.e., relative market share). However, the axes are based on a subjective measure composed of several indicators (e.g., product life cycle, competitor strategies, new technologies, and economic conditions) rather than just one objective measure as in the BCG Matrix.

Geographic segmentation Segmentation technique that focuses on the consumer's geographic area of residence.

Global distribution systems (GDS) Systems used by hospitality and travel firms to facilitate transactions within the distribution channel.

Globalization Firms expand outside of their traditional domestic markets (i.e., expanding worldwide).

Goals Goals are broad statements of what the firm seeks to accomplish.

Gross rating points Gross rating points compare media vehicles and programs. This rating is calculated by multiplying the rating points (i.e., percentage of households, according to surveys, listening to a program or station at a particular time) by the number of times that program or station is heard or viewed during a given period, usually four weeks.

Growth stage The second stage of the product life cycle represented by rapidly rising sales and profits as the cost per unit decreases for providing the product or service.

Historical appraisal An examination of the current trends in the market's size and scope, and the market shares of the competitors.

Hospitality marketing mix Hospitality marketing mix consists of five components: product–service mix, presentation mix, communication mix, pricing mix, and distribution mix.

Hypertext A method of linking related information without a hierarchy or menu system.

Idea generation The process of generating new ideas for products and services from internal and external sources.

Imitative strategy A reactive strategy that involves copying a new product or service before it can have a large impact in the market.

Implication questions Implication questions get the prospect to realize how any problems or dissatisfaction with the current supplier are negatively affecting his or her business.

Incentive trip An all-expenses-paid vacation offered by corporations to reward employees for outstanding performance.

Inception stage The inception stage of the tourist area life cycle is when the more adventurous travelers find destinations that are not frequented by the masses. These travelers are normally looking for places that have not become major tourism destinations.

Indirect channel Involves at least one intermediary that is responsible for one or more channel functions.

Inferential analysis An analysis of cause-and-effect relationships used to test hypotheses.

Information technology The use of computer systems and applications to improve operating efficiency and effectiveness.

Innovation The process of converting new ideas into products and services that offer value to consumers.

Input-output model A common approach for estimating the economic impacts of tourism by directly surveying tourists to obtain data on their spending habits.

Integrated marketing communications (IMC) A strategic approach designed to achieve the objectives of a marketing campaign using the elements of the promotion mix to convey a unified message to the firm's various audiences.

Intensive distribution The widest channel strategy, where firms attempt to make products and services available through as many outlets as possible.

Intermediaries Specialists in certain functions in the distribution process that can add value to the product or service with their knowledge and expertise.

Internal influences Personal characteristics, beliefs, and experiences that guide a consumer's decision making.

Internal marketing Encompasses all marketing activities used by a firm in an effort to improve the effectiveness of its employees.

Internal relations plan The component of the communications plan developed to improve employee morale and the work environment.

Introduction stage The first stage of the product life cycle involving the launch of new products and services.

Involvement stage The second stage in the tourist area life cycle occurs when there is limited interaction between tourists and the local community, resulting in only basic services.

Judgment sample The researcher makes a determination as to a subset of population members that will represent the population. This process is similar to the one used in choosing the members for a focus group.

Key account management A management model in which the level of attention increases for customers who are producing the largest share of the revenue and profits, or who have the potential to do so.

Knowledge gap Occurs when management's perception of what consumers expect is different from the consumers' actual expectations.

Law of demand The inverse relationship between price and quantity demanded that exists for most products and services.

Legitimate power Legitimate power is obtained through contractual arrangements that specify the members' expected behaviors. The most common form of legitimate power in the hospitality industry is franchising.

Local advertising Advertising placed in local media to reach a local target market.

Longitudinal study A study used to measure the same population over an extended period of time.

Margin of error The difference between forecasted value and actual value.

Market demand The total volume that would be bought by a clearly specified customer group in a defined geographic area in a defined period.

Market development strategy A strategy that focuses on achieving growth by pursuing new markets for existing products and services.

Market growth rate The average annual growth rate over a specified time period that can be viewed as a proxy for industry attractiveness, or future growth potential.

Market introduction A new product or service is made available for sale in the marketplace with an associated marketing program.

Market penetration strategy A market penetration strategy focuses on increasing the market share of existing products in current markets.

Market segmentation Pursuing a marketing strategy where the total potential market is divided into homogeneous subsets of customers, each of which responds differently to the marketing mix.

Market share The percentage of the market that the firm's product–service mix will capture.

Marketing The process of creating, pricing, promoting, and distributing products and services to consumers in a mutual exchange of value.

Marketing communications Marketing communications include a wide variety of approaches, which consist of, but are not limited to, advertising, promoting, direct marketing, telemarketing, and personal selling.

Marketing concept The marketing concept is based on the premise that firms determine customer wants and needs, and then design products and services that meet those wants and needs, while also meeting the goals of the firm.

Marketing information systems (MIS) The structure of people, equipment, and procedures used to gather, analyze, and distribute information used by an organization to make informed decisions.

Marketing management cycle The dynamic process involving marketing planning, execution, and evaluation.

Marketing mix The four components (price, product, place, and promotion) that are controlled by organizations and used to influence consumers to purchase goods and services.

Marketing planning The process of analyzing potential markets and developing marketing programs using marketing mix strategies to compete in chosen markets.

Marketing program The set of strategies based on the manipulation of the marketing mix to meet target market preferences.

Marketing research process A process used to collect data about marketing programs, external environments, and consumer markets in an attempt to improve the quality of marketing decisions.

Marketing strategy   Encompasses the overall plan for achieving marketing objectives.

Maslow's hierarchy of needs   Five motivational needs that individuals seek to fulfill, progressing in order from basic to complex.

Mass customization   When a firm customizes the experience for each individual consumer.

Maturity stage   The third stage of the product life cycle where the organization has expanded as much as the market will allow, and volume, measured in annual gross sales, levels off.

Measurability   The overall size of the target market segment and the projected total demand or purchasing power of the target market.

Media planning process   The process firms use to determine and implement media strategies that help achieve the desired goals and objectives for its products and services.

Meeting planners   A person who organizes and plans meetings that will be attended by groups of individuals.

Menu engineering   Analysis of menu items based on cost, volume, and profitability.

Menu sales mix analysis   The simplest method used to evaluate menu effectiveness by counting the number of times each item is sold.

Merchandising   Advertising or displaying products in ways that enhance consumer interest and service delivery.

Meta tags   Keywords are used by search engines to identify content and then rank the content in order of relevancy for users. These key words are embedded into the coding of each web page.

Metropolitan statistical area (MSA)   A self-contained urban area with a population of at least 50,000 that is surrounded by rural areas.

Milline formula   An equation used to compare the costs of advertising in different newspapers [(price per *agate line* × 1,000,000)/circulation]. Based on the milline rate, or advertising cost per line per million circulation.

Mission statement   Expresses the firm's purpose and the qualities that differentiate it from its competitors.

Monopolistic competition   A common, competitive structure where there are many buyers and sellers with differentiated products.

Monopoly   A competitive structure in an industry with one seller and many buyers.

Motive   A person's inner state that directs the individual toward satisfying a perceived need.

Moving average   This technique uses short-term forecasts (e.g., monthly) and takes the average of the most recent periods to predict future sales.

Multiple-category question   A multiple-category question contains more than two options for the respondent. Demographic information, such as education and income, is often obtained using this type of question.

Multiplier analysis   Procedure to estimate the additional impact generated in a tourist destination for every dollar spent on the tourist product itself.

National advertising   Advertising aimed at a national audience by using network television and radio, or national print media such as magazines or newspapers.

Natural or organic search optimization   This approach to optimization of web pages is based on developing Web pages so that the search engines will successfully find your content and position it prominently on search results.

Need   A lack of something or the difference between someone's desired and actual states.

Need-payoff questions   A set of questions designed to highlight the positive outcome of purchasing your product (e.g., "If my hotel were to provide your attendees with better food and closer proximity to tourist attractions, do you think you would get better attendance and collect more registration fees?").

Negotiation   Communication between two or more individuals or parties seeking an outcome that is mutually beneficial.

Negotiating skills   Negotiating skills are a set of interpersonal and analytical skills that allow a person to create an exchange that results in the mutual benefit of the involved parties.

Neutral pricing   The practice of setting a price consistent with a product's perceived economic value.

New product committee   A new product committee consists of individuals representing cross-functional areas of the firm. Usually, representatives provide input from operations, marketing, finance, and accounting.

New product department   Some firms establish full-time new products departments. It is still important for members of this department to solicit input from all cross-functional areas of the firm.

New product development
Developing new products and services is time-consuming and risky, but it is essential to the continued long-term success of a firm.

Noncompensatory strategies
Consumer decision-making strategies that place an emphasis on examining attributes independently without allowing trade-offs.

Nonprobability sample   Nonprobability samples are based on judgment and the selection process is subjective.

Objectives   Objectives are more detailed statements of what the firm intends to achieve.

Observation   A process involving watching consumers and documenting their behavior.

Odd/even pricing   Setting prices just below even dollar amounts to give the perception that the product is less expensive.

Oligopoly   A competitive structure in an industry with a few sellers and many buyers.

Open-ended question   Does not provide the respondent with any options, categories, or scales to use in answering the question.

Opinion leaders   People whose opinions impact the lifestyle choices and purchasing behaviors of others.

Opt-in and opt-out   The approach to building e-mail distribution lists that empowers consumers to choose whether to participate (opt-in) or withdraw (opt-out).

Order getters   Salespeople who are responsible for creating sales and developing new accounts.

Order takers   Salespeople who attend to customer inquiries and repeat purchases.

Organizational buying   The process organizations follow to acquire the goods and services they use to produce and deliver their own products and services.

Outdoor advertising plant   A company that buys or leases real estate (where it erects standard-size boards) or rents walls of buildings. It then sells use of space at these locations to advertisers.

Paid keyword search   This approach involves paying the search engine companies to show advertisements for your site when users initiate relevant searches.

Pay-per-click   When an advertiser pays the host each time a user clicks on an advertisement and opens the advertiser's web page.

Penetration pricing   The practice of setting a low price relative to a product's perceived economic value.

Perceived value   The worth or utility of a product or service held in the minds of consumers.

Percentage-of-sales method   A given percentage of a sales forecast is allocated to promotion and advertising.

Perception   The process by which stimuli are recognized, received, and interpreted.

Perceptual map   A technique used to construct a graphic representation of how consumers in a market perceive a competing set of products relative to each other.

Perfect competition   A competitive structure in an industry with many buyers and sellers of homogeneous products that are almost exactly the same.

Peripheral services   Additional goods and services that expand the core offering and can be used to obtain a competitive advantage.

Personal selling   An interpersonal process where a salesperson attempts to create a mutually satisfactory exchange with a buyer using various sales techniques.

Personality   An individual's distinctive psychological characteristics that lead to relatively consistent responses to his or her environment.

Place   This component, sometimes called *distribution,* refers to the manner in which the products and services are being delivered to consumers. It involves decisions related to the location of facilities and the use of intermediaries.

Point-of-sale (POS) displays Advertisements or promotions placed in retail outlets where customers select products in an attempt to stimulate demand through impulse purchases.

Point-of-sale (POS) systems A computerized system for recording sales and transactions.

Population The entire group, or target market, that is being studied for the purpose of answering the research questions.

Position statement Describes the firm's mission to its external stakeholders in terms of the benefits of the firm's offerings.

Positioning The process of determining how to differentiate a firm's product offerings from those of its competitors in the minds of consumers.

Positioning statement The positioning statement is used to differentiate the organization's product–service mix from that of the competition.

Poststagnation The period in the tourist area life cycle after the beginning of the stagnation stage. Tourist destinations try to find ways to rejuvenate the area by adding new attractions or focusing on a niche market.

Preemptible rates Charges for broadcast advertising spots that may be bumped to different time periods by advertisers paying higher rates. They vary in cost by the amount of notice the station must give the advertiser before moving an advertisement: the longer the notice, the higher the rate.

Preference data Data obtained by asking consumers to indicate their preferences for a list of alternative brands.

Premiums Something that is given away or sold at a reduced cost to bring in new guests, to encourage more frequent visits by current guests, and to build positive word of mouth about the operation.

Prestige pricing Setting relatively high prices based on quality-related attributes valued by a particular segment of consumers.

Price Price refers to the value placed by a firm on its products and services.

Price discrimination laws Price discrimination laws forbid firms from charging purchasers different prices for commodities of like grade and quality in an attempt to substantially lessen competition.

Price elasticity of demand A measure of the percentage change in demand for a product resulting from a percentage change in price.

Price lining Refers to the practice of having a limited number of products available at different price levels based on quality.

Pricing objectives Organizational objectives focused on financial performance, volume, competition, and image that are directly related to pricing decisions.

Primary data Data that are collected for a current study or project and tailored to meet the specific information needs for that study or project.

Primary metropolitan statistical area (PMSA) An urbanized county or multi-county area with a population of more than 1 million individuals.

Privatization A process by which the government allows an industry or business to change from governmental or public ownership or control to a private enterprise.

Proactive strategies Strategies that anticipate changes in the marketplace.

Probability sample Is more scientific, and a population member's chance of being selected can be calculated. Probability sampling methods include simple random sample, systematic sample, and stratified sample.

Problem questions Queries designed to uncover any concerns or dissatisfaction the prospect has with the current supplier.

Procedural dimension This refers to the procedures used in the service delivery process.

Product A good, idea, information, or service created to satisfy a consumer's want or need.

Product bundling An approach where goods and services are combined into one offering, typically at a lower price than if the individual goods and services were purchased separately.

Product development strategy A strategy that focuses on achieving growth by developing new products for existing markets.

Product levels The varying levels of goods and services that combine to form the final product.

Product life cycle A theory that describes how a product progresses from its infancy as a new product to its eventual decline.

Product line A firm's portfolio of products and services.

Product managers Managers who assume complete responsibility for determining marketing objectives and marketing strategies for a specific brand.

Product screening Screening the list of potential products or services to select those with the greatest opportunity for success.

Product–service mix The strategic blend of a firm's tangible and intangible attributes.

Profit control data This is a function of sales and costs and should be broken down by market segment.

Projected demand The total market demand multiplied by the firm's market share for a particular product–service mix.

Promotion mix The basic elements (advertising, public relations, sales promotions, and personal selling) used by organizations to communicate with consumers.

Promotional budgets Provide a detailed projection of future expenditures; act as short- and long-range planning guides for management; and help monitor and control promotional expenses by comparing actual expenses against projections.

Property analysis checklist A form used to evaluate a hotel's basic features such as location, guest-room accommodations, meeting facilities, general facilities and services, and transportation.

Prospecting and qualifying The process of identifying and qualifying prospects who are most likely to purchase a company's products.

Psychographic segmentation Segmentation technique that focuses on consumers' lifestyles, attitudes, and personalities.

Psychological pricing Setting prices based on consumer perceptions of value.

Public relations A nonpersonal stimulation of demand for a product or service by providing commercially significant news about the product or service in a published medium or obtaining favorable presentation in a medium that is not paid for by the sponsor.

Publicity A form of public relations used solely to attract media attention.

Pull promotional strategy A sales promotion strategy aimed at stimulating the interest of consumers and having them pull the product through the channels of distribution.

Pulsing advertising Constant low-level flow of advertising with intermittent periods of blitz advertising.

Purchasing power The extent to which consumers have the ability to purchase products and services.

Pure e-commerce companies Refers to firms that operate solely on the Internet. They do not operate any physical facilities.

Push promotional strategy A sales promotion strategy used to push the product–service mix through the service delivery system or channels of distribution. This approach encourages increased purchases and increased consumption by consumers.

Question marks Products and services that have low relative market shares in industries with high market growth rates.

Quota sample Chosen to fill certain quotas that are predetermined by the researcher.

Reach The number or percentage of people exposed to a specific publication. The reach is usually measured throughout publication of a number of issues.

Reactive strategies Strategies that respond to changes in the marketplace.

Recall Techniques, such as telephone surveys, direct-mail surveys, and personal interviews, used to determine consumers' relative awareness of a specific operation or firm.

Recovery strategies Strategies used to recover from service failures. Common service recovery strategies include conduct cost/benefit analysis, encourage and respond to complaints, anticipate the need for recovery, train employees, and empower the front line of employees.

Reference group A group with whom an individual identifies to the point where the group dictates a standard of behavior. Every individual is influenced directly and indirectly. Marketing research has identified three types of reference groups: comparative, status, and normative.

Reference value The cost of the competing product that the consumer perceives as the closest substitute.

Referent power Referent power occurs when a channel member has a certain prestige or image that would benefit another member as a result of their association.

Regression analysis   This technique identifies the causal factors, or independent variables, that can be used to predict the level of sales, or the dependent variable.

Relationship marketing   Marketing based on the proposition that it is important to focus on customer loyalty and retention as well as customer acquisition.

Relative market share   A firm's market share relative to its largest competitor.

Research and development strategy A proactive strategy where firms conduct research to aid in the design and development of new products or services.

Research design   A master plan specifying the methods and procedures for collecting and analyzing the needed information.

Research ethics   The code of behavior set by society and the research industry to define appropriate behavior for firms and individuals engaged in the research process.

Reservation price   The maximum price that a consumer is willing to pay for a product or service.

Resource allocation models   Models used by firms to determine the most effective use of company resources within their product portfolios.

Responsive strategy   A reactive strategy where firms adapt to the demands of customers.

Return on investment (ROI)   Data calculated by dividing return, or net profit, by the amount of the investment.

Revenue management   Involves combining people and systems in an attempt to maximize revenue by coordinating the processes of pricing and inventory management.

Revenue model   A type of electronic commerce business model that focuses on how the firm will generate revenue or income.

Revenue per available room (REVPAR)   An efficiency measure used by hotels to evaluate revenue based on capacity and occupancy rate.

Reward power   Reward power is the ability of one channel member to influence the behavior of another member through the use of incentives. These incentives can be in the form of discounts, trade promotions, or some other form of promotional support.

Sales blitz   A selling activity that targets specific groups within a condensed time frame.

Sales control data   Data focused on the firm's sales by market segment, market share, and sales inputs.

Sales force forecast   This technique aggregates the sales forecast of each salesperson or unit.

Sales forecasting   The process for determining current sales and estimating future sales for a product or service.

Sales promotion   Includes marketing activities other than advertising, personal selling, and public relations that attempt to stimulate short-term consumer demand and increase sales.

Salient attributes   Attributes that are the most important to consumers in evaluating the alternative products or service offerings.

Sample   The subset of the population that is drawn in such a way so as to represent the overall population.

Sample size   The chosen number of sample units to be included in a research study.

Sampling   Offering products and services for free to create awareness and generate interest.

Sampling error   The difference between the sample results and actual population measures.

Sampling unit   The basic level of investigation in a research study.

Satellite account method   The process used to identify an overall estimate of tourism contribution to the state and national economies by utilizing data from a country's System of National Accounts.

Scaled-response question   This form of a closed-ended question involves a statement or question followed by a rating scale. One of the more popular scaled-response questions is the Likert scale, which has respondents indicate their level of agreement with a statement on a five-point scale, with 1 being "strongly disagree" and 5 being "strongly agree."

Search engine optimization Strategically incorporating key words in web page content so that a firm's website will land at the top of a prospect's search results.

Search feeds   A resource used by some firms to reach more web users, who pay a fee to provide website data directly to a search provider to ensure its content is included in the search engine's index.

Search qualities   Attributes that the consumer can investigate prior to making a purchase.

Second but better strategy   An adapted version of the imitative strategy where the firm's primary goal is to improve on the competitor's product.

Secondary data   Data that have already been collected by another source and made available to interested parties either for free or at a reasonable cost.

Secondary data analysis   The process of reviewing existing information that is related to the research problem.

Segmented pricing   Varying prices across market segments based on certain characteristics of consumers or the buying situation.

Selective distribution   Refers to the middle channel width, where a firm uses more than one outlet but restricts availability of the product or service to a limited number of outlets.

Selling   Focuses mainly on the firm's desire to sell products, and to a lesser extent on the needs of the potential buyer.

Service   An intangible product that is sold or purchased in the marketplace.

Service blueprint   A flowchart that details the delivery points of contact with customers.

Service failures   Occur when a firm does not succeed in meeting customers' expectations.

Service gap   The gap that exists when there is a difference between customers' expectations of a service and their perceptions of the actual service once it is consumed.

Service quality   A perception resulting from attitudes formed by customers' long-term overall evaluations of performance.

Service recovery strategies   Strategies used to recover from service failures and satisfy customers.

Services marketing   The use of marketing principles to create and deliver intangible items to consumers.

Showing   A showing refers to the coverage of a market. A 100 showing is complete coverage of a market; a 50 showing is half of it.

Signature items   Menu items that are heavily promoted for which a food service operation is known.

Similarity-dissimilarity data   Data that involve asking consumers to make direct comparisons between alternative brands based on the degree of similarity.

Simple random sample   A totally random process where each population member has an equal chance of being selected.

Situation questions   Questions aimed at gathering background information and facts about the prospect, his or her needs, and the organization he or she represents.

Skim pricing   The practice of setting a high price relative to a product's perceived economic value.

SMERF group   An acronym for a combination of several market segments: social, military, educational, religious, and fraternal.

Social media   Internet-based applications that allow organizations and individuals to exchange information in virtual communities and networks.

Social network   Individuals and organizations build personal web pages to share content and communicate with friends, colleagues, fans, and customers.

Social sustainability   The ability of a country or a society to maintain an adequate standard of living indefinitely.

Spam   Any e-mail received that is unwanted or unsolicited by the recipient.

Specialty advertising   Materials bearing the firm's name and logo that are given or sold to a targeted consumer group.

SPIN selling   A sales approach developed by Neil Rackham that focuses on the prospect's situation, problem, implication, and need payoff.

Stagnation stage   The last stage of the tourist area life cycle occurs when peak numbers of tourists and capacity levels are reached, and the infrastructure and the facilities start to erode.

Standard operating procedure (SOP)   Established workflow followed by management and staff in a given situation or for a specific operation.

Stakeholders relations plan   The component of the communications plan developed to foster business partnerships and alliances.

Standards gap   The discrepancy that can occur between management's perception of what customers expect and how they design the service delivery process to meet those expectations.

Stars   Products and services with high relative market shares in industries that show good potential for future growth.

Strategic business unit (SBU) Business centers consisting of products that share common characteristics, market conditions, and competitors.

Strategic marketing plans   These plans result from a careful examination of a firm's core business strategy and primary marketing objectives.

Strategic window   Limited periods of time when marketing opportunities present themselves and the firm is in a position to take advantage of those opportunities.

Stratified sample   The population is separated into different strata based on an important population characteristic and a sample is taken from each stratum using a random or systematic process.

Substantiality   The size of the segment must be large enough to warrant special attention to meet the needs of the segment and to achieve the marketing objectives of the firm.

Suggestive-selling   Attempting to enhance an initial sale by recommending compatible products or services.

Supply chain   All suppliers and vendors, intermediaries, procurement and delivery systems, and retail outlets that assist firms in obtaining products and services and using them to add value in producing and delivering the final service to customers.

Supporting products   Additional goods and services that can be bundled with the core service in an attempt to increase the overall utility or value for consumers.

Survey of buying intentions   Firms use marketing research to ask potential customers about their future purchase intentions and then estimate future sales.

Surveys   Data collection instruments designed to gather specific information for a particular research problem through a series of questions and statements.

Sustainability   The ability of individuals or organizations to endure and function over the long term.

Sustainable development Development that meets the needs of the present without compromising the ability of future generations to meet their own needs.

Sweepstakes   Prizes are awarded solely based on chance.

SWOT analysis   An analysis of a firm's strengths and weaknesses relative to competitors, and the potential threats and opportunities posed by the external environment.

System failures   When a failure or service breakdown occurs in a core service provided by the firm.

Systematic sample   A starting point is randomly chosen and then every nth member is selected for the sample.

Tactical marketing plans   These plans focus on implementing the broad strategies that are established in the strategic marketing plan.

Target-return pricing   Setting a price to yield a target rate of return on a firm's investment.

Telemarketing   The use of telecommunication technology to conduct marketing campaigns aimed at certain target markets.

Test marketing   The limited introduction of a new product or service in select locations. A common form of field experiment consisting of manipulations in the marketing mix in communities that represent the competitive environment and consumer profile of the overall target population.

Time series analysis   This method uses statistical techniques to fit a trend line to the pattern of historical sales.

Tourist area life cycle (TALC)   The evolutionary stages for tourist destinations that illustrate their rise and decline, from the initial exploration by tourists to eventual stagnation.

Trademark   A brand that has been given legal protection and is protected for exclusive use by the owner of the trademark.

Trade-outs   When firms trade services in lieu of cash.

Trend extrapolation   The simplest method for forecasting sales is the linear projection of past sales.

Triple bottom line   An accounting and recording system used by firms to monitor sustainability performance on all three components—people, planet, and profits.

Unique destination proposition (UDP)
A statement to describe the unique elements that are available at the destination in an attempt to differentiate it from other destinations.

Unique selling proposition (USP)
Promoting a unique element of the product–service mix.

Unsolicited employee actions
Unexpected actions, both good and bad, of employees that are observed or experienced by customers.

Up-selling   A technique that involves encouraging consumers to purchase relatively more expensive products and services, or those that provide a greater profit margin.

Value proposition   A component of electronic commerce business models that focuses on how the firm creates value for the buyer.

Venture teams   Similar to new product committees, but formed to complete a specific product assignment. Venture teams bring together expertise from operations, marketing, accounting and finance, and, if necessary, architecture and construction.

Vertical marketing system   In a vertical marketing system, channel members work together as if they were one organization, coordinating their efforts for the purpose of achieving a higher degree of efficiency, thereby reducing the overall costs of providing products and services.

Wheel of retailing   The evolution of an organization from a low-end provider to a high-end provider.

Win-win relationship   A situation that results when both parties are satisfied at the end of a negotiation.

Word of mouth   A spoken communication between consumers that involves their perceptions about a product or service.

Yield Management   Using a model to maximize the revenue, or yield, obtained from a service operation, given limited capacity and uneven demand.

Index

Note: Page numbers with f indicate figures; those with t indicate tables.